D1172796

Love

*Walking with Jesus
from Eden to Eternity*

Makes a Way

Love
Walking with Jesus from Eden to Eternity

Makes a Way

Herbert Edgar Douglass

A Daily Devotional

Pacific Press® Publishing Association
Nampa, Idaho
Oshawa, Ontario, Canada
www.pacificpress.com

Cover design by Gerald Lee Monks
Cover art by Darrel Tank
Inside design by Ken McFarland

Copyright © 2007 by
Pacific Press® Publishing Association
Printed in the United States of America
All rights reserved

Scriptures quoted from the NKJV are from the Holy Bible, New King
James Version, copyright © 1979, 1980, by Thomas Nelson, Inc.
Used by permission.

Additional copies of this book may be obtained
by calling toll-free 1-800-765-6955
or on line at http://www.adventistbookcenter.com

Library of Congress Cataloging-in-Publication Data

Douglass, Herbert E.
Love makes a way : walking with God from Eden to eternity : a daily
devotional / Herbert Edgar Douglass.
p. cm.
ISBN-13: 978-0-8163-2231-2 (hard cover)
ISBN 10: 0-8163-2231-7

1. Devotional calendars—Seventh-day Adventists. 2. Seventh-day
Adventists—Prayers and devotions. 3. Adventists—Prayers and
devotions. I. Title.
BV4811.D625 2007
242'.2—dc22

2007026123

07 08 09 10 11 • 5 4 3 2 1

Dedication

To all the men and women through the years who have deepened their trust in our heavenly Father because of the writings of Ellen G. White, God's messenger for these end times.

Foreword

Ellen White's most distinctive contribution, flowing through seventy years of her writing and speaking ministry, was the unique insight God gave her into the great controversy between Christ and Satan that began in heaven and will be forever ended in a new heaven and a new earth.

The clearest presentation of this universe-wide controversy is embedded in her five-volume set, the Conflict of the Ages—*Patriarchs and Prophets, Prophets and Kings, The Desire of Ages, The Acts of the Apostles,* and *The Great Controversy.* Rounding out the picture are three books that contain additional material on the life of Jesus—*Steps to Christ, Christ's Object Lessons,* and *Thoughts From the Mount of Blessing.*

Each daily reading in this volume summarizes a single chapter of these eight books, creating a fast-paced overview of the great controversy theme in the course of the year. It is like taking a walk with God and letting Him show you how His love has made a way to remedy the devastation sin has caused in His universe. If you are able to find the time to read the complete chapter in Ellen White's words, as well as the reading for the day, you will prolong your walk with God and realize an even greater spiritual benefit.

It is my prayer that you will sense the power in these words, the laser-sharp touch that connects God's thoughts with your personal needs and hopes. For me, the impact of this journey through these eight books has become an encounter with the Divine like none I have experienced before. Now, I understand better than ever Ellen White's own comment regarding these eight volumes: "Sister White is not the originator of these books. They contain the instruction that during her lifework God has been giving her. They contain the precious, comforting light that God has graciously given His servants to be given to the world" (*Selected Messages*, Book 3, p. 50).

As you trace God's footsteps in these pages, you will sense the overarching "central theme of the Bible, the theme about which every other in the whole book clusters. . . the restoration in the human soul of the image of God. . . . He who grasps this thought has before him an infinite field for study. He has the key that will unlock to him the whole treasure house of God's word" (*Education*, pp. 125, 126).

Herbert Edgar Douglass, Th.D.
Lincoln Hills, California

Why Was Sin Permitted?

Patriarchs and Prophets, Chapter 1.

"The Lord is righteous in all his ways, and holy in all his works" (Psalm 145:17).

The great controversy between good and evil began in heaven as an outgrowth of love that flourishes only in freedom. When the controversy is over, the universe will have seen a demonstration of this love in such a display that it will prevent another rebellion from ever happening again. Every manifestation of creative power is an expression of God's love—especially His decision to create intelligent beings who could say No to Him!

Because love freely given is the foundation of true happiness, God desires from all created intelligences the response of love. Because genuine love is loyalty and appreciation, freely offered, God takes no pleasure in forced love or forced obedience.

But Lucifer, the summit of all God's creation, perverted this freedom and pervasive love. Little by little, Lucifer began to indulge the desire for self-exaltation. He envied one of the Godhead, whom we know today as Jesus. Fellow angels and God, Himself, pled with Lucifer, but He continued to foster deep, strange thoughts. With his extraordinary mind he began to devise a plan to win the allegiance of the angels by insinuating that God was unfair. Lucifer's big promise was to offer freedom from the "restraints" of God's government.

God knew that it was necessary for Lucifer's plans to be developed further and that if He eliminated Lucifer from the universe, angels would immediately believe that Lucifer was right when he charged that God was a power-hungry tyrant.

Key Thought: "God could employ only such means as were consistent with truth and righteousness. Satan could use what God could not—flattery and deceit. . . . It was therefore necessary to demonstrate before the inhabitants of heaven, and of all the worlds, that God's government is just, His law perfect. Satan had made it appear that he himself was seeking to promote the good of the universe. The true character of the usurper and his real object must be understood by all. He must have time to manifest himself by his wicked works" (*Patriarchs and Prophets,* p. 42).

Today's Lesson: God values our love and obedience only when we give it willingly. He will never force us to obey.

The Creation

Patriarchs and Prophets, Chapter 2.

"Come now, and let us reason together, saith the Lord" (Isaiah 1:18).

All creation, everywhere in the universe, God spoke into existence. This included each galaxy, star, and planet. But foremost in His planning on Planet Earth was the creation of the human race, male and female, both reflecting His own image. Their nature was in harmony with God's will, their minds capable of comprehending divine things. Their affections were pure; their appetites and passions were under the control of reason.

God celebrated the marriage between Adam and Eve, one of the two original gifts to mankind in Eden that still exist—the seventh-day Sabbath and marriage. The first couple were given the Garden of Eden as their home—resplendent with all varieties of flowers and trees, with birds and animals as their companions.

The seventh-day Sabbath would become their weekly celebration as they reflected upon God's great work of creation. Without threat or fear, they saw the evidences of God's wisdom and goodness, filling their hearts with love and reverence for their Maker.

Their job description included the care of the garden—"to dress it and to keep it." God knew that pleasant and invigorating labor would be a blessing to them. Adam and Eve were also students, receiving daily instruction from heavenly angels and God Himself. They were full of vigor imparted by the Tree of Life, and their intellect was but a little less than that of the angels. As they studied life throughout the universe, their hearts were filled with an even deeper love and gratitude to their Creator.

Key Thought: "God might have created man without the power to transgress His law; He might have withheld the hand of Adam from touching the forbidden fruit; but in that case man would have been, not a free moral agent, but a mere automaton. Without freedom of choice, his obedience would not have been voluntary, but forced. . . . It would have been unworthy of man as an intelligent being, and would have sustained Satan's charge of God's arbitrary rule" (*Patriarchs and Prophets,* p. 49).

Today's Lesson: Freedom of choice is so important to God that He was willing to risk the possibility that human beings would choose to disobey.

The Temptation and Fall

Patriarchs and Prophets, Chapter 3.

"And I will put enmity between thee and the woman, and between thy seed and her seed; it shall bruise thy head, and thou shalt bruise his heel" (Genesis 3:15).

After Satan was cast out of heaven, he turned to beautiful Planet Earth and its blissful first couple. His plan was to incite them to disobedience, bringing on them guilt and the consequences of sin. All of this would bring dishonor upon God—exactly what he had wanted in heaven.

Heavenly angels revealed to Adam and Eve the history of Satan's fall. They wanted them to beware of his subtle, deceitful ways and to understand that life itself is a gift that is maintained by obedience to the just laws of the universe. The angels also told them that to yield to Satan's temptations would open the door, making them helpless to resist Satan's further enticements—that their whole lives would become depraved and hopeless.

Nevertheless, Eve's curiosity led her to the tree of knowledge of good and evil. She was captivated by Satan's subtle praises and excited by the new powers that Satan promised if she would only eat the forbidden fruit. But Eve and the rest of her offspring have learned to their regret that disobedience may give them greater liberty, but it brings even greater sorrow.

Deciding to stand by his wife, Adam soon found that their disobedience robbed them of peace and gave them a sense of sin, a dread of the future, and a nakedness of soul. They clung to the thought that God loved them so much He would pardon their transgression and that they would not be subject to the inherent consequences of their folly. They even tried to blame God for their predicament.

Key Thought: "In the judgment men will not be condemned because they conscientiously believed a lie, but because they did not believe the truth, because they neglected the opportunity of learning what is truth. Notwithstanding the sophistry of Satan to the contrary, it is always disastrous to disobey God" (*Patriarchs and Prophets,* p. 55).

Today's Lesson: In the moment of temptation it is difficult to recognize the terrible consequences that can result from one wrong step.

The Plan of Redemption

Patriarchs and Prophets, Chapter 4.

"And all that dwell upon the earth shall worship him,
whose names are not written in the book of life of the
Lamb slain from the foundation of the world"
(Revelation 13:8).

The disobedience of Adam and Eve had been foreseen by the Godhead. Because sin carries its own self-destructing virus, God knew that a plan to save mankind was necessary, but it would require divine intervention. One of the Godhead (He whom we know today as Jesus) would Himself assume the guilt and shame of sin and rescue the ruined race. Further, He would show that God could be self-denying and unselfish.

Jesus would become human, incredible as it sounds, and endure the fiercest attacks of Satan, even to the point of dying horribly on a Roman cross. In so doing, He would prove Satan a liar. Every time we look at the Cross, we want to trust God more for giving us a future with a fresh start. He died for us so that we would not have to die the sinner's death. Further, Jesus would prove that God was fair in giving us a code of obedience that would lead the obedient to real joy, health, and hope. We call this wonderful arrangement the atonement that God provides for sinners.

From the first, the great controversy had been over the law of God. Satan tried to prove that God was unfair, that His laws were faulty. Christ's life and death would show that the divine statutes were not defective or subject to change without penalty.

Key Thought: "But the plan of redemption had a yet broader and deeper purpose than the salvation of man. It was not for this alone that Christ came to the earth; it was not merely that the inhabitants of this little world might regard the law of God as it should be regarded; but it was to vindicate the character of God before the universe" (*Patriarchs and Prophets,* p. 68).

Today's Lesson: As we allow God to work out His plan in our lives, we can help to vindicate His character before the universe.

Cain and Abel Tested

Patriarchs and Prophets, Chapter 5.

"And the Lord had respect unto Abel and to his offering"
(Genesis 4:4).

Cain and Abel differed widely in character. Abel was loyal to God and saw justice in His dealings with the fallen race. Cain cherished feelings of rebellion and murmured against God because of sin's curse. His mind ran along the same channels as Satan's, cherishing self-exaltation and questioning God's authority.

Both Cain and Abel were tested to prove their loyalty to God. The system of offerings would test their faith in Jesus, whom the slain lamb represented. The two sons built identical altars, but Abel's offering was consumed by fire from heaven, while Cain's offering of fruit received no token from heaven.

Abel pleaded with his older brother to respect God's will, but Cain resented his counsel. Cain's offering was presented as a favor done to God—a thank offering for which He expected divine approval. He did not sense a need for a Redeemer.

Cain and Abel represent two classes that will exist till the close of time—one realizes the need for a Savior; those in the other venture to depend on their own merits. Those who follow Cain are the greater portion of the world. Nearly every false religion is based on one principle—that men and women can depend on their own efforts for salvation.

From Adam's day, the great controversy has concerned obedience to God's will. True faith, like Abel's, relies wholly upon Christ and is revealed by obedience to all of God's requirements.

God came close to Cain, pleading with Him to be reasonable. Reason and conscience told Cain that Abel was right, but he was enraged and finally killed his brother. Such has been this world's history—the wicked hate those who are better than themselves.

Key Thought: "The brighter the heavenly light that is reflected from the character of God's faithful servants, the more clearly the sins of the ungodly are revealed, and the more determined will be their efforts to destroy those who disturb their peace" (*Patriarchs and Prophets,* p. 74).

Today's Lesson: Sin is unwilling to listen to reason, and often those who know themselves to be in the wrong attempt to silence their conscience by attacking those whose obedient lives are a rebuke to their own disobedience.

Seth and Enoch

Patriarchs and Prophets, Chapter 6.

"After [Enoch] begot Methuselah, Enoch walked with God three hundred years, . . . And Enoch walked with God; and he was not, for God took him" (Genesis 5:22, 24, NKJV).

Seth followed the noble example of Abel, yet he, too, inherited his parents' fallen nature. To Seth was born Enos, but the Scriptures tell us that now "men began to call on the name of the Lord" (Genesis 4:26, NKJV), signifying that as population increased, the distinction between those who followed God and those who did not became more marked.

Cain's extended family built cities; Adam continued his pastoral life, as did Seth. For some time the two distinct families kept separate. But eventually the children of each began to intermarry—the children of Seth became enamored with the daughters of Cain's descendants. Mingling with the depraved, they became like them, disregarding the Sabbath and enjoying polygamy.

Adam lived on for nearly a thousand years, his life one of sorrow, humility, and contrition. Yet, He remained faithful to his Lord, imparting His unparalleled knowledge to his descendants. The antediluvians possessed extraordinary mental and physical vigor, reaching high standards of religious and scientific knowledge.

Through it all, Seth's line understood their mission—to develop characters of righteousness and to teach lessons of godliness. Enoch, one of the holy line, learned from Adam the dark chapter of the lost Garden and leaned on God for grace to remain faithful. The birth of his first son taught him even more of God's love.

Day by day Enoch longed for a closer union with God until God took him to heaven, the first from earth to enter there. By translating Enoch, the Lord taught us all-important lessons—that God does reward the faithful, that it is possible to live obedient lives, and that God will reward with eternal life those who are willingly obedient.

Key Thought: "In the midst of a life of active labor, Enoch steadfastly maintained his communion with God. The greater and more pressing his labors, the more constant and earnest were his prayers" (*Patriarchs and Prophets,* p. 86).

Today's Lesson: Parents have a decided influence on their children, but ultimately each person decides for himself how he will live his life. Adam's sons chose distinctly different paths in their relationship to God.

The Flood

Patriarchs and Prophets, Chapter 7.

"By faith Noah, being warned of God of things not seen as yet, moved with fear, prepared an ark to the saving of his house" (Hebrews 11:7).

Before the Flood the earth was still beautiful, and the human race retained much of its original vigor. Men and women of great stature devised wonderful inventions. But they had lost their awe of God and came to deny His existence. As God looked at His creation, He saw a world filled with wickedness and continual evil (see Genesis 6:5).

Methuselah, Noah, and others did their best to keep the knowledge of the true God alive. One hundred and twenty years before the Flood, the Lord directed Noah to build an ark in preparation for a worldwide flood and to warn men and women of what was coming.

During this time of construction Noah continued to appeal to all those who laughed at the idea of a boat on dry ground. But at last silence fell upon the mocking throng as animals—large and small—moved toward the construction site and entered the ark. Then unseen hands slowly closed the huge door.

For seven days, no sign of the coming storm appeared. Faith was tested. But on the eighth day came dark clouds, thunder, and lightning—and then the rain. Rivers overflowed their banks, and jets of water burst from the earth.

Jesus said, "As in the days that were before the flood . . . so shall also the coming of the Son of man be" (Matthew 24:38, 39). So similar is our world today to the world before the Flood. Multitudes feel under no moral obligation to curb their sensual desires, and they become the slaves of lust. However, when world leaders are pointing to long ages of peace and prosperity and people are absorbed in business and pleasure, rejecting and mocking God's messengers—then destruction comes, and the Lord will appear the second time.

Key Thought: "All who will put away their sins by repentance toward God and faith in Christ are offered pardon" (*Patriarchs and Prophets,* p. 102).

Today's Lesson: As Jesus predicted, world conditions today are increasingly a mirror image of society in Noah's day just before the Flood.

After the Flood

Patriarchs and Prophets, Chapter 8.

***"Noah removed the covering [roof] of the ark, and looked,
and, behold, the face of the ground was dry"
(Genesis 8:13).***

Water had risen twenty-five feet above the highest mountain. For five long months the boat had been tossed violently until God caused the ark to drift into a spot protected by several mountains. Noah patiently waited for the Lord's command to leave its refuge. At last, an angel opened the massive door.

Upon leaving the ark, Noah's first act was to build an altar and offer a sacrifice for his deliverance. He heard God promise that the earth would never again be destroyed by a flood—that the rainbow would be humanity's token of that promise. Even now, the rainbow is a reminder to us of God's great mercies toward repentant sinners.

Two lessons Noah teaches us: Out of his small stock of cattle he cheerfully gave a part to the Lord, and before building a house for himself, he built an altar to God.

The entire surface of the earth was changed at the Flood. To cover the bodies of men and animals destroyed in the Flood, God caused a violent wind to heap up trees, rocks, and earth above the dead. Immense forests were buried that eventually became coal and extensive quantities of oil. These frequently ignite. The fury of intense heat, mixed with water, causes earthquakes and volcanoes, and these will become more frequent and terrible just before Jesus' second coming and the end of the world, as signs of its speedy destruction.

At the world's end, enormous earthquakes and volcanoes will destroy the wicked, but the righteous will be preserved in the midst of this horror, even as Noah was preserved in the ark. Says the psalmist, "Because thou hast made the Lord, which is my refuge, even the most High, thy habitation; there shall no evil befall thee" (Psalm 91:9).

Key Thought: "These wonderful manifestations [signs in the natural world] will be more and more frequent and terrible just before the second coming of Christ and the end of the world, as signs of its speedy destruction" (*Patriarchs and Prophets,* p. 109).

Today's Lesson: The Flood makes it clear that sin has consequences. Righteousness results in life; sin results in death.

The Literal Week

Patriarchs and Prophets, Chapter 9.

"The invisible things of him from the creation of the world are clearly seen, being understood by the things that are made, even his eternal power and Godhead"
(Romans 1:20).

Like the Sabbath, the week originated at Creation, and it has been preserved and brought down to us today. God Himself measured off the first week as a sample for successive weeks to the close of time, and like every other, it consisted of seven literal days. God employed six days in the work of creation; upon the seventh, He rested and blessed this day, setting it apart as a sacred day of rest.

The Ten Commandments recognize Creation as the basis for the week; the fourth commandment makes it clear that each day in the creation week was a literal, twenty-four-hour day. Assumptions that the first "week" required millions of years have made obscure what God has stated in clear language. The sacred record declares that each successive day of Creation week consisted of the evening and the morning, like all other days that have followed.

Apart from Bible history, geology can prove nothing. Relics found in the earth do give evidence of conditions differing in many respects from the present; but the time when these conditions existed can be learned only from the inspired record. The geological evidence and the fossil record should demonstrate to later generations that humans and animals perished in a disastrous worldwide flood.

It may be innocent to speculate beyond what God's Word has revealed, if our theories do not contradict facts found in the Scriptures, but those who leave the Word of God and seek to account for His created works upon scientific principles only are drifting upon an unknown ocean without chart or compass. The greatest minds, if not guided in their research by the Word of God, become bewildered in their attempts to trace the relations of science and revelation.

Key Thought: "Those who take the written word as their counselor will find in science an aid to understand God" (*Patriarchs and Prophets,* p. 116).

Today's Lesson: God expects us to stretch our minds in studying the earth and sky to understand better His works.

The Tower of Babel

Patriarchs and Prophets, Chapter 10.

"And the Lord came down to see the city and the tower, which the children of men builded" (Genesis 11:5).

Noah foretold the history of the races begun in his three sons—Shem, Ham, and Japheth. The line of Shem was to be the chosen people. Through the descendants of Ham and through his son Canaan would come the most degrading forms of heathenism. Eventually their descendants would become the servants of the descendants of Noah's other two sons. Japheth's line would expand and be blessed in its relations with the children of Shem.

Noah's prophecy was no arbitrary denunciation or declaration of favor—he did not fix the character and destiny of his sons. It merely reflected the results of their life choices. As a rule, children inherit the dispositions and tendencies of their parents.

For a time, Noah's descendants lived among the mountains where the ark had rested. Eventually, apostasy appeared, which led many to leave for the plains of Shinar, along the banks of the Euphrates with its fertile soil. Here they built a city—a metropolis of a universal empire, with plans to build a tower of stupendous height.

The tower builders disbelieved God's promise that He would never again bring a worldwide flood. When their tower had been partially completed, work suddenly stopped dramatically. Workers at the highest levels could no longer communicate with those at the base. Wrong material was sent up, and the work stopped in confusion and dismay. No one could account for the introduction of different languages, which led to strife and bloodshed.

The tower builders had become darkened by idolatry. As they turned away from God, the divine attributes of justice, purity, and love were supplanted by oppression, violence, and brutality.

For the sake of the faithful ones among them, the Lord delayed His judgments, giving all the people time to reveal their true characters.

Key Thought: "Men hang with admiration upon the lips of eloquence while it teaches that the transgressor shall not die, that salvation may be secured without obedience to the law of God" (*Patriarchs and Prophets,* p. 124).

Today's Lesson: The two key errors found throughout the Christian world today are the belief in an immortal soul and the idea that obedience isn't important in our walk with God.

The Call of Abraham

Patriarchs and Prophets, Chapter 11.

"Get thee out of thy country, and from thy kindred, and from thy father's house, unto a land that I will shew thee" (Genesis 12:1).

Adam, Seth, Enoch, Methuselah, Noah, Shem, in unbroken line, had preserved from age to age the previous revelations of God's will. God had spoken to Abraham and gave him a distinct knowledge of the requirements of His law and of the salvation that would be accomplished through Christ.

Abraham had to be separated from his early associations. He could not even explain his decision so as to be understood by his friends. Abraham's unquestioning obedience is one of the most striking evidences of faith found in the Bible. He had not the least outward assurance of the divine promise, but he abandoned all that was dear and went forward, not knowing where God would lead.

Men and women today are still tested as was Abraham. We may not hear a voice directly from heaven, but God calls us by His written Word and providential events. A life of ease and the influence of friends and home can hinder the development of the very traits essential for fulfilling God's call. Those who, like Abraham, are willing to follow God's leading no matter the cost have the faith of Abraham.

Wherever Abraham camped in the new land of Canaan, he built an altar alongside his tent, calling all those with him for evening and morning sacrifice. He could not explain the leadings of Providence, but he held fast the promise: "I will bless thee, and make thy name great; and thou shalt be a blessing" (Genesis 12:2).

To escape famine, Abraham led his family to Egypt, where the Lord would teach him and his family lessons of submission, patience, and faith.

Key Thought: "It is by close, testing trials that God disciplines His servants. . . . In His providence He brings them into positions that test their character and reveal defects and weaknesses that have been hidden from their own knowledge" (*Patriarchs and Prophets,* p. 129).

Today's Lesson: God does not tempt us, but He does allow situations to test our loyalty so that we will be stronger when temptations come.

Abraham in Canaan

Patriarchs and Prophets, Chapter 12.

"Abraham believed God, and it was counted unto him for righteousness" (Romans 4:3).

Abraham returned to Canaan from Egypt "very rich in cattle, in silver, and in gold" (Genesis 13:2). Lot was still with him, but their increased possessions brought increased trouble. Abraham, sensing the emerging strife and to preserve peace, offered Lot the choice of land.

Lot manifested no gratitude for Abraham's generosity and chose the most fertile region in all Palestine, the Jordan valley where there were cities—wealthy, beautiful, and dazzling in worldly gain. Soon afterward, Abraham moved to Hebron, continuing his simple life in his gardens and wide pastures.

Abraham soon was honored by the surrounding nations as a prince and a wise and able chief. He did not shut himself away from his neighbors, although his life and character were in marked contrast to those of the worshipers of idols. As a worthy example of His Lord, Abraham was also wise in diplomacy, as well as brave and skillful in war.

When war broke out and the cities of the plains where Lot lived were plundered, Abraham sought the Lord's counsel. Leading a coalition of Canaanite princes, Abraham overtook the invaders and rescued Lot's family, along with the rich booty of war. But when he refused the rewards of battle, his neighbors noted his lofty integrity. Through Abraham's example, they saw that righteousness is not cowardice and that Abraham's religion made him courageous in maintaining the right and defending the oppressed.

One of Abraham's continuing concerns was that he still did not have an heir. Oppressed with doubt about God's promise to make him the father of many nations, He begged for some visible token, and God revealed to him in a dream the plan of redemption.

Key Thought: "Of Abraham it is written that 'he was called the friend of God,' 'the father of all them that believe' " (*Patriarchs and Prophets,* p. 140).

Today's Lesson: Abraham's example teaches us to continue patiently serving God even when nothing good seems to be happening in our lives. If we persevere, we will see God fulfill His promises.

The Test of Faith

Patriarchs and Prophets, Chapter 13.

"My son, God will provide himself a lamb for a burnt offering" (Genesis 22:8).

Abraham had accepted without question the promise of a son, but he did not wait for God to fulfill His word in His own time and way. God permitted a delay in order to test Abraham's faith, but he failed to endure the trial. Sarah, wanting to help God, told her husband to take Hagar as a second wife.

When Abraham was nearly one hundred years old, the promise of a son was repeated but this time through Sarah. Because Abraham's faith was not yet perfect, God subjected him to another test—the strongest that anyone was ever called to endure.

When Abraham was a hundred and twenty years old, tired and longing for rest, God told him to take Isaac, in full manhood, and offer him as a burnt offering. Obedient Abraham quietly awakened his equally obedient teenage son, and they traveled in silence to a distant mountain. On the third day the promised cloud hovered over Mount Moriah, and Abraham knew that he was following God's will.

When Isaac asked where the lamb was, Abraham could only reply, "My son, God will provide himself a lamb for a burnt offering!" Then Isaac learned his fate, and laid himself on the altar without resisting!

After the last tear and embrace, Abraham lifted his knife, but an angel's voice stayed his arm. "Lay not thine hand upon the lad," the angel ordered. Just then, Abraham saw a "ram caught in a thicket," which quickly became the necessary offering.

It was to impress Abraham's mind with the reality of the gospel, as well as to test his faith, that God commanded him to slay his son. Thus, Abraham understood from personal experience the greatness of God's involvement in humanity's redemption.

Key Thought: "God desired to prove the loyalty of his servant before all heaven, to demonstrate that nothing less than perfect obedience can be accepted, and to open more fully before them the plan of salvation" (*Patriarchs and Prophets,* p. 155).

Today's Lesson: God often provides a "ram in the thicket" at just the right time for those who trust Him.

Destruction of Sodom

Patriarchs and Prophets, Chapter 14.

"They that will be rich fall into temptation and a snare, and into many foolish and hurtful lusts, which drown men in destruction and perdition" (1 Timothy 6:9).

S odom was the fairest city of the Jordan valley. Lacking for nothing, the idle lives of those living in Sodom made them a prey to Satan's temptations. When Lot moved to Sodom, its corruption had not reached its peak.

As Sodom's last night approached, two heavenly strangers entered the city looking for a night's rest. Many houses refused them, but gracious Lot provided them the hospitality for which he was known. Soon a large, lawless crowd was at his front door, inflamed by the vilest passions. Lot's appeal for restraint was like oil upon the flames, but the angels rescued him.

The angels explained to Lot that Sodom was soon to be destroyed. Still, he delayed leaving his luxurious home. To leave and become a wanderer was overwhelming. The angels actually took him, his wife, and his daughters by their hands and led them out of the city.

"Do not look back," the angels warned. Hesitancy would be fatal. But Lot's wife's heart clung to Sodom, and she perished with it. Christians today hesitate with the same concerns. Some say they don't want to be saved unless their companion and children are saved with them. But the very fact that others are ignoring God's warnings should rouse us all to greater diligence.

Beautiful Sodom became a desolate place, never again to be inhabited—a lasting lesson that there is a limit beyond which men and women may not go in sin. Like Lot's family, there are many today who profess to know God yet who deny Him in their characters and their daily lives.

Key Thought: "God may bear long while the account goes on, and calls to repentance and offers of pardon may be given; yet a time will come when the account will be full; when the soul's decision has been made; when by his own choice, man's destiny has been fixed" (*Patriarchs and Prophets,* p. 165).

Today's Lesson: It is possible to be outwardly keeping the commandments of God, yet be looking back at "Sodom."

The Marriage of Isaac

Patriarchs and Prophets, Chapter 15.

"Can two walk together, except they be agreed?"
(Amos 3:3).

Abraham, now an old man, knew that fulfilling God's promise depended on Isaac, now 40, finding the right wife. Isaac had learned to trust his father's wisdom and affection and trusted his judgment. Abraham's thoughts turned to his family in Mesopotamia, knowing that some there still worshiped the true God.

Abraham had watched with regret the influence of Ishmael's wives and Lot's wife, and he longed for Isaac to have a happy home. The result of Isaac's marriage to Rebecca is described in Genesis as a beautiful picture of domestic happiness: "Isaac brought her into his mother Sarah's tent, and took Rebekah, and she became his wife; and he loved her: and Isaac was comforted after his mother's death" (Genesis 24:67).

What a contrast between Isaac and many youth of today, even among professed Christians. Young people often feel that choosing a mate is a matter in which self alone should be consulted. Long before they have reached adulthood, they think themselves competent to make their own choice. A few years of married life are usually sufficient to show them their error, but often too late to prevent its sad results. Marriage too often becomes a galling yoke.

Like attracts like; like appreciates like. Let the love for truth, purity, and goodness be early implanted in the mind, and the youth will seek the society of those who possess these characteristics.

True love is a high and holy principle, altogether different in character from that love which is awakened by impulse and which suddenly dies when severely tested. By faithfulness to duty in the parental home, youth are prepared for homes of their own.

Key Thought: "The happiness and prosperity of the marriage relation depends upon the unity of the parties; but between the believer and the unbeliever there is a radical difference of tastes, inclinations, and purposes" (*Patriarchs and Prophets,* p. 174).

Today's Lesson: Fathers and mothers may act out in their home life characteristics that replicate their own childhood experiences, but which may not always prove to be in the best interests of their children.

Jacob and Esau

Patriarchs and Prophets, Chapter 16.

"Go out to the field, and take me some venison, and make me savoury meat, . . . that my soul may bless thee before I die" (Genesis 27:3, 4).

Jacob and Esau present a striking contrast in character and in life. Esau loved self-gratification and was impatient with restraint. Jacob, thoughtful, diligent, and caretaking, ever thinking more of the future than the present, was content with the shepherd's life.

Both were taught to regard the family's birthright as a matter of great importance, for it included not only an inheritance of worldly wealth but spiritual preeminence and the promise that the Redeemer would be born of this line.

Though the birthright should go to firstborn Esau, he had no love for the religious life. He viewed the birthright as a yoke of bondage and desired nothing more than to do as he pleased.

Jacob longed for the birthright, not for the material wealth but for the spiritual blessing—to be the progenitor of the promised Messiah. But although he esteemed eternal above temporal blessings, Jacob did not have an experimental knowledge of God. His heart had not been renewed by divine grace.

When Esau returned home famished after a hunt, Jacob offered to provide a meal in exchange for his birthright. So, for his favorite dish of red pottage, Esau confirmed the transaction with an oath. His whole interest was in the present moment.

Later, Esau married two wives devoted to their false gods—marriages that brought bitter grief to his parents. But none of these character weaknesses changed Isaac's mind that Esau should have the birthright.

When Isaac planned to bestow the birthright on Esau secretly, Rebekah, confident this was not God's will, devised a plan to deceive Isaac. Jacob reluctantly agreed to follow her leading, but once their deed was accomplished, both Rebekah and Jacob gained only trouble and sorrow.

Key Thought: "God had declared that Jacob should receive the birthright, and His word would have been fulfilled in His own good time" (*Patriarchs and Prophets,* p. 180).

Today's Lesson: It is easy to allow immediate gratification to overwhelm our conscience, settling for second best rather than doing what we know is right and best.

Jacob's Flight and Exile

Patriarchs and Prophets, Chapter 17.

"Behold, I am with thee, and will keep thee in all places whither thou goest, and will bring thee again into this land; for I will not leave thee, until I have done that which I have spoken to thee of" (Genesis 28:15).

Threatened by Esau, Jacob fled for his life after Isaac had renewed his covenant blessing, telling Jacob to find a wife from his mother's family in Mesopotamia.

On the evening of the second day, feeling like an outcast and utterly lonely, Jacob went to sleep with a stone for a pillow. He dreamed of a bright ladder resting on the earth and reaching to heaven. He heard God's voice as He opened the future, and he learned that God's purposes were reaching their accomplishment through him!

All that Jacob learned in that dream became the framework of his study for the rest of his life. He called that place *Bethel*, or "the house of God." With renewed faith and energy Jacob continued his journey until he met his uncle, Laban. After a few weeks of demonstrating his skills, arrangements were made for him to marry Rachel, Laban's daughter, after seven years of service for his uncle.

After the seven years, Laban slyly substituted Leah for Rachel. The next morning, Jacob confronted his father-in-law, and Laban promised him Rachel if Jacob would work another seven years. This opened a continuing rivalry between two sister-wives.

After twenty years in Mesopotamia, Jacob told Laban that it was time to leave. On one hand, Laban and his sons were envious of Jacob's prosperity and would make a departure difficult; on the other, Jacob feared encountering Esau. But in a dream, God told Jacob to return to the land of his fathers—and that God would be with him.

Key Thought: "Fathers did not think it safe to trust the happiness of their daughters to men who had not made provision for the support of a family" (*Patriarchs and Prophets,* p. 188).

Today's Lesson: We may possibly destroy more than we gain by demanding our rights when we are subjected to unfairness—as Jacob was. Can we trust God to make things right?

The Night of Wrestling

Patriarchs and Prophets, Chapter 18.

"I will not let thee go, except thou bless me"
(Genesis 32:26).

Though assured of God's guidance, Jacob was returning to his home in Palestine, ever mindful of how he had deceived his father—and of Esau's anger. Jacob sent messengers ahead with a conciliatory message for Esau, but they returned with the news that Esau was approaching with four hundred men!

Terror overwhelmed Jacob. He divided his enormous flocks into two groups, hoping that one of them would get through. In addition, he sent generous presents to Esau with a friendly message.

When Jacob reached the Jabbok River, he sent his family across while he remained behind to spend the night in prayer. Bitter was the knowledge that his own sin had brought the innocent into peril. Suddenly a strong hand grasped him. In the dark the two struggled, without a word being spoken. Jacob's only solace was remembering God's promises. At the break of day, the stranger touched Jacob's thigh, and he was crippled instantly. Through humiliation, repentance, and self-surrender, sinful Jacob prevailed with the Majesty of heaven.

Jacob saw more clearly than ever that he had not trusted God's providences regarding the birthright—that he had used his own efforts to bring about what God had planned to accomplish in His own way. But the crisis in Jacob's life had passed.

Jeremiah referred to this experience by the Jabbok as "the time of Jacob's trouble" (see Jeremiah 30:7). After the close of probation, after every person's case has been decided, God's restraining hand will be withdrawn from the earth. Even for the righteous it will be "the time of Jacob's trouble." While God's loyalists will have a deep sense of their unworthiness, they will have no concealed wrongs to reveal. It is now that we are to learn the lesson of prevailing prayer and unyielding faith.

Key Thought: "Jacob's experience during that night of wrestling and anguish represents the trial through which the people of God must pass just before Christ's second coming" (*Patriarchs and Prophets,* p. 201).

Today's Lesson: The decisions we make each day have implications for eternity. Before probation closes for the world, our choices are determining whether we will be mature "wheat" or immature "tares" forever.

The Return to Canaan

Patriarchs and Prophets, Chapter 19.

"Not every one that saith unto me, Lord, Lord, shall enter into the kingdom of heaven; but he that doeth the will of my Father which is in heaven" (Matthew 7:21).

Crossing the Jordan, Jacob settled for a time in Shechem, where Abraham had made his first altar more than a century earlier. Here also Jacob dug the well where, seventeen centuries later, Jesus rested from the noon heat and brought the gospel to a Samaritan woman.

Before going to Bethel as the Lord directed, Jacob determined that his household should be free from idolatry: "Put away the strange gods,. . . and change your garments" (Genesis 35:2). With deep emotion Jacob reviewed the wonderful dealings of God with him; his children were touched by a subduing power, and they responded by giving to "Jacob all the strange gods which were in their hand, and all their earrings which were in their ears" (verse 4).

Two days' journey to Hebron brought Jacob heavy grief—the death of Rachel, his deep love. Shortly before she died, she gave birth to Benjamin. Finally Jacob reached Mamre and his father Isaac. Both Jacob and Esau were at the bedside of their dying father.

Both sons had been instructed in the knowledge of God, but each had walked in different paths that continued to diverge more and more widely. It was no arbitrary choice on the part of God that shut out Esau from the blessings of salvation.

Key Thought: "God has set forth in His word the conditions upon which every soul will be elected to eternal life—obedience to His commandments, through faith in Christ. God has elected a character in harmony with His law, and anyone who shall reach the standard of His requirement will have an entrance into the kingdom of glory. . . . The provisions of redemption are free to all; the results of redemption will be enjoyed by those who have complied with the conditions" (*Patriarchs and Prophets,* pp. 207, 208).

Today's Lesson: In the great controversy, either in heaven or here on earth, we are on the winning side if we choose to be in harmony with the God of heaven; otherwise, it is all self-destruction.

Joseph in Egypt

Patriarchs and Prophets, Chapter 20.

"How then can I do this great wickedness, and sin against God?" (Genesis 39:9).

In only a few hours, Joseph, the cherished son, became a helpless slave on the way to a foreign land. For a time, he was overcome with grief and terror.

But after a few more hours, the Lord helped him to see what had gone wrong in his relations with his brothers. Accustomed to his father's tenderness, he had become self-sufficient and exacting. Now, remembering how God had provided for his father, he trusted his father's God to be his God, as well. One day had transformed Joseph from a petted child into a man—thoughtful, courageous, and self-possessed.

He was sold to Potiphar, the captain of the king's guard, where he remained for ten years as a trusted steward. But Joseph's faith and integrity were soon tested by the guile of Potiphar's wife—his whole future depended upon the decision of the moment. But Joseph's first thought was of God, regardless of earthly consequences.

Obviously, Potiphar did not believe his wife's accusations. He did not kill Joseph, but for the sake of keeping up appearances he abandoned him in a foul prison. For two years Joseph remained a prisoner until God gave the king of Egypt two dreams that the professional wise men could not interpret. Then the chief butler remembered a dream that Joseph had interpreted for him and told the king of this remarkable Hebrew captive.

Joseph's interpretation informed the king of seven years of plenty and then seven years of famine that lay ahead and how the king could avert a great calamity. In all the realm, Joseph was the only man gifted with the wisdom to handle the crisis. His character bore the tests of adversity and prosperity alike. Moral excellence and fine mental qualities are not the result of accident.

Key Thought: "How was Joseph enabled to make such a record of firmness of character, uprightness, and wisdom?—In his early years he had consulted duty rather than inclination" (*Patriarchs and Prophets,* p. 222).

Today's Lesson: Every one has many opportunities to enjoy instant gratification in many ways, but only those who have built up a habit of clear thinking will survive temptations.

Joseph and His Brothers

Patriarchs and Prophets, Chapter 21.

"I am Joseph your brother, whom you sold into Egypt. But now, do not therefore be grieved nor angry with yourselves because you sold me here; for God sent me before you to preserve life" (Genesis 45:4, 5, NKJV).

Under Joseph's direction, immense storehouses were created throughout Egypt, anticipating the surplus of the next seven years. But after seven years of plenty, the famine began, extending even to the land of Canaan where Joseph's family dwelt.

Joseph's brothers journeyed to Egypt to purchase grain, bowing down before their brother without recognizing him. Interrogating them keenly, Joseph asked questions designed to reveal whether they retained their haughty spirit and also to gain information regarding his father. Joseph talked through an interpreter but listened easily to what his brothers were saying. He discovered that they were indeed sorry for their treatment of him. He ordered them to go back to their father with all the grain they could carry but kept Simeon in prison until they returned with their younger brother Benjamin.

In Canaan, the famine grew worse, and Jacob reluctantly agreed to allow Benjamin to go to Egypt with his other sons. Joseph wept in secret when he saw Benjamin. But he tested his brothers' integrity further until he was satisfied that they were indeed repentant for their past sins. After Joseph revealed who he was, he assured them that God had carried out His purposes in spite of their sin and that He had used them and Joseph to preserve lives in the famine. Then he sent them back to Canaan to bring their father and the entire family to Egypt to be safe during the rest of the famine years.

Key Thought: "Men whom God favored, and to whom He entrusted great responsibilities, were sometimes overcome by temptation and committed sin, even as we at the present day strive, waver, and frequently fall into error. Their lives, with all their faults and follies, are open before us, both for our encouragement and warning" (*Patriarchs and Prophets,* p. 238).

Today's Lesson: "Be sure your sin will find you out" (Numbers 32:23). This is generally true, although some do seem to get away with sin unscathed. The odds are not good, however!

Moses

Patriarchs and Prophets, Chapter 22.

**"He supposed his brethren would have understood
how that God by his hand would deliver them: but they
understood not" (Acts 7:25).**

Joseph provided for his family during the years of famine. They had not sold their cattle and lands to Pharaoh, nor did they pay taxes as did the Egyptians. But as the years passed, another pharaoh arose who began to worry about the growing Israelite population. He set taskmasters over them. Then, still worried about the Israelites' numbers and independent spirit, Pharaoh ordered Hebrew boys to be killed at birth.

Jochebed and Amram were determined to keep their baby Moses alive. God arranged for Pharaoh's daughter to find the infant in the bulrushes and preserve his life. He even made it possible for Jochebed to continue to care for him until Moses was 12. Those 12 years set the course of Moses' life. Every mother should realize that the destiny of her children lies largely in her hands.

As the pharaoh's adopted son, Moses received the highest civil and military training possible, educated to become the next pharaoh of Egypt. This training required initiation into the mysteries of Egyptian religion, but he reasoned with the priests, showing the folly of worshiping senseless objects.

At 40 years of age, Moses' life took a sharp turn, and he was forced to flee to the eastern desert. Here, for the next forty years, he learned patience and tempered his passions under the guidance of the Holy Spirit and the wise influence of Jethro, his father-in-law.

Key Thought: "Moses was fitted to take pre-eminence among the great of the earth, to shine in the courts of its most glorious kingdom . . . As historian, poet, philosopher, general of armies, and legislator, he stands without a peer. Yet with the world before him, he had the moral strength to refuse the flattering prospects of wealth and greatness and fame, 'choosing rather to suffer affliction with the people of God, than to enjoy the pleasures of sin for a season' " (*Patriarchs and Prophets,* p. 246).

Today's Lesson: God chooses men and women for special service who have cultivated and dedicated their natural capacities. When we are ready, He will give us more responsibilities.

The Plagues of Egypt

Patriarchs and Prophets, Chapter 23.

"I have made you as God to Pharaoh, and Aaron your brother shall be your prophet" (Exodus 7:1, NKJV).

Aaron, instructed by angels, went to Moses near Horeb, and they discussed what the Lord had been telling them about returning to Egypt and how He would be leading the Israelites out of Egypt.

Obviously, Pharaoh was not pleased with the message from these brothers. The issue became a crisis when Moses explained to the Sabbath-breaking Israelites that obedience to God was the first condition of deliverance. Pharaoh, believing that refusing to work on the seventh day of the week was a sign of revolt, made their work even more oppressive.

However, the Hebrews expected their freedom without any special trial of their faith—they were not yet prepared for deliverance. Many were content to remain in bondage rather than meet the difficulties ahead in a strange land. For this reason God did not deliver them by the first plague for two reasons: He wanted to reveal Himself more clearly to the Israelites, and He wanted Pharaoh's tyrannical spirit to be seen more fully by all concerned.

Before each plague Moses described its nature and consequences, so Pharaoh might save himself and his country if he chose to yield. Other nations would hear of these events and tremble at the God of the Israelites.

Key Thought: "God gave to Pharaoh the most striking evidence of divine power; but the monarch stubbornly refused to heed the light. Every display of infinite power rejected by him, rendered him the more determined in his rebellion. . . . As he continued to venture on in his own course, . . . his heart became more and more hardened. . . .

"He who has once yielded to temptation will yield more readily the second time. Every repetition of the sin lessens his power of resistance, blinds his eyes, and stifles conviction. . . . God works no miracle to prevent the harvest [of rebellious choices]" (*Patriarchs and Prophets,* p. 268).

Today's Lesson: Jesus depicted the end result of the great controversy in terms of choices we make. Thoughts become acts, and acts become character—and character determines our destiny.

31

The Passover

Patriarchs and Prophets, Chapter 24.

"Thus saith the Lord, Israel is my son, even my firstborn: and I say unto thee, Let my son go, that he may serve me: and if thou refuse to let him go, behold, I will slay thy son, even thy firstborn" (Exodus 4:22, 23).

This text is a remarkable statement that Moses made to Pharaoh. But God is merciful and gave Pharaoh and all Egypt six specific warnings that He was serious about delivering His people. Moses' final plea for the release of the Hebrews concluded with a warning that God would kill all the firstborn of Egypt if Pharaoh persisted in his refusal.

Then the Lord, through Moses, gave directions to the Israelites to prepare for their deliverance. But first they were to kill a lamb and sprinkle its blood on their doorposts throughout Goshen. The hasty meal they would eat before leaving would be called the "Lord's passover."

This special meal was to be commemorated by Israelites in all future generations. The celebration would be both commemorative and symbolic, pointing back to their deliverance from Egypt but also looking forward to the greater deliverance from the bondage of sin accomplished by Jesus Christ. Eating the flesh of the lamb symbolized belief in Christ's gift of pardon but also in His constant gift of spiritual strength that changes us into His likeness.

Many Egyptians acknowledged the God of the Hebrews as their only God and begged for shelter in the Hebrew homes when the "destroying angel" passed through the land. Gladly were they welcomed, and together the Israelites and these Egyptians went forth out of the land.

Key Thought: "By obedience the people were to give evidence of their faith. So all who hope to be saved by the merits of the blood of Christ should realize that they themselves have something to do in securing their salvation. While it is Christ only that can redeem us from the penalty of transgression, we are to turn from sin to obedience" (*Patriarchs and Prophets,* p. 279).

Today's Lesson: Christ's sacrifice provides an all-sufficient covering of righteousness to all who are truly grateful and turn to Him in willing, joyful obedience.

The Exodus

Patriarchs and Prophets, Chapter 25.

"Israel saw the great work which the Lord had done in Egypt; so the people feared the Lord, and believed the Lord and His servant Moses" (Exodus 14:31, NKJV).

During the plagues, the Israelites had been preparing for their deliverance, not only with provisions but also in organizing how the large multitude—six hundred thousand men on foot plus women and children—would assemble in various groups. In addition, the people took their flocks and herds. Before leaving, they asked the Egyptians, who were glad to see them leave, for their unpaid labor—and were not refused.

Instead of the direct route to Canaan, the Lord led them southward, toward the Red Sea. By day, a cloud shielded them from the burning heat; by night, the pillar of fire illuminated their camp. Across a dreary, desertlike expanse they journeyed until they camped beside the sea.

Pharaoh's counselors urged that the Israelites were not going to return and that it was folly to believe that the Hebrew God had killed the Egyptian children. A huge attack force was quickly assembled and hastened after the Israelites.

As the Egyptians approached, the cloudy column descended between the Israelites and the Egyptians, forcing Pharaoh's army to halt. The wall of cloud became a light for the Hebrews. The Red Sea parted, walled up on each side, and didn't close until the Hebrews were safe and the Egyptians destroyed.

Key Thought: "Those who defer obedience till every shadow of uncertainty disappears and there remains no risk of failure or defeat, will never obey at all. Unbelief whispers, 'Let us wait till the obstructions are removed, and we can see our way clearly;' but faith courageously urges an advance, hoping all things, believing all things. . . .

"The path where God leads the way may lie through the desert or the sea, but it is a safe path" (*Patriarchs and Prophets,* p. 290).

Today's Lesson: The cloud that protected from the blazing sun and the pillar of fire that provided illumination for the night are mighty illustrations of how the Lord provides the "cloud" and the "fire" today to protect us from the evil one and from our own tendency to fear and to grumble.

From the Red Sea to Sinai

Patriarchs and Prophets, Chapter 26.

"He clave the rocks in the wilderness, and gave them drink as out of the great depths. He brought streams also out of the rock, and caused waters to run down like rivers" (*Psalm 78:15, 16*).

From the Red Sea, the Israelites marched through dreary, bare, desolate deserts. For three days they and all their flock had been without water. First, Marah had bitter water, and that caused great bitterness against Moses. Moses took the problem to the Lord, and the answer was to cast a tree branch into the waters—another great evidence that the Lord was leading them.

Soon they came to Elim with its twelve wells of water and many palm trees, where they made their first encampment. Provisions were beginning to run low, and the murmuring began again. The Lord was permitting difficulties so the Israelites would quickly turn to Him for all their needs. The main problem was that they were magnifying their difficulties and not willing to trust God for the future.

Soon God provided them with daily manna in the mornings and quail in the evenings. In these providential miracles they were also reminded of Sabbath sacredness by a triple blessing: a double portion of manna on Friday, none on Sabbath, and the Friday supply remained sweet and pure until the first day of the week.

Soon they were in view of Mount Sinai, where they would stay for nearly a year. Here God would begin His instructions that would begin to change them into His earthly representatives.

Key Thought: "God would have His people in these days review with a humble heart and teachable spirit the trials through which ancient Israel passed, that they may be instructed in their preparation for the heavenly Canaan" (*Patriarchs and Prophets,* p. 293).

Today's Lesson: Let's not be like the Israelites who saw God's miraculous hand divide the Red Sea and provide manna and water throughout their wilderness wandering—yet grumbled when faced with the next earthly challenge. How soon we tend to despair in spite of evidences of God's hand in our lives!

The Law Given to Israel

Patriarchs and Prophets, Chapter 27.

"You shall be to Me a kingdom of priests and a holy nation" (Exodus 19:6).

Alone, Moses climbed the steep and rugged path up Sinai. He heard the awesome message God wanted delivered to the encamped Israelites—that He wanted them to be His church and a nation under His government (see Exodus 19:3-6).

Never has this planet had a sound and light show that compared with the giving of the Ten Commandments; even Moses said, "I exceedingly fear and quake" (Hebrews 12:21). Then all the Israelites heard God's voice, beginning with a reminder that He is the One who delivered them out of Egypt—their Guide and Deliverer, the One who could be trusted.

The Ten Commandments were not exclusively for the benefit of the Israelites. God honored them by making them the guardians of the law as a sacred trust for the entire world. It is interesting that the Sabbath commandment was not introduced as a new institution but as having been founded at creation—to be remembered and observed as the memorial of God's creation.

Unfortunately, the Israelites, blinded and debased by slavery and heathenism, were not prepared to appreciate fully the far-reaching principles of God's ten precepts. So they could be led to understand more fully the commandments, additional precepts were given that would illustrate and apply the principles of the commandments.

Moses also received directions for building a sanctuary in which the divine presence would be specially manifested. The Israelites would always be reminded of a personal God who was leading them.

Key Thought: "The precepts of the decalogue are adapted to all mankind, and they were given for the instruction and government of all. Ten precepts, brief, comprehensive, and authoritative, cover the duty of man to God and to his fellow man; and all based upon the great fundamental principle of love. . . . In the ten commandments these principles are carried out in detail, and made applicable to the condition and circumstances of man" (*Patriarchs and Prophets,* p. 305).

Today's Lesson: God's commandments are a strong hedge to keep us from embarrassing mistakes or foolish blunders.

Idolatry at Sinai

Patriarchs and Prophets, Chapter 28.

"Make us gods, which shall go before us; for as for this
Moses, the man that brought us up out of the land of
Egypt, we wot [know] not what is become of him"
(Exodus 32:1).

W hen Moses had not returned from the cloud-enclosed Sinai,
the people thought he had deserted them or had been
consumed.

Feeling their helplessness, they returned to their old superstitions.
The "mixed multitude" led in the murmuring and in expressing desire
for an image to represent God. Aaron protested mildly, but his timidity
only urged on the blind frenzy.

A golden ox, a reminder of the gods of Egypt, was created, and the
unreasoning camp gave itself up to gluttony and licentious reveling.
Today we see pliant individuals who, while holding positions of
authority in the church, still yield to the desires of the unconsecrated
and thus encourage them in sin.

The nations around the Israelites had heard of their wonderful
deliverance from Egypt and waited to see what their God would yet do
for them. But the Israelites frustrated God's plans.

On returning to the camp, Moses, hot with anger, threw down the
tablets with the Ten Commandments, destroyed the golden idol, and
demanded that those on the Lord's side stand on his right. Only the
tribe of Levi had not shared in the rebellion and Moses, acting on
divine authority, commanded that they kill those who had persisted in
the rebellion. Punishment must be speedily visited upon transgression
to prevent such scenes from being repeated.

Key Thought: "The glory reflected in the countenance of Moses
illustrates the blessings to be received by God's commandment-
keeping people through the mediation of Christ. It testifies that the
closer our communion with God, and the clearer our knowledge of
His requirements, the more fully shall we be conformed to the divine
image, and the more readily do we become partakers of the divine
nature" (*Patriarchs and Prophets,* p. 330).

Today's Lesson: It is sobering to watch how God deals with
rebellion within the church that has promised to represent Him to the
world. Where would I have stood: with the Levites—or with those who
tried to devise their own ways to worship?

Satan's Enmity Against the Law

Patriarchs and Prophets, Chapter 29.

"Hearken unto me, ye that know righteousness, the people in whose heart is my law" (Isaiah 51:7).

We all know the sad story of how Satan seduced one-third of the angels over the issue of whether God could be trusted—and how he tricked Eve and then Adam into also distrusting God.

God's response was what we call the plan of salvation. Humanity was to be given a second probation; God's plan would make it possible for men and women to be brought back into harmony with Him and render obedience to His law. In the gospel plan, we are never brought into a position where yielding to evil becomes a necessity.

While in Egypt where animals were venerated, the Hebrews were not permitted to present their sacrificial offerings. Thus, for hundreds of years, their minds had not been directed to the great Sacrifice, resulting in a massive loss of knowledge that their forefathers had known so well. Knowledge of God's law had become mingled with heathen customs, so that the commandments were misunderstood and unacknowledged.

Each of the Ten Commandments has been distorted by Satan—then and now—as we well know. Soon Satan and the result of His fight against God's law will be fully laid open to the entire universe, and God's law will stand vindicated.

Key Thought: "From the opening of the great controversy it has been Satan's purpose to misrepresent God's character and to excite rebellion against His law, and this work appears to be crowned with success. . . . Through Satan's temptations the whole human race have become transgressors of God's law, but by the sacrifice of His Son a way is opened whereby they may return to God. Through the grace of Christ they may be enabled to render obedience to the Father's law. Thus in every age, from the midst of apostasy and rebellion, God gathers out a people that are true to Him—a people 'in whose heart is His law.' Isaiah 51:7" (*Patriarchs and Prophets,* p. 338).

Today's Lesson: Christ's life and death have made it possible for each of us to be a part of that people whom God is gathering in preparation for His return.

The Tabernacle and Its Services

Patriarchs and Prophets, Chapter 30.

"Let them make me a sanctuary; that I may dwell among them" (Exodus 25:8).

God especially endowed chosen men with skill and wisdom for the construction of the sacred building. God Himself gave them the plan—a miniature representation of the heavenly sanctuary. Obviously, no earthly model could represent the vastness and glory of the heavenly sanctuary, but it could "represent" the important truths concerning the plan of salvation.

Where did all the expensive materials come from? God had told Moses that "of every man that giveth it willingly with his heart ye shall take my offering" (Exodus 25:2). The Israelites gave so freely of their golden ornaments, their fine linen, and their various prized animal skins that Moses had to restrain their enthusiasm.

The tabernacle was constructed so that it could be taken apart and carried by the Israelites as they continued their journey to the Promised Land. It was divided into two apartments with an open space in front, called the court, which was enclosed by costly linens. These curtains were half as high as the tabernacle, so the Israelites could always see what God had directed to be His "dwelling place."

These two divisions, the Holy Place and the Most Holy Place, represented the two great divisions of Christ's mediatorial work for mankind—each occupying a period of time. The blood of Christ, represented by the slain lamb, did not cancel sin (though the sin was forgiven); it stood on record until the final atonement. Each feature of the sanctuary service depicts the reality of God's provisions for our salvation.

Key Thought: "In the ministration of the tabernacle, and of the temple that afterward took its place, the people were taught each day the great truths relative to Christ's death and ministration, and once each year their minds were carried forward to the closing events of the great controversy between Christ and Satan, the final purification of the universe from sin and sinners" (*Patriarchs and Prophets,* p. 358).

Today's Lesson: We live in the real-time Day of Atonement to which the earthly sanctuary service points. We need to have the same ardor for building God's sanctuary in our hearts as the Israelites had for building the earthly sanctuary.

The Sin of Nadab and Abihu

Patriarchs and Prophets, Chapter 31.

"Woe unto them that call evil good, and good evil; that put darkness for light, and light for darkness" (Isaiah 5:20).

It's hard to believe, but after the sanctuary had been completed and after fire came down from heaven to consume the first offering on the altar, and after the united shout of praise and adoration—sudden and terrible calamity happened to the family of Aaron, the high priest.

Aaron's two sons, Nadab and Abihu, used "strange fire" when they burned the fragrant incense—that is, they used common, ordinary fire and not the sacred fire that God Himself had kindled and commanded to be used for this purpose. As a result, fire went out from the Lord and devoured the men in plain sight of the people.

Their sin showed a disregard for the Lord's clear instruction, especially when they had already had numerous occasions to behold God's glory. One could say what they did was a minor mistake, but God had to teach Israel that even "small" acts of disobedience could not be overlooked, even if committed by church leaders.

The sons of Aaron had flattered themselves that with their high office they could sin with impunity, but this was a fatal deception. Aaron had a yielding disposition, and he had not taught his sons self control from their youth. Without appropriate discipline, they had been permitted to follow inclination.

Key Thought: "The divine rebuke is upon that false sympathy for the sinner which endeavors to excuse his sin. It is the effect of sin to deaden the moral perceptions, so that the wrongdoer does not realize the enormity of transgression, and without the convicting power of the Holy Spirit he remains in partial blindness to his sin. . . . Those who destroy the effect of the warning by blinding the eyes of sinners to the real character and results of sin often flatter themselves that they thus give evidence of their charity" (*Patriarchs and Prophets,* p. 361).

Today's Lesson: Indulgent parents encourage their children to think that they are entitled receive special favors. Often parents find it easier to indulge the wants of their children than to provide needed discipline in their lives.

The Law and the Covenants

Patriarchs and Prophets, Chapter 32.

"If ye will obey my voice indeed, and keep my covenant, then . . . ye shall be unto me a kingdom of priests, and an holy nation" (Exodus 19:5, 6).

When Adam and Eve sinned, the law was not changed, but a remedial system was established to bring humanity back to obedience. After He wrote the Ten Commandments in stone, God commanded Moses to write additional judgments and laws outlining detailed instructions for these former slaves who had shown themselves to be so easily led astray. These directions were the principles of the Ten Commandments amplified and given in a specific manner so no one need err.

The Bible often refers to two covenants—one changeless and the other provisional. Fidelity to God's law remains the condition for eternal life. However, the first covenant, the covenant of grace, offered pardon and assisting grace for obedience through faith in Christ. The terms of the second, or "old" covenant were "obey and live." This covenant the Israelites promised to keep, but their promise was quickly broken. Still, those who were indeed repentant could turn to the "better promises" of the covenant of grace that promised forgiveness and grace to bring them back into harmony with the principles of God's law.

Key Thought: "Though this covenant was made with Adam and renewed to Abraham, it could not be ratified until the death of Christ. It had existed by the promise of God since the first intimation of redemption had been given; it had been accepted by faith; yet when ratified by Christ, it is called a *new* covenant. The law of God was the basis of this covenant, which was simply an arrangement for bringing men again into harmony with the divine will, placing them where they could obey God's law" (*Patriarchs and Prophets,* pp. 370, 371).

Today's Lesson: We are trying to live under the "old" covenant whenever we echo the words of Israel—"All that the Lord has said, we will do and be obedient." Those living under the "new" covenant trust God's promise that He alone can make them obedient through the grace of pardon and the grace of power.

From Sinai to Kadesh

Patriarchs and Prophets, Chapter 33.

*"So I took the chief of your tribes, wise men, and known,
and made them heads over you, captains over thousands,
and captains over hundreds, and captains over fifties,
and captains over tens, and officers among your tribes"
(Deuteronomy 1:15).*

A fter a year of construction, the sanctuary and the various arrangements essential to the Israelites' civil and religious systems were completed, and the first Passover was celebrated.

The camp was arranged in exact order, separated into three great divisions with the position of each tribe specified. The mixed multitude were not permitted to occupy the same quarters with Israel's tribes but were located on the outer edges of the camp.

Sanitary regulations were strictly enforced to ensure scrupulous cleanliness. Whenever the camp moved, Moses and Aaron led the way, followed by the sons of Kohath carrying the sacred ark that contained the Ten Commandments. The priests, carrying silver trumpets, stood nearby.

As time passed, Aaron and Miriam became blinded by jealousy over the appointment of seventy elders to help Moses in leading the Israelites. They were filled with contempt for Zipporah, Moses' wife. Moses silently bore these insults without complaint for many months, but at last God stepped in. Miriam became leprous, and Aaron was severely rebuked.

Key Thought: "At the giving of the manna, just before Israel reached Sinai, the Lord had granted them flesh in answer to their clamors; but it was furnished them for only one day.

"God might as easily have provided them with flesh as with manna, but a restriction was placed upon them for their good. . . . The perverted appetite was to be brought into a more healthy state, that they might enjoy the food originally provided for man—the fruits of the earth, which God gave to Adam and Eve in Eden. It was for this reason that the Israelites had been deprived, in a great measure, of animal food. . . . Had they been willing to deny appetite, in obedience to His wise restrictions, feebleness and disease would have been unknown among them" (*Patriarchs and Prophets,* pp. 377, 378).

Today's Lesson: The Lord has given instructions regarding diet and good health in order to bless His people physically, mentally, and spiritually.

The Twelve Spies

Patriarchs and Prophets, Chapter 34.

"All the children of Israel murmured against Moses and against Aaron: and the whole congregation said unto them, Would God that we had died in the land of Egypt! Or would God we had died in this wilderness"
(Numbers 14:2).

Eleven days after leaving Mt. Sinai, the Israelites camped at Kadesh. Here, the people proposed that spies be sent into the Promised Land. One man from each tribe was selected.

After forty days, the spies returned with wonderful samples of grapes, figs, and pomegranates. But they also reported great dangers—walled cities and even giants. The people's mood became one of despair. They forgot the daily miracles and the One who had brought them this far.

Caleb and Joshua urged the people to go up at once and possess the land. But ten spies painted an ever-bleaker picture. Revolt and open mutiny developed—even to the point of accusing God of deceiving them with false hopes. With satanic hatred, the Israelites rushed to stone Caleb and Joshua, but God's presence, illuminating the tabernacle, stopped them. God told Moses to inform the people that just as the spies took forty days to scout the land, so Israel was to turn back toward the Red Sea and wander for forty years in the wilderness.

Once again changing their fickle minds, the rebellious leaders now attempted to conquer the Canaanites but were terribly defeated.

Key Thought: "Forced to submission at last, the survivors 'returned, and wept before the Lord;' but 'the Lord would not hearken' to their voice. Deuteronomy 1:45. By their signal victory the enemies of Israel, who had before awaited with trembling the approach of that mighty host, were inspired with confidence to resist them. . . . That first defeat of Israel, by inspiring the Canaanites with courage and resolution, had greatly increased the difficulties of the conquest. Nothing remained for Israel but to fall back from the face of their victorious foes, into the wilderness, knowing that here must be the grave of a whole generation" (*Patriarchs and Prophets,* p. 394).

Today's Lesson: We all have had foolish moments when we think we can reach our dreams without doing it God's way. Could God fully support your plans?

The Rebellion of Korah

Patriarchs and Prophets, Chapter 35.

"Korah . . . took men: And they rose up before Moses, with certain of the children of Israel, two hundred and fifty princes of the assembly, famous in the congregation, men of renown: And they gathered themselves together against Moses and against Aaron, and said unto them, Ye take too much upon you, seeing all the congregation are holy, every one of them, and the Lord is among them: wherefore then lift ye up yourselves above the congregation of the Lord?" (Numbers 16:1–3).

Korah was a Levite and Moses' cousin—a man of ability and influence. He was dissatisfied with his position as a caretaker of the sanctuary and aspired to the dignity of the priesthood. He found many sympathizers among those who did not accept God's decree that they would remain in the wilderness for forty more years and who secretly opposed the authority of Moses and Aaron.

When the showdown came, Korah and 250 princes who supported him called the people together to witness their victory over Moses and Aaron. But Moses, at God's direction, warned Korah and his followers that the Lord would show His support for Moses and Aaron by causing the earth to open her mouth and swallow up Korah and the rebellious princes. The earthquake and the fire which followed it destroyed Korah, the princes, and their followers—14,000 rebels in all!

Using the same methods Satan had employed in heaven, Korah deceived many into believing that they had been wronged by Moses and that right was on their side. They fondly cherished a new order of things in which praise would take the place of reproof and ease would replace anxiety and conflict.

Key Thought: "They accused Moses of pretending to act under divine guidance, as a means of establishing his authority; and they declared that they would no longer submit to be led about like blind men, now toward Canaan, and now toward the wilderness, as best suited his ambitious designs" (*Patriarchs and Prophets,* p. 399).

Today's Lesson: Korah's rebellion is repeated today by those who look for excuses to be suspicious of church leaders, claiming to be righteous while at the same time undermining those God has appointed to direct His church.

In the Wilderness

Patriarchs and Prophets, Chapter 36.

"Yet thou in thy manifold mercies forsookest them not in the wilderness: the pillar of the cloud departed not from them by day, to lead them in the way; neither the pillar of fire by night, to shew them light, and the way wherein they should go. Thou gavest also thy good spirit to instruct them, and withheldest not thy manna from their mouth, and gavest them water for their thirst. Yea, forty years didst thou sustain them in the wilderness, so that they lacked nothing; their clothes waxed not old, and their feet swelled not" (Nehemiah 9:19–21).

An awful forty years! Not even a single celebration of the Passover! But the tabernacle service continued, and God continued to supply His people's needs. The only records we have of these forty years are instances of rebellion against God. Not one of those who were doomed to wander in the wilderness would enter the Promised Land—except Caleb and Joshua.

The mixed multitude was a source of continual temptation and trouble—the first to stir up strife and the first to complain. When open, willful violation of the Sabbath laws occurred, God ordered the violators to be stoned, but even this did not halt the great carelessness shown toward His law.

Even the new generation—those born during the wilderness wanderings—failed to learn their lesson and did not turn to God with a sincere purpose. As a result, God declared that they would be scattered among the heathen after they entered the land of promise and were settled in Canaan.

Key Thought: "Here Miriam died and was buried. From that scene of rejoicing on the shores of the Red Sea, when Israel went forth with song and dance to celebrate Jehovah's triumph, to the wilderness grave which ended a lifelong wandering—such had been the fate of millions who with high hopes had come forth from Egypt. Sin had dashed from their lips the cup of blessing. Would the next generation learn the lesson?" (*Patriarchs and Prophets,* p. 410).

Today's Lesson: We need to avoid following Israel's example in the wilderness—calling upon the Lord only in tough situations and soon forgetting their promises when the trial passed.

FEBRUARY 6

The Smitten Rock

Patriarchs and Prophets, Chapter 37.

"They drank of that spiritual Rock that followed them: and that Rock was Christ" (1 Corinthians 10:4).

For forty years God provided Israel with water. Beginning with the miracle near Sinai and extending throughout their journey, water gushed from nearby rocks. What a lesson for us! As the life-giving waters flowed from the smitten rock, so from Christ, "smitten of God" (Isaiah 53:4), streams of salvation flow for a lost race.

This remarkable, continuing miracle was celebrated by the Israelites after they were established in Canaan. On each of the seven days of the Feast of Tabernacles, the priests went out with a Levite choir to draw water from the spring of Siloam.

Jesus made use of this symbolic service to direct the minds of the people to the eternal water that He came to give them: "If any man thirst, let him come unto me, and drink" (John 7:37). When we abide in Christ, we have within us a never-failing fountain of grace and strength. Moses pointed to Christ as the rock of salvation (see Deuteronomy 32:15). The psalmist sang of God as "the rock of my strength," a "rock that is higher than I" (see Psalm 62:7; 61:2).

Key Thought: "All who profess godliness are under the most sacred obligation to guard the spirit, and to exercise self-control under the greatest provocation. The burdens placed upon Moses were very great; few men will ever be so severely tried as he was; yet this was not allowed to excuse his sin. God has made ample provision for His people; and if they rely upon His strength, they will never become the sport of circumstances. The strongest temptation cannot excuse sin. However great the pressure brought to bear upon the soul, transgression is our own act. It is not in the power of earth or hell to compel anyone to do evil. Satan attacks us at our weak points, but we need not be overcome. However severe or unexpected the assault, God has provided help for us, and in His strength we may conquer" (*Patriarchs and Prophets,* p. 421).

Today's Lesson: There is no excuse for sin—not heredity, not environment, and not tough times. By God's grace, we may resist temptation.

The Journey Around Edom

Patriarchs and Prophets, Chapter 38.

"Him that cometh to me I will in no wise cast out"
(John 6:37).

At the end of their wilderness wandering, the Israelites were again on the border at Kadesh. From there, the easiest and quickest route to reach Canaan lay through Edom.

If the Israelites had fully obeyed the Lord since leaving Egypt, all the nations around them would have feared their presence. But their sad record, especially their foolish war with the Amalekites, relaxed those fears. The Edomites refused to let them pass, no longer afraid of their mysterious power.

So, the Israelites turned south, going over the same miserable land they had seen for many years, even to Sinai (or Mount Horeb). Here Aaron would be buried, never seeing the Promised Land that had beckoned him for forty years.

Even now, the Israelites continued to forget how the Lord had led them from the crossing of the Red Sea to the present. Because of their unbelief, God removed His protection against the poisonous serpents that were all around them in the desert. Soon almost every tent contained someone dead or dying.

The people, now humbled, pled with Moses to ask the Lord to protect them. God told Moses to make a serpent of brass and said that all who looked at it in faith would find relief. The people well knew that the healing virtue came from God alone—but still, many lamented their dire situation.

Key Thought: "Many are unwilling to accept of Christ until the whole mystery of the plan of salvation shall be made plain to them. . . . Many wander in the mazes of philosophy, in search of reasons and evidence which they will never find, while they reject the evidence which God has been pleased to give. . . . God will never remove every occasion for doubt. He gives sufficient evidence on which to base faith, and if this is not accepted, the mind is left in darkness" (*Patriarchs and Prophets,* p. 432).

Today's Lesson: Those who are willing to look to God in faith, trusting Him even when all is not clear, will receive the eternal life He has promised.

47

The Conquest of Bashan

Patriarchs and Prophets, Chapter 39.

"Fear him not: for I will deliver him, and all his people, and his land, into thy hand; and thou shalt do unto him as thou didst unto Sihon king of the Amorites, which dwelt at Heshbon" (Deuteronomy 3:2).

After circling around Edom the Israelites entered an elevated plain, swept by cool breezes from the hills. Crossing the brook Zered, they passed to the east of Moab, where the descendants of Lot lived. As with the Edomites, Israel was not to do battle with the Moabites or the Ammonites.

Pushing northward, Moses sent a friendly message to Sihon, the Amorite king who had a well-trained army, but he received a decided refusal to allow Israel to pass through Amorite territory. Moses kept his eye on the cloudy pillar, meanwhile preparing the Israelites for battle.

The Amorites had plenty of evidence that God was with Israel, but they rejected the light and clung to their idols. The Israelites crossed the Arnon and won a great victory; soon they possessed the land of the Amorites.

Next the cloudy pillar moved north, facing the powerful kingdom of Bashan, whose inhabitants were descended from giants and whose king, Og, was remarkable for size and strength. Og's army looked invincible, but Moses was calm and firm and inspired his people to trust the omnipotent arm of God. The Bashanites were defeated and were blotted from the earth—they had given themselves up to iniquity and abominable idolatry.

Key Thought: "Everyone who seeks to follow the path of duty will at times be assailed by doubt and unbelief. The way will sometimes be so barred by obstacles, apparently insurmountable, as to dishearten those who will yield to discouragement; but God is saying to such, Go forward. Do your duty at any cost. The difficulties that seem so formidable, that fill your soul with dread, will vanish as you move forward in the path of obedience, humbly trusting in God" (*Patriarchs and Prophets,* p. 437).

Today's Lesson: The trials and difficulties that seem so impossible for us to overcome will vanish before us if we move forward in faith, trusting God for deliverance.

Balaam

Patriarchs and Prophets, Chapter 40.

"Balaam . . . loved the wages of unrighteousness; but was rebuked for his iniquity: the dumb ass speaking with man's voice forbad the madness of the prophet" (*2 Peter 2:15, 16*).

Although the Moabites had not been molested by the Israelites, they were greatly troubled by their successes. With Israel on its borders, Moab sought an alliance with the Midianites to defeat the Israelites. Their strategy included sending for Balaam, an inhabitant of Mesopotamia who reportedly possessed supernatural powers.

Balaam, once a good man and a prophet of God, had apostatized in pursuit of his covetousness. But He knew that he could do nothing against a people led by the God of Israel. When the messengers arrived, the Lord told him that night, "Thou shalt not go with them; thou shalt not curse the people; for they are blessed." And Balaam refused to go with the messengers.

Balak, assuming that Balaam simply wanted to be coaxed with more money and honor, sent a larger group to convince him. This time, the Lord allowed Balaam to go, but Balaam warned the messengers that the words he would speak would be prompted by God. When Balaam saw the encampment of the Israelites, he was astonished at their prosperity. With that he should have severed all connection with Moab—but covetousness and the gifts he hoped to obtain prevailed.

Key Thought: "The tempter is ever presenting worldly gain and honor to entice men from the service of God. He tells them it is their overconscientiousness that keeps them from prosperity. . . . One wrong step makes the next easier, and they become more and more presumptuous. . . . Many flatter themselves that they can depart from strict integrity for a time, for the sake of some worldly advantage, and that having gained their object, they can change their course when they please. Such are entangling themselves in the snare of Satan, and it is seldom that they escape" (*Patriarchs and Prophets*, p. 440).

Today's Lesson: Many today have the same yearning to be "successful" that Balaam had. They take one "innocent" step after another without realizing how difficult it is to retrace one's steps without a complete surrender to God.

Apostasy at the Jordan

Patriarchs and Prophets, Chapter 41.

"She hath cast down many wounded; yea, many strong men have been slain by her" (Proverbs 7:26).

While Moses was occupied in planning for the occupation of Canaan, the Israelites generally had time on their hands to interact with the people in the towns on the other side of the Jordan. Balaam suggested a grand festival to be sponsored by the king of Moab, and it was secretly arranged that Balaam would induce the Israelites to attend. Beguiled with music and dancing, passions were in full sway, helped along with indulgence in wine.

Those who had stood up against their enemies in battle were overcome by the wiles of heathen women. The rulers and leading men were among the first to transgress. Suddenly, a terrible pestilence broke out, killing tens of thousands and awakening the people to the enormity of their sin. God commanded that the leaders in the apostasy be put to death, and their bodies were hung up in sight of all Israel.

The Midianites—the chief seducers in this shameful orgy—were speedily punished. Five of their kings were slain—as was Balaam.

God's people have always had to contend with sensual indulgence, one of Satan's most successful temptations. Today, on the borders of the heavenly Canaan, this appeal of debasing vice is especially seductive.

Key Thought: "It was when the Israelites were in a condition of outward ease and security that they were led into sin. They failed to keep God ever before them, they neglected prayer and cherished a spirit of self-confidence. . . . A long preparatory process, unknown to the world, goes on in the heart before the Christian commits open sin. The mind does not come down at once from purity and holiness to depravity, corruption, and crime. . . . By the indulgence of impure thoughts man can so educate his mind that sin which he once loathed will become pleasant to him" (*Patriarchs and Prophets,* p. 459).

Today's Lesson: The apostasy at the Jordan illustrates that we must work with the Holy Spirit to avoid anything that would suggest impure thoughts—especially in today's world.

The Law Repeated

Patriarchs and Prophets, Chapter 42.

"I pray thee, let me go over, and see the good land that is beyond Jordan, that goodly mountain, and Lebanon. But the Lord was wroth with me for your sakes, and would not hear me: and the Lord said unto me, Let it suffice thee; speak no more unto me of this matter"
(Deuteronomy 3:25, 26).

Before he turned over to Joshua his position as the visible leader of Israel, Moses was directed to rehearse to the Israelites the history of their deliverance from Egypt, their wilderness experiences, and the occasion of the giving of the Ten Commandments.

As Moses reviewed the past forty years, the people of Israel listened with a new confidence in him. They could now see that their suspicion, pride, ambition, and selfishness made them unprepared to properly represent their Lord in their attempt to possess Canaan—that the delay was not God's fault but theirs.

God also gave Moses a look into the far future, to the terrible scenes of Israel's final overthrow as a nation and the destruction of Jerusalem by the Roman armies. He ended his long speech with sacred verse—a song he directed the people to commit to memory and to teach to their children. The parents were to so impress the words of this song upon the susceptible minds of their children that they might never be forgotten.

Key Thought: "After the public rehearsal of the law, Moses completed the work of writing all the laws, the statutes, and the judgments which God had given him, and all the regulations concerning the sacrificial system. The book containing these was placed in charge of the proper officers, and was for safe keeping deposited in the side of the ark. Still the great leader was filled with fear that the people would depart from God. In a most sublime and thrilling address he set before them the blessings that would be theirs on condition of obedience, and the curses that would follow upon transgression" (*Patriarchs and Prophets*, p. 466).

Today's Lesson: God has given us solemn responsibilities to impart to our children and grandchildren the great truths of His role in the history of His last-day church.

The Death of Moses

Patriarchs and Prophets, Chapter 43.

"So Moses the servant of the Lord died there in the land of Moab, according to the word of the Lord. And he buried him in a valley in the land of Moab, over against Beth-peor; but no man knoweth of his sepulchre" *(Deuteronomy 34:5, 6).*

The history of Israel displayed in the clearest terms how God's love and mercy is mingled with His strict, impartial justice. When God told Moses that he would not be leading Israel into the Promised Land, Moses resolved to resign his life into the hands of his Creator without a murmur. But God had one more duty for Moses to perform before he was to die alone on Mount Nebo. He was to pronounce a blessing upon each tribe and introduce his successor to Israel. Carrying out that assignment revealed the majesty of Moses' character.

In his final address to the people, Moses portrayed what lay ahead for them in the land of promise. He foresaw the first advent of Jesus and the awful reception He would receive. He saw that the Lord's followers, like Abraham, would be called to guard God's law and the gospel of Jesus and to make them known to the world.

Key Thought: "Never, till exemplified in the sacrifice of Christ, were the justice and the love of God more strikingly displayed than in His dealings with Moses. God shut Moses out of Canaan, to teach a lesson which should never be forgotten—that He requires exact obedience, and that men are to beware of taking to themselves the glory which is due to their Maker. He could not grant the prayer of Moses that he might share the inheritance of Israel, but He did not forget or forsake His servant. The God of heaven understood the suffering that Moses had endured; He had noted every act of faithful service through those long years of conflict and trial. On the top of Pisgah, God called Moses to an inheritance infinitely more glorious than the earthly Canaan" (*Patriarchs and Prophets,* p. 479).

Today's Lesson: Even a man as faithful and heroic as Moses was accountable for his sins; only Jesus can forgive us and empower us to overcome our transgressions.

Crossing the Jordan

Patriarchs and Prophets, Chapter 44.

"There shall not any man be able to stand before thee all the days of thy life: as I was with Moses, so I will be with thee: I will not fail thee, nor forsake thee" (Joshua 1:5).

Joshua, now the acknowledged leader of Israel, had acted as prime minister under Moses. His quiet, unpretending fidelity and his steadfastness when others wavered gave evidence of his fitness to succeed Moses. Furthermore, Joshua was well known as a warrior, and his martial gifts and virtues were now especially valuable.

Before the Israelites lay the Jordan River, its banks now overflowing with the melting of mountain snows. Across the river was the heavily fortified city of Jericho. But Joshua knew that God would make a way for His people to perform whatever He might command.

When the time came to move forward, those carrying the ark containing the Ten Commandments led the way, separated from the rest of Israel by a half mile. As soon as their feet stepped into the river, the waters of the Jordan were swept back until the riverbed lay bare. Then the priests stood in the middle of the river until all Israel had passed by. This miracle made an enormous impression—on both Israel and its enemies, filling the surrounding nations with terror.

At Gilgal, their first encampment in the Promised Land, the Israelites celebrated the first Passover since their rebellion at Kadesh. The manna ceased the next day; they could now eat from the produce of the land of Canaan.

Key Thought: "Heathen nations had reproached the Lord and His people because the Hebrews had failed to take possession of Canaan, as they expected, soon after leaving Egypt. Their enemies had triumphed because Israel had wandered so long in the wilderness, and they had mockingly declared that the God of the Hebrews was not able to bring them into the Promised Land. The Lord had now signally manifested His power and favor in opening the Jordan before His people, and their enemies could no longer reproach them" (*Patriarchs and Prophets,* p. 486).

Today's Lesson: When we feel alone and a failure, the Lord often works in our behalf to part the Jordan River in our lives.

The Fall of Jericho

Patriarchs and Prophets, Chapter 45.

"By faith the walls of Jericho fell down" (Hebrews 11:30).

Jericho, one of the strongest and wealthiest fortresses in Canaan, was also a principal seat of idol worship—a vile and degraded center devoted to Ashtaroth, the moon goddess.

God gave specific instructions regarding Jericho's destruction. The Israelites were not to assault the city; for six days they were simply to march around it in an orderly manner. On the seventh day, they were to march around the city seven times and await the mighty blast of the trumpets. At the sound of the trumpets, the earth shook, and the walls of solid stones crashed down, paralyzing the inhabitants of Jericho with terror.

All Israel realized that the conquest had been wholly the Lord's doing—that they were simply His instruments. God had made His plans known in advance only to Joshua; He was building the faith of the Israelites so that they would trust Joshua—and Him.

Following the defeat at Ai, the Lord made clear that secret sin was in the camp. After solemn investigation, Achan confessed his sin and was immediately executed. His theft of the spoils of war in conquering Jericho directly defied God's explicit warning to Israel not to keep for themselves "the accursed thing."

Achan's sin was covetousness—one of the most common and most lightly regarded of sins. For one man's sin, the displeasure of God will rest upon His church, keeping back the blessings that the church needs to finish the gospel program.

Key Thought: "When the records of heaven shall be opened, the Judge will not in words declare to man his guilt, but will cast one penetrating, convicting glance, and every deed, every transaction of life, will be vividly impressed upon the memory of the wrongdoer. The person will not, as in Joshua's day, need to be hunted out from tribe to family, but his own lips will confess his shame. The sins hidden from the knowledge of men will then be proclaimed to the whole world" (*Patriarchs and Prophets,* p. 498).

Today's Lesson: Sinful habits that are not overcome continue to delay the Lord's plan to finish His work in these last days.

The Blessings and the Curses

Patriarchs and Prophets, Chapter 46.

"And ye shall teach them your children, speaking of them when thou sittest in thine house, and when thou walkest by the way, when thou liest down, and when thou risest up" (Deuteronomy 11:19).

After Achan was removed, God told Joshua to organize the warriors and successfully take Ai. But now it was time for a solemn religious service of renewed commitment on the Plain of Shechem, the valley between Ebal and Gerizim—a time for the solemn recognition of God's law and His leadership. The plain was a fitting theater for the ceremony, with lovely greenery and gorgeous flowers to cheer the wilderness-weary throng. And their antiphonal responses would reverberate from the two mountains.

Not many weeks before, Moses had given the whole book of Deuteronomy to the Israelites, but now Joshua read the law again. From then on, every seventh year, the whole law was to be read to all Israel. Why? Because Satan is ever at work, perverting what God has spoken. That is why the Lord is explicit, making His requirements so plain that none need err.

Religious teachers should be well-informed in the facts and lessons of Bible history and the warnings and requirements of the Lord. They should use simple language, adapted to the comprehension of children. Parents, above all, should recognize that they have the primary responsibility for instructing their children. But this means that they themselves must be eagerly interested in what the Bible says.

Key Thought: "Every chapter and every verse of the Bible is a communication from God to men. We should bind its precepts as signs upon our hands and as frontlets between our eyes. If studied and obeyed, it would lead God's people, as the Israelites were led, by the pillar of cloud by day and the pillar of fire by night" (*Patriarchs and Prophets,* p. 504).

Today's Lesson: God, through Moses and Joshua, made it very plain that the people should maintain a high awareness and constant review of biblical truths. How serious am I in my daily walk to set aside time to focus on the Bible so that even the familiar does not become hazy over time?

League With the Gibeonites

Patriarchs and Prophets, Chapter 47.

"Joshua made peace with [the Gibeonites], and made a league with them, to let them live: and the princes of the congregation sware unto them. And it came to pass at the end of three days after they had made a league with them, that they heard that they were their neighbours, and that they dwelt among them" (Joshua 9:15, 16).

The Gibeon ambassadors had represented themselves to be from a distant country that had heard about the Israelites' remarkable success. Their clothing and sandals were worn and patched, and their wine bottles were in disrepair. They convinced the Hebrew leaders who did not check with the Lord. Three days later, the Hebrew princes learned that they had been deceived. However, they had sworn by the Lord that they would not harm the Gibeonites. So, the Gibeonites were permitted to live but only as servants to perform menial services in the sanctuary and to cut wood and carry water. The Gibeonites were glad to purchase life on any terms—even perpetual servitude.

But their troubles were not over. The kings of Canaan confederated to destroy the four Gibeonite cities. The Gibeonites called on their new Israelite allies for help. Joshua, after seeking counsel from the Lord, marched the Israelites to Gibeon's defense. The Canaanite kings fled in terror and were struck down with fierce hailstones.

Realizing that the day would end before he could finish the battle, Joshua asked the Lord to cause the sun to "stand still" until all the Amorites had been conquered. Through divine aid, he overcame Israel's enemies and faithfully followed God's plan.

Key Thought: "It was no light humiliation to those citizens [the Gibeonites] of a 'royal city,' 'all the men whereof were mighty,' to be made hewers of wood and drawers of water throughout their generations. But they had adopted the garb of poverty for the purpose of deception, and it was fastened upon them as a badge of perpetual servitude. Thus through all their generations their servile condition would testify to God's hatred of falsehood" (*Patriarchs and Prophets*, p. 507).

Today's Lesson: Prayer is the open secret of spiritual power. Those who have accomplished much for God have been often in prayer.

The Division of Canaan

Patriarchs and Prophets, Chapter 48.

*"So Joshua smote all the country of the hills, and of the
south, and of the vale, and of the springs, and all their
kings: he left none remaining, but utterly destroyed all
that breathed, as the Lord God of Israel commanded. . . .
And all these kings and their land did Joshua take at one
time, because the Lord God of Israel fought for Israel"
(Joshua 10:40, 42).*

Although the power of the Canaanites had been broken, they had not yet been fully dispossessed. But Joshua was not to continue his military conquests. It was now the duty of each tribe to subdue fully its own inheritance. If each tribe remained faithful, the Lord would drive out their enemies.

The bounds of the twelve tribes would be decided by lot. Only the Levites, devoted to the sanctuary service, were not counted in this allotment. Instead, they were given forty-eight cities in different parts of the country for their inheritance.

But before the distribution, 85-year-old Caleb, representing his tribe, asked for Hebron—a land that had not yet been conquered. Hebron was the home of the dreaded Anakim—the giants who had terrified the ten spies forty years earlier—and Caleb wanted to set an example that would honor God and encourage the other tribes.

Key Thought: "The wisdom displayed by the Reubenites and their companions is worthy of imitation. While honestly seeking to promote the cause of true religion, they were misjudged and severely censured; yet they manifested no resentment. They listened with courtesy and patience to the charges of their brethren before attempting to make their defense, and then fully explained their motives and showed their innocence. Thus the difficulty which had threatened such serious consequences was amicably settled.

"Even under false accusation those who are in the right can afford to be calm and considerate. God is acquainted with all that is misunderstood and misinterpreted by men, and we can safely leave our case in His hands" (*Patriarchs and Prophets,* p. 520).

Today's Lesson: The Lord is still looking for those like Caleb and the Reubenites to witness to His power in supporting their courage and genuine faith. Do I allow God to work through me?

The Last Words of Joshua

Patriarchs and Prophets, Chapter 49.

*"The Lord your God is he that hath fought for you. . . .
And Israel served the Lord all the days of Joshua and all
the days of the elders that overlived Joshua, and which
had known all the works of the Lord, that he had done for
Israel" (Joshua 23:3; 24:31).*

Some years had passed since the Hebrews had settled into their special areas, but soon the same evils that had brought earlier judgments upon Israel became apparent. Old and worn, Joshua was filled with anxiety for the future of his people. He called them for a farewell speech, repeating the same blessings and warnings that Moses had given in his last speech.

Joshua understood that Satan has many plausible theories designed to mislead—such as the idea that God's love is so great that He will excuse sin in His people. Or that the warnings of God's Word serve a certain purpose but are never to be literally fulfilled. The history of Israel, however, reveals that so-called "love" which would set aside justice is not love but weakness and compromise—especially when such "love" does not make plain that the sure result of wrongdoing is misery and death. From the standpoint of the great controversy, such a perversion of God's love would fill the unfallen universe with consternation.

Key Thought: "Joshua desired to lead them [the Israelites] to serve God, not by compulsion, but willingly. Love to God is the very foundation of religion. To engage in His service merely from hope of reward or fear of punishment would avail nothing. Open apostasy would not be more offensive to God than hypocrisy and mere formal worship. . . . It was only by faith in Christ that they could secure pardon of sin and receive strength to obey God's law. They must cease to rely upon their own efforts for salvation, they must trust wholly in the merits of the promised Saviour, if they would be accepted of God" (*Patriarchs and Prophets,* pp. 523, 524).

Today's Lesson: God not only promises to pardon our sins, He also promises to empower us to overcome sin. By His grace we can meet temptation victoriously.

Tithes and Offerings

Patriarchs and Prophets, Chapter 50.

"All the tithe of the land, whether of the seed of the land, or of the fruit of the tree, is the Lord's: it is holy unto the Lord" (Leviticus 27:30).

The tithing system did not originate with the Hebrews. From earliest times, the Lord claimed a tithe—a tenth—as His, and this claim was recognized and honored by those who responded gratefully to His generosity and protecting care. The system of tithes and offerings was intended to impress the mind with a great truth—that God is the source of every blessing that we enjoy in life.

In ancient Israel, the tithe was to be used exclusively to support the Levites. In addition to the tithe, offerings were to be used for sanctuary upkeep. The contributions required of the Hebrews for religious and charitable purposes amount to fully one-fourth of their income. But the faithful observance of these regulations regarding tithes and offerings was one of the conditions of their prosperity.

Those who have faithfully followed God's direction in the matter of tithes and offerings have found Malachi's promise to be a living reality: "I will rebuke the devourer for your sakes, and he shall not destroy the fruits of your ground" (Malachi 3:11).

The principle laid down by Christ is that our offerings to God should be in proportion to the light and privileges we enjoy. We are God's stewards. To those who proved themselves faithful stewards He will commit greater trusts: "Them that honour me I will honour" (1 Samuel 2:30).

Key Thought: "The work of the gospel, as it widens, requires greater provision to sustain it than was called for anciently; and this makes the law of tithes and offerings of even more urgent necessity now than under the Hebrew economy. If His people were liberally to sustain His cause by their voluntary gifts, instead of resorting to unchristian and unhallowed methods to fill the treasury, God would be honored, and many more souls would be won to Christ" (*Patriarchs and Prophets,* p. 529).

Today's Lesson: We may pay tithe in order to impress God—or to honor Him. God wants us to trust Him as a child trusts its father.

God's Care for the Poor

Patriarchs and Prophets, Chapter 51.

"At the end of every seven years thou shalt make a release" (Deuteronomy 15:1).

A second tithe provided for the poor and to assist in the expenses of assembling the people for religious services. This second tithe—whether of money or produce or firstlings of the flocks—was brought to the sanctuary for a religious feast to which the Levite, the stranger, the fatherless, and the widow were invited. Every third year, this second tithe was to be used at home in entertaining the Levite and the poor—a special fund for charity and hospitality.

This second tithe, with its special recognition of the poor and unfortunate, greatly distinguished the laws given by Moses from the laws of the heathen kingdoms. As long as Israel followed God's instructions, no beggars would need to be among them.

Further, the poor were given the right to a certain portion of the produce of the soil. A hungry person could eat the grain or fruit from his neighbor's field or orchard or vineyard to satisfy his hunger. All the gleanings of harvested fields, orchards, and vineyards belonged to the poor.

Every seventh year, special provision was made for the poor. In this sabbatical year, the crops were not to be planted or vineyards dressed. Whatever the land produced spontaneously, the people might eat fresh, but they were not to lay up any portion in storehouses. How would this work? In the sixth year the Lord would make ample provision for a super crop.

Key Thought: "If the law given by God for the benefit of the poor had continued to be carried out, how different would be the present condition of the world, morally, spiritually, and temporally! Selfishness and self-importance would not be manifested as now, but each would cherish a kind regard for the happiness and welfare of others; and such widespread destitution as is now seen in many lands would not exist" (*Patriarchs and Prophets,* p. 536).

Today's Lesson: We can be God's instruments to care for the disadvantaged by the way we allocate our personal funds. God's blessings are given that we may, in turn, bless others who need our help.

The Annual Feasts

Patriarchs and Prophets, Chapter 52.

"Three times thou shalt keep a feast unto me in the year" (Exodus 23:14).

Although surrounded by Canaanites and others who were eager to seize their land, all the able-bodied men of Israel were required to go three times each year to the sanctuary to observe the annual feasts. The Lord promised to restrain their enemies while they were away from their homes.

The first of these feasts, the Passover, occurred in the spring and marked the beginning of the Feast of Unleavened Bread, which lasted for seven days. The second annual gathering was Pentecost, also known as the feast of harvest. And the third, the Feast of Tabernacles, acknowledged God's bounty in the products of the orchard, the olive grove, and the vineyard. This feast was an occasion for rejoicing. It took place just after the great Day of Atonement, when the people received assurance that their iniquity was cleansed and would be remembered no more.

These yearly assemblies encouraged the young and old in God's service and strengthened the ties binding the tribes of Israel to God and to each other. For those who lived at a distance from the sanctuary, more than a month of every year must have been devoted to attending these annual feasts.

Key Thought: "The people of Israel praised God at the Feast of Tabernacles, as they called to mind His mercy in their deliverance from the bondage of Egypt and His tender care for them during their pilgrim life in the wilderness. They rejoiced also in the consciousness of pardon and acceptance, through the service of the Day of Atonement, just ended. But when the ransomed of the Lord shall have been safely gathered into the heavenly Canaan, forever delivered from the bondage of the curse, under which 'the whole creation groaneth and travaileth in pain together until now' (Romans 8:22), they will rejoice with joy unspeakable and full of glory. Christ's great work of atonement for men will then have been completed, and their sins will have been forever blotted out" (*Patriarchs and Prophets,* p. 542).

Today's Lesson: When we meet with God's people wherever they gather to worship and fellowship, God has promised to bless us and make us a blessing to others.

FEBRUARY 22

The Earlier Judges

Patriarchs and Prophets, Chapter 53.

"When Israel was strong, they put the Canaanites to tribute, and did not utterly drive them out" (Judges 1:28).

The Lord had fulfilled His promises to Israel; Joshua had broken the power of the Canaanites and had distributed their land to the tribes. But the twelve tribes failed to dispossess the Canaanites. Instead, they made arrangements for the Canaanites to pay tribute to Israel—forgetting God's warning regarding their prevailing idolatry.

God had placed His people in Canaan as a mighty force to stay the tide of moral evil, that it might not flood the world. And as long as Israel remained obedient, God would subdue their enemies before them. But disregarding their high destiny, Israel chose the course of ease and self-indulgence. They intermarried with the Canaanities, and idolatry spread like the plague.

A remnant remained true to the Lord, and from them He raised up faithful and valiant men to put down idolatry and to deliver the people from their enemies. Gideon was distinguished for courage and integrity; he heard the call from God to deliver His people from the Midianites. Gideon's first task was to declare war upon idolatry before going out to battle with his enemies, and he succeeded at both responsibilities.

Key Thought: "Like Israel, Christians too often yield to the influence of the world and conform to its principles and customs, in order to secure the friendship of the ungodly; but in the end it will be found that these professed friends are the most dangerous of foes. The Bible plainly teaches that there can be no harmony between the people of God and the world. 'Marvel not, my brethren, if the world hate you.' 1 John 3:13. . . . Satan works through the ungodly, under cover of a pretended friendship, to allure God's people into sin, that he may separate them from Him; and when their defense is removed, then he will lead his agents to turn against them and seek to accomplish their destruction" (*Patriarchs and Prophets,* p. 559).

Today's Lesson: If we have the courage and humility of Gideon, God will be able to use us in these last days to demonstrate fortitude and moral clarity to a world in desperate need.

Samson

Patriarchs and Prophets, Chapter 54.

"And Samson said unto his father, Get her for me; for she pleaseth me well" (Judges 14:3).

In the angel's promise to Manoah and his wife, Samson's parents, we find ample evidence for the profound effect of prenatal influence. Samson's mother was to be controlled by principles of temperance and self-denial; she was not to follow the usual practice of gratifying every wish and impulse. Both fathers and mothers transmit their own mental and physical characteristics, their dispositions and appetites, to their children.

In choosing his wife, Samson did not ask whether he could better glorify God when uniting with an idolater. God promises wisdom to all who listen, but there is no promise to those bent on pleasing self.

After Samson won a few remarkable battlefield victories, the Israelites made him a judge. He ruled Israel for twenty years. But he lost his self-control and foolishly thought his strength would protect him even though he visited a Philistine harlot. Even then, God still spoke to him, filling him with remorse.

But Samson's infatuation with loose women overpowered his better judgment. His experience with Delilah was a classic example of a "fatal attraction." Overcome by the Philistines and with eyes put out, he ended his days in hard labor. At the last, he attempted to do the right thing. Those who died with him "were more than they which he slew in his life" (Judges 16:30).

Samson's life teaches us that God will care for all of us and prepare us to do a special work for Him—as long as we are willing to live under His providential hand.

Key Thought: "Physically, Samson was the strongest man upon the earth; but in self-control, integrity, and firmness, he was one of the weakest of men. Many mistake strong passions for a strong character, but the truth is that he who is mastered by his passions is a weak man. The real greatness of the man is measured by the power of the feelings that he controls, not by those that control him" (*Patriarchs and Prophets,* pp. 567, 568).

Today's Lesson: Everyone has his weakest link. What is my weakest link, and how does Satan work his charm to help me cherish what I should despise?

The Child Samuel

Patriarchs and Prophets, Chapter 55.

"Then Eli answered and said, Go in peace: and the God of Israel grant thee thy petition that thou hast asked of him" *(1 Samuel 1:17).*

Elkanah, a wealthy Levite, feared the Lord, but he wanted a son to perpetuate his name. His first wife, Hannah, was a woman of deep faith—gentle and unassuming—but she bore no children. So Elkanah repeated Abraham's mistake and took Penninah for his wife. Penninah eventually bore him sons and daughters.

Penninah saw the devotion that Elkanah had for Hannah and gloated over her rival's childless state—year after year. Finally, Hannah could endure this no longer and pled with the Lord for His help. Noticed by Eli, the high priest, Hannah told him of her grief, and she heard his promise—that she would be rewarded with a son.

Hannah called her boy Samuel ("asked of God"). As soon as Samuel was old enough to be separated from his mother, she kept her vow and presented him to Eli for the service of God. This was a great sacrifice for Hannah. The Holy Spirit came upon her, and she prayed a prophetic prayer (see 1 Samuel 2:1–10).

She had faithfully taught her son to reverence God and to regard himself as the Lord's, always lifting his thoughts heavenward. Every year she journeyed to Shiloh and brought Samuel another handmade robe. Her prayers were rewarded: "The child Samuel grew on, and was in favour both with the Lord, and also with men" (1 Samuel 2:26).

Key Thought: "The youth of our time may become as precious in the sight of God as was Samuel. By faithfully maintaining their Christian integrity, they may exert a strong influence in the work of reform. Such men are needed at this time. God has a work for every one of them. Never did men achieve greater results for God and humanity than may be achieved in this our day by those who will be faithful to their God-given trust" (*Patriarchs and Prophets,* p. 574).

Today's Lesson: What a remarkable story of a mother's faithfulness! As a parent, am I faithful to my responsibilities in teaching and leading my children heavenward?

Eli and His Sons

Patriarchs and Prophets, Chapter 56.

"Now Eli was very old, and heard all that his sons did unto all Israel; and how they lay with the women that assembled at the door of the tabernacle of the congregation. . . . And this shall be a sign unto thee, that shall come upon thy two sons, on Hophni and Phinehas; in one day they shall die both of them" (1 Samuel 2:22, 34).

Eli was both high priest and judge over all Israel, but he did not rule his own house. Loving peace and ease, he did not exercise authority as he should have in correcting the evil habits and passions of his children. Eli became subject to his own children.

As a result, Hophni and Phinehas had no proper appreciation of the character of God. Their service in the sanctuary, they considered a common thing. Eli had neither corrected their lack of reverence for his authority nor their disrespect for the solemn services of the sanctuary. He settled, instead, for blind affection.

The irreverence shown by Eli's sons was quickly picked up by the people, until they "abhorred the offering of the Lord" (1 Samuel 2:17). In fact, filled with indignation at the corrupt behavior of Hophni and Phinehas, many Israelites ceased to come to the appointed place of worship.

Key Thought: "Eli did not manage his household according to God's rules for family government. He followed his own judgment. The fond father overlooked the faults and sins of his sons in their childhood, flattering himself that after a time they would outgrow their evil tendencies. Many are now making a similar mistake. They think they know a better way of training their children than that which God has given in His word. They foster wrong tendencies in them, urging as an excuse, 'They are too young to be punished. Wait till they become older, and can be reasoned with.' Thus wrong habits are left to strengthen until they become second nature" (*Patriarchs and Prophets,* pp. 578, 579).

Today's Lesson: Every parent must face up to the challenges that Eli evaded. What lessons can I learn from Eli—and incorporate into my life—so my children receive better parental leadership than Eli's sons received from their father?

The Ark Taken by the Philistines

Patriarchs and Prophets, Chapter 57.

"Samuel took a stone, and set it between Mizpah and Shen, and called the name of it Ebenezer, saying, Hitherto hath the Lord helped us" (1 Samuel 7:12).

It was a gloomy time for Israel. "The word of the Lord was precious [scarce] in those days; there was no open vision" (1 Samuel 3:1). But God had not given up on Israel. Eli had failed Him, but God saw in Samuel the right man for the right time.

After a military disaster, the elders of Israel told the army to take the ark from Shiloh and attack the Philistines. But the Philistines made a fierce counterattack and captured the ark after slaying thirty thousand Israelites. The Israelites had not realized that having faith in the ark was not the same as having faith in God—their worship of the ark led to formalism, hypocrisy, and idolatry.

But the Philistines, for their part, discovered that the ark was more than a magic box. When they put it in Dagon's temple, the statue of the Philistine god fell down mutilated. Every time the ark was moved, serious plagues broke out, and the Philistines wanted to return it. But for seven years the Israelites made no effort for its recovery. The Philistines finally left the ark in an open field near an Israelite city. Amazingly, the Israelites had no sense of its importance; when they curiously opened it, many immediately died. Eventually, the ark ended up in the home of the Levite, Abinadad, where it remained for many years.

Key Thought: "For nations as well as for individuals, the path of obedience to God is the path of safety and happiness, while that of transgression leads only to disaster and defeat. The Philistines were now so completely subdued that they surrendered the strongholds which had been taken from Israel and refrained from acts of hostility for many years. Other nations followed this example, and the Israelites enjoyed peace until the close of Samuel's sole administration" (*Patriarchs and Prophets,* p. 591).

Today's Lesson: It would be well to review in our experience, how many times we have had reason to set up a memorial, so that in time to come we could remember: "Hitherto hath Jehovah helped me."

The Schools of the Prophets

Patriarchs and Prophets, Chapter 58.

"The fear of the Lord is the beginning of wisdom: and the knowledge of the Holy is understanding" (Proverbs 9:10).

The Lord had commanded the Hebrews to teach their children His requirements and to make them aware of their history. This responsibility was not to be delegated to another. Children were to be trained to see God both in nature and in the words of revelation.

For those who wanted to search deeper into the truths of God's Word and to become teachers themselves, further schooling was provided in the schools of the prophets. Samuel founded these schools to serve as a barrier against the widespread corruption that existed in the society of his day.

In these schools, students sustained themselves in a work-education program—the Israelites did not consider work to be strange or degrading. Every pupil was taught some trade, even though he was to be educated for holy office. Students were taught the duty of prayer and how to pray; they learned how to exercise faith in their Creator and how to understand and obey the teachings of the Holy Spirit. In the schools of the prophets, music served a holy purpose.

The true object of education is to restore the image of God in each student. Getting back to the perfection in which we were first created is the great object of life—the object that underlies every other. In these schools, God expected the highest possible degree of excellence in everything that was undertaken. Instead of appealing to pride and selfish ambition, teachers were to awaken in their students a love for goodness, truth, and beauty.

An intimate relationship connects the mind and the body. In order to reach a high standard of moral and intellectual attainment, the laws that control our physical being must be heeded.

Key Thought: "The Lord Himself directed the education of Israel. His care was not restricted to their religious interests; whatever affected their mental or physical well-being was also the subject of divine providence, and came within the sphere of divine law" (*Patriarchs and Prophets,* p. 592).

Today's Lesson: The principles of true, godly education are needed today as much as at any time in the history of the world.

The First King of Israel

Patriarchs and Prophets, Chapter 59.

"Nevertheless the people refused to obey the voice of Samuel; and they said, Nay; but we will have a king over us; that we also may be like all the nations; and that our king may judge us, and go out before us, and fight our battles" (1 Samuel 8:19, 20).

God saw that Israel would eventually want a king, but He would not consent to a change in the principles that had been governing Israel since leaving Egypt.

One of Israel's problems was that they were attracted by the pomp and display of heathen kings, and they tired of their own simplicity and their subjection to an unseen Ruler. But worse, Samuel's two sons were repeating the mistakes of Eli's sons—their injustice as judges became a pretext for the people to urge a change in the government. Samuel apparently had been unaware of his sons' abuses.

The Lord said to Samuel, "Hearken unto the voice of the people in all that they say unto thee: for they have not rejected thee, but they have rejected me, that I should not reign over them" (1Samuel 8:7). The days of Israel's greatest prosperity had been when they acknowledged God as their King—when the laws He had given them were recognized as superior to those of other nations.

The personal qualities of Saul, the future monarch, gratified the pride of heart that prompted the people's desire for a king. He started well—winning battles and giving the honor to God. But there was more to come.

Key Thought: "Samuel's life of purity and unselfish devotion was a perpetual rebuke both to self-serving priests and elders and to the proud, sensual congregation of Israel. Although he assumed no pomp and made no display, his labors bore the signet of Heaven. He was honored by the world's Redeemer, under whose guidance he ruled the Hebrew nation. But the people had become weary of his piety and devotion; they despised his humble authority and rejected him for a man who should rule them as a king" (*Patriarchs and Prophets,* p. 607).

Today's Lesson: Church leaders today need to have the inner qualifications of a close connection with God and a humble, teachable spirit.

The Presumption of Saul

Patriarchs and Prophets, Chapter 60.

***"It may be that the Lord will work for us: for there is no
restraint to the Lord to save by many or by few"
(1 Samuel 14:6).***

Saul's first major mistake was to slack off from his early victories
and not proceed at once to subdue Israel's remaining warlike
neighbors. In Saul's second year of kingship, the Philistines gathered
an enormous force at Michmash, threatening Israel. Samuel told Saul
to do nothing for seven days until he came to offer sacrifices to God.

God wanted Saul and the Israelites to spend this time searching their
hearts and repenting of their sins. It was to be a time of preparation
for God to work in their behalf. Instead, Saul waited impatiently
for the prophet. And when Samuel did not appear as soon as Saul
expected, the king offered the sacrifices himself, clad in his war armor.
He thought Samuel would approve, but he received only the prophet's
condemnation.

With many Israelite soldiers now deserting him, Saul retired to his
fortress at Geba. A divine impulse prompted his son, Jonathan, to look
for ways of outwitting the huge Philistine force. Under God's leading,
Jonathan and his armor-bearer initiated an attack, and God supported
them with what sounded like a great multitude with horsemen and
chariots. Panic seized the Philistines, and God enabled the limited
Israelite force to win a great victory.

Saul saw that the Israelites now preferred Jonathan above him.
He discontinued his war with the Philistines and became moody and
dissatisfied.

Key Thought: "Often those who are seeking to exalt themselves
are brought into positions where their true character is revealed. So
it was in the case of Saul. His own course convinced the people that
kingly honor and authority were dearer to him than justice, mercy, or
benevolence. Thus the people were led to see their error in rejecting
the government that God had given them. They had exchanged the
pious prophet, whose prayers had brought down blessings, for a king
who in his blind zeal had prayed for a curse upon them" (*Patriarchs
and Prophets,* pp. 625, 626).

Today's Lesson: Jealousy blinds us to the reality of our own
shortcomings and failures by causing us to focus on the shortcomings
of others.

Saul Rejected

Patriarchs and Prophets, Chapter 61.

"Now therefore behold the king whom ye have chosen, and whom ye have desired! and, behold, the Lord hath set a king over you" (1 Samuel 12:13).

Even though Saul had failed at Gilgal in not waiting for Samuel to offer sacrifices, his errors were not irretrievable. In His mercy, the Lord would grant him another opportunity to learn the lesson of unquestioning faith and obedience.

The time had come to utterly destroy the Amalekites who had only one purpose—to destroy Israel. Saul's victory over the Amalekites was his most brilliant victory, but his mistake was to exalt himself as did other conquering kings by bringing back alive his trophy, Agag—the fierce Amalekite king. Further, Saul allowed the Israelites to save the best of the Amalekite flocks and beasts of burden.

Samuel was greatly distressed, and Saul's excuses were self-condemning. Before Saul's entire army, the prophet raised his voice to express God's displeasure with the king: "Hath the Lord as great delight in burnt offerings and sacrifices, as in obeying the voice of the Lord? Behold, to obey is better than sacrifice, and to hearken than the fat of rams. . . . Because thou hast rejected the word of the Lord, he hath also rejected thee from being king" (1 Samuel 15:22, 23).

Key Thought: "Yet the Lord, having placed on Saul the responsibility of the kingdom, did not leave him to himself. He caused the Holy Spirit to rest upon Saul to reveal to him his own weakness and his need of divine grace; and had Saul relied upon God, God would have been with him. . . . But when Saul chose to act independently of God, the Lord could no longer be his guide, and was forced to set him aside. Then He called to the throne 'a man after His own heart' (1 Samuel 13:14)—not one who was faultless in character, but who, instead of trusting to himself, would rely upon God, and be guided by His Spirit; who, when he sinned, would submit to reproof and correction" (*Patriarchs and Prophets,* p. 636).

Today's Lesson: God cannot accept a divided loyalty that renders only partial obedience to His commandments.

The Anointing of David

Patriarchs and Prophets, Chapter 62.

"The Lord said unto Samuel, How long wilt thou mourn for Saul, seeing I have rejected him from reigning over Israel? Fill thine horn with oil, and go, I will send thee to Jesse the Bethlehemite: for I have provided me a king among his sons" (1 Samuel 16:1).

While young David cared for his sheep, he sang songs of his own composing, accompanied by his harp. When Samuel came to David's house, he surveyed each of David's brothers. But the Lord told him: "Look not on his countenance, or on the height of his stature; because I have refused him: for the Lord seeth not as man seeth; for man looketh on the outward appearance, but the Lord looketh on the heart" (1 Samuel 16:7).

At last, when Samuel saw David—handsome, manly, and modest—the Lord said, "This is he." At God's direction, Samuel anointed David in secret. Instead of making David proud, this new honor provided fresh inspiration as he composed songs of praise to God.

Key Thought: "David, in the beauty and vigor of his young manhood, was preparing to take a high position with the noblest of the earth. His talents, as precious gifts from God, were employed to extol the glory of the divine Giver. . . . Clearer conceptions of God, opened before his soul. Obscure themes were illuminated, difficulties were made plain, perplexities were harmonized, and each ray of new light called forth fresh bursts of rapture, and sweeter anthems of devotion, to the glory of God and the Redeemer. The love that moved him, the sorrows that beset him, the triumphs that attended him, were all themes for his active thought; and as he beheld the love of God in all the providences of his life, his heart throbbed with more fervent adoration and gratitude, his voice rang out in a richer melody, his harp was swept with more exultant joy; and the shepherd boy proceeded from strength to strength, from knowledge to knowledge; for the Spirit of the Lord was upon him" (*Patriarchs and Prophets,* p. 642).

Today's Lesson: Humility and a desire to be used by God will qualify us to fill God's plan for our life as David filled the role God envisioned for him.

David and Goliath

Patriarchs and Prophets, Chapter 63.

"Then answered one of the servants, and said, Behold, I have seen a son of Jesse, the Bethlehemite, that is cunning in playing, and a mighty valiant man, and a man of war, and prudent in matters, and a comely person, and the Lord is with him" (1 Samuel 16:18).

Saul had never experienced true repentance; his haughty spirit became increasingly desperate until he was on the verge of losing his reason. His counselors urged him to seek David to calm his troubled spirit with his songs and harp—and David charmed away Saul's melancholy.

When Israel declared war against the Philistines, David's father directed him to carry a message to his older brothers who were in the army at the scene of battle. As David drew near, he heard Goliath's taunts and was astonished at the passivity of the Israelites, who had been listening to these insults for forty days.

When David told Saul that he would face Goliath, Saul tried to dissuade him. Failing that, he outfitted David with suitable armor. But David declined, trusting in his staff, his sling, and in the Lord. When Goliath heard David's voice expressing his fearlessness, he rushed forward, pushing up his helmet for better vision. David aimed his stone at exactly this vulnerable spot. Goliath fell, and David wasted no time in cutting off his proud head.

Key Thought: "David was growing in favor with God and man. . . . He had new themes for thought. He had been in the court of the king and had seen the responsibilities of royalty. He had discovered some of the temptations that beset the soul of Saul and had penetrated some of the mysteries in the character and dealings of Israel's first king. . . . But while he was absorbed in deep meditation, and harassed by thoughts of anxiety, he turned to his harp, and called forth strains that elevated his mind to the Author of every good, and the dark clouds that seemed to shadow the horizon of the future were dispelled" (*Patriarchs and Prophets,* pp. 643, 644).

Today's Lesson: When God calls us to defend the truth against its enemies, we can be confident that He will provide all the resources we need to accomplish the task He assigns.

March 4

David a Fugitive

Patriarchs and Prophets, Chapter 64.

"Every one that was in distress, and every one that was in debt, and every one that was discontented, gathered themselves unto him; and he became a captain over them: and there were with him about four hundred men"
(1 Samuel 22:2).

After Goliath was slain, Saul kept David with him, where he was entrusted with important responsibilities. This experience in the king's court gave David a knowledge of affairs that would prove valuable for his future greatness.

Jonathan, Saul's son, found David to be a trusted friend; this, too, was part of God's providence and plan. But when Saul learned of this friendship, he was so infuriated that he hurled the spear he had intended for David at his own son. Jonathan told David to flee from Saul's wrath. Thus began a long and difficult time for David. Hunted and persecuted, he saw in every man a spy and a betrayer. His distress and perplexity almost hid the heavenly Father from his sight. Yet, this experience was also teaching David to realize his weaknesses and the necessity of depending constantly upon God.

David found refuge among the mountains of Judah, but he remained always on the run. Meanwhile, in Saul, jealousy turned into envy, then into raging hatred, and eventually to an obsession with revenge and murder—exactly the downward slide that Satan had taken in heaven.

Key Thought: "One great defect in the character of Saul was his love of approbation. This trait had had a controlling influence over his actions and thoughts; everything was marked by his desire for praise and self-exaltation. His standard of right and wrong was the low standard of popular applause. No man is safe who lives that he may please men, and does not seek first for the approbation of God. It was the ambition of Saul to be first in the estimation of men; and when this song of praise was sung, a settled conviction entered the mind of the king that David would obtain the hearts of the people and reign in his stead" (*Patriarchs and Prophets,* p. 650).

Today's Lesson: We need to be able to honestly evaluate our own lives—and by God's grace eradicate objectionable traits of character.

The Magnanimity of David

Patriarchs and Prophets, Chapter 65.

"He said unto his men, The Lord forbid that I should do this thing unto my master, the Lord's anointed, to stretch forth mine hand against him, seeing he is the anointed of the Lord" (1 Samuel 24:6).

Time after time, David's location was revealed to Saul. In the wilderness of Engedi, David had only six hundred men against Saul's three thousand. Hiding in a secluded cave, David and his men were surprised when Saul entered alone for personal relief. Quietly, David cut off part of Saul's garment, not wanting to hurt the Lord's anointed.

As soon as Saul left the cave to resume his search, David appeared at the opening of the cave and called to Saul, "My lord the king!" Then he held up the piece that had been cut from his robe. For a short time, Saul was humbled and returned home. But David knew that Saul could not be trusted; feelings of reconciliation do not always prove to be lasting in minds not controlled by the Holy Spirit.

The second instance of David's respect for Saul occurred when David and his attendant entered Saul's camp. The king lay surrounded by his sleeping soldiers. David took Saul's spear and jar of water. Once again, from a safe place, David called to Saul and to his army, declaring his unwillingness to kill Saul when it would have been so easy to do so.

Key Thought: "Although David's faith had staggered somewhat at the promises of God, he still remembered that Samuel had anointed him king of Israel. He recalled the victories that God had given him over his enemies in the past. He reviewed the great mercy of God in preserving him from the hand of Saul, and determined not to betray a sacred trust. Even though the king of Israel had sought his life, he would not join his forces with the enemies of his people" (*Patriarchs and Prophets*, p. 674).

Today's Lesson: Magnanimity is one of the most difficult fruits of the Holy Spirit, because we often are pained victims of those who deliberately have done us wrong. What can I do today to develop this quality in my character?

MARCH 6

The Death of Saul

Patriarchs and Prophets, Chapter 66.

"Why hast thou deceived me? for thou art Saul"
(1 Samuel 28:12).

T he last days of King Saul are most troubling, for they mirror what will happen to anyone who openly turns his or her back upon the clear counsel of God.

On the plain of Jezreel the armies of the Philistines and the armies of the Israelites had gathered for a decisive battle. At this same site, years before, Gideon with his three hundred had overwhelmed the Midianites. But the spirit that stirred Gideon was far different than the spirit that inspired Saul, who realized that God had forsaken him. He "was afraid, and his heart greatly trembled" (1 Samuel 28:5).

In his despair Saul turned to a spiritualist living in Endor. Trying to disguise himself, Saul was in bondage to his own twisted mind. The spiritualist was not fooled, yet she practiced her supernatural power. With the aid of the master deceiver, she produced what appeared to be the prophet Samuel. Saul and the impersonating spirit spoke to each other, and Saul heard the prediction of his own death.

By consulting the spirit of darkness, Saul had destroyed himself, spiritually and eventually physically. The battle went badly; his three sons were killed, and Saul was wounded. The king took his own life by falling on his sword, thus ending his life in failure, dishonor, and despair.

Key Thought: "All through his course of rebellion Saul had been flattered and deceived by Satan. It is the tempter's work to belittle sin, to make the path of transgression easy and inviting, to blind the mind to the warnings and threatenings of the Lord. Satan, by his bewitching power, had led Saul to justify himself in defiance of Samuel's reproofs and warning. But now, in his extremity, he turned upon him, presenting the enormity of his sin and the hopelessness of pardon, that he might goad him to desperation. Nothing could have been better chosen to destroy his courage and confuse his judgment, or to drive him to despair and self-destruction" (*Patriarchs and Prophets,* pp. 680, 681).

Today's Lesson: No one wants to die in dishonor and without hope. Am I making the choices today that will assure my standing with God—now and forever?

Ancient and Modern Sorcery

Patriarchs and Prophets, Chapter 67.

"Saul died for his transgression which he committed against the Lord, even against the word of the Lord, which he kept not, and also for asking counsel of one that had a familiar spirit, to inquire of it; and inquired not of the Lord: therefore he slew him, and turned the kingdom unto David the son of Jesse" (1 Chronicles 10:13, 14).

Many believe that Samuel was actually present at the interview with Saul—that Samuel had been in heaven and was summoned to earth by the power of God. Nearly all forms of sorcery and witchcraft claim to communicate with the dead. Spiritualism forms the cornerstone of heathen idolatry, and the ancient practices continue today under more modern names. It takes hold of the sympathies of those who have laid their loved ones in the grave, deceiving those who are not anchored in Bible truth. In the last days the world will see a display of the "signs and wonders" of modern spiritualism.

Satan indeed can "foretell" the future, in the sense that he can reason from cause to effect, predicting with a degree of accuracy some of the future events of a person's life. And he can arrange future events to fit his "forecast."

Key Thought: "There are many who become restless when they cannot know the definite outcome of affairs. They cannot endure uncertainty, and in their impatience they refuse to wait to see the salvation of God. Apprehended evils drive them nearly distracted. They give way to their rebellious feelings, and run hither and thither in passionate grief, seeking intelligence concerning that which has not been revealed. . . . Their spirit would be calmed by communion with God. The weary and the heavy-laden would find rest unto their souls if they would only go to Jesus; but when they neglect the means that God has ordained for their comfort, and resort to other sources, hoping to learn what God has withheld, they commit the error of Saul, and thereby gain only a knowledge of evil" (*Patriarchs and Prophets,* p. 687).

Today's Lesson: Satan deceives many by impersonating their dead loved ones, teaching them that the dead are not really dead. In this way, he undermines faith in God.

David at Ziklag

Patriarchs and Prophets, Chapter 68.

"David took hold on his clothes, and rent them; and likewise all the men that were with him: And they mourned, and wept, and fasted until even, for Saul, and for Jonathan his son, and for the people of the Lord, and for the house of Israel; because they were fallen by the sword" (2 Samuel 1:11, 12).

Saul had thought that David had been a part of the huge Philistine army that he feared, but David and his six hundred men had been removed from the battle because some of the Philistine kings feared that David would betray them. That brought great relief to David, but it did not remove his remorse for siding with the Philistines instead of trusting God to deal with Saul.

When David and his six hundred men returned to their home in Ziklag, they found the city sacked by the Amalekites and all the women and children taken captive. His men blamed David for their situation and were ready to stone him. David felt cut off from everything dear to him on earth. In his despair, he determined to see if God had something to tell him regarding what he should do.

David sent for Abiathar, the priest, who told him that he should pursue the Amalekites and that he would succeed. So it was that all was recovered. When news arrived that Saul and Jonathan had died in the Philistine war, David wept and fasted with his band of men. His grief was sincere. There was no exultation, no rejoicing, while David composed a treasured psalm—2 Samuel 1:19–27.

Key Thought: "David's grief at the death of Saul was sincere and deep, evincing the generosity of a noble nature. He did not exult in the fall of his enemy. The obstacle that had barred his access to the throne of Israel was removed, but at this he did not rejoice. Death had obliterated the remembrance of Saul's distrust and cruelty, and now nothing in his history was thought of but that which was noble and kingly" (*Patriarchs and Prophets,* pp. 695, 696).

Today's Lesson: We need to be able to remember the good points of a person's life rather than recalling the darker memories.

David Called to the Throne

Patriarchs and Prophets, Chapter 69.

"And David went on, and grew great, and the Lord God of hosts was with him" (2 Samuel 5:10).

After Saul died, David was no longer a fugitive. But he looked to God for direction regarding where he should go and what he should do. The Lord said, "Hebron." So, David took his six hundred men and their families to Hebron, where he was welcomed as Israel's future king by the tribe of Judah. But David made no effort to establish his authority by force over the other tribes.

Ishbosheth, the son of Saul, was proclaimed king by the other tribes. He was supported by Abner, one of Saul's army commanders, and Mahanaim on the other side of the Jordan became his capital. For two years Ishbosheth extended his rule over all Israel except the tribe of Judah. As the armies of the two houses struggled for supremacy, David grew stronger while Ishbosheth's forces grew weaker. Eventually, Abner deserted Ishbosheth, promising to bring all the tribes under David's rule. But Joab, commander of David's forces, grew jealous of Abner's newfound favor and murdered him. David buried Abner with full honors, and this magnanimous act won the admiration of all Israel.

Following the murder of Ishbosheth by two of his captains, the leading men of Israel came to Hebron to declare their allegiance to David. Thus, through God's providence, the way was opened for David to come to the throne.

Nearly half a million souls thronged Hebron and its environs to see David anointed by the high priest as their rightful king. God's promise to David was fulfilled, and Israel had a king by divine appointment.

Key Thought: "'So all the elders of Israel came to the king to Hebron; and King David made a league with them in Hebron before the Lord.' Thus through the providence of God the way had been opened for him to come to the throne. He had no personal ambition to gratify, for he had not sought the honor to which he had been brought" (*Patriarchs and Prophets*, p. 701).

Today's Lesson: David's experience teaches us to wait patiently for God to work out the next steps in His plan for our lives.

MARCH 10

The Reign of David

Patriarchs and Prophets, Chapter 70.

"Be of good courage, and let us behave ourselves valiantly for our people, and for the cities of our God: and let the Lord do that which is good in his sight"
(1 Chronicles 19:13).

As soon as David became king, he sought a more appropriate location for the nation's capital. Not far from Hebron was Jebus (Moriah), protected by a group of hills. Here Abraham had proved his loyalty to God by his willingness to sacrifice Isaac. Long the home of the Jebusites, Moriah seemed impregnable until Joab and his forces conquered the city and renamed it Jerusalem.

Meanwhile, Hiram, king of wealthy Tyre, recognized the rapid rise of Israelite power and sought an alliance with David, offering architects, workmen, and materials to help build a palace in Jerusalem.

Once David was firmly established upon the throne, he turned to fulfilling a cherished promise—to bring the ark of God to Jerusalem. With ceremony, the ark was placed on a new cart drawn by oxen, followed by thirty thousand of the leading men of Israel, singing and playing musical instruments. But when the ark appeared about to fall, Uzzah presumptuously tried to steady it and died immediately. David was astonished and questioned God's justice.

The leaders had forgotten God's explicit instructions about how the ark was to be carried. Only the Kohathites were to carry it, but even they were not to touch it. The ark was to be covered and two staves placed through the rings on its sides. Then the Kohathites were to bear it "upon their shoulders" (Numbers 7:9).

Uzzah's death taught all Israel the lesson that God accepts only service that is carried out in accordance with His directions. Uzzah was guilty of gross presumption and a failure to recognize the necessity of strict obedience.

Key Thought: "Israel had become a mighty nation, respected and feared by surrounding peoples. In his own realm David's power had become very great. He commanded, as few sovereigns in any age have been able to command, the affections and allegiance of his people. He had honored God, and God was now honoring him" (*Patriarchs and Prophets,* p. 716).

Today's Lesson: God is love, but we must not presume upon His gracious character of mercy.

David's Sin and Repentance

Patriarchs and Prophets, Chapter 71.

"There is a way that seems right to a man, but its end is the way of death" (Proverbs 14:12, NKJV).

Self-confidence and self-exaltation prepared the way for David's fall. The subtle allure of flattery, power, and luxury left its mark on him. Monarchs rarely feel obliged to exercise the same restraint they expect of their subjects. The same is true of those in positions of power today, whether they rule a nation or a corporation.

The work of the enemy is not abrupt; it is not sudden or startling at the outset. It begins as a secret undermining of the strongholds of principle. It begins in apparently small things—neglecting to be true to God.

Bathsheba's fatal beauty proved to be a snare to the king. She was the wife of Uriah, one of David's bravest and most faithful officers. Soon, David's sin with Bathsheba was in danger of being made known. To hide his great sin, he deliberately contrived to have Uriah killed.

God sent Nathan the prophet to reprove David. His message to the king was terrible in its severity. The sentence of death that David deserved was transferred to the child of his sin. The suffering and death of the child was a far more bitter punishment than his own death would have been. Nathan pointed out further that David's sin had given "great occasion to the enemies of the Lord to blaspheme" (2 Samuel 12:14).

Psalm 51 is an expression of David's repentance in response to God's message of reproof. The king's repentance was sincere and deep—bringing him more fully into harmony with God and sympathy with his fellowmen than before he fell.

Key Thought: "This passage in David's history is full of significance to the repenting sinner. It is one of the most forcible illustrations given us of the struggles and temptations of humanity, and of genuine repentance toward God and faith in our Lord Jesus Christ. Through all the ages it has proved a source of encouragement to souls that, having fallen into sin, were struggling under the burden of their guilt" (*Patriarchs and Prophets,* p. 726).

Today's Lesson: No matter how deeply we fall into sin, God offers forgiveness if we truly repent.

The Rebellion of Absalom

Patriarchs and Prophets, Chapter 72.

"Thou art the man. Thus saith the Lord God of Israel, . . .
Wherefore hast thou despised the commandment of the
Lord, to do evil in his sight?" (2 Samuel 12:7, 9).

David's flagrant sin against Uriah and Bathsheba had its terrible consequences. Feeling condemned for his own sin, David did not punish Amnon, his firstborn, for raping his sister. But Absalom, another of David's sons, took matters into his own hands and had Amnon killed for his crime against his sister. Belatedly, David sensed that he should begin showing leadership in his own family and banished Absalom from his presence. Thus began the alienation between David and his energetic, ambitious son Absalom that ended with such heartache for all involved.

When Joab interceded for the young man, David agreed to allow Absalom to return to Jerusalem, but he still refused to see his son. Among the people, sympathy ran strong for Absalom; they considered him a hero and sympathized with him against his father. Absalom did nothing to discourage this attitude. Meanwhile, David seemed morally paralyzed. Where once he had been courageous and decided, it now seemed that he desired only retirement and solitude.

The praise of Absalom was on the lips of all, but David suspected nothing until it was too late. Conspiracy became open rebellion, and David was eventually forced to sorrowfully leave Jerusalem and concede the throne to Absalom.

For David, it seemed that all the labor of his life was being swept away. But this bitter experience taught him to see clearly that God does not excuse sin. And he did not lose his trust in God in spite of all that he suffered.

Key Thought: "The Lord did not forsake David. This chapter in his experience, when, under the cruelest wrong and insult, he shows himself to be humble, unselfish, generous, and submissive, is one of the noblest in his whole experience. Never was the ruler of Israel more truly great in the sight of heaven than at this hour of his deepest outward humiliation" (*Patriarchs and Prophets,* p. 738).

Today's Lesson: It is possible that parents may love their children so much that they do them great harm by not correcting them when necessary.

The Last Years of David

Patriarchs and Prophets, Chapter 73.

"Is it not I that commanded the people to be numbered? Even I it is that have sinned and done evil indeed; but as for these sheep, what have they done? let thine hand, I pray Thee, O Lord my God, be on me, and on my father's house; but not on thy people, that they should be plagued" (1 Chronicles 21:17).

Worldly success and honor had so weakened David's character that he was repeatedly overcome by Satan. His decision to number the Israelites showed sinful pride and a distrust of God's ability to provide for the welfare of His people.

The prophet Gad presented David with a choice of divine punishments for his pride: "Choose thee either three years' famine; or three months to be destroyed before thy foes, . . . or else three days the sword of the Lord, even the pestilence" (1 Chronicles 21:11, 12). David replied, "Let us fall now into the hand of the Lord" (2 Samuel 24:14). The pestilence destroyed seventy thousand in Israel.

At seventy years of age, David's strength was waning. Solomon was selected to be David's successor, but his older brother, Adonijah, rebelled against this decision and was joined in rebellion by Joab and many other sympathizers. Again, David's dereliction of parental duty had allowed Adonijah to become unprincipled and reckless. David abdicated in favor of Solomon, who was immediately proclaimed king, crushing the conspiracy.

David's greatest desire had been to build a temple to properly honor God. But he accepted God's plan to have Solomon carry out this project, using the materials and the detailed plans David had provided.

Key Thought: "The psalms of David pass through the whole range of experience, from the depths of conscious guilt and self-condemnation to the loftiest faith and the most exalted communing with God. His life record declares that sin can bring only shame and woe, but that God's love and mercy can reach to the deepest depths, that faith will lift up the repenting soul to share the adoption of the sons of God" (*Patriarchs and Prophets,* p. 754).

Today's Lesson: God will overrule our poor choices and renew our walk with Him if, like David, we turn to Him in sincere, genuine repentance.

Solomon

Prophets and Kings, Chapter 1.

"Thus saith the Lord, Let not the wise man glory in his wisdom, neither let the mighty man glory in his might, let not the rich man glory in his riches: But let him that glorieth glory in this, that he understandeth and knoweth me, that I am the Lord which exercise lovingkindness, judgment, and righteousness, in the earth: for in these things I delight, saith the Lord" (Jeremiah 9:23, 24).

During the reigns of David and Solomon, Israel was strong among the nations and had many opportunities to wield a mighty influence for truth and right. Barriers were broken down, conversions took place, and God's church on earth prospered. David encouraged young Solomon to show mercy and lovingkindness in all his dealing with others.

For many years Solomon followed his father's counsel and walked uprightly. He prayed that God would give him "an understanding heart to judge thy people, that I may discern between good and bad" (1 Kings 3:9). But the Lord gave Him more—the riches and honor that Solomon did not ask for! Further, God promised him long life.

For many years Solomon's experience was marked with devotion to God, with uprightness and firm principles. The name of Jehovah was greatly honored during the first part of Solomon's reign. During this time, Israel was the light of the world, showing forth God's greatness to surrounding nations.

Solomon became an expert in natural history, animate and inanimate; everywhere he saw a revelation of God's wisdom and power. Solomon's divinely inspired understanding was expressed in "three thousand proverbs: and his songs were a thousand and five" (1 Kings 4:32).

Key Thought: "So long as he remains consecrated, the man whom God has endowed with discernment and ability will not manifest an eagerness for high position, neither will he seek to rule or control. Of necessity men must bear responsibilities; but instead of striving for the supremacy, he who is a true leader will pray for an understanding heart, to discern between good and evil" (*Prophets and Kings,* p. 31).

Today's Lesson: God is just as willing today to give His loyal followers wise discernment as He was to grant wisdom to Solomon. Wisdom is more to be desired than power, wealth, or fame.

The Temple and Its Dedication

Prophets and Kings, Chapter 2.

"The Lord hath said that he would dwell in the thick darkness. But I have built an house of habitation for thee, and a place for thy dwelling forever" (2 Chronicles 6:1, 2).

For seven years Jerusalem was filled with workers leveling the site for the temple and laying broad foundations. Simultaneously, thousands were manufacturing its rich furnishings under Hiram of Tyre. All the stone shaping was done in the quarries, and all the articles of gold, silver, and brass were cast off site, so that on the building site itself, no noise was heard.

Solomon's splendid temple was a fit emblem of God's living church on earth. Like the wilderness tabernacle, Solomon's temple was a type, a symbol, of God's people who were created to be His real dwelling place on earth (see 1 Corinthians 3:10–12; Psalm 144:12).

The dedication of the new temple was set for the seventh month when the people from every part of the kingdom customarily assembled for the Feast of Tabernacles—predominantly an occasion for rejoicing. One of the first signs of God's approval was the embracing cloud that surrounded the temple—a great affirmation for all Israel and the invited guests from many foreign countries.

Solomon led out in worship, offering the dedicatory prayer—a prayer that should be read often (see 2 Chronicles 6). When his prayer ended, "fire came down from heaven, and consumed the burnt offering and the sacrifices" (2 Chronicles 7:1).

Had Israel remained true to God, this glorious building would have stood forever, a perpetual sign of God's special favor to His chosen people.

Key Thought: "Although God dwells not in temples made with hands, yet He honors with His presence the assemblies of His people. He has promised that when they come together to seek Him, to acknowledge their sins, and to pray for one another, He will meet with them by His Spirit. . . . Unless they worship Him in spirit and truth and in the beauty of holiness, their coming together will be of no avail" (*Prophets and Kings,* p. 50).

Today's Lesson: God is infinitely great but also as close to us as the cloud with which He honored Solomon's temple at its dedication.

March 16

Pride of Prosperity

Prophets and Kings, Chapter 3.

"Neither shall he multiply wives for himself, lest his heart turn away; nor shall he greatly multiply silver and gold for himself" (Deuteronomy 17:17, NKJV).

Very few men or women have had so much—or lost so much—as did Solomon. His earlier years were unblemished. But gradually he began to think like other earthly monarchs, seeking political strength by marrying wives from the surrounding pagan nations. He rationalized that these political unions would bring these nations to a knowledge of the true God! He told himself that his example would lead these hundreds of wives from idolatry to a knowledge of the truth about God. Vain hope!

Solomon thought he was strong enough to resist the influence of these heathen women, but events proved him wrong. So gradual was his apostasy that before he was aware of it, he had wandered far from God. An ambition to excel all other nations in power and grandeur led Solomon to pervert for selfish purposes the heavenly gifts he had hitherto employed for the glory of God.

From being the wisest and most merciful of rulers, Solomon degenerated into being an oppressive, despotic tyrant. He levied tax upon tax upon the people to support his luxurious court. Worse, to please his wives, Solomon erected imposing idolatrous shrines on the Mount of Olives, where the most degrading vices of heathenism were practiced. He lost the mastery of himself. He tried to unite light with darkness. He became enervated and effeminate and even entertained atheistic doubts.

Key Thought: "In the midst of prosperity lurks danger. Throughout the ages, riches and honor have ever been attended with peril to humility and spirituality. It is not the empty cup that we have difficulty in carrying; it is the cup full to the brim that must be carefully balanced. Affliction and adversity may cause sorrow, but it is prosperity that is most dangerous to spiritual life. Unless the human subject is in constant submission to the will of God, unless he is sanctified by the truth, prosperity will surely arouse the natural inclination to presumption" (*Prophets and Kings,* pp. 59, 60).

Today's Lesson: Even "minor" decisions may gradually lead to wholesale presumption and apostasy. Unholy ambition is one of Satan's most successful lures.

Results of Transgression

Prophets and Kings, Chapter 4.

"It was a true report which I heard in my own land about your words and your wisdom. However I did not believe their words until I came and saw with my own eyes; and indeed, the half of the greatness of your wisdom was not told me. You exceed the fame of which I heard. . . . Because your God has loved Israel, to establish them forever, therefore He made you king over them, to do justice and righteousness" (2 Chronicles 9:5, 6, 8, NKJV).

In his later years, Solomon forgot who had given him his wisdom and political greatness. He miserably failed to accomplish God's plan to use him to reveal more thoroughly the principles of the great controversy.

Among the primary causes of Solomon's failure was his failure to maintain the spirit of self-sacrifice. When Moses had asked for support in the building of the wilderness tabernacle, God endowed certain men, particularly Bezaleel and Aholiab, with the wisdom and skill to build the sanctuary and all of its special utensils.

To a large degree, the descendants of these workmen inherited the abilities conferred on their forefathers. But they gradually lost their hold upon God and their desire to serve Him unselfishly. They asked for higher wages and indulged a spirit of covetousness. When Solomon needed skilled craftsmen for the temple, he had to turn to Hiram, a Phoenician descendant of Aholiab, whose demand for higher wages was gradually accepted—and similar expectations spread throughout the kingdom.

In Solomon's life, the trend away from self-sacrifice led to self-glorification. The missionary spirit was replaced by a spirit of commercialism. And God's intended witness to the world was eclipsed.

Key Thought: "The men who stand, as it were, on a lofty pinnacle, and who, because of their position, are supposed to possess great wisdom—these are in gravest peril. Unless such men make God their dependence, they will surely fall" (*Prophets and Kings,* p. 60).

Today's Lesson: The principle of self-denial needs daily watering—it stands at the gate of almost every decision we make. To reason that we are entitled to this or that is the sure road to numbness of spirit and the eclipse of genuine companionship with the Lord.

Solomon's Repentance

Prophets and Kings, Chapter 5.

"Whatever my eyes desired I did not keep from them. I did not withhold my heart from any pleasure, for my heart rejoiced in all my labor; And this was my reward from all my labor. Then I looked on all the works that my hands had done and on the labor in which I had toiled; and indeed all was vanity and grasping for the wind. There was no profit under the sun" (Ecclesiastes 2:10, 11, NKJV).

So complete was Solomon's apostasy that his case seemed hopeless. He turned from the joy he had found early in his reign in communion with God to search for satisfaction in the pleasures of his senses.

But the Lord had not completely forsaken Solomon. Through a prophet, God told him that because he had not kept the commandments, his kingdom would be torn into pieces after his death. Solomon awakened as if from a dream. He began to make every effort to retrace his steps toward the purity and holiness from which he had fallen.

Like all who are truly repentant, Solomon found it difficult to put his past sins from his memory. He could not help being concerned about past mistakes. Through the spirit of inspiration, he wrote the book of Ecclesiastes, recording for future generations the history of his wasted years, with their lessons of warning. In this way, Solomon's lifework was not wholly lost.

Key Thought: Solomon's repentance was sincere; but the harm that his example of evil-doing had wrought could not be undone. During his apostasy there were in the kingdom men who remained true to their trust, maintaining their purity and loyalty. But many were led astray; and the forces of evil set in operation by the introduction of idolatry and worldly practices could not easily be stayed by the penitent king. His influence for good was greatly weakened. Many hesitated to place full confidence in his leadership. . . . Emboldened by his apostasy, many continued to do evil, and evil only. And in the downward course of many of the rulers who followed him may be traced the sad influence of the prostitution of his God-given powers" (*Prophets and Kings,* pp. 84, 85).

Today's Lesson: Forgiveness is always available, but the consequences of our sins continue.

The Rending of the Kingdom

Prophets and Kings, Chapter 6.

*"The king [Rehoboam] answered the people roughly, and
forsook the old men's counsel that they gave him; and
spake to them after the counsel of the young men, saying,
My father made your yoke heavy, and I will add to your
yoke: my father also chastised you with whips, but I will
chastise you with scorpions" (1 Kings 12:13, 14).*

After Solomon's death, his son Rehoboam went to Shechem, where
he expected to receive formal recognition as king from all the
tribes. Also present at Shechem was Jeroboam, whom the Bible
calls a mighty man of valor. God gave the prophet Ahijah a startling
message to deliver to Jereboam: "Behold, I will rend the kingdom
out of the hand of Solomon, and will give ten tribes to thee" (1 Kings
11:31).

Rehoboam's early training had been grossly neglected. His mother
was an Ammonite, and he had developed a vacillating character.
The fearful results of Solomon's union with idolatrous women were
vividly demonstrated in Rehoboam's life and in his final apostasy.
He chose not to take counsel from the elders of Solomon's court but
turned to the younger men with whom he had grown up. For three
years Rehoboam prospered, profiting from the lesson he learned at
Shechem. But gradually he put his trust in the power of his position,
giving way to his inherited weaknesses, until he crossed over the line
to idolatry and apostasy.

The interplay of the forces at work in the later history of Israel
clearly revealed the satanic forces that were determined to destroy
the influence of God's once-noble witness to the nations. But the idol
worshipers were at last to learn that false gods are powerless to save.

Key Thought: "The pen of inspiration has traced the sad record of
Solomon's successor as one who failed to exert a strong influence for
loyalty to Jehovah. Naturally headstrong, confident, self-willed, and
inclined to idolatry, nevertheless, had he placed his trust wholly in
God, he would have developed strength of character, steadfast faith,
and submission to the divine requirements" (*Prophets and Kings,*
p. 93).

Today's Lesson: By God's grace, we may develop a living faith in
His leading and overcome those tendencies that would lead us away
from following Him fully.

MARCH 20

Jeroboam

Prophets and Kings, Chapter 7.

"As I live, saith the Lord God, I have no pleasure in the death of the wicked" (Ezekiel 33:11).

When Jeroboam served under Solomon as a public servant, he had shown aptitude and sound judgment. But he ultimately failed to make God his trust. His greatest fear was that his subjects in the northern tribes would be won over by the ruler occupying David's throne in Jerusalem. He especially feared that if the ten northern tribes continued to visit the Jerusalem temple for the yearly feasts, they might renew their allegiance to the Jerusalem government.

So, in one bold stroke Jeroboam created two new centers of worship—one at Bethel and another at Dan. Further, in order to appeal to the religious imagination of those in the northern kingdom, he made two calves of gold to be visual symbols of the presence of the invisible God—something akin to the visual appeal of the Jerusalem temple.

But Jeroboam failed to see the fundamental weakness of his plan: He was setting before his people the same kind of idolatrous symbols that were rampant in the pagan world. Many of the faithful, including the Levites, deserted to the southern kingdom. When Jeroboam attempted to duplicate the annual feasts at Jerusalem, a prophet of God predicted that the king's defiance would not pass unrebuked. Immediately, the altar with its sacrifice "was rent, and the ashes poured out" (1 Kings 13:5).

Key Thought: "The Lord did not give Israel up without first doing all that could be done to lead them back to their allegiance to Him. . . . Through His prophets He gave them every opportunity to stay the tide of apostasy and to return to Him. . . . Even in the darkest hours some would remain true to their divine Ruler and in the midst of idolatry would live blameless in the sight of a holy God. These faithful ones were numbered among the goodly remnant through whom the eternal purpose of Jehovah was finally to be fulfilled" (*Prophets and Kings,* p. 108).

Today's Lesson: We cannot "improve" upon God's clear instructions by trying to substitute our own ideas and practices—even with the best of intentions. God's way is the only safe way.

National Apostasy

Prophets and Kings, Chapter 8.

"It is nothing with thee to help, whether with many, or with them that have no power: help us, O Lord our God; for we rest on thee, and in thy name we go against this multitude. O Lord, thou art our God; let not man prevail against thee" (2 Chronicles 14:11).

The house of Jeroboam ended in a wholesale slaughter carried out by his generals during the reign of his son, Nadab. For the next forty years, the rulers who followed in the northern kingdom continued in the same fatal course of evil-doing.

Meanwhile, Asa was ruling in the southern kingdom of Judah. Wherever he found altars to strange gods, he removed them, so that "the kingdom was quiet before him" (2 Chronicles 14:5). Asa's test came when the Ethiopians invaded Judah with overwhelming force. Setting his forces in battle array, Asa placed his trust in God. He had sought God in days of prosperity, and now he relied upon Him in the day of adversity. Asa's prayer is one that every Christian should be able to pray in times of crisis.

Two years before Asa's death, Ahab began his terrible reign in the northern kingdom. During this period of great apostasy, Ahab boldly led his people to set aside their confused forms of worship at Dan and Bethel—only to substitute the worship of Jehovah for Baal worship! With Jezebel's encouragement, Ahab erected heathen altars in many high places, where the priests and others performed their degrading practices.

Key Thought: "Through the influence of Jezebel and her impious priests, the people were taught that the idol gods that had been set up were deities, ruling by their mystic power the elements of earth, fire, and water. All the bounties of heaven—the running brooks, the streams of living water, the gentle dew, the showers of rain which refreshed the earth and caused the fields to bring forth abundantly—were ascribed to the favor of Baal and Ashtoreth, instead of to the Giver of every good and perfect gift" (*Prophets and Kings,* pp. 115, 116).

Today's Lesson: When many of those around us—in our family, church, or workplace—are losing their way, God can enable us to resist their influence and remain faithful to Him.

Elijah the Tishbite

Prophets and Kings, Chapter 9.

**"If I shut up heaven that there be no rain, or if I command
the locusts to devour the land, or if I send pestilence
among my people; If my people, which are called by my
name, shall humble themselves, and pray, and seek my
face, and turn from their wicked ways; then will I hear
from heaven, and will forgive their sin, and will heal their
land" (2 Chronicles 7:13, 14).**

In his mountain retreat east of the Jordan, Elijah watched the northern
kingdom slide ever deeper into idolatry. As Elijah prayed earnestly
for God to deliver His people, the Lord answered his prayers—by
entrusting Elijah himself with a message of divine judgment to deliver
to Ahab. It was an assignment Elijah had not expected and did not
want, but he accepted it.

On his way to the palace, Elijah crossed many flowing streams and
rich landscapes; it took faith to believe God's prediction of a severe
drought. Striding past the palace guards, the bold prophet stood before
the astonished Ahab and solemnly announced God's warning. Then,
his message delivered, he disappeared as quickly as he had arrived.

Two years passed, and the severe effects of a long drought lay
heavy on the land. But the Israelites were so far into idolatry that
they continued to believe their priests and their excuses. They did not
repent or learn the lessons God wanted to teach them.

Key Thought: "God had sent messengers to Israel, with appeals
to return to their allegiance. Had they heeded these appeals, had they
turned from Baal to the living God, Elijah's message of judgment would
never have been given. . . . Their pride had been wounded, their anger
had been aroused against the messengers, and now they regarded
with intense hatred the prophet Elijah. If only he should fall into their
hands, gladly they would deliver him to Jezebel—as if by silencing
his voice they could stay the fulfillment of his words! In the face of
calamity they continued to stand firm in their idolatry" (*Prophets and
Kings,* pp. 127, 128).

Today's Lesson: Those who deliberately and repeatedly disregard
God's counsel will reach a point where they are no longer able to
discern the reality of their situation.

The Voice of Stern Rebuke

Prophets and Kings, Chapter 10.

"Arise, get thee to Zarephath, which belongeth to Zidon, and dwell there: behold, I have commanded a widow woman there to sustain thee" (1 Kings 17:9).

Elijah had been miraculously fed for many months by the Brook Cherith, but now the brook had run dry. The widow whom God had designated to care for His prophet was not an Israelite, but she was a believer in the true God and walked in all the light shining on her pathway. Amazingly, Elijah could not find safety in Israel but had to find refuge in a foreign country.

The widespread famine had affected the widow, as well, and when Elijah arrived, he discovered how little food she had. In fact, the remaining oil and meal would make only one final meal for her and her son. After that, starvation seemed to be their only prospect. So, Elijah's request for a little food was a true test of her faith. And what a reward she received in response to her remarkable faith! Her barrel of meal and her jar of oil did not fail until the famine ended and the rains returned.

Three years had gone by since Elijah had stood before Ahab and announced God's judgments against Israel. Now, when the prophet and the king again came face to face, Ahab's first question was, "Art thou he that troubleth Israel?" (1 Kings 18:17). How typical for the wrongdoer to hold God's messenger responsible for the consequences of his own departure from righteousness!

But Elijah turned the question back on Ahab and requested that he gather 450 prophets of Baal and the 400 prophets that ate at Jezebel's table for a meeting on Mount Carmel.

Key Thought: "Today there is need of the voice of stern rebuke; for grievous sins have separated the people from God. Infidelity is fast becoming fashionable. . . . The smooth sermons so often preached make no lasting impression; the trumpet does not give a certain sound. Men are not cut to the heart by the plain, sharp truths of God's word" (*Prophets and Kings,* p. 140).

Today's Lesson: In times of crisis, God is looking for those who are prepared to take an unambiguous stand for the right regardless of consequences.

Carmel

Prophets and Kings, Chapter 11.

"Elijah came unto all the people, and said, How long halt ye between two opinions? if the Lord be God, follow him: but if Baal, then follow him. And the people answered him not a word" (1 Kings 18:21).

Elijah alone stood before Ahab, the false prophets, and the assembled hosts of Israel. Unashamed, he asked the question, "How long?" But no one dared to reveal loyalty to Jehovah.

Then the prophet asked for two bullocks to be slain and laid on the two altars—one bullock for God and one for Baal. The test would be which offering would be destroyed by fire—God's sacrifice or Baal's. All day long the false prophets called upon Baal, carrying out their senseless ceremonies. Of course, Satan would have willingly had lightning strike their offering, but God restrained his power.

Finally, at the hour of the evening sacrifice, Elijah had the people draw near. Then three times he emptied four barrels of water over the Lord's altar and sacrifice, soaking the wood and the bullock and filling a trench around the altar. And then the prophet prayed a simple prayer. Flames of fire descended from heaven in a spectacular display of God's power, consuming the sacrifice and evaporating even the water standing in the trench around the altar.

With one voice, the people cried out, "The Lord, he is the God; the Lord, he is the God" (1 Kings 18:39). The priests of Baal refused to repent, and the angry multitudes killed them at Elijah's command—not one escaped.

Key Thought: The Lord abhors indifference and disloyalty in a time of crisis in His work. The whole universe is watching with inexpressible interest the closing scenes of the great controversy between good and evil. The people of God are nearing the borders of the eternal world; what can be of more importance to them than that they be loyal to the God of heaven?. . . . Fidelity to God is their motto" (*Prophets and Kings,* p. 148).

Today's Lesson: When multitudes are mocking God's loyalists in the end time, the Lord will still have a remnant who will stand undaunted, without any visible means of support, as they take their places in the great controversy.

From Jezreel to Horeb

Prophets and Kings, Chapter 12.

"The angel of the Lord came back the second time, and touched him, and said, 'Arise and eat, because the journey is too great for you' " (1 Kings 19:7, NKJV).

Often after a man or woman has expended enormous physical and emotional energy—even when doing a great work for the Lord—an opposite reaction sets in that tends to counteract the previous enthusiasm.

After His glorious victory over the priests of Baal, Elijah prayed for rain to end the long-lasting drought. Six times he sent his servant to a point overlooking the Mediterranean to search for signs of rain before the servant returned with word of a small cloud. Elijah told Ahab to return quickly to his palace; then, energized by the Spirit, he ran ahead of Ahab's horses for sixteen miles through the downpour! More energy expended!

But Elijah soon learned that Jezebel was furious and determined to kill him. Bewildered, he fled for his life. Exhaustion and despair replaced energy and confidence. Elijah should have trusted that God would protect him from the queen's hatred, remembering how the Lord had cared for him for three years. But in his depression, God was forgotten, and Elijah's spirit was crushed by such bitter disappointment that he wanted to die! But God was very near to His beloved prophet, even in his blackness of despair.

Key Thought: "Into the experience of all there come times of keen disappointment and utter discouragement—days when sorrow is the portion, and it is hard to believe that God is still the kind benefactor of His earthborn children; days when troubles harass the soul, till death seems preferable to life. It is then that many lose their hold on God and are brought into the slavery of doubt, the bondage of unbelief. Could we at such times discern with spiritual insight the meaning of God's providences we should see angels seeking to save us from ourselves, striving to plant our feet upon a foundation more firm than the everlasting hills, and new faith, new life, would spring into being" (*Prophets and Kings,* p. 162).

Today's Lesson: In our darkest moments God is still near. He has promised never to leave us or forsake us.

March 26

"What Doest Thou Here?"

Prophets and Kings, Chapter 13.

"Yet I have reserved seven thousand in Israel, all whose knees have not bowed to Baal, and every mouth that has not kissed him" (1 Kings 19:18, NKJV).

God knew that Elijah had yet to trust wholly in Him, even after his victory on Carmel. The prophet had been devastated by the threat of an infuriated woman. God's next move in arousing Elijah to reality was to call him from his cave. Each of us has experienced his or her own cave when discouragement has settled in the soul like a dense fog. God chose to reveal Himself to Elijah, not through the hurricane, the earthquake, or the fire but through His "still small voice" (1 Kings 19:12). That "still small voice," the quiet voice of the Holy Spirit, alone can transform and develop character.

But now Elijah must recognize that there was stern work to be done. All those in Israel must have the opportunity to take their position on the Lord's side. One of Elijah's duties was to anoint Elisha, and they worked together for some time.

Apostasy prevails today as in Elijah's time. Multitudes are still following Baal—human speculation is exalted in the place of God's Word, popular leaders receive praise and honor, material security is worshiped, and the teachings of science are given preference over the truths of revelation. Amidst these challenges, God is asking parents, teachers, and pastors, "What doest thou here?"

Key Thought: "When we are encompassed with doubt, perplexed by circumstances, or afflicted by poverty or distress, Satan seeks to shake our confidence in Jehovah. It is then that he arrays before us our mistakes and tempts us to distrust God, to question His love. He hopes to discourage the soul and break our hold on God. . . .

"To wait patiently, to trust when everything looks dark, is the lesson that the leaders in God's work need to learn. Heaven will not fail them in their day of adversity" (*Prophets and Kings,* p. 174).

Today's Lesson: In these last days, God's still small voice calls each of us to turn from our preoccupation with self and its concerns in order to let the Lord use us as He sees fit.

"In the Spirit and Power of Elias"

Prophets and Kings, Chapter 14.

"Now all these things happened unto them for ensamples: and they are written for our admonition, upon whom the ends of the world are come" (1 Corinthians 10:11).

History is being repeated. The world today has its Ahabs and Jezebels. No visible shrines may be apparent, but many are following the gods of this world—riches, fame, pleasure, and pleasing pulpit messages that permit men and women to follow the inclinations of an unregenerate heart. Behind it all, multitudes have a wrong conception of God and His attributes; they are as truly serving a false god as were the worshipers of Baal. The faith that actuated Paul, Peter, and John is regarded today as old-fashioned, mystical, and unworthy of intelligent, modern thinkers.

Satan's master stroke has been to thwart God's purpose by leading men and women to disobey His law, while at the same time they are professing to obey it. When the fourth commandment is genuinely obeyed, idolatry cannot exist.

In the closing work of God in the earth, the standard of His law again will be exalted. And in the hour of the world's greatest need, the God of Elijah will raise up men and women to bear a message that will not be silenced. The line of demarcation between those who serve God and those who serve Him not will be as clearly drawn as it was on Mount Carmel in the days of Elijah.

Key Thought: "Many a star that we have admired for its brilliance will then go out in darkness. Those who have assumed the ornaments of the sanctuary, but are not clothed with Christ's righteousness, will then appear in the shame of their own nakedness.

"Among earth's inhabitants, scattered in every land, there are those who have not bowed the knee to Baal.... God has in reserve a firmament of chosen ones that will yet shine forth amidst the darkness, revealing clearly to an apostate world the transforming power of obedience to His law" (*Prophets and Kings,* pp. 188, 189).

Today's Lesson: God is looking for men and women with the spiritual and moral clarity to speak up for Him as Elijah did on Carmel.

Jehoshaphat

Prophets and Kings, Chapter 15.

***"Hear me, O Judah, and ye inhabitants of Jerusalem;
Believe in the Lord your God, so shall ye be established;
believe his prophets, so shall ye prosper"
(2 Chronicles 20:20).***

Jehoshaphat succeeded his father, Asa, as king of Judah. Asa had a terrific record of almost always doing what was "right in the eyes of the Lord" (1 Kings 15:11), and Jehoshaphat faithfully followed his father's example. He eventually destroyed all the remaining pockets of Baal worship in the kingdom. Jehoshaphat realized that Judah's prosperity depended on a continuous educational program teaching God's laws and the promise of His blessings to the people.

In one of his weak moments, Jehoshaphat promised Ahab that he would join Ahab in a war against the Syrians, thinking that they would regain Ramoth, one of the old cities of refuge. But Jehoshaphat wanted to seek counsel from the Lord before the battle. Ahab's prophets all told the two kings to "go up; for God will deliver it into the king's hand" (2 Chronicles 18:5). Faithful Micaiah disagreed, prophesying that he saw Israel scattered in defeat— but still, the kings went ahead. The result was as Micaiah predicted. Ahab was killed in the battle, and Jehoshaphat returned to Jerusalem.

Jehoshaphat's later years were spent strengthening Judah's spiritual and military defenses. One of his signal successes was the establishment of efficient courts of justice. In an attack by a huge army of Ammonites, Moabites, and Edomites, Jehoshaphat led the kingdom of Judah in placing the battle completely in the hands of God. The Lord blessed His people with an astounding victory over their enemies.

Key Thought: "God was the strength of Judah in this crisis, and He is the strength of His people today. We are not to trust in princes, or to set men in the place of God. We are to remember that human beings are fallible and erring, and that He who has all power is our strong tower of defense. In every emergency we are to feel that the battle is His" (*Prophets and Kings,* p. 202).

Today's Lesson: God needs men and women today who will, in times of great stress, place the battle in God's hands and let Him work out the solution.

The Fall of the House of Ahab

Prophets and Kings, Chapter 16.

***"All the people of the land rejoiced: and the city was quiet,
after that they had slain Athaliah with the sword"
(2 Chronicles 23:21).***

Ahab's dominant trait—evil selfishness—continued its disastrous influence on his successors. While Elijah was still a prophet in Israel, Ahab set his mind on a nearby vineyard belonging to Naboth. However, Naboth refused to sell the land that had been in his family for generations; furthermore, the Levitical code declared that no land in Israel could be transferred permanently by sale or exchange.

When he didn't get his way, Ahab pouted, and Jezebel decided to take matters into her own hands. She falsely accused Naboth of blaspheming God and cursing the king and arranged to have him executed for his supposed crimes. Elijah heard about the murder and confronted Ahab, declaring that as a result of this sin, evil would come to him and destroy his posterity. As for Jezebel, the Lord declared that dogs would eat her body by the palace wall. Three years later Ahab was slain by the Syrians, and Jezebel met the fate decreed for her.

Ahab's son, Ahaziah, learned nothing from the sins of his father. When he fell ill, he turned to the god of Ekron instead of to the Creator of the universe. Elijah told him he would not recover. Ahaziah's open sin and his punishment should have been a strong warning to all Israel. Even to this day, the mysteries of heathen worship are continued in secret associations, spiritualism, and many occult practices that are increasingly embedded in Protestant religions.

Key Thought: "During the father's reign, Ahaziah had witnessed the wondrous works of the Most High. He had seen the terrible evidences that God had given apostate Israel. . . . Ahaziah had acted as if these awful realities were but idle tales. Instead of humbling his heart before the Lord, he had followed after Baal, and at last he had ventured upon this, his most daring act of impiety" (*Prophets and Kings,* pp. 209, 210).

Today's Lesson: In His Word God has given us examples—both negative and positive—and He expects us to learn from these as we make decisions in our own lives.

The Call of Elisha

Prophets and Kings, Chapter 17.

*"Elijah said to Elisha, 'Ask! What may I do for you, before
I am taken away from you?' And Elisha said, 'Please let a
double portion of your spirit be upon me' "
(2 Kings 2:8, NKJV).*

E lijah was told to anoint Elisha to be his successor. Elisha's father
was a wealthy farmer whose household was among the few in
Israel who had not bowed to Baal. Elijah found Elisha plowing in
the field—a disciplined son of a wise father.

Elisha had the capabilities of a leader and the meekness of one
ready to serve. His parents had taught him how to cooperate with God,
and he was learning that success depends not so much on talent as
on energy and willingness. Elisha was well aware of Elijah's work—
especially what had happened during the showdown on Mount Carmel
with the priests of Baal. When Elijah threw his mantle around him,
Elisha instantly knew the meaning of the prophet's act.

Having made his decision, Elisha never looked back upon the
pleasures and comforts of his godly home; he knew that God had called
him into service. Elisha was not given some great work at first—just
commonplace duties. But he showed his willingness to do anything
that the Lord directed. Every day he was learning from a master soul
winner. Conversations between Elijah and Elisha must have been
unforgettable.

Elijah gave Elisha several opportunities to turn back to the comforts
of home. Unknown to Elijah, Elisha and the students in the school of
the prophets knew of Elijah's coming translation. In spite of Elijah's
strong suggestion to turn back, Elisha was determined to stay with
Elijah until his translation. All he wanted was a double portion of
Elijah's spirit—his courage and endurance.

Key Thought: "Elijah was a type of the saints who will be living
on the earth at the time of the second advent of Christ and who will be
'changed, in a moment, in the twinkling of an eye, at the last trump,'
without tasting of death. 1 Corinthians 15:51, 52" (*Prophets and Kings,*
p. 227).

Today's Lesson: If we do well the work lying closest at hand, God
will fit us for greater responsibilities.

The Healing of the Waters

Prophets and Kings, Chapter 18.

"Then he went out to the source of the water, and cast in the salt there, and said, 'Thus says the Lord: "I have healed this water; from it there shall be no more death or barrenness."' So the water remains healed to this day, according to the saying of Elisha which he spoke"
(2 Kings 2:21, 22, NKJV).

Not far from Jericho, in the midst of fruitful groves, was one of the schools of the prophets. As part of his new duties, Elisha was responsible for the well-being of these schools. During one of his visits, he was told that the "city is pleasant. . . . but the water is naught, and the ground barren" (2 Kings 2:19).

Elisha asked for a new bowl and some salt, which he proceeded to scatter at the source of the water. The "healing" of the waters of Jericho occurred not because of what Elisha did but because of what God would do to bless the school, as well as the inhabitants of Jericho.

Many are the spiritual lessons in this incident—the new bowl, the salt, and the spring of water were all symbolic, teaching us how God intends to heal Israel of its spiritual maladies. Many years later, Jesus said that His followers were to be the "salt of the earth" (see Matthew 5:13).

Salt must be mingled with the substance to which it is added; it must penetrate and infuse it in order to preserve it. So, it is through personal contact the saving power of the gospel reaches and transforms men and women. Weak, erring human beings show to the world the ability of the redeeming power of God's grace to develop within them the character of Christ.

Key Thought: "The religion of Christ reveals itself as a vitalizing, pervading principle, a living, working, spiritual energy. When the heart is opened to the heavenly influence of truth and love, these principles will flow forth again like streams in the desert, causing fruitfulness to appear where now are barrenness and dearth" (*Prophets and Kings,* p. 234).

Today's Lesson: We may be God's agents to infuse His love and grace into those around us—in our homes, neighborhoods, and churches.

A Prophet of Peace

Prophets and Kings, Chapter 19.

"Now it happened, as they were eating the stew, that they cried out and said, 'O man of God, there is death in the pot!' And they could not eat it. So he said, 'Then bring some flour.' And he put it into the pot, and said, 'Serve it to the people, that they may eat.' And there was nothing harmful in the pot" (2 Kings 4:40, NKJV).

God gave Elijah the voice of fearless reproof, but Elisha was assigned a more peaceful mission—to build up the work Elijah had begun. However, at the beginning of Elisha's ministry, young rabble-rousers mocked him, ridiculing his bald head and the ascent of Elijah to heaven. Elisha, the kind, gentle teacher, pronounced a curse on the young people, and two bears pounced on forty-two of them. This one instance of terrible severity was sufficient to command respect throughout Elisha's life. Authority must be maintained in the face of mockery and contempt.

The Shunem experience revealed Elisha's tenderness. The family prepared a room for the prophet to stay in when he needed it. When their only child died, Elisha stretched himself across the boy until he was restored to life by the power of Christ—the same power Jesus will demonstrate when He raises the dead at His coming.

Like Jesus, Elisha combined the work of healing with that of teaching, and people saw the deep moving of the Holy Spirit in his life. In so many ways he was an early symbol of Jesus Christ.

Key Thought: "When the Lord gives a work to be done, let not men stop to inquire into the reasonableness of the command or the probable result of their efforts to obey. The supply in their hands may seem to fall short of the need to be filled; but in the hands of the Lord it will prove more than sufficient. . . .

"The gift brought to Him with thanksgiving and with prayer for His blessing, He will multiply as He multiplied the food given to the sons of the prophets and to the weary multitude" (*Prophets and Kings,* p. 243).

Today's Lesson: Through our daily activities we can represent the Lord Jesus to those with whom we associate.

APRIL 2

Naaman

Prophets and Kings, Chapter 20.

"A false witness shall not be unpunished, and he that speaketh lies shall not escape" (Proverbs 19:5).

After the battle between Ahab and Benhadad, the king of Syria, frequent border raids continued to occur. In one of these, a teenaged Israelite girl was taken captive and made a slave to Naaman's wife. She carried out her tasks faithfully and was sympathetic toward Naaman, the Syrian general, who was afflicted with leprosy. She knew about the many miracles performed by Elisha, and she told her mistress of the power of God's prophet. Here we see the influence of early home training in spiritual things.

This young girl's confidence in Elisha moved Naaman to seek permission from Benhadad to visit the Israelite man of God. He brought with him an enormous array of gifts.

When Naaman reached Elisha, he expected to see some wonderful manifestation of healing power from heaven. But the prophet merely told him to wash in the Jordan. Naaman was offended, and he refused. But his servant urged him to do as the prophet had directed. Pride struggled in Naaman's heart with a new experience—faith. After seven dips, he was a clean man.

Flushed with gratitude, he tried to reward Elisha with his rich gifts, but the prophet would take no payment for a blessing that had come from God. Gehazi—Elisha's servant—however, yielded to greed and temptation. He lied to Naaman in order to obtain some of the gifts the general had brought. But in the end he received Naaman's leprosy—not his gifts! Truth is of God; deception in all its forms is of Satan.

Key Thought: "Today in every land there are those who are honest in heart, and upon these the light of heaven is shining. If they continue faithful in following that which they understand to be duty, they will be given increased light, until, like Naaman of old, they will be constrained to acknowledge that 'there is no God in all the earth,' save the living God, the Creator" (*Prophets and Kings,* p. 253).

Today's Lesson: God's grace is available to all. Sometimes those we think the most unlikely recipients are on the verge of the kingdom, waiting for us to witness to them of His power.

Elisha's Closing Ministry

Prophets and Kings, Chapter 21.

"Fear not: for they that be with us are more than they that be with them. And Elisha prayed, and said, Lord, I pray thee, open his eyes, that he may see" (2 Kings 6:16, 17).

Elisha supported the spiritual reforms of Jehu and led many Israelites away from their Baal worship. He met with much opposition, yet none could deny the force of his words.

On one occasion, the king of Syria was determined to find Elisha and kill him, because the prophet continued to thwart Syrian attacks against Israel. Learning that Elisha was in Dothan, the Syrian king gathered his chariots and a huge army against the city. In terror, Elisha's servant saw the encircling army. But Elisha assured his servant there was no need to fear—the forces of heaven were with them, and God would use this occasion to demonstrate His great power and gracious magnanimity.

God blinded the Syrian army, and Elisha organized a lavish dinner for them. And Israel was free from Syrian attacks for some time.

Elisha was known as God's messenger. Throughout his ministry, his courage never wavered, and he turned many in Israel back to a trust in God. He was loyal to God until he died.

Key Thought: "It was not given Elisha to follow his master in a fiery chariot. Upon him the Lord permitted to come a lingering illness. During the long hours of human weakness and suffering his faith laid fast hold on the promises of God, and he beheld ever about him heavenly messengers of comfort and peace. As on the heights of Dothan he had seen the encircling hosts of heaven, the fiery chariots of Israel and the horsemen thereof, so now he was conscious of the presence of sympathizing angels, and he was sustained. Throughout his life he had exercised strong faith, and as he had advanced in a knowledge of God's providences and of His merciful kindness, faith had ripened into an abiding trust in his God, and when death called him he was ready to rest from his labors" (*Prophets and Kings,* p. 263).

Today's Lesson: Our lives may reflect the same trust, courage, and faithfulness that Elisha demonstrated—and brighten the lives of those around us.

"Nineveh, That Great City"

Prophets and Kings, Chapter 22.

"Then God saw their works, that they turned from their evil way; and God relented from the disaster that He had said He would bring upon them, and He did not do it"
(Jonah 3:10, NKJV).

Nineveh was one of the greatest cities of the ancient world. Though it was well-known for its crime and wickedness (see Nahum 3:1), God wanted the Ninevites to have at least one more chance to hear the truth, and He chose Jonah as His messenger.

Jonah resisted God's call, and Satan overwhelmed him with discouragement. Jonah tried to flee to Tarshish, but God did not desert him. Through a series of trials and strange providences, God brought Jonah to Ninevah and revived his faith.

When the reluctant prophet finally arrived in the great city, he proclaimed God's message—that in forty days the city would be overthrown. All the inhabitants heard the startling announcement, and every heart trembled because of their sins. Amazingly, the people of Nineveh, from the king down, "repented at the preaching of Jonah" (Matthew 12:41, NKJV).

Jonah should have been the first to rejoice. But instead, he dwelt on the possibility that he would be seen as a false prophet because of God's grace toward Nineveh. Discouragement once more overwhelmed him, and God had to give Jonah a lesson in trust and humility. That lesson is also for us today, when the cities of the world are in need of the knowledge of God as were the Ninevites of old.

Key Thought: "God allows men a period of probation; but there is a point beyond which divine patience is exhausted, and the judgments of God are sure to follow. The Lord bears long with men, and with cities, mercifully giving warnings to save them from divine wrath; but a time will come when pleadings for mercy will no longer be heard, and the rebellious element that continues to reject the light of truth will be blotted out, in mercy to themselves and to those who would otherwise be influenced by their example" (*Prophets and Kings,* p. 276).

Today's Lesson: We need to focus more on the power and goodness of God than on the obstacles and "impossibilities" that seem to stand in our way.

The Assyrian Captivity

Prophets and Kings, Chapter 23.

"They have set up kings, but not by me: they have made princes, and I knew it not" (Hosea 8:4).

The closing years of Israel, the northern kingdom, were marked with violence and bloodshed. King after king was assassinated, and every principle of justice was set aside.

Through Elijah, Elisha, Hosea, and Amos, God sent message after message, urging full and complete repentance and threatening disaster as the awful consequence of disobedience. Amos registered his frustration: "They hate him that rebuketh in the gate, and they abhor him that speaketh uprightly. . . . They afflict the just, they take a bribe, and they turn aside the poor in the gate from their right" (Amos 5:10, 12).

The ten tribes were now to reap the fruits of the apostasy that had started with the altars set up at Bethel and Dan. Amos's prediction that "Israel shall surely go into captivity" (Amos 7:17) was literally fulfilled in the destruction of the kingdom by the Assyrians. In the terrible judgments that fell on the northern tribes, the Lord had a wise and merciful purpose—multitudes in Assyria would come to know God's character and the benefits of His law through the witness of a faithful few of the Israelite captives.

Key Thought: "The iniquity in Israel during the last half century before the Assyrian captivity was like that of the days of Noah, and of every other age when men have rejected God and have given themselves wholly to evil-doing. The exaltation of nature above the God of nature, the worship of the creature instead of the Creator, has always resulted in the grossest of evils. Thus when the people of Israel, in their worship of Baal and Ashtoreth, paid supreme homage to the forces of nature, they severed their connection with all that is uplifting and ennobling, and fell an easy prey to temptation. With the defenses of the soul broken down, the misguided worshipers had no barrier against sin and yielded themselves to the evil passions of the human heart" (*Prophets and Kings,* pp. 281, 282).

Today's Lesson: The great controversy continues to demonstrate today that sin has sure and certain consequences. Faithfulness to God is the only path to peace and happiness.

"Destroyed for Lack of Knowledge"

Prophets and Kings, Chapter 24.

"My people are destroyed for lack of knowledge: because thou hast rejected knowledge, I will also reject thee; . . . seeing thou hast forgotten the law of thy God"
(Hosea 4:6).

The clear truth is that God's favor toward Israel had always been conditional upon its obedience. This covenant relationship had been emphasized at Sinai and repeated again on the borders of the Promised Land. Moses, as recorded in Deuteronomy, specifically warned the people against the temptations that would assail them in the future and of the evils that would result from disobedience and from joining the nations around them—either spiritually or politically. He pointed out that their obedience would be their strength and blessing. These warnings and predictions were fulfilled, in part, in the time of the judges but met a more complete and literal fulfillment in the captivity of Israel by Assyria and that of Judah by Babylon.

Had Israel and Judah heeded the messages of the prophets, they would have been spared the humiliation that followed. They earned their captivity!

In symbolic language Hosea set before the ten tribes God's plan to restore every penitent soul who would unite with His church on earth and grant them the blessings they enjoyed in the days of their loyalty to Him in the Promised Land.

Key Thought: "From 'every nation, and kindred, and tongue, and people' there will be some who will gladly respond to the message, 'Fear God, and give glory to Him; for the hour of His judgment is come.' They will turn from every idol that binds them to earth, and will 'worship Him that made heaven, and earth, and the sea, and the fountains of waters.' They will free themselves from every entanglement and will stand before the world as monuments of God's mercy. Obedient to the divine requirements, they will be recognized by angels and by men as those that have kept 'the commandments of God, and the faith of Jesus.' Revelation 14:6, 7, 12" (*Prophets and Kings,* pp. 299, 300).

Today's Lesson: God's covenant relationship with His people is still the same today as it was throughout Israel's history. We face the same choices Israel faced—obedience and life or disobedience and death.

The Call of Isaiah

Prophets and Kings, Chapter 25.

"[Jothan] did that which was right in the sight of the Lord:
he did according to all that his father Uzziah had done.
Howbeit the high places were not removed: the people
sacrificed and burned incense still in the high places"
(2 Kings 15:34, 35).

The long reign of Uzzah (also known as Azariah) in the land of Judah and Benjamin was characterized by a prosperity greater than that of any other ruler since the death of Solomon. But Judah's outward prosperity was not accompanied by a corresponding revival of spiritual power among the people.

Such was the situation when Isaiah was called to his prophetic mission—a time filled with peril for God's people. For sixty years, Isaiah witnessed the demise of the northern kingdom and repeated invasions of Judah by the Assyrians. But the dangers within were more serious than the dangers without. Many of the same evils that led to Israel's fall were prevalent also in Judah.

During the last year of Uzzah's life, God gave Isaiah a vision of Himself sitting on a throne high and lifted up, surrounded by a multitude united in solemn invocation: "Holy, holy, holy, is the Lord of hosts: the whole earth is full of his glory" (Isaiah 6:3). Isaiah realized His insufficiency, but he also recognized that God was calling him to be a faithful prophet who would proclaim both encouragement and warning to the people.

Key Thought: "This assurance of the final fulfillment of God's purpose brought courage to the heart of Isaiah. What though earthly powers array themselves against Judah? What though the Lord's messenger meet with opposition and resistance? Isaiah had seen the King, the Lord of hosts; he had heard the song of the seraphim. . . . Throughout his long and arduous mission he carried with him the memory of this vision. For sixty years or more he stood before the children of Judah as a prophet of hope, waxing bolder and still bolder in his predictions of the future triumph of the church" (*Prophets and Kings,* p. 310).

Today's Lesson: The more clearly we see God, the more clearly we will understand our spiritual duties—and the great grace and blessings He offers.

APRIL 8

"Behold Your God!"

Prophets and Kings, Chapter 26.

"Seek ye the Lord while he may be found, call ye upon him while he is near: Let the wicked forsake his way, and the unrighteous man his thoughts: and let him return unto the Lord, and he will have mercy upon him; and to our God, for he will abundantly pardon" (Isaiah 55:6, 7).

In Isaiah's day, the spiritual understanding of mankind was dark through misapprehension of God. Satan led men to look upon their Creator as the author of sin and suffering and death. Those whom he had thus deceived imagined that God was hard and exacting. Satan misrepresented heaven's law of love as a restriction upon human happiness. Further, Satan had inspired leaders to declare that its precepts could not be obeyed and that its penalties were arbitrary. You can see who seemed to be winning in the great controversy.

In losing sight of the true character of God, the Israelites were without excuse. They simply kept forgetting the Red Sea, God's help for forty years in the wilderness, and many other miraculous experiences. So, God raised up prophets to remind them in clear, bold messages.

When Isaiah saw the character of God in his temple vision, he also saw a view of his own unworthiness and the assurance of forgiveness. He arose a changed man. Hereafter, in his messages, Isaiah made clear that the misunderstood God was really the great Healer of spiritual disease.

Key Thought: "The inhabitants of Judah were all undeserving, yet God would not give them up. By them His name was to be exalted among the heathen. Many who were wholly unacquainted with His attributes were yet to behold the glory of the divine character. It was for the purpose of making plain His merciful designs that He kept sending His servants the prophets with the message, 'Turn ye again now everyone from his evil way'. . . . 'For Mine own sake, even for Mine own sake, will I do it: for how should My name be polluted? and I will not give My glory unto another.' Isaiah 48:9, 11" (*Prophets and Kings,* p. 319).

Today's Lesson: Misconceptions of God are widespread in the world—and in the church—today. What misconceptions may I still be harboring?

Ahaz

Prophets and Kings, Chapter 27.

"Woe to thee, O land, when thy king is a child"
(Ecclesiastes 10:16).

The accession of Ahaz to the throne brought Isaiah and his associates face to face with conditions more appalling than any that had hitherto existed in the realm of Judah. Princes were proving untrue to their trust; false prophets were arising with messages to lead astray. The priests were carrying out their duties for monetary gain. Yet, in spite of the depths to which they had fallen, the leaders of apostasy still kept up the forms of divine worship and claimed to be God's people. The prophet Micah viewed the situation and exclaimed: "The good man is perished out of the earth: and there is none upright among men" (Micah 7:2).

Both Micah and Isaiah presented appeals that should have broken many hearts. When we read these two prophets today, we should receive them as the voice of God to every soul. The sins of Judah are no different than those that are so prevalent today. If we were living in Judah in Isaiah's day, would we have responded to his messages?

When Ahaz was besieged by Assyria, instead of appealing to the Lord, he sacrificed to the gods of Damascus, hoping that the Syrian gods might help him! He even closed the temple doors! No longer were the sacred candlesticks kept burning; no longer were offerings made for the sins of the people. The morning and evening sacrifices had ceased. No wonder God could not bless His people!

Key Thought: "In Judah there dwelt some who maintained their allegiance to Jehovah, steadfastly refusing to be led into idolatry. It was to these that Isaiah and Micah and their associates looked in hope as they surveyed the ruin wrought during the last years of Ahaz. Their sanctuary was closed, but the faithful ones were assured: 'God is with us.' 'Sanctify the Lord of hosts Himself; and let Him be your fear, and let Him be your dread. And He shall be for a sanctuary.' Isaiah 8:10, 13, 14" (*Prophets and Kings,* p. 330).

Today's Lesson: When the faith of many is extinguished, those who remain faithful to God shine even more brightly. Am I determined to let God live in and through me?

APRIL 10

Hezekiah

Prophets and Kings, Chapter 28.

"Hezekiah . . . wrought that which was good and right and truth before the Lord his God. And in every work . . . in the service of the house of God, and in the law, and in the commandments, to seek his God, he did it with all his heart, and prospered" (2 Chronicles 31:20, 21).

Hezekiah's reign was a sharp contrast to that of his father, Ahaz. As soon as he became king, he restored the temple services that had been so long neglected, working with the Levites who had remained true to their sacred calling. He appealed to the priests to unite with him in bringing about the necessary reforms and to begin quickly.

In the first religious service conducted after the temple's restoration, the rulers of the city united with Hezekiah and the priests and the Levites in seeking forgiveness for the sins of the nation. The people now listened to the words of Micah and Isaiah with new confidence. For many years the Passover had not been observed as a national festival, and Hezekiah did what seemed impossible—he invited the faithful in the northern kingdom to join with those in Jerusalem. The streets were cleared of the idolatrous shrines placed there during the reign of Ahaz.

"There was great joy in Jerusalem: for since the time of Solomon the son of David king of Israel there was not the like in Jerusalem" (2 Chronicles 30:26).

Key Thought: "The reign of Hezekiah was characterized by a series of remarkable providences which revealed to the surrounding nations that the God of Israel was with His people. The success of the Assyrians in capturing Samaria and in scattering the shattered remnant of the ten tribes among the nations, during the earlier portion of his reign, was leading many to question the power of the God of the Hebrews. . . . Not until some years later, toward the close of Hezekiah's reign, was it to be demonstrated before the nations of the world whether the gods of the heathen were finally to prevail" (*Prophets and Kings,* p. 339).

Today's Lesson: Reform is the result of consecrated leadership. What can I do today—in my home or church—to be an influence for good?

The Ambassadors From Babylon

Prophets and Kings, Chapter 29.

"Hezekiah humbled himself for the pride of his heart, both he and the inhabitants of Jerusalem, so that the wrath of the Lord came not upon them in the days of Hezekiah" (2 *Chronicles 32:26).*

In the midst of his prosperous reign, Hezekiah suddenly was stricken with a fatal disease. Knowing that he had served the Lord faithfully, he now pled with the Lord for relief. In response, the Lord sent Isaiah to tell Hezekiah that his prayers had been heard—that he would be healed and that fifteen years were to be added to his life. Hezekiah broke out in a memorable song, recorded in Isaiah 38: 10–20, expressing his gratitude to God for His great mercies.

Far to the east, Babylonian astronomers noticed that the shadow on the sundial had been turned back ten degrees—the very sign God had promised Hezekiah to prove to him that his prayers had been heard. The king of Babylon, greatly impressed, sent ambassadors to Hezekiah to congratulate him on his recovery and to learn more of His God who could produce such a wonder.

This visit from the Babylonians gave Hezekiah a great opportunity to extol the living God. But pride and vanity took over, and he laid open to their covetous eyes the treasures with which God had enriched His people. There was nothing that Hezekiah did not show them! This visit was a test of his gratitude and devotion, but he failed.

This foolish move by Hezekiah proved disastrous. The Babylonians now knew the extent of Judah's riches, and they determined to take them by conquest. Hezekiah may have been sorry when he realized the missed opportunity, but the damage had been done.

Key Thought: "The story of Hezekiah's failure to prove true to his trust at the time of the visit of the ambassadors is fraught with an important lesson for all. Far more than we do, we need to speak of the precious chapters in our experience, of the mercy and loving-kindness of God, of the matchless depths of the Saviour's love" (*Prophets and Kings,* p. 347).

Today's Lesson: Our witness to God's blessings should focus more on the spiritual benefits He brings than on the physical or material blessings.

Deliverance From Assyria

Prophets and Kings, Chapter 30.

"Be strong and courageous, be not afraid nor dismayed for the king of Assyria, nor for all the multitude that is with him: for there be more with us than with him: With him is an arm of flesh; but with us is the Lord our God to help us, and to fight our battles" (2 Chronicles 32:7, 8).

In Hezekiah's earlier years he continued to pay tribute to Assyria in harmony with the agreement entered into by his father, Ahaz. At the same time, he made sure of a plentiful supply of water within the walls of Jerusalem; the tunnel he built is visible yet today and is known as "Hezekiah's tunnel." He built up Jerusalem's walls and prepared military weapons. Hezekiah's faith spread through the land, and "the people rested themselves upon the words of Hezekiah" (2 Chronicles 32:8).

Finally the expected crisis came. The Assyrians divided their forces into two armies—one to meet an Egyptian army and the other to besiege Jerusalem. Now God became Judah's only hope, because the expected help from Egypt had been cut off.

The Assyrians insolently demanded the surrender of the city, hurling insults against Judah's God. Isaiah sent Hezekiah a message: "Be not afraid of the words which thou hast heard" (2 Kings 19:6). The Assyrian king sent a sarcastic, insulting letter to Hezekiah, and he spread it out before the Lord in the temple, knowing that the honor of God was at stake.

Deliverance came at night, when an angel "smote in the camp of the Assyrians an hundred fourscore and five thousand" (2 Kings 19:35). The honor of Jehovah was vindicated in the eyes of the surrounding nations.

Key Thought: "When the king of Judah received the taunting letter, he took it into the temple and 'spread it before the Lord' and prayed with strong faith for help from heaven, that the nations of earth might know that the God of the Hebrews still lived and reigned. . . . The honor of Jehovah was at stake; He alone could bring deliverance" (*Prophets and Kings,* p. 355).

Today's Lesson: When we face overwhelming problems—financial, family, job-related—we may spread them out before the Lord as did Hezekiah and trust in His promised power.

Hope for the Heathen

Prophets and Kings, Chapter 31.

"In thy seed shall all the nations of the earth be blessed"
(Genesis 22:18).

Throughout his ministry, Isaiah bore a clear message—probably clearer than any other prophet—concerning God's purposes for the heathen. But this testimony was not in harmony with the accepted theology of his day in Judah. Often the descendants of Abraham seemed unable or unwilling to understand God's purpose for the heathen nations around them. Yet, this was the reason God had called the Hebrews into existence as His special people—to be a witness for Him to the world.

As the Hebrews were advancing into the Promised Land, they discovered that some among the heathens—like Rahab—were already learning that Jehovah alone was the true God.

God recognizes no distinctions of nationality, race, or caste. All people are of one family by creation, and all are one through redemption. Had Israel been true to her trust, all the nations of earth would have shared in her blessings. But in Isaiah's day, the love of the true God was little known; error and superstition flourished.

But a merciful and fair God was doing as much as Israel would allow Him to do to illuminate others with the light "which lighteth every man that cometh into the world" (John 1:9). Many honest-hearted heathen responded to that light and desired a better way; ultimately, they will be judged by the light they had. God loves everyone—Hebrew or Gentile—and He will not permit any soul to be disappointed who is sincerely longing for something higher and nobler than anything the world can offer.

Key Thought: "At times those who have no knowledge of God aside from that which they have received under the operations of divine grace have been kind to His servants, protecting them at the risk of their own lives. The Holy Spirit is implanting the grace of Christ in the heart of many a noble seeker after truth, quickening his sympathies contrary to his nature, contrary to his former education" (*Prophets and Kings,* pp. 376, 377).

Today's Lesson: God is working on every heart. How can He use me today to bring a fuller knowledge of His love and grace to someone who is seeking?

Manasseh and Josiah

Prophets and Kings, Chapter 32.

**"*Manasseh made Judah and the inhabitants of Jerusalem to err, and to do worse than the heathen*"
(*2 Chronicles 33:9*).**

Here is another sad instance in which a faithful father was followed by a wicked son. And it is also another example of how easily leadership can sway a majority into evil ways. But not everyone forgot the faithfulness God had shown during Hezekiah's reign, and they resisted Manasseh and his cronies. "Manasseh shed innocent blood very much, till he had filled Jerusalem from one end to another" (2 Kings 21:16). Isaiah was one of the first to be slain.

As a down payment on what lay ahead for the southern kingdom, God permitted the Assyrians to capture Manasseh for a time. Remarkably, this affliction led Manasseh to his knees, and he surrendered his heart to God. But it came too late in his life to reverse the idolatrous practices of his people.

Amon, Manasseh's son, came to the throne and continued the worst habits of his father, leading to his own assassination after only two years. Amon's son, young Josiah, only eight years old, began his reign of thirty-one years. Josiah's reverence for God is astonishing in view of all that he had seen in the palace from his earliest years.

During this time the true-hearted in Judah questioned whether God's promises could ever be fulfilled. The prophets were now foretelling the utter destruction of their fair city.

Key Thought: "Habakkuk was not the only one through whom was given a message of bright hope and of future triumph as well as of present judgment. During the reign of Josiah the word of the Lord came to Zephaniah, specifying plainly the results of continued apostasy, and calling the attention of the true church to the glorious prospect beyond. His prophecies of impending judgment upon Judah apply with equal force to the judgments that are to fall upon an impenitent world at the time of the second advent of Christ" (*Prophets and Kings,* p. 389).

Today's Lesson: The tone for a nation—or a church—is often set by its leaders. Godly leaders can exert great influence, and so can the ungodly. As individuals, however, we must each make our own choices in life.

The Book of the Law

Prophets and Kings, Chapter 33.

"The king stood by a pillar, and made a covenant
before the Lord, to walk after the Lord, and to keep his
commandments and his testimonies and his statutes with
all their heart and all their soul, to perform the words of
this covenant that were written in this book"
(2 Kings 23:3).

This reform, in the eighteenth year of Josiah's reign, was brought about in a wholly unexpected manner through the discovery and study of the book of Deuteronomy that had for many years been strangely misplaced and lost.

Nearly a century before, during the first Passover celebrated by Hezekiah, provision had been made for the daily public reading of the book of the law to the people by teaching priests. But Manasseh had thought differently, and through careless neglect, this document had been lost. It was rediscovered by Hilkiah, the high priest, while the temple was undergoing extensive repairs.

For years Josiah had been earnestly purging the Baal shrines wherever he found them in Judah. But when the book of Deuteronomy was discovered, Josiah knew that he now had a powerful ally to continue his work of reform.

After gathering his countrymen around him, Josiah himself read this book of the law. His voice revealed a broken heart, and his hearers were greatly moved. But the zeal of Josiah and the piety of his followers could not change the hearts of many who stubbornly refused to turn from idolatry to the worship of the true God.

Key Thought: "Thus Josiah, from his earliest manhood, had endeavored to take advantage of his position as king to exalt the principles of God's holy law. And now, while Shaphan the scribe was reading to him out of the book of the law, . . . the king resolved to walk in the light of its counsels, and also to do all in his power to acquaint his people with its teachings and to lead them, if possible, to cultivate reverence and love for the law of heaven" (*Prophets and Kings,* p. 398).

Today's Lesson: God's Word is powerful and has been the basis for a spiritual reformation in many places and in different ages. It has power to transform our individual lives, as well.

Jeremiah

Prophets and Kings, Chapter 34.

"Ask for the old paths, where is the good way, and walk therein, and ye shall find rest for your souls"
(Jeremiah 6:16).

In the thirteenth year of Josiah's reign, Jeremiah was called to be a prophet while still a youth. For forty years Jeremiah stood before Judah as a mighty witness for truth. Through it all, he was despised, hated, and rejected of men, while he witnessed the literal fulfillment of his own prophecies of impending doom on Jerusalem.

God permitted Jeremiah to look beyond the distressing scenes of the present to Israel's glorious return from captivity, when God would renew His covenant with His people. He emphasized often that faith and obedience and good works alone are acceptable in the sight of a holy God.

Jeremiah called attention repeatedly to the counsels given in Deuteronomy. More than any other of the prophets, he emphasized the teachings of the Mosaic law and showed how these might bring the highest spiritual blessing to the nation and to every individual heart.

But his countrymen would not accept his warnings; they called him a traitor and worthy of death. Jeremiah's sensitive soul was crushed by derision and physical abuse, but he daily let the Holy Spirit strengthen him to endure.

Key Thought: "What a lesson is this to men holding positions of responsibility today in the church of God! What a solemn warning to deal faithfully with wrongs that bring dishonor to the cause of truth! Let none who claim to be the depositaries of God's law flatter themselves that the regard they may outwardly show toward the commandments will preserve them from the exercise of divine justice. Let none refuse to be reproved for evil, nor charge the servants of God with being too zealous in endeavoring to cleanse the camp from evil-doing. A sin-hating God calls upon those who claim to keep His law to depart from all iniquity. A neglect to repent and to render willing obedience will bring upon men and women today as serious consequences as came upon ancient Israel" (*Prophets and Kings,* p. 416).

Today's Lesson: It may not be easy to grasp at the time, but God is with us equally in the tough times as He is when life is proceeding smoothly.

Approaching Doom

Prophets and Kings, Chapter 35.

"His word was in mine heart as a burning fire shut up in my bones, and I was weary with forbearing, and I could not stay" (Jeremiah 20:9).

The first years of Jehoiakim's rule were filled with signs of approaching doom. Assyria and Egypt, in which the kings of Judah had relied in the past, were soon to be replaced on the world stage by Babylon. At first only a few Judeans—followed by thousands and then ten of thousands—were made captive and marched to Babylon. Among these captives were Daniel and his three friends. Three Jewish kings—Jehoiakim, Jehoiachin, and Zedekiah—were to become vassals of the Babylonian ruler.

The faithful listened not only to the predictions of doom but looked ahead with the eye of faith to the time of restoration after seventy years of captivity. Faith in the promises of God was drilled into the children of the faithful. Thus young Daniel and his three friends were clear-headed about the future, even though the present would call for great endurance.

During these difficult hours, God commanded Jeremiah to commit to writing his many sermons. To Baruch, the scribe, Jeremiah dictated what we now know as the book called by his name.

Key Thought: "God's plan is not to send messengers who will please and flatter sinners; He delivers no messages of peace to lull the unsanctified into carnal security. Instead, He lays heavy burdens upon the conscience of the wrongdoer and pierces his soul with sharp arrows of conviction. Ministering angels present to him the fearful judgments of God, to deepen the sense of need and to prompt the agonizing cry, 'What must I do to be saved?' Acts 16:30. But the Hand that humbles to the dust, rebukes sin, and puts pride and ambition to shame, is the Hand that lifts up the penitent, stricken one. With deepest sympathy He who permits the chastisement to fall, inquires, 'What wilt thou that I shall do unto thee?' " (*Prophets and Kings,* p. 435).

Today's Lesson: God's punishments are designed to bring about repentance and forgiveness. In the history of Israel and Judah we can learn to see His hand in our own lives—and how to respond to His leading.

The Last King of Judah

Prophets and Kings, Chapter 36.

"I will overturn, overturn, overturn, it: and it shall be no more, until he come whose right is it; and I will give it him" (Ezekiel 21:27).

Jeremiah counseled Zedekiah and all Judah, including those taken to Babylon, to submit quietly to the temporary rule of their conquerors. But this advice was contrary to the inclinations of the human heart, and Satan took advantage of the circumstances to incite false prophets—both in Jerusalem and in Babylon—to announce that the yoke of bondage would soon be broken and the nation's former prestige soon restored.

Listening and acting on these flattering deceptions would have led to fatal moves on the part of the king and the exiles and would have frustrated God's merciful designs on their behalf. Any insurrection on the part of the Hebrews would lead to a further restriction of their liberties. Submission to the rule of Babylon was the lightest punishment that a merciful God could inflict upon so rebellious a people, but if they rebelled against this decree of servitude, they would feel the full rigor of His chastisement.

Against determined opposition, Jeremiah stood firmly for the policy of submission. The prophet had to contend not only with false prophets but with the priests, as well. "Both prophet and priest are profane; yea, in my house have I found their wickedness" (Jeremiah 23:11).

Key Thought: "While Jeremiah continued to bear his testimony in the land of Judah, the prophet Ezekiel was raised up from among the captives in Babylon, to warn and to comfort the exiles, and also to confirm the word of the Lord that was being spoken through Jeremiah. During the years that remained of Zedekiah's reign, Ezekiel made very plain the folly of trusting to the false predictions of those who were causing the captives to hope for an early return to Jerusalem. He was also instructed to foretell, by means of a variety of symbols and solemn messages, the siege and utter destruction of Jerusalem" (*Prophets and Kings,* p. 448).

Today's Lesson: Each individual needs a personal connection with God in order to be able to discern His will. God has promised the Holy Spirit to guide us as we look for direction.

Carried Captive Into Babylon

Prophets and Kings, Chapter 37.

"A small number that escape the sword shall return out of the land of Egypt into the land of Judah, and all the remnant of Judah, that are gone into the land of Egypt to sojourn there, shall know whose words shall stand, mine, or theirs" (Jeremiah 44:28).

In the ninth year of Zedekiah's reign, Nebuchadnezzar besieged Jerusalem with a vengeance. In God's plan it was time for the remnant of Judah to go into captivity—to learn through adversity the lessons they had refused to learn under more favorable circumstances. Among the righteous still living in Jerusalem were some who were determined to safeguard the sacred Ark of the Covenant containing the tablets of stone on which God had traced with His own finger the precepts of the Ten Commandments. To place it beyond the reach of ruthless hands, they hid it in a cave. That sacred ark has never been disturbed from that day to this.

In the last days of Judah, Jeremiah was thrown into a dungeon by jealous, frustrated counselors to the king. Zedekiah was greatly worried about the situation in Judah; secretly, the king visited Jeremiah and asked: "Is there any word from the Lord?" Jeremiah answered, "There is: for, said he, thou shalt be delivered into the hand of the king of Babylon" (Jeremiah 37:17). Sensing that the prophet was right, Zedekiah commanded that Jeremiah be released from the dungeon and allowed to live in the prison courtyard.

The king dared not openly manifest any faith in Jeremiah. He was too weak to brave the disfavor of his princes and of the people by submitting to the will of God.

Key Thought: "The sorrow of the prophet over the utter perversity of those who would have been the spiritual light of the world, his sorrow over the fate of Zion and of the people carried captive to Babylon, is revealed in the lamentations he has left on record as a memorial of the folly of turning from the counsels of Jehovah to human wisdom" (*Prophets and Kings,* p. 461).

Today's Lesson: In these last days, fidelity to God demands the same unflinching, unwavering endurance Jeremiah exhibited. As God sustained His prophet then, so will He sustain us today.

Light Through Darkness

Prophets and Kings, Chapter 38.

"Behold, I am the Lord, the God of all flesh: is there any thing too hard for me?" (Jeremiah 32:27).

These were dark days for Judah. Had it not been for the encouragement of such prophets as Jeremiah, Daniel, and Ezekiel, the future would have appeared hopeless. But through these prophets of the exile, God continued to make clear His eternal purpose in the great controversy. A faithful remnant in Judah continued to present His side of the controversy with Satan.

Though continually beaten down by his countrymen, Jeremiah, in his older years, acted out a parable that illustrated before the inhabitants of Jerusalem God's ultimate purpose for His people. In the presence of witnesses, he purchased an ancestral field in nearby Anathoth. Since this land was in an area already under the control of the Babylonians, Jeremiah's action seemed to be foolish. Besides, he was advanced in years and could never hope to receive personal benefit from the purchase.

But Jeremiah's purchase was designed to make a point. With the eye of faith, he demonstrated his trust in God's assurance that He still had a purpose for His people in Judah. His act would inspire others to maintain hope and trust those same inspired words. Yet, even after this amazing act of faith, Jeremiah wondered if he had acted presumptuously and given others false hope (see Jeremiah 32:17–27). God answered the concerns of His loyal servant in words that still ring with hope for us today (see verses 37–44).

Key Thought: "Humbled in the sight of the nations, those who once had been recognized as favored of Heaven above all other peoples of the earth were to learn in exile the lesson of obedience so necessary for their future happiness. Until they had learned this lesson, God could not do for them all that He desired to do. 'I will correct thee in measure, and will not leave thee altogether unpunished,' He declared in explanation of His purpose to chastise them for their spiritual good. Jeremiah 30:11" (Prophets and Kings, p. 475).

Today's Lesson: Faith lies close to presumption, and it is easy to mistake one for the other. Only a close connection with heaven can keep us in the center of God's will.

In the Court of Babylon

Prophets and Kings, Chapter 39.

"Them that honour me I will honour" (1 Samuel 2:30).

Among the Israelites carried to Babylon at the beginning of the seventy years of captivity were young men who were true to principle, whose highest goal was honoring God. Nebuchadnezzar saw in these four young men remarkable abilities that he wanted to train for government service in his kingdom.

The king didn't demand that the Hebrew youth change their religion in favor of his own; he hoped to bring this about gradually. At the very beginning of their training they had to make decisions—their food came from the king's own table and had been offered to idols. Nor was it the kind of food that would be best for them mentally or physically. They had been educated since childhood to live temperately and judiciously regarding food and other aspects of mental and physical health. Besides, they knew that if they yielded in what appeared to be a small test, they would open the door to yield in greater matters.

At graduation time, the four completed their course with exceptional honors—no one else came near their achievements. Their university years were years of maturing as they improved every opportunity to become intelligent in all lines of learning. Before they could fulfill God's plan for them in Babylon, they had to become prepared to take on the heavy responsibilities the king would give them. But through it all, God's larger purpose was being achieved—they were representing His character in the highest circles of Babylon. These four Hebrews understood that intellectual power, physical stamina, and length of life depends on God's immutable laws.

Key Thought: "True success in any line of work is not the result of chance or accident or destiny. It is the outworking of God's providences, the reward of faith and discretion, of virtue and perseverance. Fine mental qualities and a high moral tone are not the result of accident. God gives opportunities; success depends upon the use made of them" (*Prophets and Kings,* p. 486).

Today's Lesson: Life is made up of seemingly small decisions. But these choices have significant effects—both for this life and the next. Faithfulness in little things will fit us for larger responsibilities.

Nebuchadnezzar's Dream

Prophets and Kings, Chapter 40.

"Truly your God is the God of gods, the Lord of kings, and a revealer of secrets, since you could reveal this secret" (Daniel 2:47, NKJV).

Soon after Daniel and his three friends entered the king's service, Nebuchadnezzar had a remarkable dream that disturbed him very much. He could not find any of his wise men who could help him understand this dream—although they made their living promising to do just such things as part of their special "wisdom."

The king was furious with these imposters and commanded they be executed. Daniel was included in this group of "wise men" and asked for an audience with the king. After praying with his three companions, Daniel offered to interpret the king's dream. Listening, Nebuchadnezzar was convinced that Daniel had given him the true meaning he had been seeking. The king's first decision was to halt the execution of his wise men. As the days went by, these men should have been very grateful to Daniel, but jealousy overrode their gratitude, and they determined to avenge their embarrassment sooner or later.

With remarkable tact and courtesy, Daniel unfolded the next twenty-five hundred years of world history as he explained the king's dream. It wasn't easy to tell Nebuchadnezzar that his kingdom would fall to another. Had the rulers of Babylon, the richest of all earthly kingdoms, continued to recognize Nebuchadnezzar's insights, God could have painted an entirely different future. But they trusted in their glory, and God could not do for them what He wanted to do.

The student of history today can behold the literal fulfillment of divine prophecy in Nebuchadnezzar's dream.

Key Thought: "To understand these things,—to understand that 'righteousness exalteth a nation;' that 'the throne is established by righteousness,' and 'upholden by mercy;' to recognize the outworking of these principles in the manifestation of His power who 'removeth kings, and setteth up kings,'—this is to understand the philosophy of history. Proverbs 14:34; 16:12; 20:28; Daniel 2:21" (*Prophets and Kings,* p. 502).

Today's Lesson: God's purposes and plans are carried out in human history. Bible prophecy draws the curtain aside and gives us a glimpse of the divine design, but we need to be careful not to speculate beyond what has been revealed.

The Fiery Furnace

Prophets and Kings, Chapter 41.

"When thou passest through the waters, I will be with thee; and through the rivers, they shall not overflow thee: when thou walkest through the fire, thou shalt not be burned; neither shall the flame kindle upon thee"
(Isaiah 43:2).

Unfortunately, Nebuchadnezzar's confidence in Daniel's God faded in time; his heart was not yet cleansed of his desire for self-exaltation. His "wise men," seeing that the king had returned to idolatry, proposed a test that would feed his vanity. He had dreamed of a statue made of different metals. They suggested an imposing statute made entirely of gold and urged that the king command every important person in the kingdom to gather and worship it. Satan was determined to defeat God's purpose of making the captive Israelites a means for blessing the heathen nations.

When the time came, everyone bowed down to the statue as a sign of devotion—all but the three Hebrews. Embarrassed, the king did his best to persuade these three special young men, but they were determined. Furious, the king directed the furnace to be heated seven times hotter.

But God did not forsake His faithful three. In that fire, even the king could see a fourth figure whom he identified as the "Son of God." Amazing! All this, because through the preceding years, Daniel and his friends had explained to Nebuchadnezzar the great story of the Redeemer to come. The greatness of the king was evident when he descended from his throne to call the three Hebrews in the furnace to come out and be recognized as servants of the Most High God.

Key Thought: "As in the days of Shadrach, Meshach, and Abednego, so in the closing period of earth's history the Lord will work mightily in behalf of those who stand steadfastly for the right. He who walked with the Hebrew worthies in the fiery furnace will be with His followers wherever they are. His abiding presence will comfort and sustain" (*Prophets and Kings,* p. 513).

Today's Lesson: In the last days, a death decree will be pronounced against those who choose to remain loyal to God's commands—and He will protect them even as He did the three young Hebrews on the plain of Dura.

True Greatness

Prophets and Kings, Chapter 42.

"I, Nebuchadnezzar, praise and extol and honour the King of heaven, all whose works are truth, and his ways judgment: and those that walk in pride he is able to abase" *(Daniel 4:37).*

In spite of feeling the Spirit working on his heart, Nebuchadnezzar was tempted to turn from the path of humility and yield to pride. God gave him another dream to warn him of his peril. This dream depicted a huge tree with branches stretching to the ends of the earth. But the king saw the tree cut down and seven years go by with only a stump remaining in the ground.

Once more Nebuchadnezzar appealed to his "wise men" for an interpretation—without results. And once more the king turned to Daniel, whom he greatly esteemed. Daniel tactfully unfolded the dream's meaning: The great tree represented Nebuchadnezzar himself, who would suddenly become like a beast of the field for seven years until he understood that the Most High God rules in the kingdom of men. The most cheerful part of the dream was the fact that Nebuchadnezzar's kingdom would be waiting for him after the seven years of humiliation.

Daniel urged the king to repent and thus possibly avert the threatened judgment. For a time, Nebuchadnezzar seemed impressed, but a heart not transformed by God's grace soon loses the impressions of the Holy Spirit.

A year went by, and as Nebuchadnezzar was boasting of Babylon's glory, he was struck down and humbled before the watching world. As predicted, his reason did return after seven years, and he humbly acknowledged that Daniel's God is greater than all other gods.

Key Thought: "Under the rebuke of Him who is King of kings and Lord of lords, Nebuchadnezzar had learned at last the lesson which all rulers need to learn—that true greatness consists in true goodness. He acknowledged Jehovah as the living God, saying, 'I Nebuchadnezzar praise and extol and honor the King of heaven, all whose works are truth, and His ways judgment: and those that walk in pride He is able to abase' " (*Prophets and Kings,* p. 521).

Today's Lesson: True greatness consists in true goodness. God cannot live in a heart that is full of pride and selfishness.

The Unseen Watcher

Prophets and Kings, Chapter 43.

"Let thy gifts be to thyself, and give thy rewards to another; yet I will read the writing unto the king, and make known to him the interpretation" (Daniel 5:17).

Through the folly and weakness of Belshazzar, the grandson of Nebuchadnezzar, proud Babylon was about to fall. Although he had every opportunity to know of Daniel's relationship with his grandfather, Belshazzar's love of pleasure and self-glorification was a stronger influence than any fleeting knowledge of Daniel and Daniel's God.

Even with the enemy armies of the Medes and Persians surrounding the city, Belshazzar felt secure in mighty Babylon. He "made a great feast to a thousand of his lords" (Daniel 5:1) and reveled in a riotous orgy. He and his guests drank from the gold and silver vessels that his grandfather had taken from the Hebrew temple.

In the midst of the party, a mysterious hand traced strange letters on the wall. The laughter came to a halt. The guests were terrified—none more so than Belshazzar. No one could read the meaning of the words on the wall. At this point the queen mother remembered Daniel, and he was called. Before turning to the mysterious writing, Daniel first reminded Belshazzar of his grandfather's experiences and then rebuked him for his great wickedness. Turning to the writing on the wall, he told the terrified onlookers that Babylon would soon be conquered by the Medes and Persians.

While they were still in the banquet hall, news reached the king that the Medes and Persians were already inside the city.

Key Thought: "In that last night of mad folly, Belshazzar and his lords had filled up the measure of their guilt and the guilt of the Chaldean kingdom. No longer could God's restraining hand ward off the impending evil. . . . Because of the strange perversity of the human heart, God had at last found it necessary to pass the irrevocable sentence. Belshazzar was to fall, and his kingdom was to pass into other hands" (*Prophets and Kings,* p. 530).

Today's Lesson: God doesn't give up on us as long as something within our hearts still responds to His repeated invitations. But neither will He force Himself on us if we continue to reject Him.

In the Lions' Den

Prophets and Kings, Chapter 44.

"Daniel prospered in the reign of Darius, and in the reign of Cyrus the Persian" (Daniel 6:28).

Amazingly, when Darius the Mede conquered Babylon, he immediately made Daniel the executive vice president of the empire! Such honors, of course, aroused the jealousy of the other leading men in Babylon, and Daniel's blameless conduct excited their enmity even more. These high officials prepared a trap for Daniel based on their knowledge of his prayer life.

When he heard of the new decree that prohibited praying to any man or god except Darius the king for thirty days, Daniel recognized the duplicity of his enemies. But he continued praying to God three times a day, with his window open toward Jerusalem, as he always had.

The king, too, learned to his sorrow of the motive behind the decree and was greatly displeased. But nothing could be done about it; the decree must stand. The king believed Daniel's God could save him. "Thy God whom thou servest continually," he assured Daniel, "he will deliver thee" (Daniel 6:16). In His wisdom, God permitted this awful treatment so that Daniel's deliverance would be even more telling and the power of the Lord more clearly revealed.

After a sleepless night, the king went to the lions' den early the next morning and found what he had hoped to find—a divinely-protected executive vice president. Swiftly, Daniel's accusers were cast into the same den; they were mutilated before they even hit the floor.

Key Thought: "From the story of Daniel's deliverance we may learn that in seasons of trial and gloom God's children should be just what they were when their prospects were bright with hope and their surroundings all that they could desire. . . . A man whose heart is stayed upon God will be the same in the hour of his greatest trial as he is in prosperity, when the light and favor of God and of man beam upon him. Faith reaches to the unseen, and grasps eternal realities" (*Prophets and Kings,* p. 545).

Today's Lesson: Daniel's experience teaches us that those who are loyal to God can be assured that His presence will always be with them to sustain them in the worst of circumstances.

The Return of the Exiles

Prophets and Kings, Chapter 45.

"I know the thoughts that I think toward you, says the Lord, thoughts of peace and not of evil, to give you a future and a hope" (Jeremiah 29:11, NKJV).

When the Medes and Persians overthrew Babylon, loyal Jews knew that their deliverance from captivity was drawing near. More than a century before, Isaiah had predicted their release and even mentioned Cyrus by name (see Isaiah 44:28; 45:1–3, 13). They studied with even more seriousness the prophecies of Jeremiah, especially those concerning the seventy years assigned to their captivity (see Jeremiah 25:12).

As Cyrus saw the larger meaning of these prophecies, he was profoundly moved and determined to fulfill his divinely appointed mission. In his decree, Cyrus recognized the God of heaven and wrote that God had charged him to restore the temple in Jerusalem. Whatever was needed for its rebuilding could be requisitioned from the king's treasury! This good news reached every corner of the empire.

About fifty thousand from among the Jews in exile, including the priests and Levites, determined to take advantage of the opportunity to return to Jerusalem. Zerubbabel served as governor and Joshua as high priest. The builders worked with the immense stones from Solomon's temple, and when the foundation stone was positioned, a great celebration took place. But sounds of weeping were soon heard from those who remembered the first temple and all its splendor. Instead of rejoicing over God's gracious providence, they focused on discontent and discouragement.

Key Thought: "It is when the vital principles of the kingdom of God are lost sight of, that ceremonies become multitudinous and extravagant. It is when the character building is neglected, when the adornment of the soul is lacking, when the simplicity of godliness is despised, that pride and love of display demand magnificent church edifices, splendid adornings, and imposing ceremonials. But in all this God is not honored. . . . Not all the beauty of art can bear comparison with the beauty of temper and character to be revealed in those who are Christ's representatives" (*Prophets and Kings,* p. 565, 566).

Today's Lesson: We need to be aware of the proper balance between the beauty of holiness and the holiness of beauty—recognizing which is more important.

APRIL 28

"The Prophets of God Helping Them"

Prophets and Kings, Chapter 46.

"Is it time for you, O ye, to dwell in your cieled houses, and this house lie waste? Now therefore thus saith the Lord of hosts; Consider your ways" (Haggai 1:4, 5).

Close by the area where the Jews were rebuilding the temple under Cyrus's decree lived the Samaritans—a mixed race resulting from the intermarriage of pagan colonists from Assyria with the remnant of the ten tribes that had been left in Samaria and Galilee. During this period of restoration, the Samaritans were known as "the adversaries of Judah and Benjamin" (Ezra 4:1, 2).

Seeing that only a remnant of 50,000 Hebrews had come from Babylon to undertake a work seemingly beyond their strength, the Samaritans offered to help. But had the Jewish leaders accepted this offer, they would have opened the door for the entrance of idolatry.

Zerubbabel and his associates had been reading the Scriptures, and they were determined that never again would the Jews break their covenant with God. They resolved that they would keep themselves unmistakably distinct from the pagans around them. It is still true today that the open enemies of God's people are not those who are most to be feared. Those who, like the Samaritans, come with smooth speeches, apparently seeking a friendly alliance, have the greater power to deceive.

At times the temple was neglected, while the people built their own homes and struggled for material prosperity. The Jews were in a pitiable state. During this dark hour, Haggai and Zechariah were raised up to meet the crisis. In stirring speeches, they revealed the cause of Israel's troubles—the people were neglecting to put God's interest first.

Key Thought: "God has a purpose in sending trial to His children. He never leads them otherwise than they would choose to be led if they could see the end from the beginning, and discern the glory of the purpose that they are fulfilling. All that He brings upon them in test and trial comes that they may be strong to do and to suffer for Him" *(Prophets and Kings, p. 578).*

Today's Lesson: God must have first place in our lives—in terms of our time and financial resources, as well as in our spiritual commitment.

Joshua and the Angel

Prophets and Kings, Chapter 47.

"Take away the filthy garments from him. And unto him he said, Behold, I have caused thine iniquity to pass from thee, and I will clothe thee with change of raiment"
(Zechariah 3:4).

As the work on the temple continued, Satan held up before the weary builders their imperfections of character and filled them with discouragement.

Zechariah presents an impressive picture of Satan opposing Christ face to face, and he shows the Lord's power to vanquish the accuser of His people. Zechariah pictures Joshua, the high priest, "clothed with filthy garments" (Zechariah 3:3), standing before the angel of the Lord, pleading for God's mercy. Satan stands up boldly to resist him, pointing to Israel's transgressions and insisting the people cannot be restored to God's favor. Joshua cannot defend himself or his people, but the angel, who is Christ Himself, silences the accuser. Joshua's intercession is accepted, and the command is given: "Take away the filthy garments. . . . I will clothe thee with change of raiment" (verse 4).

The change of clothing represents the imputed righteousness of Christ. But Jesus is not finished: "If thou wilt walk in my ways, and if thou wilt keep my charge, then thou shalt also judge my house" (verse 7). If obedient, Joshua would be honored as the ruler over the temple and all its services. And if the Israelites continued to be obedient, they would be "men wondered at" (verse 8), honored as the chosen of God among the nations. Satan knows that those who ask God for pardon and grace will obtain it.

Key Thought: "Nothing in this world is so dear to the heart of God as His church. It is not His will that worldly policy shall corrupt her record. He does not leave His people to be overcome by Satan's temptations. He will punish those who misrepresent Him, but He will be gracious to all who sincerely repent. To those who call upon Him for strength for the development of Christian character, He will give all needed help" (*Prophets and Kings,* p. 590).

Today's Lesson: There is no sin God cannot—or will not—forgive for those who sincerely seek His pardon. He promises to cover our sins with Christ's robe of righteousness.

"Not by Might, nor by Power"

Prophets and Kings, Chapter 48.

"I will shake all nations, and the desire of all nations shall come: and I will fill this house with glory, saith the Lord of hosts" (Haggai 2:7).

Zerubbabel labored under great difficulties in the work of rebuilding Jerusalem and the temple. Besides the lack of commitment on the part of many of the Hebrews who had returned from Babylon, he was also surrounded by Samaritan adversaries intent on hindering progress. But God supported His leader when problems mounted, sending him messages of encouragement through His prophets.

In all ages, God's people have faced seemingly insurmountable obstacles as they have attempted to carry out heaven's plans. The Lord has allowed these trials as a test of faith. Indeed, it is when difficulties press upon us most strongly that we most need to trust in God and the power of the Holy Spirit. And if God's people will press forward in faith, they will find their burdens and trials disappearing before them. The Savior has promised, "Nothing shall be impossible unto you" (Matthew 17:20).

Zerubbabel persevered under God's guidance until the work was completed and the restored temple was dedicated. True, this second temple did not equal the first in magnificence, nor was it hallowed by those visible tokens of the divine presence that distinguished Solomon's temple. But the promise of Haggai was that the glory of the "latter house shall be greater than of the former" (Haggai 2:9) because it was this temple to which the Messiah, the Son of God Himself, would come. If only the Jews had understood these prophecies of Haggai and Zechariah!

Key Thought: "The second temple was honored, not with the cloud of Jehovah's glory, but with the presence of the One in whom dwelt 'all the fullness of the Godhead bodily'—God Himself 'manifest in the flesh.' Colossians 2:9; 1 Timothy 3:16. . . . The 'Desire of all nations' had indeed come to His temple, when the Man of Nazareth taught and healed in the sacred courts" (*Prophets and Kings, p.* 597).

Lesson for Today: We may face great trials in life, but God has promised never to leave us or forsake us. He will provide the strength to face the burdens of each day.

In the Days of Queen Esther

Prophets and Kings, Chapter 49.

"Who knoweth whether thou art come to the kingdom for such a time as this?" (Esther 4:14).

When Cyrus issued his decree in favor of the Jews returning to their homeland, the majority of the Jewish exiles had settled throughout the Medo-Persian Empire, and they chose to remain, preferring their present comforts rather than the hardships of restoring their desolated homes.

Some twenty years later, Darius Hystaspes issued another decree—as favorable as the decree of Cyrus—supporting the return of the Jews. Zechariah urged those Jews scattered in many lands to respond. Meanwhile, Xerxes the Great became king, and Jew-hating subordinates were assuming new powers. Jews who had not responded to the first two decrees were now facing death!

Satan worked through Haman, the Agagite—a high official in Xerxes' court. Haman hated the influence of Mordecai, a Jew, and determined to kill him—as well as all the Jews in the empire.

But in God's providence, the queen was Esther, a Jewish girl, although the fact that she was Jewish was not known. In the crisis, Mordecai challenged Esther to carry out a plan that would reverse the death decree against the Jews that Haman had engineered with the king's blessing. Esther's plan worked. The king countermanded his earlier decree to kill all the Jews throughout the empire. Haman was executed, and Mordecai was given the position of honor formerly occupied by Haman.

The trying experiences of God's people in the days of Esther cast a long shadow forward to the last days. The death decree that will finally go forth against God's remnant people will be similar to the one issued against the Jews in Esther's day.

Key Thought: "Today the enemies of the true church see in the little company keeping the Sabbath commandment, a Mordecai at the gate. The reverence of God's people for His law is a constant rebuke to those who have cast off the fear of the Lord and are trampling on His Sabbath" (*Prophets and Kings,* p. 605).

Today's Lesson: When God calls us to a difficult or unpleasant task, it is easy to ignore His will and remain in our comfortable circumstances—as did those Jews who remained in Medo-Persia.

MAY 2

Ezra, the Priest and Scribe

Prophets and Kings, Chapter 50.

"Blessed be the Lord God of our fathers, which hath put such a thing as this in the king's heart, to beautify the house of the Lord which is in Jerusalem" (Ezra 7:27).

About seventy years after the first return of the exiles under Zerubbabel and Joshua, Artaxerxes Longimanus came to the Medo-Persian throne and issued the third—and final—decree for the restoration of Jerusalem.

Ezra was born of Aaron's line and had been trained as a priest. He had also acquired familiarity with the writings of the Medo-Persian "wise men." But Ezra was not satisfied with his spiritual condition; he longed to be in full harmony with God. This commitment led him to study the writings of prophets and kings, searching to understand why God had permitted Jerusalem to be destroyed and His people to be carried into captivity in a heathen land.

After his study, Ezra experienced a thorough conversion, and he was determined to use the knowledge he had gained to bring blessing and light to his people. He gathered all the copies of the Scriptures that he could find and had them transcribed and distributed. He shared his religious convictions with the emperor, who, in turn, made Ezra his special representative. Ezra's influence with the king led to the third decree to restore Jerusalem—with all the expenses paid out of the king's treasury!

In preparation for the return, Artaxerxes arranged for preferred treatment for all the temple personnel. He also made provision for the appointment of civil officers who would govern Israelites after the Jewish code of laws, and he gave Ezra authority to teach the laws of God and to execute judgment against lawbreakers. And he generously financed the travel expenses of those returning to Jerusalem. Simply amazing!

Key Thought: "The care exercised by Ezra in providing for the transportation and safety of the Lord's treasure, teaches a lesson worthy of thoughtful study. . . . In the appointment of faithful officers to act as treasurers of the Lord's goods, Ezra recognized the necessity and value of order and organization in connection with the work of God" (*Prophets and Kings,* p. 617).

Today's Lesson: Leaders like Ezra are needed in God's work today.

A Spiritual Revival

Prophets and Kings, Chapter 51.

"And [I] said, 'O my God: I am too ashamed and humiliated to lift up my face to You, my God; for our iniquities have risen higher than our heads, and our guilt has grown up to the heavens' " (Ezra 9:6, NKJV).

Ezra's arrival in Jerusalem was none too early. He quickly learned that many of those who had returned under the previous decrees had lost sight of the sacredness of God's law, and some of the leaders were living in open sin.

One of the chief problems, Ezra learned, was intermarriage with the surrounding non-Jewish peoples. Even some priests and Levites were guilty. Such intermarriage had been one of the chief causes of apostasy prior to the Babylonian captivity. In his public prayers for the people, Ezra clearly expressed his disappointment with the sins he had seen since returning. His sorrow and that of his associates greatly affected the people, and they "wept very bitterly" (Ezra 10:1, NKJV). This was the beginning of a wonderful reformation. Wherever Ezra labored, a revival in the study of the Scriptures occurred.

In our own day, setting aside the plain truths of the Bible has led many to turn away from God's law. The idea that men and women have been released from obedience to God's commandments has weakened the force of moral obligations. The last battle of the great controversy between truth and error will be fought over the conflict between human laws and God's laws.

Key Thought: "The agencies which have united against truth are now actively at work. God's Holy Word, which has been handed down to us at so great a cost of suffering and bloodshed, is little valued. . . . Thousands who pride themselves on their knowledge regard it as an evidence of weakness to place implicit confidence in the Bible, and a proof of learning to cavil at the Scriptures and to spiritualize and explain away their most important truths" (*Prophets and Kings,* p. 625).

Today's Lesson: Every true reformation and revival focuses attention on God's Word and endorses the need for heartfelt obedience to His commandments.

MAY 4

A Man of Opportunity

Prophets and Kings, Chapter 52.

"When Sanballat the Horonite and Tobiah the Ammonite official heard of it, they were deeply disturbed that a man had come to seek the well-being of the children of Israel" (Nehemiah 2:10, NKJV).

Nehemiah was a Hebrew exile who held an influential position in the Persian court, but his heart was in Jerusalem. Through messengers from Jerusalem, Nehemiah kept abreast of the current situation—especially the difficulties facing the Jews there. The fact that the city walls were still largely in ruins greatly increased the problems the returning exiles had to deal with.

Overwhelmed with sorrow, Nehemiah could neither eat nor drink. He prayed day and night. He feared that failure in Jerusalem would bring embarrassment and dishonor to the God of Israel. For four months, Nehemiah waited for an opportunity to request from the king a leave of absence so he could go to Jerusalem. The king could read Nehemiah's face. Finally he asked him, "Why is thy countenance sad?" (Nehemiah 2:2).

After a short prayer for God's guidance, Nehemiah told the king of the difficulties facing the Jews in Jerusalem—and that he would like to go there to help change the situation. The king responded positively to Nehemiah's request.

With his usual prudence and forethought, Nehemiah proceeded to Jerusalem without telling anybody of his plans. He asked the king for royal letters and a military escort for the journey. He made sure that his commission included the king's approval and authority for everything he wanted to do and to purchase.

Key Thought: "Nehemiah did not depend upon uncertainty. The means that he lacked he solicited from those who were able to bestow. And the Lord is still willing to move upon the hearts of those in possession of His goods, in behalf of the cause of truth. Those who labor for Him are to avail themselves of the help that He prompts men to give. . . . The donors may have no faith in Christ, no acquaintance with His word; but their gifts are not on this account to be refused" (*Prophets and Kings,* p. 634).

Today's Lesson: God's work requires not only faith but energy and decisiveness. Good leaders work with diligence through the difficulties that are always present.

The Builders on the Wall

Prophets and Kings, Chapter 53.

"So we built the wall, and the entire wall was joined together up to half its height, for the people had a mind to work" (Nehemiah 4:6, NKJV).

Nehemiah arrived safely in Jerusalem, escorted by a military guard. Knowing that bitter enemies were ready to oppose him and his plans for rebuilding the wall, Nehemiah didn't confide his mission to anyone at first—until he was able to choose a few men whom he could trust.

On the third night after his arrival, Nehemiah quietly rode his mule around the city to see the situation for himself. Painful memories came to mind as he viewed the broken defenses of his beloved Jerusalem. What a contrast to Israel's past greatness!

Although he had a royal commission authorizing him to rebuild, he sought to win the confidence of the people. He knew he needed to gain their hearts if he were to be successful. As he spoke to them of the city's condition, they were surprised that he was so well informed. They didn't know of his night-time survey.

Nehemiah then told the people of the emperor's support for rebuilding the city wall and the authorization he had been given. And he asked them directly whether they would join him in taking advantage of this opportunity. His energy, enthusiasm, and determination were contagious. When the enemies of Israel heard of Nehemiah's plans, they laughed. But the Jews took new courage under Nehemiah. Working night and day—with their weapons by their sides—they finished the city wall in fifty-two days, to the consternation of their enemies.

Key Thought: "The opposition and discouragement that the builders in Nehemiah's day met from open enemies and pretended friends is typical of the experience that those today will have who work for God. Christians are tried, not only by the anger, contempt, and cruelty of enemies, but by the indolence, inconsistency, lukewarmness, and treachery of avowed friends and helpers. . . . And the same enemy that leads to contempt, at a favorable opportunity uses more cruel and violent measures" (*Prophets and Kings,* pp. 644, 645).

Today's Lesson: Every neglected opportunity to serve God is recorded; every act of faith and love is duly noted and held in everlasting remembrance.

MAY 6

A Rebuke Against Extortion

Prophets and Kings, Chapter 54.

"So they said, 'We will restore it, and will require nothing from them; we will do as you say.' Then I called the priests, and required an oath from them that they would do according to this promise" (Nehemiah 5:12, NKJV).

Before the wall was completed, Nehemiah had to deal with another problem. Due to the unsettled conditions, food was scarce, and the poor had to pay exorbitant prices and buy food for their families on credit. They also had to borrow money at high interest rates to pay their share of the heavy taxes imposed by the kings of Persia. And, of course, the wealthy among the Jews were taking advantage of the situation to enrich themselves further at the expense of the poor.

All this made Nehemiah very angry (see Nehemiah 5:6). He called a great assembly to work on a solution, even though many of the wealthy who were abusing their fellow Jews were the very ones Nehemiah relied on to finance the rebuilding project. He tactfully but decisively urged a better way to care for the needs of everyone—and the crisis was over.

The lesson is for all time: Those who take advantage of the ignorance, the weakness, or misfortune of another will shut out the light of the Holy Spirit to his heart.

Key Thought: "Even among those who profess to be walking in the fear of the Lord, there are some who are acting over again the course pursued by the nobles of Israel. Because it is in their power to do so, they exact more than is just, and thus become oppressors. And because avarice and treachery are seen in the lives of those who have named the name of Christ, because the church retains on her books the names of those who have gained their possessions by injustice, the religion of Christ is held in contempt. . . . The church is in a great degree responsible for the sins of her members. She gives countenance to evil if she fails to lift her voice against it" (*Prophets and Kings,* p. 651).

Today's Lesson: Our liberality toward those in need proves that we are sincerely grateful for the blessings and mercies God extends to us.

Heathen Plots

Prophets and Kings, Chapter 55.

"Then I sent to [Sanballat], saying, 'No such things as you say are being done, but you invent them in your own heart' " (Nehemiah 6:8, NKJV).

Sanballat and his confederates dared not make open war upon the Jews, because they were well aware that Nehemiah had the complete support of the king of Persia. Rather than direct confrontation, he tried to entice Nehemiah to meet with him in a nearby village. Nehemiah responded that he was far too busy building the wall and had no time for conferences.

Next, Sanballat tried something more sinister: He said that rumors were circulating to the effect that the Jews in Jerusalem were planning to secede from Persian control and that the rebuilding of the city was proof of their intentions. Nehemiah replied that such talk was manufactured by Sanballat himself.

His next ploy was to use hired men—Jews within the city—who professed to be friends of Nehemiah. They would give Nehemiah false and evil counsel as though it came from the Lord. Nehemiah was not fooled, yet besides the enemy without, he had to contend with men of high reputation, Jews, who sent letters to the enemy betraying his plans. All this was the result of the intermarriage of Jews with idolaters.

Secret opposition by supposed friends is most to be feared at all times in the history of God's church. Those who use such malicious mischief to weaken the hands of fellow workers bring upon themselves a stain that is not easily removed from the character.

Key Thought: "In Nehemiah's firm devotion to the work of God, and his equally firm reliance on God, lay the reason of the failure of his enemies to draw him into their power. The soul that is indolent falls an easy prey to temptation; but in the life that has a noble aim, an absorbing purpose, evil finds little foothold. The faith of him who is constantly advancing does not weaken; for above, beneath, beyond, he recognizes Infinite Love, working out all things to accomplish His good purpose" (*Prophets and Kings,* p. 660).

Today's Lesson: We should not allow anything to divert us from the work God has given us. Truth is stronger than error and will prevail.

Instructed in the Law of God

Prophets and Kings, Chapter 56.

"And all the people went their way to eat, and to drink, and to send portions, and to make great mirth, because they had understood the words that were declared unto them" (Nehemiah 8:12).

Aged Ezra looked down from a wooden platform upon a sea of heads as he prayed a prayer of thankfulness to the Lord. He knew that many in his audience did not clearly understand the Hebrew language because they were children of mixed marriages between Jews and the surrounding pagan people. So, for the next few days, Ezra read the words of Scripture and carefully explained it.

The first part of each day was devoted to religious exercises, and the afternoon was given to recounting God's blessings. Portions of food were shared with the poor. This spiritual revival went on for ten days, until the tenth day of the month and the Day of Atonement arrived.

The whole congregation entered into a covenant with the Lord to keep all His commandments. Further, this covenant was written on a scroll as a memorial of the commitment they had made, and in the name of the people, the priests, Levites, and princes signed it.

Provision also was made to support the public worship of God. In addition to the tithe, the people pledged to contribute a stated sum annually for the service of the sanctuary. Also, before the day was over, the people pledged themselves to stop desecrating the Sabbath. At this time, Nehemiah did not exercise his authority to prevent pagan traders from entering Jerusalem. But he did bind the Jewish people with a solemn covenant not to transgress the Sabbath by purchasing anything from these traders, hoping that this would put an end to their traffic.

Key Thought: "Nehemiah's efforts to restore the worship of the true God had been crowned with success. As long as the people were true to the oath they had taken, as long as they were obedient to God's word, so long would the Lord fulfill His promise by pouring rich blessings upon them" (*Prophets and Kings,* p. 668).

Today's Lesson: No matter how far we may have wandered from God, we need not despair. Pardon may be ours if we sincerely repent.

Reformation

Prophets and Kings, Chapter 57.

"It grieved me sore: therefore I cast forth all the household stuff of Tobiah out of the chamber. Then I commanded, and they cleansed the chambers: and thither brought I again the vessels of the house of God, with the meat offering and the frankincense" (Nehemiah 13:8, 9).

Solemnly and publicly, the people pledged themselves to obey God's law. But not long after Nehemiah had returned to Persia, idolaters gained renewed power—even among the temple leadership. Eliahshib, the high priest, permitted Tobiah, an Ammonite and Israel's bitter enemy, to live in a temple apartment that had been used to store tithes and offerings!

When Nehemiah returned, he took prompt measures to expel the intruder. But there were even more serious matters. Tithes and offerings had been misapplied; temple workers were not getting their proper support and had left to work elsewhere. When the people of Judah saw that Nehemiah was now in charge, the workers came back, and the people again brought their offerings to the temple.

Another problem facing Nehemiah was the disregard of the Sabbath by many, especially those who traded with pagan merchants. Nehemiah fearlessly rebuked this evil and commanded that Jerusalem's gates should be shut before the Sabbath hours arrived and remain shut until the Sabbath ended.

Intermarriage with pagans continued to be a widespread problem among the Jewish population. Nehemiah insisted that these mixed families had to leave Jerusalem—starting with the priesthood and the rulers. Many chose to join the Samaritans, where they erected a temple on Mount Gerizim that would compete with the Jerusalem temple.

Nehemiah is an example of one who did not cover evil with false love. Such are still needed today.

Key Thought: "In the work of reform to be carried forward today, there is need of men who, like Ezra and Nehemiah, will not palliate or excuse sin, nor shrink from vindicating the honor of God. . . . They will remember that God is no respecter of persons, and that severity to a few may prove mercy to many" (*Prophets and Kings,* p. 675).

Today's Lesson: In these last days, God's remnant people will stand as "repairers of the breach" made in God's law by the lack of moral clarity so rampant in modern society.

The Coming of a Deliverer

Prophets and Kings, Chapter 58.

"But thou, Bethlehem Ephratah, though thou be little among the thousands of Judah, yet out of thee shall he come forth unto me that is to be ruler in Israel; whose goings forth have been from of old, from everlasting" (Micah 5:2).

The great controversy between Satan and God has been intense in every age, from our first parents in Eden to the zenith of ferocity when Jesus faced Satan on earth. The only hope for God's people was centered on the coming of a Deliverer to free all humanity from sin. And that hope was made most clear in the symbol of the slain lamb in the sanctuary service.

It was God's plan that the hope of deliverance and restoration should be imparted to the whole world through the Israelites as they faithfully proclaimed His law and atoning sacrifice. The Old Testament is full of these promises, passed down through the generations by the patriarchs and prophets. Through the wilderness tabernacle and the Jerusalem temple, Israelites were daily instructed in the great truths of Christ as Redeemer, Priest, and King. Once each year their minds were carried forward to the closing events of the great controversy— the grand lesson of the Day of Atonement.

Through it all, Satan was untiring in misrepresenting God— especially the messages of the sanctuary services. Throughout the time of the Old Testament, God's people had to face the most determined opposition, as we have seen in their history. And that hellish shadow will get even more fierce as the end of time draws near.

Key Thought: "Not without the most determined opposition was the divine purpose carried out. In every way possible the enemy of truth and righteousness worked to cause the descendants of Abraham to forget their high and holy calling, and to turn aside to the worship of false gods. And often his efforts were all but successful. For centuries preceding Christ's first advent, darkness covered the earth, and gross darkness the people" (*Prophets and Kings,* p. 687).

Today's Lesson: The experiences of God's people in the past are to serve as examples to us in the last days—that we may learn valuable lessons both from their mistakes and from their triumphs of faith.

"The House of Israel"

Prophets and Kings, Chapter 59.

"Israel shall blossom and bud, and fill the face of the world with fruit" (Isaiah 27:6).

God's promise to Abraham—and to all Israel—that He would bless him and that he would be a blessing (see Genesis 12:2) should have been fulfilled in large measure during the centuries following the return of the Israelites from their captivity. It was God's plan that the whole earth should be prepared for Christ's first advent, just as it should be prepared for His second advent.

These promises to Israel were conditional on obedience. The sins of the Israelites prior to their Babylonian captivity were not to be repeated. If they would put into practice the principles of righteousness, rich would be the rewards both temporally and spiritually. During the days of Zerubbabel, Ezra, and Nehemiah, it seemed that they had learned their lesson well. Too well, perhaps!

Determined to avoid idolatry, they made walls around themselves that hindered an outflow of truth about God. They saw clearly that obedience to the law of God brought temporal prosperity, but for the most part, their obedience was not the result of faith and love. They did not become the light of the world, because they shut themselves away from the world in order to safeguard themselves against idolatry. Time and again they kept for themselves the blessings that God intended them to share with the world.

In their self righteousness they trusted to their own works—to the sacrifices and ordinances themselves—instead of relying upon the merits of the Savior to whom all these things pointed. Nevertheless, God's purposes would prevail—if not through Israel, then through others.

Key Thought: "That which God purposed to do for the world through Israel, the chosen nation, He will finally accomplish through His church on earth today. He has 'let out His vineyard unto other husbandmen,' even to His covenant-keeping people, who faithfully 'render Him the fruits in their seasons.' Never has the Lord been without true representatives on this earth who have made His interests their own" (*Prophets and Kings,* pp. 713, 714).

Today's Lesson: God is counting on His people to show the world the peace and freedom that come in understanding His pardoning love and power.

MAY 12

Visions of Future Glory

Prophets and Kings, Chapter 60.

"He will swallow up death in victory; and the Lord God will wipe away tears from off all faces; and the rebuke of his people shall he take away from off all the earth: for the Lord hath spoken it" (Isaiah 25:8).

One of the magnificent expressions of God's compassion for His followers is His continuing revelation of His eternal purpose. In the darkest hours, the assurances of His guiding presence and the ultimate joy of seeing Him face to face have kept the faithful singing on their deathbeds or when dying in the fires of persecution.

The deep sense that God is the "Great Forgiver," as well as the "Great Sustainer," provides a peace beyond human understanding. Facing the darkest hours of the church's struggle with the powers of evil, those who trust in God will not fear, because "when the blast of the terrible ones is as a storm against the wall," God will be to His church "a refuge from the storm" (Isaiah 25:4).

God also is merciful to those who have not yet decided to commit themselves to be members of His loyal followers. Through inspired messengers He warns those unprepared to meet Him in peace: "Behold, the Lord maketh the earth empty, and maketh it waste, and turneth it upside down, and scattereth abroad the inhabitants thereof . . . because they have transgressed the laws, changed the ordinance, broken the everlasting covenant" (Isaiah 24:1, 5).

The day of God's judgment against sinners is the day of final deliverance for His church.

Key Thought: "To us who are standing on the very verge of their fulfillment, of what deep moment, what living interest, are these delineations of the things to come—events for which, since our first parents turned their steps from Eden, God's children have watched and waited, longed and prayed! . . . Let us by faith behold the blessed hereafter as pictured by the hand of God" (*Prophets and Kings,* p. 731).

Today's Lesson: In the world, we are so often surrounded with the worst of human sensuality and self-gratification. It becomes all the more important that we keep our eyes and ears filled with all that is pure, honest, and self-denying.

God's Love for Man

Steps to Christ, Chapter 1.

"Who is a God like You, pardoning iniquity and passing over the transgression of the remnant of His heritage? He does not retain His anger forever, because He delights in mercy. He will again have compassion on us, and will subdue our iniquities" (Micah 7:18, 19, NKJV).

Though a small book, *Steps to Christ* is rich in meaning as it explains the basic issues in the great controversy and how to place ourselves on the side of Christ and find forgiveness and redemption. Through Christ, all that has been lost as a result of sin is to be restored—on earth and in our individual lives.

Satan has done his malignant best to misrepresent God. In heaven he was so artful in his deceptions that one-third of the angels (see Revelation 12:4) believed that God was severe and unforgiving. He convinced angels—and now he convinces humans—that God's chief attribute is stern justice—that He is a severe judge, a harsh, exacting creditor. Satan has pictured God as One who is watching with jealous eye to discern the errors and mistakes of men and women so that He may visit judgments on them.

The truth of the matter is that God loves us—sinners as well as those who have accepted His grace—with an incomprehensible love. Jesus came to this dark world to remove the shadows Satan had placed over the Father's character. Jesus became a human like us in order to tell the truth about God. As we understand God's love for us, we will joyfully respond with love, praise, and faithfulness. More than that, in connection with Christ, we may become worthy of the name "children of God" (John 1:12, NKJV). Jesus took our sins so God could be justified in redeeming us!

Key Thought: "Christ was to identify Himself with the interests and needs of humanity. He who was one with God has linked Himself with the children of men by ties that are never to be broken . . . ,bearing our human form before the Father's throne" (*Steps to Christ*, p. 14).

Today's Lesson: God's love for fallen, sinful human beings is the theme of the Bible from beginning to end. It saturates every page.

MAY 14

The Sinner's Need of Christ

Steps to Christ, Chapter 2.

"The carnal mind is enmity against God; for it is not subject to the law of God, nor indeed can be" (Romans 8:7, NKJV).

God created Adam and Eve perfect. Their minds and natures were in complete harmony with Him; their thoughts were pure and holy. But disobedience disrupted this perfect harmony. Selfishness replaced love. Before sin, they loved to meet with their Creator and commune with Him. They found their greatest delight in His presence. But after their disobedience, they tried to hide from Him, because they were afraid. And because of the transgression of our first parents, men and women became the captives of Satan and sin—and would have remained so forever had not God intervened. We are born with a sinful nature at enmity against God and His truth.

The unrenewed heart finds no joy in God and cannot be happy in His presence. Heaven would hold no joy for the sinner. Indeed, it would be torture to him, for his nature is alien to its spirit of unselfish love.

Sinful human beings cannot escape their condition in their own strength. Our hearts are naturally evil, and we cannot change them. But God has made a way of escape for us. He loves us more than earthly parents love their children. He gave us His most precious gift when Jesus left heaven to come and save us from our sins. He bids us come to Him and find forgiveness, transformation of our lives, and eternal salvation. Jesus is the only solution to the sin problem.

Key Thought: "In vain are men's dreams of progress, in vain all efforts for the uplifting of humanity, if they neglect the one Source of hope and help for the fallen race. 'Every good gift and every perfect gift' (James 1:17) is from God. There is no true excellence of character apart from Him. And the only way to God is Christ. He says, 'I am the way, the truth, and the life: no man cometh unto the Father, but by Me.' John 14:6" (*Steps to Christ,* p. 21).

Today's Lesson: Because we are powerless to change our sinful natures in our own strength, we must be born again through the power of the Holy Spirit.

Repentance

Steps to Christ, Chapter 3.

"Search me, O God, and know my heart: try me, and know my thoughts: and see if there be any wicked way in me, and lead me in the way everlasting" (Psalm 139:23, 24).

The question is: How are we to come to Christ? How can a person be just with God? That is, how shall the sinner be made righteous? Often that question is asked in the Bible, and the answer is always "Repent." Only through Christ can we be brought into harmony with God.

Repentance includes sorrow for sin and a turning away from it. We shall not renounce sin unless we see its sinfulness; until we turn away from it in heart, there will be no real change in the life. Many fail to understand the true nature of repentance. Multitudes sorrow that they have sinned and even make an outward reformation, because they fear that their wrongdoing will bring embarrassment upon themselves. But this is not repentance in the Bible sense. Such lament the embarrassment rather than the sin. This was Esau's grief when he saw that the birthright was lost to him forever. Balaam, terrified by the angel standing in his pathway with drawn sword, acknowledged his guilt lest he should lose his life. But he felt no genuine repentance for his sin. Judas Iscariot, after betraying his Lord, exclaimed, "I have sinned in that I have betrayed the innocent blood" (Matthew 27:4). But he did not truly repent.

Every habit, unrepented of, only makes it easier to repeat that sin.

Key Thought: "Christ is ready to set us free from sin, but He does not force the will; and if by persistent transgression the will itself is wholly bent on evil, and we do not desire to be set free, if we will not accept His grace, what more can He do? We have destroyed ourselves by our determined rejection of His love. 'Behold, now is the accepted time; behold, now is the day of salvation.' 'Today if ye will hear His voice, harden not your hearts.' 2 Corinthians 6:2; Hebrews 3:7, 8" (*Steps to Christ,* p. 34).

Today's Lesson: Asking for forgiveness without a willingness to allow God to change our lives and overcome sin is not true repentance.

MAY 16

Confession

Steps to Christ, Chapter 4.

"He that covereth his sins shall not prosper: but whoso confesseth and forsaketh them shall have mercy"
(Proverbs 28:13).

The conditions of obtaining God's mercy are simple, just, and reasonable. The Lord does not require us to do something spectacular in order to be forgiven. Long, wearisome pilgrimages or painful penances cannot commend our souls to a loving, forgiving God. He is even more eager to forgive us than we are to be forgiven! Those who have not acknowledged their guilt and humbled their souls before God in repentance have not yet fulfilled the first condition of acceptance. If we have not confessed our sins, abhorring our iniquity, with true humiliation of soul and brokenness of spirit, we have never truly sought forgiveness for our sins. And if we have never sought it, we have never found the peace God waits to bestow on us.

God has given explicit instructions on this subject. Confession of sin—public or private—should be heartfelt and freely expressed. It is not to be made carelessly or lightly. It is not to be forced from anyone who does not realize the terrible character of sin.

True confession is always specific and acknowledges particular sins. Some sins should be confessed to God alone; others may be sins that should be confessed to the person who has been wronged. Still others may be of a public nature and should be publicly confessed. But all confession should be definite and to the point, acknowledging the very sins committed.

Key Thought: "When sin has deadened the moral perceptions, the wrongdoer does not discern the defects of his character nor realize the enormity of the evil he has committed; and unless he yields to the convicting power of the Holy Spirit he remains in partial blindness to his sin. His confessions are not sincere and in earnest. To every acknowledgment of his guilt he adds an apology in excuse of his course, declaring that if it had not been for certain circumstances he would not have done this or that for which he is reproved" (*Steps to Christ,* p. 40).

Today's Lesson: God always responds when we sincerely confess our sins. The Bible is clear that if we confess, He will forgive (see 1 John 1:9).

Consecration

Steps to Christ, Chapter 5.

"Ye shall seek me, and find me, when ye shall search for me with all your heart" (Jeremiah 29:13).

God wants to heal us and set us free. But since this requires an entire transformation—a renewal—of our whole nature, we must yield ourselves completely to Him in order for Him to work in us the transformation He intends us to experience. The battle against self is the greatest battle ever fought. Yielding ourselves, surrendering everything in our lives to God's will, requires a struggle. But we must submit to God before we can be renewed in holiness.

Anything that draws our hearts away from God must be given up. A desire for wealth—the love of money—is a golden chain that binds many to Satan. Others worship their reputations and the honors of the world. The idol of still others is a life of selfish ease and freedom from responsibility. But all these slavish bonds must be broken. We cannot belong half to God and half to the world.

And when we give up "everything," what do we really give up? A sin-polluted heart for Jesus to cleanse by His own blood and to save by His matchless love! And yet, humans think it hard to give up everything!

Key Thought: "The government of God is not, as Satan would make it appear, founded upon a blind submission, an unreasoning control. It appeals to the intellect and the conscience. . . . God does not force the will of His creatures. . . . A mere forced submission would prevent all real development of mind or character; it would make man a mere automaton. Such is not the purpose of the Creator. He desires that man, the crowning work of His creative power, shall reach the highest possible development. . . . He invites us to give ourselves to Him, that He may work His will in us. It remains for us to choose whether we will be set free from the bondage of sin, to share the glorious liberty of the sons of God" (*Steps to Christ,* pp. 43, 44).

Today's Lesson: God does not ask us to give up anything that it is in our best interest to keep—here or in eternity.

Faith and Acceptance

Steps to Christ, Chapter 6

"A new heart also will I give you, and a new spirit will I put within you" (Ezekiel 36:26).

We need to be in harmony with God, to be like Him. We need the peace He promises. But money cannot buy it; wisdom cannot achieve it. We can't have it merely by hoping for it. All this a gracious God has given us freely—"without money and without price" (Isaiah 55:1).

But how do we receive His gifts? "Give" yourself to God. Ask Him to wash away your sins and give you a new heart. Now believe that He does this *because He has promised!* While on earth, Jesus healed people of their diseases when they had faith in His power. He helped them in ways that they could see, thus inspiring them with confidence that He could help them in things they could not see—His power to forgive sins. Through the simple act of believing God, you allow the Holy Spirit to generate a new life in you. Now you are God's child, born into His family.

Once you have given yourself to God, don't draw back. Every day ask Him to give you His Holy Spirit and to keep you by His grace. Say, "I belong to Christ; I have given myself to Him."

Key Thought: "You cannot atone for your past sins; you cannot change your heart and make yourself holy. But God promises to do all this for you through Christ. You *believe* that promise. You *confess* your sins and give yourself to God. You *will* to serve Him. Just as surely as you do this, God will fulfill His word to you. If you believe . . . that you are forgiven and cleansed,—God supplies the fact; you are made whole, just as Christ gave the paralytic power to walk when the man believed that he was healed. It is so if you believe it.

"Do not wait to feel that you are made whole, but say, 'I believe it; it is so, not because I feel it, but because God has promised' " (*Steps to Christ,* p. 51).

Today's Lesson: We may trust God's promises with the same simple faith of a young child who trusts his parents implicitly.

The Test of Discipleship

Steps to Christ, Chapter 7.

"If any man be in Christ, he is a new creature: old things are passed away; behold, all things are become new" (2 Corinthians 5:17).

We cannot do anything to change our hearts or to bring ourselves into harmony with God. We must not trust to ourselves or our good works. Yet, our lives will reveal whether the grace of God is dwelling within us. A change will be seen in our characters, our habits, and how we spend our time and energy. The contrast between what we used to be and what we now are will be clear. Character is revealed, not by occasional good deeds and occasional misdeeds but by the tendency of the habitual words and acts.

Unless there is a change for the better in our lives, there is no genuine repentance. We can be sure we have passed from death into life if we confess our sins, make restitution where necessary, and love God and our fellowman sincerely. When we come to Christ and become recipients of His pardoning grace, love springs up in our hearts. Every burden is light, because the yoke that Christ asks us to wear—His yoke—is easy. Duty becomes a delight and sacrifice a pleasure.

As we come to Christ, we must guard ourselves against two errors. The first is trying to bring ourselves into harmony with God by depending on our own works, on anything we can do. All that we can do *without Christ* is polluted with selfishness and sin. The opposite—and no less dangerous—error is to feel that believing in Christ releases us from keeping God's law, that our works have nothing to do with our redemption since we receive the grace of Christ by faith alone. True obedience is not a mere outward compliance; it is the service of love.

Key Thought: "We have nothing in ourselves of which to boast. We have no ground for self-exaltation. Our only ground of hope is in the righteousness of Christ imputed to us, and in that wrought by His Spirit working in and through us" (*Steps to Christ,* p. 63).

Today's Lesson: The life will show whether one's faith in Christ is genuine or a mere mental assent.

Growing Up Into Christ

Steps to Christ, Chapter 8.

**"Therefore, laying aside all malice, all guile, hypocrisy,
envy, and all evil speaking, as newborn babes, desire
the pure milk of the word, that you may grow thereby, if
indeed you have tasted that the Lord is gracious"
(1 Peter 2:1–3, NKJV).**

In living a holy life, we are just as dependent upon Christ as the branch is dependent on the tree to grow fruit. Apart from Him, we have no life. We have no power to resist temptation or to grow in grace and holiness. But by abiding in Him we may flourish. Drawing our life from Him, we will not wither nor be fruitless.

Many have an idea that they must do some part of the work in their own power. They have trusted in Christ to forgive their sins, but now they are trying to live a godly life by their own efforts. But every such effort must fail. Jesus says, "Without me ye can do nothing" (John 15:5). Our growth in grace, our joy, our usefulness—all depend upon our union with Christ.

But how do we "abide" in Christ? In the same way we received Him at first—by faith. "As ye have therefore received Christ Jesus the Lord, so walk ye in him" (Colossians 2:6). We could not atone for our sins or change our hearts. But we gave ourselves to God; we believed that He did the work for us. *By faith* we became Christ's child—and now *by faith* we are to grow up in Him. We are to give all—give ourselves to God to obey all His commandments. And we are to take all—Christ, the fullness of God's blessings, to abide in our hearts, to be our strength, our righteousness, our everlasting Helper, giving us the power to obey.

Key Thought: "Consecrate yourself to God in the morning; make this your very first work. Let your prayer be, 'Take me, O Lord, as wholly Thine. I lay all my plans at Thy feet. Use me today in Thy service. Abide with me, and let all my work be wrought in Thee.' This is a daily matter" (*Steps to Christ,* p. 70).

Today's Lesson: Abiding in Christ is the same as breathing—it becomes natural!

The Work and the Life

Steps to Christ, Chapter 9.

"Let every man, wherein he is called, therein abide with God" (1 Corinthian 7:24).

Love to Jesus will be shown in a desire to work as He worked for the blessing and uplifting of humanity. The Savior's life while here on earth was not a life of ease and devotion to Himself; He toiled with persistent, earnest, untiring effort for others.

In the same way, those who have received the grace of Christ will be ready to make any sacrifice so other men and women for whom He died may share the heavenly gift of salvation. They will do all they can to make the world a better place for their having lived in it. Such an attitude is the sure outgrowth of a truly converted soul.

And working to bless others will result in blessings to ourselves. This was God's purpose in giving us a part to act in the plan of redemption. He has granted men and women the privilege of taking part in the divine nature and of being channels of blessing to their fellow human beings. Those who thus participate with God in labors of love are brought near to their Creator.

The only way to grow in grace is to do the very work Christ has given us—to engage, to the extent of our ability, in helping and blessing those who need the help we can give them. Strength comes by exercise. Those who try to maintain a Christian life by passively accepting the blessings that come through God's grace—while doing nothing for Christ or others—are like those who are trying to live physically by eating without expending energy.

Key Thought: "You are not to wait for great occasions or to expect extraordinary abilities before you go to work for God. You need not have a thought of what the world will think of you. If your daily life is a testimony to the purity and sincerity of your faith, and others are convinced that you desire to benefit them, your efforts will not be wholly lost" (*Steps to Christ,* p. 83).

Today's Lesson: The secret of joyful living is to give out to others as much as we take in from Jesus.

MAY 22

A Knowledge of God

Steps to Christ, Chapter 10.

"This is eternal life, that they may know You, the only true God, and Jesus Christ whom You have sent"
(John 17:3, NKJV).

God uses many ways to try to make Himself known to us and bring us into communion with Him. The receptive heart will be impressed with God's love and glory as revealed through the works of His hands. If we will but listen, His created works will teach us precious lessons.

In addition to God's created works, He speaks to us through His providential workings and through the influence of His Spirit upon our hearts. Further, He speaks to us in His Word—the clearest revelation of His character and His work of redemption. In His Word the history of holy individuals of old is open to us. These persons were "subject to like passions as we are" (James 5:17). We see how they struggled through discouragements like our own, how they fell under temptation as we have done and yet took heart and conquered through the grace of God—and by beholding their examples, we are encouraged to be like them in character and to walk with God as they did.

We should dwell upon the character of our dear Redeemer. As we contemplate heavenly themes, our faith and love will grow stronger and our prayers will be more and more acceptable to God. They will be intelligent and fervent. Daily, we will experience a more constant confidence in Jesus and in His power to save to the uttermost all who come unto God by Him.

Key Thought: "There is but little benefit derived from a hasty reading of the Scriptures. One may read the whole Bible through and yet fail to see its beauty or comprehend its deep and hidden meaning. One passage studied until its significance is clear to the mind and its relation to the plan of salvation is evident, is of more value than the perusal of many chapters with no definite purpose in view and no positive instruction gained" (*Steps to Christ,* p. 90).

Today's Lesson: The power of God's spoken word created this world, and the power of His written Word will make a new creation of our lives. We must keep listening!

The Privilege of Prayer

Steps to Christ, Chapter 11.

"Be anxious for nothing, but in everything by prayer and supplication, with thanksgiving, let your requests be made known to God" (Philippians 4:6, NKJV).

In order to commune with God, we must have something to say to Him concerning our actual life. Prayer is opening our hearts to God as we would to a friend. Not that it is necessary in order to make known to God what we are but in order to enable us to receive Him. Prayer does not bring God down to us; it brings us up to Him.

Jesus Himself, while He dwelt among men, was often in prayer. Our Savior identified Himself with our needs and weaknesses by often praying to His Father, seeking fresh supplies of strength so He might come forth from these seasons of prayer braced anew for duty and trial. He is our example in all things. His humanity made prayer a necessity and a privilege. He found comfort and joy in communion with His Father. And if the Savior, the Son of God, felt the need of prayer, how much more should we feeble, sinful mortals feel the necessity of fervent, constant prayer!

The darkness of the evil one encloses those who neglect to pray. The whispered temptations of the enemy entice them to sin, and it is all because they do not make use of the privilege of prayer that God has given them. Why should God's sons and daughters be reluctant to pray, when prayer is the key in the hand of faith to unlock heaven's storehouse, where are kept the boundless resources of Omnipotence? God is not a hard, exacting Taskmaster; He is our Friend.

Key Thought: "We must gather about the cross. Christ and Him crucified should be the theme of contemplation, of conversation, and of our most joyful emotion. We should keep in our thoughts every blessing we receive from God, and when we realize His great love we should be willing to trust everything to the hand that was nailed to the cross for us" (*Steps to Christ,* pp. 103, 104).

Today's Lesson: Prayer should be as natural to the Christian as breathing. Why, then, do we too often feel that we are gasping for spiritual breath?

What to Do With Doubt

Steps to Christ, Chapter 12.

***"Paul . . . has written to you . . . in all his epistles, speaking
in them of these things, in which are some things hard to
understand, which those who are untaught and unstable
twist to their own destruction, as they do also the rest of
the Scriptures" (2 Peter 3:15, 16, NKJV).***

Those young in the Christian life are often troubled with doubts. But
God never asks us to believe without giving us sufficient evidence
upon which to base our faith. His existence, His character, the
truthfulness of His Word—all are established by testimony that
appeals to our reason. Yet, God has never removed the possibility of
doubt. Our faith must rest upon evidence, not demonstration. Those
who wish to doubt will have opportunity, and those who really want
to know the truth will find plenty of evidence on which to rest their
faith.

The Bible unfolds truth with a simplicity that is perfectly adapted to
the needs and longings of the human heart. Its concepts have astonished
and charmed the most highly cultivated minds, and at the same time it
allows the humble and uneducated to find the way of salvation clearly.
The more we search the Bible, the deeper our conviction becomes
that it is the Word of the living God. Human reason bows before the
majesty of divine revelation.

Key Thought: "And everyone who has passed from death unto life
is able to 'set to his seal that God is true.' John 3:33. He can testify,
'I needed help, and I found it in Jesus. Every want was supplied,
the hunger of my soul was satisfied; and now the Bible is to me the
revelation of Jesus Christ. Do you ask why I believe in Jesus? Because
He is to me a divine Saviour. Why do I believe the Bible? Because
I have found it to be the voice of God to my soul.' We may have the
witness in ourselves that the Bible is true, that Christ is the Son of
God. We know that we are not following cunningly devised fables"
(*Steps to Christ,* p. 112).

Today's Lesson: The voice of experience is among the strongest
evidences that the Bible is God's voice speaking to us.

Rejoicing in the Lord

Steps to Christ, Chapter 13.

*"Trust in the Lord with all your heart, and lean not on
your own understanding; in all your ways acknowledge
Him, and He shall direct your paths. Do not be wise in
your own eyes; fear the Lord and depart from evil. It
will be health to your flesh, and strength to your bones"
(Proverbs 3:5–8, NKJV).*

As Christians, we are light bearers on the way to heaven. Our lives
should be such that others will have a right conception of Christ
by looking at our example. If we represent Christ correctly, we
will make His service appear attractive—as it really is. Christians who
gather up gloom and sadness to their souls, and murmur and complain,
are giving others a false representation of God and the Christian life.

Satan is pleased when he can lead us into unbelief and despondency.
He works to represent the Lord as lacking in compassion and pity. He
fills the imagination with false ideas concerning God, and instead of
dwelling upon the truth in regard to our heavenly Father, we too often
fix our minds upon Satan's misrepresentations and dishonor God by
distrusting Him.

Everyone has trials and grief; we all face temptations that are hard
to resist. Don't tell other human beings about your troubles; instead,
take them to God in prayer. Make it a rule never to utter a single word
of doubt or discouragement. You can do much to brighten the lives of
others and strengthen their efforts to live for Jesus by your words of
hope and holy cheer.

Key Thought: "We cannot but look forward to new perplexities
in the coming conflict, but we may look on what is past as well as on
what is to come, and say, 'Hitherto hath the Lord helped us' [1 Samuel
7:12]. 'As thy days, so shall thy strength be.' Deuteronomy 33:25. The
trial will not exceed the strength that shall be given us to bear it. Then
let us take up our work just where we find it, believing that whatever
may come, strength proportionate to the trial will be given" (*Steps to
Christ,* p. 125).

Today's Lesson: Night and day, we have many opportunities to
be grateful, rejoicing in the Lord for His many divine interventions!

"God With Us"

The Desire of Ages, Chapter 1.

" 'They shall call His name Immanuel' which is translated, 'God with us' " Matthew 1:23, NKJV).

From eternity, our Lord Jesus has been one with the heavenly Father. He came to earth to manifest the glory of the Father to a world that had largely lost sight of God. By coming to live with us, Jesus revealed God both to human beings and to angels. Sin has marred God's perfect work in creating this world; yet, His divine handwriting remains, and if we are attuned to Him, we can still see much of the original glory He placed in His creation.

The truth is that nothing lives to itself—except the selfish human heart. All things in nature—birds, fish, animals, plants, even the oceans—live to serve others. As do the angels in heaven. But the greatest example of loving, unselfish service is the example we see of God in the life of Jesus. It is the glory of our God to give.

It was in heaven itself that this law of service to others was first broken. Sin originated in self-seeking. Lucifer desired to be first in heaven—to gain control of heavenly beings and to draw them away from their Creator. He worked through deception in misrepresenting God's character. Jesus came to earth to tell the truth about God, and He did it not merely with words but with a life that all men and women could see every day. Satan had claimed that no created being could obey God's law and be happy. Jesus came to earth to prove Satan wrong—and He did so using no power that is not freely available to us.

Key Thought: "Our little world is the lesson book of the universe. God's wonderful purpose of grace, the mystery of redeeming love, is the theme into which 'angels desire to look,' and it will be their study throughout endless ages. Both the redeemed and the unfallen beings will find in the cross of Christ their science and their song" (*The Desire of Ages,* pp. 19, 20).

Today's Lesson: The "good news" is that by the grace of God I can live an overcoming life that results in happiness and spiritual life.

The Chosen People

The Desire of Ages, Chapter 2.

"He came unto his own, and his own received him not"
(John 1:11).

For more than a thousand years the Jewish people had waited for the Messiah; yet, when He came, they rejected Him! Why? Because He did not fit the expected job description!

God chose the Jews to preserve a knowledge of His law; they were to be as wells of salvation to the world. Their highest privilege was to reveal God to men and women. But they fixed their hopes upon worldly greatness. Had the Jews been true to their mission, God would have accomplished His purpose through them and made them "high above all nations which he hath made, in praise, and in name, and in honour" (Deuteronomy 26:19).

Not all the Israelites forgot their mission. Many of the pagans learned from the Hebrews about the promise of a Redeemer and grasped it in faith. Not a few lost their lives by refusing to dishonor the Sabbath and observe pagan festivals. Time after time, world monarchs proclaimed the supremacy of Israel's God.

After Israel's return from Babylon, much attention was given to religious instruction. Synagogues and schools were erected, but these agencies became corrupted; their multiple requirements—designed to avoid idolatry—became an end in themselves rather than the means of growing spiritually. The Jews wanted deliverance from the Romans more than they wanted deliverance from sin. Pride obscured their vision. They interpreted prophecy in accordance with their selfish desires.

Key Thought: "With all their minute and burdensome injunctions, it was an impossibility to keep the law. Those who desired to serve God, and who tried to observe the rabbinical precepts, toiled under a heavy burden. They could find no rest from the accusings of a troubled conscience. Thus Satan worked to discourage the people, to lower their conception of the character of God, and to bring the faith of Israel into contempt. He hoped to establish the claim put forth when he rebelled in heaven,—that the requirements of God were unjust, and could not be obeyed. Even Israel, he declared, did not keep the law" (*The Desire of Ages,* p. 29).

Today's Lesson: Human nature finds it much easier to be "religious" than to have a personal love relationship with God.

MAY 28

"The Fullness of the Time"

The Desire of Ages, Chapter 3.

"When the fulness of the time was come, God sent forth his Son, . . . to redeem them that were under the law, that we might receive the adoption of sons" (Galatians 4:4, 5).

The time was ripe for the birth of Jesus. Throughout the earth, the nations were united under one government, and one language was widely spoken. To a large degree, paganism was losing its hold on the masses; people were longing for a religion that could satisfy the heart.

Outside the Jewish nation were men and women seeking truth. Among these supposed "heathen" were those who had a better understanding of the Scripture prophecies concerning the Messiah than had the teachers in Israel. Many were trying to understand better these prophecies, but the bigotry of the Jews greatly hindered the spread of light.

Satan had been doing his work well. It was his purpose to wear out the forbearance of God and to extinguish His love for human beings so He would abandon the world to satanic rule. Through paganism, Satan had for ages turned men and women away from God, but his greatest triumph was in perverting the faith of Israel itself.

Unfallen worlds watched with intense interest to see if God would sweep away earth's inhabitants. And if God should do this, Satan would have won the argument that God's government made forgiveness impossible and that His laws could not be obeyed. But instead of destroying the world, God sent His Son to save it.

Key Thought: "Satan was exulting that he had succeeded in debasing the image of God in humanity. Then Jesus came to restore in man the image of his Maker. None but Christ can fashion anew the character that has been ruined by sin. He came to expel the demons that had controlled the will. He came to lift us up from the dust, to reshape the marred character after the pattern of His divine character, and to make it beautiful with His own glory" (*The Desire of Ages,* pp. 37, 38).

Today's Lesson: By our lives, we have the daily privilege of vindicating God's wisdom and honor—or of adding strength to Satan's arguments against Him.

Unto You a Saviour

The Desire of Ages, Chapter 4.

"Then the angel said to them, 'Do not be afraid, for behold, I bring you good tidings of great joy which will be to all people' " (Luke 2:10, NKJV).

T he angels had wondered at the plan of redemption. They had been amazed at the indifference of God's people whom He had called to communicate to the world the light of truth and the coming of the world's Redeemer. And they must have been further amazed that the only people who seemed interested in the coming of the Messiah were shepherds watching their flocks!

Obedient to the message and splendor of that glorious event, the shepherds hurried to Bethlehem, wondering about the meaning of what they had seen and heard. Mary knew more than all others, but even she had much to learn. The message for us today is that heaven and earth are no wider apart than when shepherds heard the angels sing.

The birth of Jesus opens up an exhaustless theme. It would have been an almost infinite humiliation for Jesus to take man's nature when Adam stood in Eden, but in Bethlehem Jesus accepted humanity after it had been weakened by four thousand years of sin. Like every man or woman, Jesus assumed the results of the great law of heredity. He came with the heredity of His earthly ancestors, to share our sorrows and temptations and to give us the example of a sinless life.

Key Thought: "Satan in heaven had hated Christ for His position in the courts of God. He hated Him the more when he himself was dethroned. He hated Him who pledged Himself to redeem a race of sinners. Yet into the world where Satan claimed dominion God permitted His Son to come, a helpless babe, subject to the weakness of humanity. He permitted Him to meet life's peril in common with every human soul, to fight the battle as every child of humanity must fight it, at the risk of failure and eternal loss" (*The Desire of Ages,* p. 49).

Today's Lesson: Christ came to be one with us in His humanity, giving us an example of a life victorious over sin—the same life He has made available to us.

MAY 30

The Dedication

The Desire of Ages, Chapter 5.

"Lord, now You are letting Your servant depart in peace, according to Your word; for my eyes have seen Your salvation" (Luke 2:29, 30, NKJV).

About forty days after Christ's birth, Joseph and Mary took Him to Jerusalem to dedicate Him to the Lord. As man's Substitute, Jesus must conform to the law in every particular.

The law for the presentation of the firstborn was especially significant, for it was a memorial of the Lord's wonderful deliverance of the Israelites from Egypt. And it prefigured a greater deliverance by Christ Himself. As the blood sprinkled on the doorposts had saved the firstborn of Israel, so the blood of Christ has power to save the world.

It was business as usual in the temple that day. Only Simeon and Anna perceived the enormous importance of Mary's child. These faithful Jews had not studied the Scriptures in vain. So many today are like the busy priests that day—they acknowledge Jesus as a historical figure but do not recognize Him as the Son of God.

Mary did not understand her Son's mission. She pondered Simeon's prophecy, especially the reference to a sword piercing her own heart. Many years would pass before she would understand.

When Simeon said that "the thoughts of many hearts may be revealed" (Luke 2:35), he was emphasizing one of the key issues in the great controversy. Christ would be facing Satan, His long-time antagonist. The principles of God's government would be in direct contrast with Satan's character and his principles. In the life and death of Jesus, the thoughts of all men and women are brought to view—and everyone passes judgment on himself or herself.

Key Thought: "In the day of final judgment, every lost soul will understand the nature of his own rejection of truth. The cross will be presented, and its real bearing will be seen by every mind that has been blinded by transgression. Before the vision of Calvary with its mysterious Victim, sinners will stand condemned. Every lying excuse will be swept away" (*The Desire of Ages,* p. 58).

Today's Lesson: In Jesus, God has already given us His greatest gift. We may be sure He will spare nothing to complete His work of redemption in us.

"We Have Seen His Star"

The Desire of Ages, Chapter 6.

"We have seen His star in the East and have come to worship Him" (Matthew 2:2, NKJV).

These wise men from the East, though pagan philosophers, had been studying the indications of Providence in nature, and God honored them for their integrity and wisdom. His light was shining in the darkness. As these men turned to the Hebrew Scriptures, they were fascinated with the prophecies of the coming Messiah and longed to understand more clearly what these words meant.

Then they saw a mysterious light in the heavens on the night God's glory flooded the hills of Bethlehem. They were convinced that something extraordinary had occurred and determined to seek further. The inward evidence of the Holy Spirit guided them on their journey.

The star—not an ordinary star or a planet but the distant company of shining angels—led them to the temple in Jerusalem, where they eagerly inquired about the newborn king. They found only surprise and fear mingled with contempt. The news of their arrival spread rapidly, and Herod was highly suspicious that these wise men were part of a plot to unseat Him. In his interview with them, he feigned great interest and found from them that Bethlehem was their goal.

When they reached Jesus, they dropped to their knees and worshiped Him, recognizing the presence of divinity. They gave Him their gifts. Then, warned by a dream that they should not return to Herod, they made their way home. Joseph also had a dream, urging him to flee to Egypt with Mary and Jesus.

Key Thought: "Pride and envy closed the door against the light.... These learned teachers would not stoop to be instructed by those whom they termed heathen.... They determined to show their contempt for the reports that were exciting King Herod and all Jerusalem. They would not even go to Bethlehem to see whether these things were so.... Here began the rejection of Christ by the priests and rabbis. From this point their pride and stubbornness grew into a settled hatred of the Saviour" (*The Desire of Ages,* pp. 62, 63).

Today's Lesson: Preconceived ideas and prejudice can so easily blind us to God's truth.

As a Child

The Desire of Ages, Chapter 7.

***"The Child grew and became strong in spirit, filled with
wisdom; and the grace of God was upon Him"
(Luke 2:40, NKJV).***

Jesus grew as all children may do. He gained knowledge as we may
also. Our Lord's powers of mind and body developed gradually, in
keeping with the laws of childhood.

God had directed the faithful in Israel to educate the youth from
babyhood regarding His goodness, as revealed in His laws, and Mary
sought ways to encourage Jesus' bright, receptive mind. Through the
Holy Spirit she received wisdom to cooperate with heavenly agencies
in the development of her Son.

In the days of Jesus, the town that did not provide for the religious
instruction of their young was regarded as under the curse of God. Yet,
the instruction provided had become formal and sterile; tradition took
the place of the Scriptures. Realizing this situation, our Lord's parents
taught Him the Scriptures personally—as well as scientific knowledge
from nature. Through all His studies, His goal was to understand the
reason of things.

Jesus was not exempt from temptation, especially as an inhabitant
of Nazareth, a town proverbial for wickedness (see John 1:46). He
was subject to all the conflicts we have to meet, that He might be an
example to us in childhood, youth, and manhood.

His parents were poor, and He was very familiar with poverty. He
learned a trade and had to compete with other carpenters. The energy
and strength of character manifested in Christ are to be developed in
us, through the same discipline that He endured. And the grace that
He received is for us.

Key Thought: "Every child may gain knowledge as Jesus did.
As we try to become acquainted with our heavenly Father through
His word, angels will draw near, our minds will be strengthened, our
characters will be elevated and refined. We shall become more like our
Saviour. . . . Communion with God through prayer develops the mental
and moral faculties, and the spiritual powers strengthen as we cultivate
thoughts upon spiritual things" (*The Desire of Ages,* pp. 70, 71).

Today's Lesson: The same resources for character development
that were available to the child Jesus are available to us and our
children today.

The Passover Visit

The Desire of Ages, Chapter 8.

"Why did you seek Me? Did you not know that I must be about My Father's business?" (Luke 2:49, NKJV).

In His twelfth year, Jesus went with his parents to Jerusalem to attend the Passover. As the young boy watched the solemn ceremonies of the temple, He saw their meaning ever more clearly. Every act seemed to be bound up with His own life. New impulses were awakening within Him. The mystery of His own mission was opening before Him. Jesus presented Himself to the teachers as one thirsting for a knowledge of God. He asked the meaning of Isaiah's prophecies—those scriptures that point to the suffering and death of the Lamb of God.

As the teachers directed their attention to this precocious learner, they were amazed at His perception. With the humility of a child, He repeated the words of Scripture, but He gave them a depth of meaning that the teachers had not conceived of. Our Lord's youthful modesty and grace disarmed their prejudices; the Holy Spirit was speaking to their hearts.

Joseph and Mary departed Jerusalem without Jesus, assuming He was among the crowd traveling to Nazareth. When they discovered their loss, they were in great distress. They remembered Herod's attempt to kill Him in His infancy. Finding Him at last in the school of the rabbis, they reproved Him. But Jesus' answer—"Don't you realize that I must be about My Father's business?"—showed that He understood His relationship to God.

Key Thought: "Jesus did not ignore His relation to His earthly parents. From Jerusalem He returned home with them, and aided them in their life of toil. He hid in His own heart the mystery of His mission, waiting submissively for the appointed time for Him to enter upon His work. For eighteen years after He had recognized that He was the Son of God, He acknowledged the tie that bound Him to the home at Nazareth, and performed the duties of a son, a brother, a friend, and a citizen" (*The Desire of Ages,* p. 82).

Today's Lesson: When we allow the demands and cares of the day to crowd out time for daily devotions, it takes decided effort to make up for the loss.

Days of Conflict

The Desire of Ages, Chapter 9.

"Thy word have I hid in mine heart, that I might not sin against thee" (Psalm 119:11).

In the years between His first Passover visit to Jerusalem and His baptism, Jesus saw ever more clearly that society's expectations were in constant collision with the requirements of God. Traditional rites possessed no virtue and offered no peace. Most people were unaware of the freedom of spirit that could be theirs by serving God in truth. Jesus did not attack the precepts or practices of the learned teachers, but when reproved for His own simple habits, He presented the Word of God as justification for His conduct.

At an early age, Jesus had begun to think and act for Himself in forming His character; not even respect and love for His parents could turn Him from obedience to God's Word. But the influence of the rabbis made His life bitter. Even in His youth He had to learn the hard lessons of silence and patient endurance.

At all times, however, Jesus manifested a cheerful piety. All this was a rebuke to the Pharisees, and they tried to force Jesus into conformity to their regulations. His attitude displeased His brothers as well, who thought that Jesus should be under their control. They accused Him of thinking Himself superior to them, and they reproved Him for setting Himself above the teachers and priests. His brothers did not like Jesus, because His standards were not their standards. His unselfishness and integrity brought forth only sneers.

Through it all, Jesus did not contend for His rights. He lived above these difficulties and did not retaliate when roughly used but bore insults patiently.

Key Thought: "Through childhood, youth, and manhood, Jesus walked alone. In His purity and His faithfulness, He trod the wine press alone, and of the people there was none with Him. He carried the awful weight of responsibility for the salvation of men. He knew that unless there was a decided change in the principles and purposes of the human race, all would be lost. This was the burden of His soul" (*The Desire of Ages,* p. 92).

Today's Lesson: The Word of God, not human interpretations or traditions, is the only safe guide for conducting our lives.

JUNE 4

The Voice in the Wilderness

The Desire of Ages, Chapter 10.

"Behold, I send My messenger before Your face, who will prepare Your way before You. The voice of one crying in the wilderness: 'Prepare the way of the Lord, make His paths straight' " (Mark 1:2, 3, NKJV).

John was born to Zacharias and Elisabeth, an elderly couple who were "both righteous before God" (Luke 1:6). Before John's birth, the angel had said, "He shall be great in the sight of the Lord, and shall drink neither wine nor strong drink; and he shall be filled with the Holy Ghost" (verse 15). As Christ's messenger, John must give a new direction to his hearers. He, himself, must be a temple for the indwelling Spirit of God. He must have a sound physical constitution and mental and spiritual strength; he must remain in control of his appetites and passions. John's abstemious life and plain dress were a rebuke to the excesses of his time.

John did not go to the rabbis for his education; in the desert he learned of nature and nature's God. Yet, from time to time, he went forth to mingle with society, always an interested observer of what was happening in the world. His words were plain, pointed, and convincing. He baptized the repentant in the waters of the Jordan as a symbol of cleansing from sin and told them that without purification of heart and life they could have no part in the Messiah's kingdom.

Key Thought: "In preparing the way for Christ's first advent, he [John] was a representative of those who are to prepare a people for our Lord's second coming. The world is given to self-indulgence.... All who would perfect holiness in the fear of God must learn the lessons of temperance and self-control. . . . This self-discipline is essential to that mental strength and spiritual insight which will enable us to understand and to practice the sacred truths of God's word. For this reason temperance finds its place in the work of preparation for Christ's second coming" (*The Desire of Ages,* p. 101).

Today's Lesson: John's message of mental, physical, and spiritual commitment is still the foundation of a life that seeks to overcome sin through the grace of God.

The Baptism

The Desire of Ages, Chapter 11.

***"Permit it to be so now, for thus it is fitting for us to fulfill
all righteousness" (Matthew 3:15, NKJV).***

The news of John's ministry spread throughout Galilee. In Nazareth, Jesus realized that His time had come. Though He and John were cousins, they had not had direct contact with each other. John was aware of the circumstances surrounding Jesus' birth, but he had no positive assurance that Jesus was the Messiah.

Jesus did not receive baptism as a confession of personal guilt. Instead, He requested baptism in order to identify Himself with sinners, taking the steps that we are to take. When He bowed in prayer after coming out of the water, Jesus knew that a new era was opening for Him. He knew, too, that this time He would not face Satan as He had in heaven. This time He would face His adversary as a member of the human race, in the same way that all men and women must face temptation. In His prayer, Jesus pled for power to fulfill His mission and asked for a sign that the Father accepted His humanity. His prayer astonished the angels in heaven.

The voice from heaven inspired John and strengthened Jesus for His mission. It was the Father's endorsement that Christ was still the divine Son, even though he had taken on humanity.

The next day, John announced Jesus as "the Lamb of God" (John 1:29), but even he did not understand the full meaning of those words.

Key Thought: "Alone He [Jesus] must tread the path; alone He must bear the burden. Upon Him who had laid off His glory and accepted the weakness of humanity the redemption of the world must rest. He saw and felt it all, but His purpose remained steadfast. . . . Notwithstanding that the sins of a guilty world were laid upon Christ, notwithstanding the humiliation of taking upon Himself our fallen nature, the voice from heaven declared Him to be the Son of the Eternal" (*The Desire of Ages,* pp. 111, 112).

Today's Lesson: Jesus took on the limitations of fallen humanity and identified Himself with the human race, so that by His victory over Satan He might provide a way of escape for us.

JUNE 6

The Temptation

The Desire of Ages, Chapter 12.

"Then Jesus was led up by the Spirit into the wilderness to be tempted by the devil" (Matthew 4:1, NKJV).

Jesus went into the wilderness to be alone and to be strengthened for the blood-stained path He must travel. Of course, He knew that Satan would also be there, because that was the whole point of the great controversy—He and Satan, old antagonists, would fight the issues out, face to face. Except for a few who understood the meaning of the sanctuary service, Satan had conquered almost the whole world. And to ensnare Jesus in his temptations would mean total victory in his rebellion against God and His law.

In the wilderness, Jesus faced Satan "in the likeness of sinful flesh" (Romans 8:3). This gave Satan a great advantage—all others in such weakness had joined his camp. All the enticements that humans find so hard to withstand would be presented to Jesus in their strongest forms—the test of appetite, the love of the world, and the love of display that leads to presumption. Jesus knew that the fate of the world depended on how He responded.

Jesus also knew—and Satan had to learn to his sorrow—that even though the human race had been decreasing in physical strength, mental power, and moral worth, Jesus would prove that humanity, with all its liabilities, would be able to live an overcoming life.

Key Thought: "In our own strength it is impossible for us to deny the clamors of our fallen nature. Through this channel Satan will bring temptation upon us. Christ knew that the enemy would come to every human being, to take advantage of hereditary weakness, and by his false insinuations to ensnare all whose trust is not in God. And by passing over the ground which man must travel, our Lord has prepared the way for us to overcome. It is not His will that we should be placed at a disadvantage in the conflict with Satan. He would not have us intimidated and discouraged by the assaults of the serpent" (*The Desire of Ages,* pp. 122, 123).

Today's Lesson: Whatever the enticement to self-indulgence, whether in appetite or passions, Jesus will give us the same strength to overcome that was available to Him.

The Victory

The Desire of Ages, Chapter 13.

"Get thee hence, Satan: for it is written, Thou shalt worship the Lord thy God, and him only shalt thou serve" (Matthew 4:10).

Satan did not appear to Christ as the familiar antagonist He had known in heaven. True to his deceptive nature, Satan assumed the appearance of an angel of light, claiming to have been sent by God to encourage and strengthen Jesus.

Failing in his first two temptations, Satan commended Jesus for His steadfast faithfulness. But now he urged Him to give one more evidence of His faith. He took the Son of God to the top of the temple, where—misquoting Scripture—Satan asked Jesus to prove His faith in God by throwing Himself down.

Of course, Jesus trusted His Father perfectly, but He would not place Himself in a position that would require the Father to save Him from death. He would not force God to come to His rescue and thus fail to give men and women an example of trust and submission. He would not ask for something God had not promised in order to prove whether He would fulfill His Word.

Faith is not presumption, for that would be using Satan's counterfeit. Faith claims God's promises and brings forth fruit in obedience. Presumption also claims God's promises but uses them as Satan did, to excuse transgression. Faith does not claim the favor of God without complying with the conditions on which mercy is to be granted.

Satan promised to give Jesus the control of this world if He would only acknowledge him as the earth's ruler. But Jesus refused to yield to Satan's enticements and thus concede failure in the great controversy.

Key Thought: "Never can the cost of our redemption be realized until the redeemed shall stand with the Redeemer before the throne of God. Then as the glories of the eternal home burst upon our enraptured senses we shall remember that Jesus left all this for us, that He not only became an exile from the heavenly courts, but for us took the risk of failure and eternal loss" (*The Desire of Ages,* p. 131).

Today's Lesson: When we yield to Satan's temptations, we are casting our vote against God in the great controversy.

"We Have Found the Messias"

The Desire of Ages, Chapter 14.

"Because I said unto thee, I saw thee under the fig tree, believest thou? Thou shalt see greater things than these" (John 1:50).

It was an electric moment for all Israel. Daniel's seventy-week prophecy regarding the Messiah was well known, and John's preaching had attracted the attention of the religious leaders in Jerusalem, who now realized that they had to investigate his work.

John assured them that he was not the Messiah but merely a voice crying in the wilderness preparing the way for the Messiah. Yet, the Jewish leaders could not reconcile their picture of the Messiah with anything connected to John's ministry.

The day following Jesus' baptism, John saw Jesus walking past and called out, "Behold the Lamb of God!" (John 1:36). Two of John's disciples, Andrew and John, followed Jesus in awe, wanting an opportunity to talk further with Him. This small nucleus of followers soon began to grow, with the addition of Peter and Philip.

When Nathanael was invited to join the group, he was disappointed to observe that Jesus bore the marks of toil and poverty. But the Holy Spirit was awakening his interest, and after a few minutes he was convinced that Jesus was the Messiah. Nathaniel is a great example for all to follow. If men and women would judge for themselves, without trusting religious teachers for guidance, Nathanael's experience would be theirs. But it took a friend to get Nathaniel to make the effort to listen to Jesus.

Key Thought: "Here Christ virtually says, On the bank of the Jordan the heavens were opened, and the Spirit descended like a dove upon Me. That scene was but a token that I am the Son of God. If you believe on Me as such, your faith shall be quickened. You shall see that the heavens are opened, and are never to be closed. I have opened them to you. The angels of God are ascending, bearing the prayers of the needy and distressed to the Father above, and descending, bringing blessing and hope, courage, help, and life, to the children of men" (*The Desire of Ages,* p. 142).

Today's Lesson: You can be the means of introducing someone to a saving relationship with Jesus.

At the Marriage Feast

The Desire of Ages, Chapter 15.

"Woman, what does your concern have to do with Me? My hour has not yet come" (John 2:4, NKJV).

Jesus did not begin His ministry with some great work before the leaders in Jerusalem. His credentials were first exhibited at a wedding feast, where He showed His social awareness and His concern for family joy.

Joseph had died, and now Mary alone carried the knowledge of Jesus' mysterious birth. Yet, even His mother had her doubts and disappointments. At the wedding feast where Mary had been assisting in the arrangements, the supply of drinks suddenly failed. Mary was greatly concerned and turned to her Son, hoping He could find a solution. All she got, at first, was what seems, in our English translations, to be a cold, discourteous response.

But Christ's answer, in accordance with contemporary eastern custom, showed respect, just as had His earlier response to His parents when they found Him in the temple at 12 years of age. On one level, He was responding to Mary's inner hope that He might be the Messiah and take the throne of Israel. But the time to reveal Himself fully had not yet come. However, to honor His mother and to strengthen the faith of His disciples, Jesus performed His first miracle.

The wine Christ provided for the country wedding in Cana was the pure, unfermented juice of the grape. His example in linking Himself with the social interests of humanity is a pattern to be followed by all who preach His Word and call themselves Christians.

Key Thought: "We should all become witnesses for Jesus. Social power, sanctified by the grace of Christ, must be improved in winning souls to the Saviour. Let the world see that we are not selfishly absorbed in our own interests, but that we desire others to share our blessings and privileges. Let them see that our religion does not make us unsympathetic or exacting. Let all who profess to have found Christ, minister as He did for the benefit of men" (*The Desire of Ages,* p. 152).

Today's Lesson: Followers of Jesus will be genuinely and unselfishly interested in the well-being of their neighbors and all of society, sharing the joys and sorrows of those around them.

In His Temple

The Desire of Ages, Chapter 16.

**"Take these things away! Do not make My Father's house
a house of merchandise" (John 2:16, NKJV).**

When Jesus attended the Passover in Jerusalem with His
disciples, He had not yet publicly announced His mission. Jews
from throughout the Roman Empire came to the feast. For the
convenience of travelers who could not bring sacrificial animals with
them, animals were for sale in the outer court of the temple. Here
also, foreign money was exchanged. And such transactions provided
opportunity for fraud and extortion.

Jesus took in the whole scene—the dishonest trading, the distress
of the poor, the desecration of the temple court. He saw far into the
future—how those representing Him would make merchandise of His
grace.

Slowly entering the temple court with an upraised scourge of cords,
Jesus commanded the crowd to leave and upended the tables of the
money changers. Jesus did not actually strike anyone with the scourge,
but the symbol of authority itself was enough to send priests, money
changers, and animal traders in a mad rush to disappear.

Eventually, the ordinary people drifted back, and many sensed that,
in some way, Jesus was their Savior. They began to realize the symbolic
significance of God's presence in the temple and the indwelling of
Christ in the human heart.

Key Thought: "In the cleansing of the temple, Jesus was
announcing His mission as the Messiah, and entering upon His work.
That temple, erected for the abode of the divine Presence, was designed
to be an object lesson for Israel and for the world. . . . Because of sin,
humanity ceased to be a temple for God. . . . But by the incarnation
of the Son of God, the purpose of Heaven is fulfilled. God dwells in
humanity, and through saving grace the heart of man becomes again
His temple. . . . In cleansing the temple from the world's buyers and
sellers, Jesus announced His mission to cleanse the heart from the
defilement of sin,—from the earthly desires, the selfish lusts, the evil
habits, that corrupt the soul" (*The Desire of Ages,* p. 161).

Today's Lesson: God's desire for every human being is to provide
a cleansed mind and heart in which He can dwell.

Nicodemus

The Desire of Ages, Chapter 17.

"Most assuredly, I say to you, unless one is born again, he cannot see the kingdom of God" (John 3:3, NKJV).

Nicodemus held a high position of trust in the Jewish nation and was an honored member of the Sanhedrin. He felt an attraction to Jesus and His teachings. After Jesus cleansed the temple, the Jewish leaders agreed that this new Teacher and His challenge demanded some sort of response. But they could not agree on what that response should be. Nicodemus counseled caution and moderation.

Wanting to talk to Jesus but not wanting to meet Him openly, Nicodemus arranged a night meeting. Jesus knew that he was an honest seeker and came directly to the point, laying bare the foundation principles of truth. He knew that Nicodemus needed spiritual regeneration more than he needed theoretical knowledge. Nicodemus was startled at the thought of a kingdom too pure for him to see in his present state. He raised objections, but Jesus did not meet argument with argument.

Instead, He helped Nicodemus to see that the most rigid obedience to the mere letter of the law as applied to the outward life entitles no one to enter the kingdom of God. The Holy Spirit guided Nicodemus to see that the remedy for sin is repentance and accepting the Spirit's overcoming power in the life.

Key Thought: "The light shining from the cross reveals the love of God. His love is drawing us to Himself. If we do not resist this drawing, we shall be led to the foot of the cross in repentance for the sins that have crucified the Saviour. Then the Spirit of God through faith produces a new life in the soul. The thoughts and desires are brought into obedience to the will of Christ. The heart, the mind, are created anew in the image of Him who works in us to subdue all things to Himself. Then the law of God is written in the mind and heart, and we can say with Christ, 'I delight to do Thy will, O my God.' Psalm 40:8" (*The Desire of Ages,* p. 176).

Today's Lesson: Spiritual health depends on continually focusing on Jesus and receiving the empowering strength of the Holy Spirit on a daily basis.

"He Must Increase"

The Desire of Ages, Chapter 18.

"This my joy therefore is fulfilled. He must increase, but I must decrease" (John 3:29, 30).

For a time John's influence was greater than that of the rulers and priests. Satan tried everything to tempt John to announce himself as the Messiah and be Israel's hero. But John refused and directed attention to Jesus instead.

As a result, John saw his popularity waning, while the crowds around Jesus increased daily. John's disciples were jealous and found reasons to criticize Jesus and His followers. John could have joined them, but he had learned to live in an atmosphere uncontaminated with selfishness and ambition. He reminded his disciples that his message had always been designed to prepare the way for the Messiah. He accepted the reality that Jesus must increase and that he must decrease.

So it is with all of Christ's followers. His true disciples will turn from the lure of applause and rivalry. They will put Jesus before all else.

Jesus saw that dark clouds were already gathering. Not wanting to add to the dissension, He withdrew to Galilee, giving us all a good example of what to do when divisions develop.

Today, God calls leaders to do a certain work, and when they have carried it as far as they are qualified to take it, the Lord brings in others to carry it still further.

Key Thought: "Looking in faith to the Redeemer, John had risen to the height of self-abnegation. He sought not to attract men to himself, but to lift their thoughts higher and still higher, until they should rest upon the Lamb of God. He himself had been only a voice, a cry in the wilderness. Now with joy he accepted silence and obscurity, that the eyes of all might be turned to the Light of life.

"Those who are true to their calling as messengers for God will not seek honor for themselves. Love for self will be swallowed up in love for Christ. No rivalry will mar the precious cause of the gospel" (*The Desire of Ages,* p. 179).

Today's Lesson: Pride is among the most difficult sins to detect and eradicate—while humility is a delicate virtue that requires careful attention to ensure its growth.

At Jacob's Well

The Desire of Ages, Chapter 19.

"Whoever drinks of this water will thirst again, but whoever drinks of the water that I shall give him will never thirst. But the water that I shall give him will become in him a fountain of water springing up into everlasting life" (John 4:13, 14, NKJV).

As Jesus passed through Samaria on the road to Galilee, it was noon, and He was weary and hungry. In a few minutes, a Samaritan woman approached the well to fill her pitcher. Jesus asked her for a drink. He was indeed thirsty, but at the same time he was using the request as a tactful way to open conversation.

Jesus avoided argument with this woman and appealed instead to her curiosity by telling her He had something she needed and that if she accepted it, she would never have to search again. He asked her to call her husband. Before He could offer her the gift of salvation, she would have to recognize her sinfulness.

When she shifted the conversation to a less personal area—raising an abstract theological question—Jesus turned the discussion back to the spiritual implications of true worship. Real worship, He told her, doesn't depend on a place but on a pure heart.

At this moment the disciples returned with food, only to be surprised by Jesus' Samaritan visitor. The woman left immediately, singing in her heart about her talk with Jesus. But she soon returned, accompanied by many of her fellow villagers, who also listened to Jesus—and believed the truths He shared.

Key Thought: "As soon as she had found the Saviour the Samaritan woman brought others to Him. She proved herself a more effective missionary than His own disciples. The disciples saw nothing in Samaria to indicate that it was an encouraging field. Their thoughts were fixed upon a great work to be done in the future. They did not see that right around them was a harvest to be gathered. But through the woman whom they despised, a whole cityful were brought to hear the Saviour" (*The Desire of Ages,* p. 195).

Today's Lesson: Every person you meet is a potential "Samaritan woman" waiting to hear the good news of salvation. God saves men and women one by one.

"Except Ye See Signs and Wonders"

The Desire of Ages, Chapter 20.

"Unless you people see signs and wonders, you will by no means believe" (John 4:48, NKJV).

In Capernaum, a Jewish nobleman whose son was close to death from a seemingly incurable disease came to plead with Jesus to heal his son. Jesus knew that the father's faith in Him was weak—that he was filled with doubt. He had decided that if Jesus healed his son, then he would believe. In contrast, the Samaritans had believed on Jesus without any outward sign.

"Unless you people see signs and wonders," Jesus said sadly, "you will by no means believe."

Immediately, the father saw that his motive in coming to Jesus had been purely selfish. His heart was changed; his faith fastened upon Jesus. And the Savior responded to his need. He assured the man that his son would live and sent him on his way. Before the nobleman arrived home, he was greeted by servants who told him the good news—the fever had left the child, and he was resting. No sign of the sickness remained. The change had occurred at the very moment Jesus spoke the word!

Jesus wanted not only to heal the man's son but to bring salvation to the nobleman's family. As a result of this experience, the nobleman wanted to learn more about Jesus, and the more he heard, the more he believed. He became a faithful follower.

Today, we may not feel that God hears us, but we are to believe His promises.

Key Thought: "Notwithstanding all the evidence that Jesus was the Christ, the petitioner had determined to make his belief in Him conditional on the granting of his own request. The Saviour contrasted this questioning unbelief with the simple faith of the Samaritans, who asked for no miracle or sign. His word, the ever-present evidence of His divinity, had a convincing power that reached their hearts. Christ was pained that His own people, to whom the Sacred Oracles had been committed, should fail to hear the voice of God speaking to them in His Son" (*The Desire of Ages,* p. 198).

Today's Lesson: We are to believe God's promise not because we *feel* that it is so, but because He has promised—and we trust Him.

178

Bethesda and the Sanhedrin

The Desire of Ages, Chapter 21.

"I can of Myself do nothing. As I hear, I judge; and My judgment is righteous, because I do not seek My own will but the will of the Father who sent Me"
(John 5:30, NKJV).

One Sabbath, on the edge of the Bethesda pool, Jesus bent over a wretched cripple, helpless for thirty-eight years, and asked, "Wilt thou be made whole?" Hope arose that Jesus would help him be the first into the pool so that he could be healed. But that was not what Jesus intended.

He simply said, "Rise, take up thy bed, and walk" (John 5:8). The man's faith took hold of the implied promise. Without questioning, he willed to obey, and all his withered muscles responded. He believed Christ's words, and in acting upon them, he received healing and strength.

After Jesus had melted into the crowd, the former cripple made his way to the temple, still carrying his mat! The Jewish leaders were furious that he was carrying a burden on the Sabbath! They had so perverted the law that it had become a heavy yoke; its intended blessings had been lost. Later, Jesus met the man and told him, "Behold, thou art made whole: sin no more, lest a worse thing come unto thee" (verse 14).

The leaders accused Jesus of breaking the Sabbath by healing the man on that day. In His answer before the Sanhedrin, Jesus clarified the principles of true Sabbath keeping and defined His relationship with His heavenly Father (see John 5:19–47).

Key Thought: "The words of Christ teach that we should regard ourselves as inseparably bound to our Father in heaven. Whatever our position, we are dependent upon God, who holds all destinies in His hands. He has appointed us our work, and has endowed us with faculties and means for that work. So long as we surrender the will to God, and trust in His strength and wisdom, we shall be guided in safe paths, to fulfill our appointed part in His great plan" (*The Desire of Ages,* p. 209).

Today's Lesson: One sure indication that we have lost sight of the true meaning of God's law is when we allow its provisions to blind us to human need.

Imprisonment and Death of John

The Desire of Ages, Chapter 22.

"But what did you go out to see? A prophet? Yes, I say to you, and more than a prophet" (Matthew 11:9, NKJV).

John was the first to herald Christ's kingdom and the first to suffer martyrdom for it. His fearless preaching brought fear to the heart of Herod, and the king eventually threw John into prison. John did not fully understand the nature of Christ's kingdom. He had fearlessly proclaimed God's Word, but Jesus seemed content simply to heal and teach. Wondering if his work had been in vain, John longed for some word from Jesus.

Jesus did not immediately respond to the disciples John sent— except to continue healing and teaching. Then He told them to return to their master and tell him what they had seen and heard. This was enough for John; he yielded himself to life or death—whatever would best serve the cause he loved.

After John's disciples left, Jesus made it clear to His hearers that God had not forsaken John. John was greater in God's plan, Jesus declared, than a prophet. The lesson comes down through the centuries: All who follow Christ will wear the crown of sacrifice—one way or another.

God allowed His faithful servant, John, to die at the hands of a vengeful woman and a weak king. John experienced no miraculous deliverance, but angels were his companions in his dungeon, and they helped him understand the prophecies and promises in God's Word.

Key Thought: "God never leads His children otherwise than they would choose to be led, if they could see the end from the beginning, and discern the glory of the purpose which they are fulfilling as co-workers with Him. Not Enoch, who was translated to heaven, not Elijah, who ascended in a chariot of fire, was greater or more honored than John the Baptist, who perished alone in the dungeon. . . . And of all the gifts that Heaven can bestow upon men, fellowship with Christ in His sufferings is the most weighty trust and the highest honor" (*The Desire of Ages,* p. 224).

Today's Lesson: No matter what gloomy circumstances we may find ourselves in, it is enough to know that Jesus understands and will sustain us.

"The Kingdom of God Is at Hand"

The Desire of Ages, Chapter 23.

***"The time is fulfilled, and the kingdom of God is at hand:
repent ye, and believe the gospel" (Mark 1:15).***

If the leaders of Israel had received Christ, He would have honored them as His messengers to carry the gospel to the world. Their jealousy and distrust ripened into hatred, leading the general public to turn away from Him.

Such has been the case ever since—church authorities keep rejecting the real Jesus in every succeeding generation. The Reformers never thought of withdrawing from the established church, but the religious leaders would not tolerate the new light.

When Jesus said, "The time is fulfilled," He was referring to the "seventy weeks" that were to be allotted to the Jewish nation (see Daniel 9:24, 25). According to the prophecy, the seventieth week began in A.D. 27, when Jesus was baptized and initiated His ministry. "In the midst of the week, he shall cause the sacrifice and oblation to cease" (verse 27). This happened when the veil in the temple was torn apart, ending the sacredness of the sacrificial service. The "seventieth week" ended in A.D. 34, when Stephen was stoned and the disciples reached out to the Gentiles.

Like those who were looking for the first advent of Christ, so it is in the preparation for His second coming. Both events are based on solid Bible prophecies. We have reached the period foretold in the Scriptures, and we must be very sure that we are truly preaching the New Testament gospel.

Key Thought: "The Jews misinterpreted and misapplied the word of God, and they knew not the time of their visitation. The years of the ministry of Christ and His apostles,—the precious last years of grace to the chosen people,—they spent in plotting the destruction of the Lord's messengers. . . . So today the kingdom of this world absorbs men's thoughts, and they take no note of the rapidly fulfilling prophecies and the tokens of the swift-coming kingdom of God" (*The Desire of Ages,* p. 235).

Today's Lesson: We stand today on the threshold of the Second Coming, and God has asked us to carry the message of Jesus' soon return to all the world.

"Is Not This the Carpenter's Son?"

The Desire of Ages, Chapter 24.

"And all bare him witness, and wondered at the gracious words which proceeded out of his mouth" (Luke 4:22).

Many times Jesus and His parents and siblings had worshiped in the synagogue at Nazareth. So, when He returned to His home town after the early days of His teaching and healing ministry, excitement was at its highest pitch. That Sabbath, in the local synagogue, He was asked to read from the scroll of Isaiah—chapter 61:1, 2. Handing back the scroll, Jesus began to speak. His words carried a power that the worshipers had never felt before.

But when He told them that the Scripture He had just read was fulfilled that day in their hearing, the listeners were forced to look at themselves—and their pride was offended. They began to turn against Jesus. How could He be the Messiah? He was simply the carpenter's son. The more Jesus talked, the angrier they became.

Jesus knew what was in their minds. He reminded them that the amount of light one has is less important than the use he makes of it. After all, the heathen who choose the right as far as they can distinguish it are in a more favorable condition than are those who have had great light but reject it. His words struck at the root of their self-righteousness.

Their unbelief led to open hostility and violence. They pulled Him from the synagogue and led him to a precipice to throw Him to His death—but angels interceded and delivered Him from their sight.

People today still have difficulty accepting truth and separating real greatness from outward show.

Key Thought: "Truth was unpopular in Christ's day. It is unpopular in our day. It has been unpopular ever since Satan first gave man a disrelish for it by presenting fables that lead to self-exaltation. Do we not today meet theories and doctrines that have no foundation in the word of God? Men cling as tenaciously to them as did the Jews to their traditions" (*The Desire of Ages,* p. 242).

Today's Lesson: Spiritual pride is the sworn enemy of truth. If we close our eyes to unpleasant truths, we are deceiving ourselves; truth does not change.

The Call by the Sea

The Desire of Ages, Chapter 25.

"*Follow Me, and I will make you fishers of men*"
(*Matthew 4:19, NKJV*).

After preaching a sermon from Peter's boat, Jesus told him to launch out into the Sea of Galilee—the same place where Peter and the others had fished unsuccessfully all night. Everyone knew that night-time was the best time to catch fish, but because Jesus said so, Peter and his brother threw out their net, even though it was morning.

Imagine their surprise when the net filled with so many fish that they needed James and John to help them bring in the catch! Peter was ashamed of his unbelief; he sensed his uncleanness in the presence of infinite purity, and he fell at Jesus' feet.

Until now, none of the disciples had followed Jesus full time, but when He invited these fishermen to leave their nets and become fishers of men, they gladly made the commitment.

These men were not educated in the schools of the day. Jesus did not despise education, for He knew that when educated men and women are controlled by the love of God and devoted to His service, intellectual culture is a blessing. But he chose men and women who were humble and not filled with self-confidence. The Holy Spirit can educate those who begin with self-distrust and who are teachable. When the disciples came forth from the Savior's training, they were no longer ignorant and uncultured. They had become like Him in mind and character.

Key Thought: "He who loves Christ the most will do the greatest amount of good. There is no limit to the usefulness of one who, by putting self aside, makes room for the working of the Holy Spirit upon his heart, and lives a life wholly consecrated to God. . . . If men in humble life were encouraged to do all the good they could do, if restraining hands were not laid upon them to repress their zeal, there would be a hundred workers for Christ where now there is one" (*The Desire of Ages,* p. 250).

Today's Lesson: Regardless of formal training, Jesus can make effective workers of those who are willing to be molded by His Spirit and who will remain humble.

At Capernaum

The Desire of Ages, Chapter 26.

"They were astonished at His teaching, for His word was with authority" (Luke 4:32, NKJV).

Jesus had nothing to do with the various dissensions among the Jews—His work was to present the truth. Jesus spoke truth in a direct and simple way, while Israel's teachers spoke with doubt and hesitancy, leaving their hearers in even greater uncertainty. Jesus was earnest rather than vehement. He varied His messages to fit His audience. He tactfully appealed to prejudiced minds and surprised them with illustrations that won their attention. He used the imagination to reach the heart. The most highly educated were charmed with His words, and the uneducated were blessed. He watched the changing expressions of His hearers.

Once Jesus was interrupted by a madman, but He rebuked the demon and freed the wretched man from his bondage. The sufferer's mind had been darkened by Satan, but the Savior's truth pierced the gloom. His neighbors knew of this man's background—that he had made life a grand carnival, fascinated by the pleasures of sin. Remorse came too late, and as do most who begin by dabbling in evil, he ended up helpless in Satan's grasp.

The religious leaders and teachers in Christ's day were powerless to resist the work of Satan, for only the power of God can overcome the wicked one. The same is true today. Many find themselves enslaved by Satan, because they have not allowed God's power to work in their lives.

Key Thought: "So it will be in the great final conflict of the controversy between righteousness and sin. While new life and light and power are descending from on high upon the disciples of Christ, a new life is springing up from beneath, and energizing the agencies of Satan. Intensity is taking possession of every earthly element. With a subtlety gained through centuries of conflict, the prince of evil works under a disguise. He appears clothed as an angel of light, and multitudes are 'giving heed to seducing spirits, and doctrines of devils.' 1 Tim. 4:1" (*The Desire of Ages,* p. 257).

Today's Lesson: The same evil powers are at work in the world today as when Christ was on earth. Satan labors with undimmed skills to destroy our spiritual discernment.

"Thou Canst Make Me Clean"

The Desire of Ages, Chapter 27.

"What reason ye in your hearts? Whether is easier, to say, Thy sins be forgiven thee; or to say, Rise up and walk?" (Luke 5:22, 23).

A mong the Jews, illness—especially leprosy—was regarded as a judgment for sin and hence was called "the finger of God." No one had any idea how it could be cured. In Christ's ministry, He met many who were suffering with this disease.

There was one leper who heard of Jesus and His power to heal diseases. But how to find Him? Lepers were shut out from the cities; the difficulties were great. But he persevered and eventually found Jesus teaching beside the lake. He watched from a distance as Jesus laid hands on the lame, the blind, and the paralyzed. He watched the healed leaping for joy and praising God. Faith and hope drove him nearer, while people scattered before his loathsome presence. Falling at Jesus' feet, he cried, "Lord, if thou wilt, thou canst make me clean" (Matthew 8:2). Laying His hand on him, Jesus replied, "I will; be thou clean" (verse 3). Immediately, the leper's flesh was healthy—his muscles firm.

Jesus' miracles of healing were illustrations of the spiritual cleansing of the soul from sin. His healing of the paralyzed man at Capernaum taught this truth, as well as did His healing of the leper. Although the paralyzed man desired physical healing, his greater longing was for relief from the burden of sin. Jesus knew this and assured him, "Thy sins are forgiven thee" (Luke 5:20).

Key Thought: "The paralytic found in Christ healing for both the soul and the body. The spiritual healing was followed by physical restoration. . . . There are today thousands suffering from physical disease, who, like the paralytic, are longing for the message, 'Thy sins are forgiven.' The burden of sin, with its unrest and unsatisfied desires, is the foundation of their maladies. They can find no relief until they come to the Healer of the soul" (*The Desire of Ages,* p. 270).

Today's Lesson: Jesus came to give us abundant life—physically and spiritually. He can heal and forgive as surely today as He did when He walked among men and women on earth.

Levi-Matthew

The Desire of Ages, Chapter 28.

"As Jesus passed on from there, He saw a man named Matthew sitting at the tax office. And He said to him, 'Follow Me.' And he arose and followed Him"
(Matthew 9:9, NKJV).

Levi-Matthew was the fifth disciple to be called into Christ's service. He had been listening to Jesus, and his heart was open. He was astonished that Jesus spoke to him while at his toll booth. Even more surprising, Matthew left all to follow the Lord's invitation. No hesitation, no questioning, no thought of his lucrative lifestyle—he simply wanted to be with Jesus.

Like the four fishermen with their successful catch of fish, Matthew left his livelihood for poverty and hardship. The lesson they and others learned is that no one can succeed in the service of God unless his whole heart is in the work.

Matthew became the talk of the town. Many were offended that a religious teacher should choose a publican as one of His closest coworkers, but widespread interest was aroused among the tax collectors. Matthew hosted a dinner in honor of Jesus. Among the three thousand converted at Pentecost after Jesus' death were many who first heard God's truth at Matthew's dinner.

The Pharisees would not consider that Jesus associated and ate with tax collectors and sinners in order to bring the light of heaven to them. They needed to learn that a legal, loveless religion can never lead souls to repentance.

Key Thought: "Thousands are making the same mistake as did the Pharisees whom Christ reproved at Matthew's feast. Rather than give up some cherished idea, or discard some idol of opinion, many refuse the truth which comes down from the Father of light. They trust in self, and depend upon their own wisdom, and do not realize their spiritual poverty. They insist on being saved in some way by which they may perform some important work. When they see that there is no way of weaving self into the work, they reject the salvation provided" (*The Desire of Ages,* p. 280).

Today's Lesson: We must be emptied of self before Christ can enter the heart. The love of Jesus will awaken new life in the heart and transform us into a new person.

The Sabbath

The Desire of Ages, Chapter 29.

"The Son of man is Lord also of the Sabbath" (Luke 6:5).

The Sabbath was embodied in the Ten Commandments, but that was not the first time it had been made known as a day of rest. The Israelites had known about the Sabbath before they came to Sinai (see Exodus 16:28). The Sabbath was not for Israel alone but for the world.

As the Jews departed from God and failed to make Christ's righteousness their own by faith, the Sabbath lost its significance to them. In Jesus' day, the Sabbath had become so perverted from its original purpose that its observance reflected the character of selfish and arbitrary men rather than the character of the loving heavenly Father. The rabbis led the people to look upon God as a tyrant and to think that the observance of the Sabbath, as He required it, made men hardhearted and cruel. It was Christ's work to clear away these misconceptions.

One Sabbath Jesus' disciples plucked some grain beside the path as they walked and ate the kernels. Spies for the rabbis reported this as a double offense—reaping grain and threshing it on the Sabbath. Jesus dismissed the arbitrary claims of the religious leaders and insisted that His disciples were innocent. That which is necessary for accomplishing God's work is appropriate on the Sabbath day. It is lawful to do well on the Sabbath, Jesus declared (see Matthew 12:12).

Key Thought: "Christ reiterated the truth that the sacrifices were in themselves of no value. They were a means, and not an end. Their object was to direct men to the Saviour, and thus to bring them into harmony with God. It is the service of love that God values. When this is lacking, the mere round of ceremony is an offense to Him. So with the Sabbath. It was designed to bring men into communion with God; but when the mind was absorbed with wearisome rites, the object of the Sabbath was thwarted. Its mere outward observance was a mockery" (*The Desire of Ages,* p. 286).

Today's Lesson: God gave the Sabbath to His people to be a blessing, not a burden. We are to keep it holy, but doing so is to be a delight.

"He Ordained Twelve"

The Desire of Ages, Chapter 30.

"And he goeth up into a mountain, and calleth unto him whom he would: and they came unto him. And he ordained twelve, that they should be with him, and that he might send them forth to preach" (Mark 3:13).

Jesus' first step in organizing God's New Testament church was to select His disciples, whom He would send forth to tell what they had seen and heard while they had been with Him.

When Jesus was preparing the disciples for their ordination, one who had not been summoned urged his presence among them—Judas Iscariot, who professed to be a follower of Christ. With earnestness he declared, "Lord, I will follow thee whithersoever thou goest" (Luke 9:57). The disciples were eager that Judas should become one of their number. His appearance was commanding, and he was a man of keen discernment and executive ability; they commended him to Jesus as someone who would greatly assist Him in His work. They were surprised that Jesus received Judas so coolly.

All the disciples had serious faults when Jesus called them. He warned and reproved them during their time together, but they never considered leaving Him.

Key Thought: "As His representatives among men, Christ does not choose angels who have never fallen, but human beings, men of like passions with those they seek to save. Christ took upon Himself humanity, that He might reach humanity. Divinity needed humanity; for it required both the divine and the human to bring salvation to the world. Divinity needed humanity, that humanity might afford a channel of communication between God and man. So with the servants and messengers of Christ. Man needs a power outside of and beyond himself, to restore him to the likeness of God, and enable him to do the work of God; but this does not make the human agency unessential. Humanity lays hold upon divine power, Christ dwells in the heart by faith; and through co-operation with the divine, the power of man becomes efficient for good" (*The Desire of Ages,* pp. 296, 297).

Today's Lesson: Jesus is still calling men and women to be His disciples. He invites you to learn of Him so that you can carry out His purposes in your sphere of influence.

The Sermon on the Mount

The Desire of Ages, Chapter 31.

"Therefore whosoever heareth these sayings of mine, and doeth them, I will liken him unto a wise man, which built his house upon a rock: And the rain descended, and the floods came, and the winds blew, and beat upon that house; and it fell not: for it was founded upon a rock" (Matthew 7:24, 25).

The Sermon on the Mount was spoken in the hearing of the multitude, but it was given especially for the disciples. In the crowd were scribes and Pharisees, poor peasants and fishermen, and the usual throngs eager to hear what Jesus had to say. All were hoping that Jerusalem would soon be exalted as the head of a universal kingdom.

But Christ disappointed everyone. In His sermon He sought to undo their false expectations. He didn't directly attack their misconceptions; instead, He taught them something infinitely better than they had known.

His first words were: "Happy are they who recognize their spiritual poverty, who know what to mourn for, who are humble, who hunger and thirst after righteousness, who are merciful, who are peacemakers, who are persecuted for righteousness' sake, and who are reviled falsely." Such people, He said, would have great reward in heaven.

In His sermon, Jesus outlined the principles of God's kingdom. He showed what makes up true righteousness and what will be its results in the Christian's life. A good tree will produce good fruit.

Key Thought: "Thus Christ set forth the principles of His kingdom, and showed them to be the great rule of life. To impress the lesson He adds an illustration. It is not enough, He says, for you to hear My words. By obedience you must make them the foundation of your character. Self is but shifting sand. If you build upon human theories and inventions, your house will fall. By the winds of temptation, the tempests of trial, it will be swept away. But these principles that I have given will endure. Receive Me; build on My words" (*The Desire of Ages,* p. 314).

Today's Lesson: One is not a Christian merely because he or she believes certain doctrines or teachings. Christ's true followers bring truth into the daily life and live out His teachings.

The Centurion

The Desire of Ages, Chapter 32.

"I say unto you, I have not found so great faith, no, not in Israel" (Luke 7:9).

A centurion's servant was stricken with palsy and dying. Although he had never seen Jesus, the reports the centurion had heard inspired him with faith. All that was spiritual within him responded to the Savior. But he felt unworthy to meet Jesus personally, so he appealed to the Jewish elders to deliver his request to Jesus on his behalf and ask Him to heal his servant.

The elders urged Jesus to fulfill the centurion's request, and the Master set out immediately. But the multitude that accompanied Him slowed Him down. When the centurion heard that Jesus was on His way, he sent a message, saying that Jesus need not come in person. "Speak the word only, and my servant shall be healed" (Matthew 8:8). He saw Jesus in His true character; he was not blind to Jesus' authority, as were the children of Abraham. And Jesus replied, "As thou hast believed, so be it done unto thee" (verse 13).

Some twenty miles away, Jesus and His disciples met a funeral party, mourning the only son of a widow. Jesus had "compassion on her" (Luke 7:13). He touched the bier, which shocked the mourners, and called for the young man to arise.

In these two incidents, Jesus showed how much He values genuine faith and how close He is to those who mourn. His compassion and power are no less today.

Key Thought: "Satan cannot hold the dead in his grasp when the Son of God bids them live. He cannot hold in spiritual death one soul who in faith receives Christ's word of power. God is saying to all who are dead in sin, 'Awake thou that sleepest, and arise from the dead.' Eph. 5:14. That word is eternal life. . . . 'God hath delivered us from the power of darkness, and hath translated us into the kingdom of His dear Son.' Col. 1:13. It is all offered us in His word. If we receive the word, we have the deliverance" (*The Desire of Ages,* p. 320).

Today's Lesson: Jesus is touched with sympathy for our sorrows. He is still a living Savior to all who believe on Him.

Who Are My Brethren?

The Desire of Ages, Chapter 33.

"Whosoever shall do the will of my Father which is in heaven, the same is my brother, and sister, and mother"
(Matthew 12:50).

Jesus' brothers were not in sympathy with Jesus and His work. Reports of His activities filled them with dismay. Spending entire nights in prayer, surrounded by people with no time to eat, and especially His attitude toward the Pharisees—all this suggested to them that Jesus' reason was becoming unsettled. They persuaded Mary to join them in confronting Jesus and insisting He stop his activities.

Just before his family arrived, Jesus healed a demon-possessed man. The Pharisees immediately declared that only the prince of demons could cast out demons! They may not have really believed their accusation, but having started down the path of unbelief, they were too proud to confess their error. Jesus responded with a warning about sinning against the Holy Spirit. It is unsafe to use arguments we may not even fully believe—because the words we use react on our thoughts and have the power to affect the character. Resisting the Holy Spirit can lead to habits that leave us at Satan's mercy.

While He was speaking to the Pharisees, Jesus was told that His brothers and mother were waiting to see Him. Their unbelief cast a shadow over His ministry. They condemned that which they could not understand. Many followers of Christ through the centuries have had to endure misapprehension, even in their own homes. Such can find comfort in knowing that Jesus had to endure the same and that He knows how to sustain them.

Key Thought: "Christ loves the heavenly beings that surround His throne; but what shall account for the great love wherewith He has loved us? We cannot understand it, but we can know it true in our own experience. And if we do hold the relation of kinship to Him, with what tenderness should we regard those who are brethren and sisters of our Lord! Should we not be quick to recognize the claims of our divine relationship?" (*The Desire of Ages,* p. 327).

Today's Lesson: It is our privilege to encourage those who find little support within their own family circle as they attempt to live for Christ.

JUNE 28

The Invitation

The Desire of Ages, Chapter 34.

"Come unto me, all ye that labour and are heavy laden, and I will give you rest" (Matthew 11:28).

In this invitation Jesus is speaking to everyone—to the scribes and Pharisees with their punctilious attention to religious forms, to the publicans and sinners seemingly content with the sensual and earthly, and to the burdened barely able to survive.

We are all weighed down with burdens that only Jesus can remove. The heaviest burden of all is sin. By experience, Jesus knows the weaknesses of humanity—our wants and the strength of temptation.

Whatever our anxieties and trials, Jesus invites us to spread them out before Him. He will open the way for us to disentangle ourselves from embarrassment and difficulty. He will not leave us to follow our own inclinations, going wherever our will leads us. He will not allow us to fall into Satan's ranks and take on his characteristics.

Many are aching under a load of care because they are trying to reach the world's standards; they wear a yoke of bondage. Jesus invites us to accept His yoke. Worry is blind and cannot discern the future, but Jesus sees the end from the beginning. In every difficulty He has prepared a way to bring relief. Our heavenly Father has a thousand ways to provide for us, of which we know nothing. If we will make God's service and honor the supreme objective of our lives, we will find perplexities vanishing before us, and God will open a plain pathway before us.

Love of self brings unrest. The more we learn of Jesus, the happier we will be.

Key Thought: "Our lives may seem a tangle; but as we commit ourselves to the wise Master Worker, He will bring out the pattern of life and character that will be to His own glory. And that character which expresses the glory—character—of Christ will be received into the Paradise of God. A renovated race shall walk with Him in white, for they are worthy" (*The Desire of Ages,* p. 331).

Today's Lesson: When we live in Jesus' peace day and night because we make His will our first choice in all things, we find rest to our souls, and heaven begins here and now.

"Peace, Be Still"

The Desire of Ages, Chapter 35.

"Why are ye fearful, O ye of little faith?" (Matthew 8:26).

All day Jesus had been teaching and healing, scarcely pausing for food or rest. He was exhausted, looking forward to resting in a solitary place across the lake. Settling into the boat, He was soon asleep.

A fierce storm developed, filling the boat with water. The disciples worked frantically to bail out the water, while Jesus slept on, undisturbed. Finally, in their desperation, they cried, "Master, carest thou not that we perish?" (Mark 4:38). How could He rest so peacefully while they were battling with death?

Jesus arose, took in the situation, and said to the angry sea, "Peace, be still" (verse 39). Jesus had not been resting unafraid because of His own almighty power. He was trusting in His Father's power. We can rest in that same kind of faith when the storms of life threaten to overwhelm us.

The next morning, the disciples faced a different kind of storm, more terrible than the night's tempest. Two madmen rushed at them as if to tear them in pieces. The disciples fled in terror. But not Jesus. He had stilled the tempest the night before, and now He was ready to quell the storm raging in the minds of these two madmen.

After freeing these men from the demons and restoring them to their right minds, Jesus sent them as missionaries to preach the gospel in Decapolis. In their own lives they bore the evidence that Jesus was the Messiah. So it is with us—we are to tell what we know, what we ourselves have seen and heard and felt of God's power.

Key Thought: "As Jesus rested by faith in the Father's care, so we are to rest in the care of our Saviour. If the disciples had trusted in Him, they would have been kept in peace. Their fear in the time of danger revealed their unbelief. In their efforts to save themselves, they forgot Jesus; and it was only when, in despair of self-dependence, they turned to Him that He could give them help" (*The Desire of Ages,* p. 336).

Today's Lesson: We need to be ready on any occasion to witness to what God has done for us.

JUNE 30

The Touch of Faith

The Desire of Ages, Chapter 36.

"Daughter, be of good comfort; thy faith hath made thee whole" (Matthew 9:22).

Pressing through the crowds around Jesus, a poor woman was barely able to get close enough to touch His robe. But it was enough. She had been suffering from a condition that the physicians had declared incurable, but she was convinced Jesus could heal her—"If I may but touch his garment, I shall be whole" (Matthew 9:21). And when she did, she knew she had been instantly cured.

Jesus stopped and called out, "Who touched me?" (Mark 5:31). He knew the difference between a casual touch and the intentional touch of faith, and He wanted to honor this woman's faith. She fell trembling at His feet and heard Him say, "Daughter, be of good comfort; thy faith hath made thee whole" (Matthew 9:22).

That woman had a great story—a personal experience—to tell. So today, our confession of Jesus' faithfulness is Heaven's chosen agency for revealing Christ to the world. The most effective testimony we can give is the testimony of our own experience. Such words have an irresistible power that works for the salvation of souls.

Key Thought: "A nominal faith in Christ, which accepts Him merely as the Saviour of the world, can never bring healing to the soul. The faith that is unto salvation is not a mere intellectual assent to the truth. He who waits for entire knowledge before he will exercise faith, cannot receive blessing from God. It is not enough to believe about Christ; we must believe in Him. The only faith that will benefit us is that which embraces Him as a personal Saviour; which appropriates His merits to ourselves. Many hold faith as an opinion. Saving faith is a transaction by which those who receive Christ join themselves in covenant relation with God. Genuine faith is life. A living faith means an increase of vigor, a confiding trust, by which the soul becomes a conquering power" (*The Desire of Ages,* p. 347).

Today's Lesson: We receive more encouragement from the smallest blessing that we personally receive from the Lord than from hearing of great blessings others have obtained. That is why a living experience with Christ is essential.

The First Evangelists

The Desire of Ages, Chapter 37.

***"Behold, I send you out as sheep in the midst of wolves.
Therefore be wise as serpents and harmless as doves"
(Matthew 10:16, NKJV).***

The disciples lived as members of Jesus' family, traveling on foot throughout Galilee and gaining an education in how to present truth and win souls. In this training, the Master's example was far more effective than any mere doctrinal instruction. Now Jesus was ready to send them out on their own.

The disciples' message was to be the same as that of John the Baptist and of Christ Himself. During His ministry, Jesus devoted more time to healing the sick than to preaching. The followers of Christ, then and now, are to labor as He did. The love of Christ, manifested in unselfish ministry, will be more effective in reclaiming sinners than any attempt to force them to do right.

On their first missionary tour, the disciples were to go only to "the lost sheep of the house of Israel" (Matthew 10:6). Also, they were to go only where Jesus had been before them and had made friends. Nothing must be allowed to divert their minds from their great work or in any way excite opposition that would close the door for further labor.

Key Thought: "The disciples might speak fluently on doctrines, they might repeat the words of Christ Himself; but unless they possessed Christlike meekness and love, they were not confessing Him. A spirit contrary to the spirit of Christ would deny Him, whatever the profession. Men may deny Christ by evilspeaking, by foolish talking, by words that are untruthful or unkind. They may deny Him by shunning life's burdens, by the pursuit of sinful pleasure. They may deny Him by conforming to the world, by uncourteous behavior, by the love of their own opinions, by justifying self, by cherishing doubt, borrowing trouble, and dwelling in darkness. In all these ways they declare that Christ is not in them. And 'whosoever shall deny Me before men,' He says, 'him will I also deny before My Father which is in heaven' " (*The Desire of Ages,* p. 357).

Today's Lesson: We need to examine ourselves daily to make sure we are truly representing the truth as it is in Jesus.

Come Rest Awhile

The Desire of Ages, Chapter 38.

"Come ye yourselves apart into a desert place, and rest a while" (Mark 6:31).

After the disciples returned from their first missionary tour, Jesus knew they needed to rest and discuss their experiences. They discussed their successes and failures, and their Teacher knew how to help them relate to both. Besides, Jesus knew that it is not wise always to be under the strain of work and excitement; in this way, personal piety is often neglected, and the powers of mind and soul and body are overtaxed.

Jesus Himself longed for quiet time with His disciples, free from the pressing crowds. One of the lessons Jesus knew the disciples needed was to remember that it is easy to take personal credit for success. Spiritual pride is one of Satan's temptations. As activity increases and men and women become successful in doing any work for God, there is danger of trusting to their own human plans and methods.

But one of the most important reasons for this spiritual retreat was to contemplate the sudden death of John the Baptist. Jesus needed time to think through the gathering shadows and to help His disciples think through all the implications of the coming troubles. This "rest" was not a picnic. The little group had much to talk about.

Key Thought: "In a life wholly devoted to the good of others, the Saviour found it necessary to withdraw from the thoroughfares of travel and from the throng that followed Him day after day. He must turn aside from a life of ceaseless activity and contact with human needs, to seek retirement and unbroken communion with His Father. As one with us, a sharer in our needs and weaknesses, He was wholly dependent upon God, and in the secret place of prayer He sought divine strength, that He might go forth braced for duty and trial. In a world of sin Jesus endured struggles and torture of soul. In communion with God He could unburden the sorrows that were crushing Him. Here He found comfort and joy" (*The Desire of Ages,* pp. 362, 363).

Today's Lesson: In the rhythm of life, work must be balanced by appropriate periods of rest. Both are needed for us to be effective in God's plan.

"Give Ye Them to Eat"

The Desire of Ages, Chapter 39.

"And they took up twelve baskets full of fragments and of the fish. Now those who had eaten the loaves were about five thousand men" (Mark 6:43, 44, NKJV).

The rest that Jesus and the disciples needed was interrupted by the multitudes, who were looking for them. Pilgrims on the way to Jerusalem to celebrate the Passover joined with Galileans, until about five thousand men, plus women and children, had gathered to hear Jesus. Mark observed that Jesus had compassion on the multitude.

The day wore on as Jesus held their attention with His fresh thoughts about God and their relationship to Him. Finally, it became obvious that everyone was hungry. No shops were in sight, of course, and Jesus told the disciples to give the crowd the food they needed. This was a test of their faith. The disciples could find only a boy with five barley loaves and two fishes. Nevertheless, Jesus directed the disciples to have the people be seated in groups of fifty and a hundred. Then He blessed the loaves and fishes and distributed them to the disciples, who passed the food to the huge crowd—until all were fed!

Jesus could have prepared a grand buffet, but He didn't want to attract people to Him by gratifying their desire for luxury. Instead, He demonstrated that selfish gratification and overindulgence are a curse on spiritual life.

Key Thought: "The disciples were the channel of communication between Christ and the people. This should be a great encouragement to His disciples today. Christ is the great center, the source of all strength. His disciples are to receive their supplies from Him. The most intelligent, the most spiritually minded, can bestow only as they receive. Of themselves they can supply nothing for the needs of the soul. We can impart only that which we receive from Christ; and we can receive only as we impart to others. As we continue imparting, we continue to receive; and the more we impart, the more we shall receive. Thus we may be constantly believing, trusting, receiving, and imparting" (*The Desire of Ages,* p. 370).

Today's Lesson: It requires determination and watchfulness to avoid letting our lives be ruled by selfish indulgence.

A Night on the Lake

The Desire of Ages, Chapter 40.

"Be of good cheer! It is I; do not be afraid"
(Matthew 14:27, NKJV).

While the grateful multitude were eating the meal Jesus had provided, certain individuals were encouraging the crowd that the time had come for Jesus to reveal Himself as the Messiah and assume the leadership of Israel. Jesus had captured the public's attention, they argued, and now He had shown that He could feed an entire army if necessary, as well as heal their wounds.

The disciples, no doubt, encouraged this grassroots support. But Jesus knew all this would only complicate further His mission on earth. Even then the priests and rulers were seeking an excuse to kill Him, accusing Him of drawing people away from them. The movement had to be checked, and Jesus ordered His disciples to leave at once in their boats while He dismissed the people.

Never had a command from Jesus seem so impossible to obey! The disciples protested, but Jesus spoke with authority. It was painful to Jesus that their understanding of His kingdom was so limited. Turning to the multitudes, Jesus commanded the people to disperse; their words of praise and exaltation died on their lips.

While on the lake, the minds of the disciples were as troubled as the growing storm. They seemed quickly to have forgotten the amazing miracle of a few hours before. But when the storm overwhelmed them, they longed for their Master.

And at the very moment they felt all was lost, Jesus appeared. Once more, the disciples had good reason to keep trusting Him.

Key Thought: "We may now suppose that our feet stand secure, and that we shall never be moved. We may say with confidence, 'I know in whom I have believed; nothing can shake my faith in God and in His word.' But Satan is planning to take advantage of our hereditary and cultivated traits of character, and to blind our eyes to our own necessities and defects. Only through realizing our own weakness and looking steadfastly unto Jesus can we walk securely" (*The Desire of Ages,* p. 382).

Today's Lesson: We need to examine our motives continually to make sure we are relating correctly to God's plan for our lives.

The Crisis in Galilee

The Desire of Ages, Chapter 41.

"Most assuredly, I say to you, you seek Me, not because you saw the signs, but because you ate of the loaves and were filled. Do not labor for the food which perishes, but for the food which endures to everlasting life, which the Son of Man will give you, because God the Father has set His seal on Him" (John 6:26, 27, NKJV).

When Christ forbade the people to declare Him king, He knew that His life had reached a turning point. Multitudes who desired to exalt Him to the throne today would turn from Him tomorrow. The disappointment of their selfish ambition would change their love to hatred and their praise to curses. Yet knowing this, He took no measures to avert the crisis.

The miracle of the loaves and fishes was reported everywhere, and even more people flocked to see Jesus. In His first remarks, He pointed out that His hearers weren't seeking Him from worthy motives—they hoped to receive temporal benefit by attaching themselves to Him.

Then Jesus led them into a discussion of what mattered most in genuine service for God. He tried to turn their minds from physical bread to the "Bread of Life"—Himself—which had come down from heaven to feed them spiritually (see John 6:35, 48, 51). The rabbis argued and ridiculed; the multitudes turned away disaffected. His disciples alone remained. They had nowhere else to go. Jesus had given them a picture of God they had never seen before.

Key Thought: "They had seen Christ by the witness of the Holy Spirit, by the revelation of God to their souls. The living evidences of His power had been before them day after day, yet they asked for still another sign. Had this been given, they would have remained as unbelieving as before. If they were not convinced by what they had seen and heard, it was useless to show them more marvelous works. Unbelief will ever find excuse for doubt, and will reason away the most positive proof" (*The Desire of Ages,* p. 386).

Today's Lesson: We may not fully understand God's leading in our life. We may suffer disappointment. But in the end, there is no alternative to trusting Jesus.

JULY 6

Tradition

The Desire of Ages, Chapter 42.

"Out of the heart proceed evil thoughts, murders, adulteries, fornications, thefts, false witness, blasphemies. These are the things which defile a man, but to eat with unwashed hands does not defile a man" *(Matthew 15:19, 20, NKJV).*

The scribes and Pharisees kept laying traps for Jesus over such matters as Sabbath breaking, but now they focused on His apparent disregard for the traditions they believed guarded the observance of God's law. Among the requirements they enforced most strenuously were the ones regarding ceremonial purification—especially those that had to do with food.

The ceremonies regarding food and eating were numberless. As long as people were occupied with trifling distinctions that God had not required, their attention was turned away from the great principles of the law. Christ and His disciples did not observe these ceremonial washings. Jesus made no attempt to defend Himself or His disciples when accused by the religious leaders. Rather, He exposed the attitude of those who were such sticklers for human rules. He specifically pointed out their hypocritical attitude toward honoring parents—the fifth commandment—compared to their zealous concern for ritual washings. He accused them of placing their requirements above the divine precepts. He explained that defilement comes from within—not from without. It is the evil deed, the evil thought, not the neglect of external, man-made ceremonies, that defiles men and women.

Key Thought: "Whenever the message of truth comes home to souls with special power, Satan stirs up his agents to start a dispute over some minor question. . . . Whenever a good work is begun, there are cavilers ready to enter into dispute over forms or technicalities, to draw minds away from the living realities. When it appears that God is about to work in a special manner for His people, let them not be enticed into a controversy that will work only ruin of souls. The questions that most concern us are, Do I believe with saving faith on the Son of God? Is my life in harmony with the divine law?" (*The Desire of Ages,* p. 396).

Today's Lesson: Although the details may be different, it is just as easy today to focus on insignificant questions of little importance, while neglecting important spiritual issues.

Barriers Broken Down

The Desire of Ages, Chapter 43.

" 'O woman, great is your faith! Let it be to you as you desire.' And her daughter was healed from that very hour" (Matthew 15:28, NKJV).

After the encounter with the Pharisees over man-made ceremonies, Jesus withdrew from the turmoil to the borders of Phoenicia, where the great port cities of Tyre and Sidon were located. Again, He desired to spend some time in rest with His disciples, but His main purpose was to help them understand that the gospel was to be preached to Gentiles, as well as to the Jews.

Even before He began His journey, Jesus was aware of the mother with a sick daughter. He knew she had heard of Him and His healing ministry, and He deliberately put Himself in her path. Jesus also knew that the disciples, like their fellow Israelites, possessed a Jewish pride that looked down on others and that they had little sympathy with the heathen world. These barriers He was determined to break down.

How did He do it? He gave the disciples a living demonstration of their typical Jewish coldness to a Gentile's request for help. When the Gentile mother requested healing for her daughter, Jesus did not respond. Indeed, He seemed to push her away. But the woman did not lose faith. She persevered, and her faith was rewarded. Through His careful treatment of this woman, Jesus led the disciples to see that He was sent not only to the lost sheep of the house of Israel but to the whole world. Those the disciples considered outcasts were also children in God's household.

The same attitudes that tried to bar certain individuals from Christ are still at work today. Whenever pride and prejudice continue to separate people, we can be sure that we are not following Christ.

Key Thought: "Caste is hateful to God. He ignores everything of this character. In His sight the souls of all men are of equal value. . . . Without distinction of age, or rank, or nationality, or religious privilege, all are invited to come unto Him and live" (*The Desire of Ages,* p. 403).

Today's Lesson: Followers of Christ today have a responsibility to stand forthrightly against prejudice and discrimination in all its forms.

The True Sign

The Desire of Ages, Chapter 44.

"Then they understood that He did not tell them to beware of the leaven of bread, but of the doctrine of the Pharisees and Sadducees" (Mathew 16:12, NKJV).

Jesus returned to Galilee after being refreshed by the confiding trust of the Syro-phoenician woman and the gratitude of the heathen people of Decapolis. But here in Galilee, among fellow Jews and in the very place where most of His miraculous works had been performed, He was met with contemptuous unbelief.

Here, the Pharisees and Sadducees, always at odds with each other, were united against Christ. They asked Him for a sign from heaven. But already He had given them many signs that confirmed His mission. Every miracle He had performed, the healing of the sick and raising the dead, were signs of His divinity.

The highest evidence that He came from God, however, was the way that His life revealed God's character. Such a godly life is the greatest of all miracles. Jesus did not use His power to vindicate Himself or to satisfy the demands of unbelief and pride. Neither does He give such power to us. The change in heart, the transformation of human character, is a miracle that reveals the power of an eternal Savior. A consistent Christian life is the greatest of miracles.

The disciples wanted Jesus to grant the leaders' demand for a sign. They knew He was fully able to provide some miraculous performance and silence His enemies. The disciples were in danger of cherishing the same self-seeking and self-glorification that so motivated the Pharisees and Sadducees.

Key Thought: "Among the followers of our Lord today, as of old, how widespread is this subtle, deceptive sin! How often our service to Christ, our communion with one another, is marred by the secret desire to exalt self! How ready the thought of self-gratulation, and the longing for human approval! It is the love of self, the desire for an easier way than God has appointed that leads to the substitution of human theories and traditions for the divine precepts" (*The Desire of Ages,* p. 409).

Today's Lesson: Only the power of God in the life can eradicate the human longing for approval and the selfishness of the human heart.

The Foreshadowing of the Cross

The Desire of Ages, Chapter 45.

***"If anyone desires to come after Me, let him deny himself,
and take up his cross, and follow Me"
(Matthew 16:24, NKJV).***

Jesus saw clearly the path from the manger to Calvary. He knew the sorrow that lay ahead, yet He kept His eyes on the final results of His mission. He was encouraged by the realization that His suffering would bring eternal blessings to the world.

Jesus was almost ready to tell the disciples more clearly about the things that lay ahead. But first, He gave them an opportunity to renew their confession of faith in Him so that they would be strengthened for the dark days lying just ahead. He asked them the question, "Whom do men say that I the Son of man am?" (Mathew 16:13).

Peter expressed the convictions of the twelve: "Thou art the Christ, the Son of the living God" (verse 16). But they were still far from understanding Christ's mission. Peter's confession is the foundation of the believer's faith. Jesus is the rock, the foundation of the church, and if we build upon His promises and strength, we can never be overthrown.

Then Jesus told them plainly of the humiliation and sufferings that lay ahead for Him. The disciples were speechless with grief and amazement; Christ's words seemed incomprehensible to them. Jesus went on to tell them that His life of sacrifice was an example of what their life should be. Selfishness leads to eternal death, but self-sacrifice means life evermore.

Key Thought: "After Peter's confession, Jesus charged the disciples to tell no man that He was the Christ. This charge was given because of the determined opposition of the scribes and Pharisees. More than this, the people, and even the disciples, had so false a conception of the Messiah that a public announcement of Him would give them no true idea of His character or His work. But day by day He was revealing Himself to them as the Saviour, and thus He desired to give them a true conception of Him as the Messiah" (*The Desire of Ages,* p. 414).

Today's Lesson: As followers of Jesus, we are to walk the same path of self-denial that He was willing to walk for us.

He Was Transfigured

The Desire of Ages, Chapter 46.

"Behold, Moses and Elijah appeared to them, talking with Him" (Matthew 17:3, NKJV).

Both Jesus and the disciples were very weary as He led the little group up a lonely mountain. Soon, Jesus drew apart and began to pray, even weeping as He prayed and reached out to His heavenly Father for strength to face the future. He had seen how downcast the disciples had been after He talked to them plainly about what lay ahead. Now He longed to give them some assurance that their faith in Him was not misplaced; He longed to strengthen their belief. But only Peter, James, and John were ready to receive the revelation He wanted to give them.

There on the mountainside, the Savior's prayer was suddenly answered. The gates of heaven were thrown open wide, and Jesus was bathed in a heavenly radiance. Peter, James, and John saw two figures—Moses and Elijah—standing near their Master. Before their excited gaze, the future kingdom of glory was represented in miniature—Christ the King, Moses, representing the risen saints, and Elijah, representing those who will be taken to heaven without dying.

The disciples misread the scene, but they rejoiced that their Teacher was honored by these heavenly messengers. They thought that Elijah had come to announce the Messiah's reign and that Jesus was about to set up His kingdom on the earth. Peter enthusiastically suggested they build some kind of memorial to this blessed occasion.

The other disciples were overcome with sleep and missed the amazing sight.

Key Thought: "Before the crown must come the cross. Not the inauguration of Christ as king, but the decease to be accomplished at Jerusalem, is the subject of their conference with Jesus. . . . Moses and Elijah. . . . had shared His longing for the salvation of men. . . . These men, chosen above every angel around the throne, had come to commune with Jesus concerning the scenes of His suffering, and to comfort Him with the assurance of the sympathy of heaven" (*The Desire of Ages,* pp. 422, 425).

Today's Lesson: If we could penetrate the veil separating heaven from earth, we would realize how close the connection is between the two and how real the unseen world actually is.

Ministry

The Desire of Ages, Chapter 47.

***"Tell the vision to no man, until the Son of man be risen
again from the dead" (Matthew 17:9).***

When Jesus and the disciples left the mountain, they were met by
the usual crowd. Jesus had already told His disciples not to tell
anyone about what had happened that night; he knew it would
only invite ridicule or idle wonder.

Jesus found a tense situation awaiting Him at the foot of the
mountain. Some of His disciples who had not been with Him the night
before were much troubled because they weren't able to cast out the
evil spirit from a boy. They had done so on their recent missionary
tour—why not now? They felt humiliated, and the scribes were making
the most of their defeat. Jesus sensed the tension as He approached.

The boy's father turned to Jesus, pleading for his son. "If thou canst
believe," Jesus told him, "all things are possible to him that believeth"
(Mark 9:23). Jesus was saying, "I have the power. Your son's healing
depends on your faith—not my power."

With a burst of tears, the father casts himself upon Christ's mercy,
crying, "Lord, I believe; help thou mine unbelief" (verse 24). Jesus
commanded the evil spirit to leave. The demon flung the boy to the
ground, lifeless, but Jesus lifted him up and presented him to his
grateful father.

Every troubled person has voiced that father's plea. And Jesus hears
and responds. But why did the disciples fail? Christ's answer was that
their faith was not deep enough. They had become careless in their
sacred work. They needed to empty self and depend entirely on God.

Key Thought: "It is faith that connects us with heaven, and brings
us strength for coping with the powers of darkness. In Christ, God has
provided means for subduing every sinful trait, and resisting every
temptation, however strong. But many feel that they lack faith, and
therefore they remain away from Christ. . . . He who healed the sick
and cast out demons when He walked among men is the same mighty
Redeemer today. Faith comes by the word of God" (*The Desire of
Ages,* p. 429).

Today's Lesson: Carelessness in daily devotions and prayer leads
to failure in serving God.

Who Is the Greatest?

The Desire of Ages, Chapter 48.

"Whosoever therefore shall humble himself as this little child, the same is greatest in the kingdom of heaven"
(Matthew 18:4).

Even though they had been with Jesus for at least two years, the disciples were still arguing over status. Jesus knew the strife this was causing and told them plainly, "If any man desire to be first, the same shall be last of all, and servant of all" (Mark 9:35).

The disciples still didn't understand the nature of Christ's kingdom, and this misunderstanding fueled their contention and jockeying for position. Their struggle for the highest places was the outworking of the same spirit that Lucifer had manifested in initiating the great controversy in heaven. Had Lucifer really desired to be like the Most High, he would never have deserted his appointed place in heaven, for the spirit of the Most High is manifested in unselfish ministry. Lucifer desired God's power but not His character.

Looking at these issues as Satan does, control becomes the prize of the strongest. The kingdom of Satan is a kingdom of force; each individual regards every other as an obstacle in the way of his or her own advancement or a steppingstone on which he or she may climb to a higher place. But in Christ's kingdom, the greatest is the one who is most willing to serve.

Key Thought: "Before honor is humility. To fill a high place before men, Heaven chooses the worker who, like John the Baptist, takes a lowly place before God. The most childlike disciple is the most efficient in labor for God. The heavenly intelligences can co-operate with him who is seeking, not to exalt self, but to save souls. He who feels most deeply his need of divine aid will plead for it; and the Holy Spirit will give unto him glimpses of Jesus that will strengthen and uplift the soul. From communion with Christ he will go forth . . . and . . . succeeds where many of the learned and intellectually wise would fail" (*The Desire of Ages,* p. 436).

Today's Lesson: The last sin, the last habit to be overcome, is the desire to be first, to be especially honored. Pride is a subtle defect that is most hard to detect.

At the Feast of Tabernacles

The Desire of Ages, Chapter 49.

"If any man thirst, let him come unto me, and drink"
(John 7:37).

The most impressive ceremony of the Feast of Tabernacles was a commemoration of the time in the wilderness journey when water had gushed from a rock to quench Israel's thirst.

Three times a year, Jews were required to assemble in Jerusalem for religious purposes. From all lands where they had been dispersed, Jewish people had come to Jerusalem for the Feast of Tabernacles. They had heard the reports of Jesus' miracles in their home countries, and many were hoping and expecting that He would be present at the feast. And after the feast had begun, He did make His appearance. As He taught, He gave evidence of His knowledge of Israel's laws and institutions. Day by day He taught the people, and on the last day of the feast, He called out, "If any man thirst, let him come unto me, and drink" (John 7:37).

Hearts were thrilled with a strange awe at His words. Many were ready to cry out with the Samaritan woman, "Give me this water, that I thirst not" (John 4:15).

Key Thought: "Jesus knew the wants of the soul. Pomp, riches, and honor cannot satisfy the heart. . . . The rich, the poor, the high, the low, are alike welcome. . . . Many of those who heard Jesus were mourners over disappointed hopes, many were nourishing a secret grief, many were seeking to satisfy their restless longing with the things of the world and the praise of men; but when all was gained, they found that they had toiled only to reach a broken cistern, from which they could not quench their thirst. Amid the glitter of the joyous scene they stood, dissatisfied and sad. That sudden cry, 'If any man thirst,' startled them from their sorrowful meditation, and as they listened to the words that followed, their minds kindled with a new hope. The Holy Spirit presented the symbol before them until they saw in it the offer of the priceless gift of salvation" (*The Desire of Ages,* p. 454).

Today's Lesson: Just as water is essential to physical life, so Jesus, the "Water of Life," is essential to our spiritual survival.

JULY 14

Among Snares

The Desire of Ages, Chapter 50.

"If anyone wants to do His will, he shall know concerning the doctrine, whether it is from God or whether I speak on My own authority" (John 7:17, NKJV).

Jesus taught that the perception and appreciation of truth depends less upon the mind than upon the heart. That is, truth must be received into the soul, where it claims the homage of the will. If truth could be submitted to the reason alone, pride would be no hindrance to its reception.

More than this, truth is to be received through the work of grace in the heart. Its reception depends on our willingness to renounce every sin that the Spirit of God reveals to us. Jesus said that those who are eager to know and follow truth will be able to distinguish between the one who speaks for God and the one who speaks merely for himself.

Then He gave a test by which we may distinguish the true teacher from the deceiver: If a person is trying to turn attention on himself and build up himself, he is not speaking for God. The spirit of self-seeking betrays its origin.

Jesus gave the rabbis an evidence of His divinity by showing them He could read their hearts: "Why go ye about to kill Me?" he asked (John 7:19). Like a flash of light these words revealed the great plunge into darkness they were about to make.

The question for the Jewish leaders was: "Is this truth?" not "Who is advocating this?" This is the question for us, as well.

Key Thought: "The human mind is endowed with power to discriminate between right and wrong. God designs that men shall not decide from impulse, but from weight of evidence, carefully comparing scripture with scripture. Had the Jews laid by their prejudice and compared written prophecy with the facts characterizing the life of Jesus, they would have perceived a beautiful harmony between the prophecies and their fulfillment in the life and ministry of the lowly Galilean" (*The Desire of Ages,* p. 458).

Today's Lesson: The truthfulness of a message is not determined by who is accepting it or by how many are accepting it. Rather, we should ask, "Is this message in harmony with God's Word?"

"The Light of Life"

The Desire of Ages, Chapter 51.

"I am the light of the world: he that followeth me shall not walk in darkness, but shall have the light of life"
(John 8:12).

At the evening sacrifice throughout the week of the Feast of Tabernacles, all the lamps in the temple court were lighted. This illumination symbolized the hope of the Jews that the Messiah would come to shed His light upon Israel.

One morning during the feast, Jesus pointed to the rising sun and declared that He was the Light of the world. The people could not fail to connect these words with Isaiah's prophecy (Isaiah 49:6) and to understand that Jesus was claiming to be the Messiah.

To the Pharisees and rulers, this was an arrogant claim, and they challenged Him. In response He referred to the Scriptures and told all those listening that the truth would make them free (see John 8:32). These words also offended the Pharisees, who were unwilling to consider the truth.

God always leaves men and women to choose whom they will serve. But when a person surrenders to Christ, there is the highest sense of freedom. The expulsion of sin is the act of the soul itself. When we desire to be set free, the powers of the soul are imbued with the divine energy of the Holy Spirit, and we obey the dictates of our will in fulfilling the will of God. This new freedom that we find in subjecting ourselves to God restores our true glory and dignity; we become what God intended humanity to be.

Key Thought: "Christ had come to open the blind eyes, to give light to them that sit in darkness. He had declared Himself to be the light of the world. . . . The people who beheld the Saviour at His advent were favored with a fuller manifestation of the divine presence than the world had ever enjoyed before. The knowledge of God was revealed more perfectly. But in this very revelation, judgment was passing upon men. Their character was tested, their destiny determined" (*The Desire of Ages,* p. 475).

Today's Lesson: Following the light is a never-ending journey in which we become more and more what God would have us to be.

The Divine Shepherd

The Desire of Ages, Chapter 52.

"I am the good shepherd, and know my sheep, and am known of mine" (John 10:14).

Jesus always found access to the minds of His hearers by the pathway of their familiar associations, whether it be water, light, seeds, or harvests. This time He used the illustration of a shepherd and his sheep.

Christ is the door to God's sheepfold. All His children, from the earliest times, have found entrance through Him. The Pharisees and rulers had not yet entered that door. They had been climbing into the fold by another way than Christ.

In all ages, philosophers and teachers have been presenting theories to satisfy the soul's need—some other means of redemption than Christ. At the same time, they have been filling the hearts of men and women with either a slavish fear of God or cold indifference to Him.

Of all creatures the sheep is one of the most timid and helpless, making the shepherd's care for his flock untiring and incessant. However large the flock, the shepherd knows every sheep. Every one has a name and responds to its name at the shepherd's call.

So, Jesus knows us individually and is touched with our troubles. He knows the very house in which we live, as if we were the only one for whom He died. The way to heaven is imprinted by the Savior's feet, and though the path may be steep and rugged, He knows exactly what we need to keep walking heavenward.

Best of all, unless we choose to leave Him, He will hold us fast. We have a never-failing Helper.

Key Thought: "It is not the fear of punishment, or the hope of everlasting reward, that leads the disciples of Christ to follow Him. They behold the Saviour's matchless love, revealed throughout His pilgrimage on earth, from the manger of Bethlehem to Calvary's cross, and the sight of Him attracts, it softens and subdues the soul. Love awakens in the heart of the beholders. They hear His voice, and they follow Him" (*The Desire of Ages,* p. 480).

Today's Lesson: When we go through tough times, whatever they may be, we can be sure that Jesus will provide just what we need to endure to the end.

The Last Journey From Galilee

The Desire of Ages, Chapter 53.

"The Son of Man did not come to destroy men's lives but to save them" (Luke 9:56, NKJV).

A s the close of His ministry drew near, Jesus changed His method of teaching and healing. Before, He had shunned excitement and publicity. But now He left Galilee and returned to Jerusalem openly. The attention of the people needed to be drawn to the sacrifice He was about to make.

This was not an easy time for the Savior. The disciples' unbelief caused Him pain, and Satan was always present to press temptations upon Him. Why should He go to Jerusalem to certain death? There were many in Galilee who were longing for His messages and His healing. He had just begun His ministry; He was a young man!

But had Jesus yielded, even for a moment, in order to save Himself, Satan would have triumphed, and the world would have been lost. The one law of Jesus' life was obedience to His Father's will.

When the Samaritans refused Him lodging, the disciples wanted to call down fire from heaven to consume them! But Jesus gave them another lesson in the big picture of the great controversy—God never compels. It is Satan, and those actuated by his spirit, who try to force the conscience. There is no more conclusive evidence that we possess the spirit of Satan than the desire to hurt and destroy those who do not appreciate our work or who act contrary to our ideas.

Key Thought: "Every warning, reproof, and entreaty in the word of God or through His messengers is a knock at the door of the heart. It is the voice of Jesus asking for entrance. With every knock unheeded, the disposition to open becomes weaker. The impressions of the Holy Spirit if disregarded today, will not be as strong tomorrow. . . . Our condemnation in the judgment will not result from the fact that we have been in error, but from the fact that we have neglected heaven-sent opportunities for learning what is truth" (*The Desire of Ages,* p. 490).

Today's Lesson: We can focus too much on Satan's power. Why not talk of the wonderful love of Jesus and the grace He offers?

JULY 18

The Good Samaritan

The Desire of Ages, Chapter 54.

**"Which of these three do you think was neighbor to him
who fell among the thieves?" (Luke 10:36, NKJV).**

In the story of the Good Samaritan, Christ illustrates the nature
of true religion. He shows that it consists not in systems, creeds,
or rites, but in the performance of loving deeds—in bringing the
greatest good to others in genuine concern.

The story Jesus told was no imaginary scene—it was something that
had actually happened and that His hearers knew to have taken place
just as Jesus told it. In fact, the priest and the Levite who had passed
by on the other side were in the crowd listening to Christ's words!

The Jews recognized that God had instructed them to love their
neighbor as themselves. But they could not agree on who was included
as a "neighbor." Obviously, they argued, non-Jews were not neighbors,
but did God's command include even all classes of Jews? Were the
ignorant and ceremonially unclean to be considered "neighbors?"
Jesus told the story of the Good Samaritan to answer this very issue.
In doing so, He drove home the fact that everyone who needs our help
is our "neighbor."

Christ showed that our neighbor does not mean merely someone
who is of the same church or faith to which we belong. "Neighbor"
does not refer to race, color, or class distinction. Our neighbor is
every person who is wounded and bruised by Satan. Our neighbor is
everyone who is the property of God.

Key Thought: "The lesson is no less needed in the world today
than when it fell from the lips of Jesus. Selfishness and cold formality
have well-nigh extinguished the fire of love, and dispelled the graces
that should make fragrant the character. Many who profess His name
have lost sight of the fact that Christians are to represent Christ.
Unless there is practical self-sacrifice for the good of others, in the
family circle, in the neighborhood, in the church, and wherever we
may be, then whatever our profession, we are not Christians" (*The
Desire of Ages,* p. 504).

Today's Lesson: As Christians, we can never pass by human
beings in distress and feel that it is of no concern to us.

Not With Outward Show

The Desire of Ages, Chapter 55.

"The kingdom of God does not come with observation; nor will they say, 'See here!' or 'See there!' For indeed, the kingdom of God is within you" (Luke 17:20, 21, NKJV).

More than three years had passed since John the Baptist had appeared and announced that the kingdom of God was at hand (see Matthew 3:2). Many of those who rejected John and had been opposing Jesus were insinuating that His mission had failed. Even the disciples had not yet fully comprehended His work. They had been searching the prophetic Scriptures diligently, but they could not connect Jesus in His humiliation with their expectation of what the Messiah would look like.

But all that changed after Calvary and Pentecost. It is as true now as in apostolic days that without the illumination of the divine Spirit, humanity cannot discern the glory of Christ. The truth and the work of God are unappreciated by a world-loving and compromising Christianity. The kingdom of God comes not with outward show.

Even today, multitudes are working to establish God's kingdom according to their own ideas. They expect His kingdom to come through legal enactments, enforced by human authority. Though the government in Christ's day was corrupt and oppressive, He attempted no civil reforms—not because He was indifferent to the institutionalized abuses around Him but because the remedy could come only through regenerated hearts.

Now, as in Christ's day, the work of God's kingdom lies not with those who are clamoring for recognition and support by earthly rulers and human laws but with those who are declaring to the people in His name those spiritual truths that will really change society.

Key Thought: "Not by the decisions of courts or councils or legislative assemblies, not by the patronage of worldly great men, is the kingdom of Christ established, but by the implanting of Christ's nature in humanity through the work of the Holy Spirit. . . . Here is the only power that can work the uplifting of mankind. And the human agency for the accomplishment of this work is the teaching and practicing of the word of God" (*The Desire of Ages,* pp. 509, 510).

Today's Lesson: God works to change society through changing individual human hearts.

Blessing the Children

The Desire of Ages, Chapter 56.

**"Let the little children come to Me, and do not forbid them;
for of such is the kingdom of heaven"
(Matthew 19:14, NKJV).**

Jesus loved children, and they loved Him. They were drawn to Him by His gentle, kindly attitude. They enjoyed being in His presence, and their sincerity refreshed His spirit.

Our Savior understood the care and burden of mothers who were seeking to train their children according to God's Word. He, Himself, had drawn them into His presence. Several women made known their desire to have Jesus bless their children, but the disciples tried to send them away. They thought that in doing so they were protecting the Master. However, Jesus gladly laid His hands on the children and blessed them, bringing a new cheerfulness to their mothers. Mothers today can receive Jesus' words, believing that He will bless their children also.

Jesus knows the burden of every parent's heart. He had earthly parents who struggled with poverty. He traveled a great distance to relieve the anxious heart of a Canaanite woman. He gave back to the widow of Nain her only son.

Jesus knew that children would listen to Him, because in His teaching He came down to their level. He planted in their minds the seeds of truth, which in later years would spring up and bear fruit unto eternal life.

Key Thought: "Let not your un-Christlike character misrepresent Jesus. Do not keep the little ones away from Him by your coldness and harshness. Never give them cause to feel that heaven will not be a pleasant place to them if you are there. Do not speak of religion as something that children cannot understand, or act as if they were not expected to accept Christ in their childhood. Do not give them the false impression that the religion of Christ is a religion of gloom, and that in coming to the Saviour they must give up all that makes life joyful" (*The Desire of Ages,* p. 517).

Today's Lesson: Parents should give their children every spiritual advantage that will help them form Christlike characters. Just because they are not yet mature doesn't mean that boys and girls may not understand God's love and truly love Him in return.

"One Thing Thou Lackest"

The Desire of Ages, Chapter 57.

"But when the young man heard that saying, he went away sorrowful: for he had great possessions"
(Matthew 19:22).

Deeply moved by Christ's words and His record of healing, the rich, young ruler desired to be one of His disciples. When Jesus passed nearby, he ran to Him and knelt at His feet, asking, "Good Master, what good thing shall I do, that I may have eternal life?" (Matthew 19:16).

The young man had a high estimate of his own righteousness; yet, he was not altogether satisfied. Jesus looked into his face and loved him, knowing that he was sincere. Further, He saw that he could be just the help He needed. In a marked degree the ruler could have represented Jesus. He possessed qualifications which, if he united himself with Jesus, would enable him to become a spiritual force among men.

However, he lacked one thing—he needed the love of God in his soul. To receive God's love, he must surrender his supreme love of self. Jesus gave him a test to which self must yield. The ruler quickly saw the importance of Christ's word, and he became sad, for riches were his idol. To give up his earthly assets for unseen, heavenly treasure was too great a risk.

Key Thought: "Christ's dealing with the young man is presented as an object lesson. God has given us the rule of conduct which every one of His servants must follow. It is obedience to His law, not merely a legal obedience, but an obedience which enters into the life, and is exemplified in the character. God has set His own standard of character for all who would become subjects of His kingdom. Only those who will become co-workers with Christ, only those who will say, Lord, all I have and all I am is Thine, will be acknowledged as sons and daughters of God. . . . He offers to use the means God has given us, to carry forward His work in the world. Only in this way can He save us" (*The Desire of Ages,* p. 523).

Today's Lesson: The same invitation—and demand—that Jesus made to the rich young ruler, He offers to all. Jesus has no favorites.

JULY 22

"Lazarus, Come Forth"

The Desire of Ages, Chapter 58.

" 'Lord, if he sleeps he will get well.' Then Jesus said to them plainly, 'Lazarus is dead' " (John 11:12, 14, NKJV).

In Bethany, at the home of Lazarus and his two sisters, Jesus often found the rest He needed and a respite from the suspicion and jealousy of the angry Pharisees. Here He could speak freely, with simplicity, and know that He would be understood. He didn't need to speak to them in parables. Mary often sat at Jesus' feet, eagerly listening, while Martha bustled about seeing to everyone's comfort.

Sorrow came to their home when Lazarus became severely ill. The sisters sent word to Jesus, knowing that He would be most concerned. He sent back the message that this sickness "is not unto death" (John 11:4). But Lazarus did die, and meanwhile, Jesus continued His usual ministry.

When Jesus finally reached Bethany four days after Lazarus had died, the sisters were in great distress. Jesus sorrowed with them, but He knew their faith would shine forth even stronger after He had performed the great miracle that lay ahead. Lazarus, his sisters, the disciples, and even the stubborn Jewish leaders would be given the most positive evidence that He was God and the Lifegiver.

Coming to the place of burial, Jesus commanded that the stone be rolled away from the tomb, and then in a loud voice, He called to His friend to come forth. And the dead man was raised to life!

Key Thought: "It was not only because of the scene before Him that Christ wept. The weight of the grief of ages was upon Him. . . . Looking down the years to come, He saw the suffering and sorrow, tears and death, that were to be the lot of men. His heart was pierced with the pain of the human family of all ages and in all lands. The woes of the sinful race were heavy upon His soul, and the fountain of His tears was broken up as He longed to relieve all their distress" (*The Desire of Ages,* p. 534).

Today's Lesson: The resurrection of Lazarus is a foretaste of what will happen when Jesus returns to earth and calls His sleeping saints to eternal life.

216

Priestly Plottings

The Desire of Ages, Chapter 59.

"Both the chief priests and the Pharisees had given a command, that if anyone knew where He was, he should report it, that they might seize Him" (John 11:57, NKJV).

The resurrection of Lazarus alarmed the Sadducees, who denied the possibility that the dead could be raised to life. The Pharisees, in contrast, believed in a resurrection, but they hated Jesus because He exposed their hypocritical pretensions. These groups of religious leaders were often at odds with one another. Now both Sadducees and Pharisees united in laying plans to seize Jesus and silence Him.

At the height of their angry discussion, Caiaphas, the high priest, rose to plead that it was better that one man should die rather than the whole nation be destroyed. Using all his persuasive powers and debating tactics, Caiaphas moved the group to agree that Jesus must be put to death. They dismissed the convictions that the Holy Spirit brought to their conscience and rationalized that killing Jesus was God's will. They were pleased with their decision. They regarded themselves as patriots seeking the nation's salvation.

But they didn't want to seize Jesus immediately, for fear of the people's reaction. Jesus knew of their plots and that they would eventually accomplish their purpose. Not wanting to hasten the crisis, He withdrew.

Key Thought: "At this council Christ's enemies had been deeply convicted. The Holy Spirit had impressed their minds. But Satan strove to gain control of them. He urged upon their notice the grievances they had suffered on account of Christ. . . . Taking no notice of their forms and ceremonies, He had encouraged sinners to go directly to God as a merciful Father, and make known their wants. Thus, in their opinion, He had set aside the priesthood. He had refused to acknowledge the theology of the rabbinical schools. He had exposed the evil practices of the priests, and had irreparably hurt their influence. . . . All this Satan now brought to their minds.

"Satan told them that in order to maintain their authority, they must put Jesus to death" (*The Desire of Ages,* pp. 540, 541).

Today's Lesson: In the great controversy, jealousy and hatred always lead to coercion and the destruction of truth.

The Law of the New Kingdom

The Desire of Ages, Chapter 60.

"Yet it shall not be so among you; but whoever desires to become great among you, let him be your servant" (Matthew 20:26, NKJV).

With the Passover approaching, Jesus knew that His betrayal and suffering was near. He explained this to the disciples more clearly than ever before, but they kept focusing on the kingdom they were sure He was about to set up on earth. They were sure it was near.

At this point, the mother of James and John entered the picture with a request that her sons should sit on Jesus' right and left in the coming kingdom. Jesus read this mother's heart. He knew her sons were deeply attached to Him. He didn't rebuke her request, but He placed it in a deeper context.

When the other disciples heard what James and John had requested through their mother, they were greatly displeased. After all, they all wanted those cherished seats! Strife was renewed as to who would be the greatest in God's kingdom.

Jesus told them that greatness in His kingdom was based on different principles than those of the world. Earthly kingdoms are based on influence, wealth, and power. But in the heavenly kingdom, position is based on service to others—best illustrated by Jesus Himself. Their desire for the highest positions reflected the kingdom of Satan.

Key Thought: "The principles and the very words of the Saviour's teaching, in their divine beauty, dwelt in the memory of the beloved disciple. To his latest days the burden of John's testimony to the churches was, 'This is the message that ye heard from the beginning, that we should love one another' [1 John 3:11].

"This was the spirit that pervaded the early church. After the outpouring of the Holy Spirit, 'the multitude of them that believed were of one heart and of one soul: neither said any of them that aught of the things which he possessed was his own.' 'Neither was there any among them that lacked' . . . Acts 4:32, 34" (*The Desire of Ages,* p. 551).

Today's Lesson: The principle of service from the heart is what Jesus demonstrated while on earth—and we are to pattern our lives after His example.

Zaccheus

The Desire of Ages, Chapter 61.

"Today salvation has come to this house, because he also is a son of Abraham; for the Son of Man has come to seek and to save that which was lost" (Luke 19:9, 10, NKJV).

Many caravans passed through Jericho on their way to the Passover. The news spread throughout the city that Jesus, who had resurrected Lazarus, was in the throng. Many in Jericho were eager to see Him.

Among these was Zaccheus, chief of the tax collectors, who was well detested by his fellow Jews. But in spite of his reputation, his heart was open to truth. He had heard John the Baptist preach about the need for repentance, and Zaccheus had been making restitution to those he had overcharged. Learning that Jesus was soon to pass his way, the short man climbed a tree in order to have a good view.

As he watched from his perch, Zaccheus saw Jesus and His disciples stop under his tree! In amazement he saw Jesus look up and call his name! He heard the Master ask to stay at his house that day! Love and loyalty to his newfound Master unsealed his lips, and Zaccheus publicly confessed his sins and promised to make more than a full restitution to those he had cheated. He did what the rich, young ruler could not bring himself to do.

Today, "holiness unto the Lord" should be written upon every financial transaction, every check, every account book. Those who are truly converted abandon all unrighteous practices—even if they may be legally sanctioned. He or she will make wrongs right.

Key Thought: "No sooner did Zaccheus yield to the influence of the Holy Spirit than he cast aside every practice contrary to integrity.

"No repentance is genuine that does not work reformation. The righteousness of Christ is not a cloak to cover unconfessed and unforsaken sin; it is a principle of life that transforms the character and controls the conduct. Holiness is wholeness for God; it is the entire surrender of heart and life to the indwelling of the principles of heaven" (*The Desire of Ages,* pp. 555, 556).

Today's Lesson: Christians should be known for their honesty and transparent business dealings, as well as strict integrity in all areas of life.

JULY 26

The Feast at Simon's House

The Desire of Ages, Chapter 62.

"Assuredly, I say to you, wherever this gospel is preached in the whole world, what this woman has done will also be told as a memorial to her" (Matthew 26:13, NKJV).

Simon of Bethany was one of the few Pharisees who had openly joined Christ's followers. He hoped Jesus was the Messiah, but he had not yet accepted Him as the Savior. Simon's character had not been transformed.

Jesus had healed him from leprosy, and it was this that had drawn him to Jesus. In gratitude, he prepared a feast in Jesus' honor. The disciples and prominent Jews of Simon's circle were invited. At the table, Jesus sat at one side of Simon, with Lazarus on the other. Martha was serving at the table, and Mary was eagerly listening to Jesus' words.

At great sacrifice, Mary had purchased an alabaster box of expensive perfume. As she anointed Jesus' head, the delicate fragrance of the perfume filled the room. Judas reacted immediately with displeasure, feeling it was a tremendous waste. Mary heard his criticism, but she also heard the Lord defend her and her generous act.

The look that Jesus cast upon Judas convinced him that Jesus penetrated his hypocrisy, and he determined to get his revenge by betraying Jesus to the Sanhedrin.

Simon himself had led Mary into sin. Jesus knew—and Simon knew that Jesus knew. On this occasion his pride was humbled.

Mary went on to be the first person to proclaim a risen Savior.

Key Thought: "Simon was touched by the kindness of Jesus in not openly rebuking him before the guests. He had not been treated as he desired Mary to be treated. He saw that Jesus did not wish to expose his guilt to others, but . . . by pitying kindness to subdue his heart. . . . He saw the magnitude of the debt which he owed his Lord. His pride was humbled, he repented, and the proud Pharisee became a lowly, self-sacrificing disciple" (*The Desire of Ages,* pp. 567, 568).

Today's Lesson: All of us—like both Simon and Mary—owe Christ a far greater debt of gratitude than we can ever appreciate or possibly repay. All we can give Him is our heart.

"Thy King Cometh"

The Desire of Ages, Chapter 63.

"This is Jesus, the prophet from Nazareth of Galilee"
(Matthew 21:11, NKJV).

On Sunday of the week that would end with His crucifixion, Jesus made His triumphal entry into Jerusalem. Hope for a new kingdom was springing up, and multitudes accompanied Him.

Previously, Jesus had walked from town to town, but now He rode into Jerusalem on a donkey colt, following the Jewish custom for a royal entry and fulfilling Zechariah's prophecy (see Zechariah 9:9). By this act, He proclaimed Himself to be Israel's king.

Lepers He had healed and blind men He had given sight—cripples, sinners, widows, and orphans whom He had forgiven and blessed—all these led the way and shouted His praises as He entered the city. Jesus now accepted homage that He had never before permitted, and the disciples received this as proof that their glad hopes were soon to be realized. But Jesus knew that the triumphal entry would bring Him to the Cross.

Also, the events of that day would cause many to search the prophecies and find the evidence for themselves that Jesus was indeed the Messiah.

Key Thought: "Jesus raised His hand,—that had so often blessed the sick and suffering,—and waving it toward the doomed city, . . . explained: 'If thou hadst known, even thou, at least in this thy day, the things which belong unto thy peace!—' Here the Saviour paused, and left unsaid what might have been the condition of Jerusalem had she accepted the help that God desired to give her. . . . If Jerusalem had known what it was her privilege to know, . . . she might have stood forth in the pride of prosperity, the queen of kingdoms, free in the strength of her God-given power. . . . The glorious destiny that might have blessed Jerusalem had she accepted her Redeemer rose before the Son of God. . . . From her walls the dove of peace would have gone forth to all nations. She would have been the world's diadem of glory" (*The Desire of Ages,* pp. 576, 577).

Today's Lesson: Jesus longs to gather us to Him and bless us. If we do not resist, He will keep us safe in His hand.

A Doomed People

The Desire of Ages, Chapter 64.

"Let no fruit grow on you ever again" (Matthew 21:19, NKJV).

Following His triumphal entry into Jerusalem, Jesus returned to Bethany, spending the entire night in prayer. In the morning, He returned to Jerusalem. Along the way He passed a fig orchard. It was the nature of these trees for the fruit to appear even before the leaves opened. Jesus noticed a fig tree that appeared much in advance of the others, but on closer inspection, it was only a mass of foliage and nothing more—and He cursed it.

The cursing of the fig tree was an acted parable—the barren tree with its deceptive foliage was a symbol of the Jewish nation. Jesus wanted to make plain the cause and certainty of Israel's doom, a nation He had specially favored with many blessings to give to the world. With their magnificent temple and ceremonies, the Israelites stood before the world as something special, but they lacked fruit. They failed to reflect the God they claimed to worship.

Key Thought: "Jesus had come to the fig tree hungry, to find food. So He had come to Israel, hungering to find in them the fruits of righteousness. He had lavished on them His gifts, that they might bear fruit for the blessing of the world. Every opportunity and privilege had been granted them, and in return He sought their sympathy and co-operation in His work of grace. . . . Had they kept the law of God, they would have done the same unselfish work that Christ did. But love to God and man was eclipsed by pride and self-sufficiency. . . . The treasures of truth which God had committed to them, they did not give to the world. In the barren tree they might read both their sin and its punishment. Withered beneath the Saviour's curse, standing forth sere and blasted, dried up by the roots, the fig tree showed what the Jewish people would be when the grace of God was removed from them" (*The Desire of Ages,* p. 583).

Today's Lesson: There are still "pretend" Christians in Christ's church—visible outwardly by their claims to follow Jesus but inwardly lacking His righteousness and its fruits.

The Temple Cleansed Again

The Desire of Ages, Chapter 65.

"Is it not written, 'My house shall be called a house of prayer for all nations'? But you have made it a 'den of thieves' " (Mark 11:17, NKJV).

At the beginning of His ministry, Jesus had driven from the temple those who defiled it by their unholy traffic. Now, at the close of His ministry, He came again to the temple and found conditions even worse than before. The very symbols pointing to the Lamb of God had been made a means of getting gain.

Jesus knew that His efforts to reform a corrupt priesthood would be in vain, but He would give this unbelieving people another evidence of His divine mission. All eyes were turned toward Him in awe, as divinity flashed through humanity. His displeasure seemed like consuming fire.

After He emptied the temple of those who defiled it, peace reigned. Once again, He began to heal the sick and teach the multitudes. The Pharisees were perplexed; One whom they could not intimidate was in command. The Sanhedrin pressed Jesus for a sign that He was the Messiah. They had before them the evidences of His authority, but still they demanded more, because He did not meet their expectations.

Key Thought: "The people who rejected Christ were soon to see their city and their nation destroyed. Their glory would be broken, and scattered as the dust before the wind. And what was it that destroyed the Jews? It was the rock which, had they built upon it, would have been their security. It was the goodness of God despised, the righteousness spurned, the mercy slighted. Men set themselves in opposition to God, and all that would have been their salvation was turned to their destruction. . . . So it will be in the great final day, when judgment shall fall upon the rejecters of God's grace. Christ, their rock of offense, will then appear to them as an avenging mountain. . . . Because of love rejected, grace despised, the sinner will be destroyed" (*The Desire of Ages,* p. 600).

Today's Lesson: To those who oppose His grace and turn from Him, Jesus is an avenging fire. But He is a gracious Redeemer and Healer of all who will accept His mercy.

Controversy

The Desire of Ages, Chapter 66.

"Then some of the scribes answered and said, 'Teacher, You have spoken well.' But after that they dared not question Him anymore" (Luke 20:39, 40, NKJV).

The Jewish leaders tried to trap Jesus by posing several contentious issues to Him. "Should Jews pay the taxes demanded by Rome?" the Pharisees asked. Christ's answer was no evasion but a candid answer: "Render . . . to God the things that are God's" (Luke 20:25, NKJV). Had the Jewish nation truly fulfilled its obligations to God, it would not have been in a position of paying tribute to a foreign power. His answer silenced the Pharisees.

The Sadducees chose to ask Jesus a theological question concerning the resurrection—which, of course, they did not believe was possible. "What would happen," they asked, "if a woman who had been married more than once was raised to life? Whom would she live with in heaven?"

Jesus' answer showed them that they did not really know the Scriptures in spite of their boasted learning. And they, too, were silenced.

A lawyer asked which was the greatest commandment, and Jesus responded with a broader view than he had expected. He gratefully acknowledged Jesus' insight. This honest man manifested an entirely different spirit than that of previous questioners—and received Jesus' approval.

Key Thought: "The scribe was near to the kingdom of God, in that he recognized deeds of righteousness as more acceptable to God than burnt offerings and sacrifices. But he needed to recognize the divine character of Christ, and through faith in Him receive power to do the works of righteousness. The ritual service was of no value, unless connected with Christ by living faith. Even the moral law fails of its purpose, unless it is understood in its relation to the Saviour. Christ had repeatedly shown that His Father's law contained something deeper than mere authoritative commands. In the law is embodied the same principle that is revealed in the gospel. The law points out man's duty and shows him his guilt. To Christ he must look for pardon and for power to do what the law enjoins" (*The Desire of Ages,* p. 608).

Today's Lesson: Faith does not require that all questions be answered, all doubts removed, before believing.

Woes on the Pharisees

The Desire of Ages, Chapter 67.

"See! Your house is left to you desolate"
(Matthew 23:38, NKJV).

Jesus' last day of teaching in the temple—this last week before Calvary—unfolded as had those that had gone before. The ordinary people were charmed by what He said; they didn't understand why the priests and rabbis disagreed so greatly with Him. Jesus knew that the true character of these Jewish teachers must be exposed more fully.

He minced no words. He pointed out the yoke of bondage that these religious leaders had laid on the Jewish nation and how they did not follow their own teachings (see Matthew 23:3). Jesus called them hypocrites, blind guides, fools, serpents, a brood of vipers, and murderers. They made a great outward show of piety, but this was only a covering to hide their worldly ambition, despotism, and base sins.

As He spoke, He saw a poor widow depositing her offering, trying not to be observed. Jesus called attention to the fact that she had given all that she had. He held up her unselfish generosity as an example to those who gave much larger gifts but did so from impure motives—and who could well afford to give more.

The Jews were famous for building tombs for their prophets—after they had persecuted them, even killing them. But rejecting Jesus would be their most tragic error.

Key Thought: "Divine pity marked the countenance of the Son of God as He cast one lingering look upon the temple and then upon His hearers. In a voice choked by deep anguish of heart and bitter tears He exclaimed, 'O Jerusalem, Jerusalem, thou that killest the prophets, and stonest them which are sent unto thee, how often would I have gathered thy children together, even as a hen gathereth her chickens under her wings, and ye would not!' This is the separation struggle. In the lamentation of Christ the very heart of God is pouring itself forth. It is the mysterious farewell of the long-suffering love of the Deity" (*The Desire of Ages,* p. 620).

Today's Lesson: The value of our gifts to Jesus is measured not by the amount we give but by the motive for our giving and the sacrifice that they represent.

In the Outer Court

The Desire of Ages, Chapter 68.

"Now there were certain Greeks among those who came up to worship at the feast. Then they came to Philip, who was from Bethsaida of Galilee, and asked him, saying, 'Sir, we wish to see Jesus' " (John 12:20, 21, NKJV).

At the hour when Christ's work bore the appearance of cruel defeat, Jesus saw in the Greeks' request a pledge of the great harvest that would take place among the Gentiles when the wall of prejudice between Jews and Gentiles would be finally broken down. These Greeks had heard of Christ's triumphal entry into Jerusalem and of His standoff in the temple with the priests and rulers. They had heard of the expectation that He would soon announce His kingdom. Now they wanted to know the truth about His mission.

Jesus used an illustration that dramatically explained why He was about to die. Year after year, the farmer separates part of his harvest— the choicest grain—and saves it as seed for the next year's crop. An onlooker could say that he was "throwing away" a significant part of his increase. But the farmer has an eye to future harvests. Likewise, it would seem that the death of Christ was a tragic end. But only by yielding up His life could He impart life to humanity.

The principle of self-sacrifice runs like a scarlet thread through God's side of the great controversy. Self-love, self-interest, must perish. But the law of self-sacrifice is the law of self-preservation.

Key Thought: "The work of human redemption is not all that is accomplished by the cross. The love of God is manifested to the universe. The prince of this world is cast out. The accusations which Satan has brought against God are refuted. The reproach which he has cast upon heaven is forever removed. Angels as well as men are drawn to the Redeemer. 'I, if I be lifted up from the earth,' He said, 'will draw all unto Me' " (*The Desire of Ages,* p. 626).

Today's Lesson: Only if a seed is placed in the ground to "die" will there be new life. As Christ died *for* our sins, we must also die *to* our sins and let Him create new life in us.

On the Mount of Olives

The Desire of Ages, Chapter 69.

"He that shall endure unto the end, the same shall be saved" (Matthew 24:13).

In His answer to the question regarding the destruction of Jerusalem and the end of the world, Jesus mingled descriptions of these two events. This entire discourse was given, not for the disciples only but for those living in the last scenes of earth's history.

"Take heed that no man deceive you," He cautioned (Matthew 24:4). The same deceptions practiced prior to the destruction of Jerusalem have been practiced through the ages and will be practiced again. Further, Jesus wanted His followers to know that the world will not get better—that wars, famines, pestilences, earthquakes, etc. would continue and grow worse. Like labor pains that increase in frequency and intensity just before birth occurs, so these disasters will reach critical levels, indicating the end is near.

Christ could foresee long centuries of darkness—centuries marked with blood and tears and agony for His church. For more than a thousand years, His followers would suffer great persecution.

He also clearly pointed out that men and women can actually hasten the time of His return by giving the gospel message to the world. We are not only to look for but to hasten His coming (2 Peter 3:12). Had the church done her appointed work as the Lord ordained, the whole world would have been warned long before now, and the Lord Jesus would have come in power and great glory.

Key Thought: "The crisis is stealing gradually upon us. . . . Men are still eating and drinking, planting and building, marrying, and giving in marriage. Merchants are still buying and selling. . . . The highest excitement prevails, yet probation's hour is fast closing, and every case is about to be eternally decided. Satan sees that his time is short. He has set all his agencies at work that men may be deceived, deluded, occupied and entranced, until the day of probation shall be ended, and the door of mercy be forever shut" (*The Desire of Ages,* p. 636).

Today's Lesson: We can know that Jesus' return is near as we look at world conditions today. Jesus' counsel is to watch and be ready.

"The Least of These My Brethren"

The Desire of Ages, Chapter 70.

"Inasmuch as ye have done it unto one of the least of these my brethren, ye have done it unto me" (Matthew 25:40).

The principle Jesus sets forth here cuts through mountains of theological discussion and lays bare a fundamental concept of the great controversy theme. If we do not get this message right, it matters little how much else we understand. According to Jesus Himself, the important issue in the judgment is not how much we know but how we have lived out the principle of self-sacrificing love for others. Those whom Christ commends in the judgment may have known little of theology, but they have cherished the principles that are the foundation of His kingdom. Even among the heathen have been those who demonstrated the spirit of kindness; before they heard the words of life, they befriended missionaries, even at the peril of their own lives. Their works were evidence that the Holy Spirit had touched their hearts.

Christ's rule of life, by which every one of us must stand or fall in the judgment, is, "Whatsoever ye would that men should do to you, do ye even so to them" (Mathew 7:12).

Key Thought: " 'When the Son of man shall come in His glory, and all the holy angels with Him, then shall He sit upon the throne of His glory: and before Him shall be gathered all nations: and He shall separate them one from another.' Thus Christ on the Mount of Olives pictured to His disciples the scene of the great judgment day. And He represented its decision as turning upon one point. When the nations are gathered before Him, there will be but two classes, and their eternal destiny will be determined by what they have done or have neglected to do for Him in the person of the poor and the suffering.

"In that day Christ does not present before men the great work He has done for them in giving His life for their redemption. He presents the faithful work they have done for Him" (*The Desire of Ages,* p. 637).

Today's Lesson: The way we treat others is the way we are treating Christ. He identifies with the disadvantaged and needy.

A Servant of Servants

The Desire of Ages, Chapter 71.

"What I am doing you do not understand now, but you will know after this" (John 13:7, NKJV).

For more than three years the disciples had watched Christ's life of unselfish service, yet they had not learned the lesson He wanted to teach them. At the last Passover supper they would share with their Master, the disciples noticed that Jesus was greatly troubled.

Jesus had much to tell His disciples that would save them from heartbreaking anguish in days to come, but He knew they could not bear what He wanted to say to them. Just a short time earlier, He had listened to their arguing over who would be the greatest in His kingdom. Now, because no servant had come to wash their dusty feet, the contention broke out afresh. Pride kept each from acting the part of a servant, so they sat in tense silence pretending nothing was amiss.

Without a word, Jesus picked up a towel and a basin of water. The unspoken rebuke was clear and unmistakable. Judas, especially, understood the lesson. He would not humble himself, but at the same time he resented Jesus doing so. He was convinced now that he had nothing to gain by continuing to follow Jesus.

The disciples needed more than clean feet; they needed to wash away alienation, jealousy, and pride from their hearts. With their current attitude, not one of them was prepared to join in the fellowship of the Passover with Jesus and each other. Neither are we prepared to receive the emblems of the Lord's Supper if pride and jealousy reside in our hearts.

Key Thought: "There is in man a disposition to esteem himself more highly than his brother, to work for self, to seek the highest place; and often this results in evil surmisings and bitterness of spirit. The ordinance preceding the Lord's Supper is to clear away these misunderstandings, to bring man out of his selfishness, down from his stilts of self-exaltation, to the humility of heart that will lead him to serve his brother" (*The Desire of Ages,* p. 650).

Today's Lesson: Of all sins, pride is the most difficult to be aware of in ourselves and the most difficult to eradicate from the life.

"In Remembrance of Me"

The Desire of Ages, Chapter 72.

"I say to you, I will not drink of this fruit of the vine from now on until that day when I drink it new with you in My Father's kingdom" (Matthew 26:29, NKJV).

The Passover was ordained to commemorate Israel's deliverance from Egyptian bondage. The Lord's Supper was given to commemorate the great deliverance brought about by the death of Christ.

Jesus had not yet given up on Judas. And Judas had not yet passed beyond the possibility of repentance. By including him in that last supper, Jesus was showing us that we are not to prevent anyone from taking part in this sacred rite. Those who have not yet declared themselves to be followers of the truth may wish to take part in the service, and they should not be forbidden as long as they are not involved in open, obvious sin. No one should pass judgment on another. In these symbolic services, Jesus meets with us and energizes us by His presence. The blessings are for all who desire them.

The foot-washing service allows us to make things right with each other and keeps the Communion service from being a season of sorrow. At the Lord's table we stand—not in the shadow of the cross—but in its saving light. It points to His second coming and is designed to keep this hope alive in our minds. It draws our attention to the great supper of the Lamb that we will eat with all of God's redeemed children—and with Jesus—in heaven.

Key Thought: "Our Lord says, Under conviction of sin, remember that I died for you. When oppressed and persecuted and afflicted for My sake and the gospel's, remember My love, so great that for you I gave My life. When your duties appear stern and severe, and your burdens too heavy to bear, remember that for your sake I endured the cross, despising the shame. When your heart shrinks from the trying ordeal, remember that your Redeemer liveth to make intercession for you" (*The Desire of Ages,* p. 659).

Today's Lesson: The Lord's Supper is an opportunity to think more deeply about what Jesus has done—and still wants to do—for us.

August 6

"Let Not Your Heart Be Troubled"

The Desire of Ages, Chapter 73.

"Let not your heart be troubled; you believe in God, believe also in Me. . . . If I go and prepare a place for you, I will come again and receive you to Myself; that where I am, there you may be also" (John 14:1, 3, NKJV).

These were among our Lord's last words to His disciples. He knew they were perplexed about references to His death and filled with foreboding. So, now He talked hope. He proceeded to give them an overall view of how the great controversy was to unfold. He emphasized that He was going away to prepare eternal homes for them—and that He was also preparing them to live happily in those homes. These are words that still bring comfort to those who are perplexed and disappointed, who are weary of their battles with temptation.

Jesus emphasized once more, for all time, that there are not many roads to heaven, that He is the only Way. He wanted His disciples— and us—to understand that during His time on earth He revealed no qualities and exercised no powers that we may not also have through faith in Him. All His followers may share in His perfect humanity if they will submit to God in faith as He did.

Key Thought: "The Spirit was to be given as a regenerating agent, and without this the sacrifice of Christ would have been of no avail. . . . Sin could be resisted and overcome only through the mighty agency of the Third Person of the Godhead, who would come with no modified energy, but in the fullness of divine power. It is the Spirit that makes effectual what has been wrought out by the world's Redeemer. It is by the Spirit that the heart is made pure. Through the Spirit the believer becomes a partaker of the divine nature. Christ has given His Spirit as a divine power to overcome all hereditary and cultivated tendencies to evil, and to impress His own character upon His church" (*The Desire of Ages,* p. 671).

Today's Lesson: It is the work of the Holy Spirit to reproduce in men and women the same character that Jesus demonstrated on earth.

Gethsemane

The Desire of Ages, Chapter 74.

**"Father, if it is Your will, remove this cup from Me;
nevertheless not My will, but Yours, be done"
(Luke 22:42, NKJV).**

As Jesus entered the Garden of Gethsemane with His disciples, He was strangely silent, His heart full of sorrow. He carried an invisible load that burdened Him beyond their comprehension. Indeed, He was now living the unthinkable—bearing the guilt and separation from a holy God that will be experienced by everyone who chooses to be lost. He cried out, "My soul is exceeding sorrowful unto death" (Mark 14:34).

As a human, He must suffer the consequences of humanity's sin. And He was showing the universe that sin's punishment is not arbitrary; that its inevitable result is eternal separation from God and from life itself.

Jesus feared that in His human nature He would be unable to endure the coming conflict with Satan. With the issues of the great controversy before Him, Christ was filled with a dread of separation from God. What was to be gained by passively walking to the cross? Three times He pled with increasing anguish for the Father to remove the terrible experience from Him. Great drops of blood fell from His face; He was overcome by the horror of a great darkness. The awful moment had come on which the destiny of the world would be decided. He experienced the second death and revealed the wages of sin to the onlooking universe.

All this occurred while the disciples slept in a strange stupor!

Key Thought: "Christ's agony did not cease, but His depression and discouragement left Him. The storm had in nowise abated, but He who was its object was strengthened to meet its fury. He came forth calm and serene. A heavenly peace rested upon His bloodstained face. He had borne that which no human being could ever bear; for He had tasted the sufferings of death for every man" (*The Desire of Ages,* p. 694).

Today's Lesson: Jesus paid the price of humanity's sin—not to a calculating God but to show the universe how fair and just God has been in dealing with sin. Jesus died the second death so you and I would never need to do so.

Before Annas and the Court of Caiaphas

The Desire of Ages, Chapter 75.

"Then they spat in His face and beat Him; and others struck Him with the palms of their hands, saying, 'Prophesy to us, Christ! Who is the one who struck You?' " **(Matthew 26:67, NKJV).**

After arresting Jesus in the Garden, the Jews took Him first to Annas, the former high priest. The rulers were afraid that the current high priest, Caiaphas, was too inexperienced to handle the matter as they wished. They deliberately excluded Nicodemus and Joseph of Arimathaea from the night's proceedings, knowing that these men were favorable toward Jesus.

The Lord suffered keenly under abuse and insult as Satan worked through human beings to try to break Jesus' hold on His Father's grace. Jesus knew that He could lay His tormentors in the dust simply by raising His hand—but He refused to deliver Himself.

In the trial, His accusers could find nothing incriminating to bring against Him. Even their false witnesses were shown to be paid informers. Finally, Caiaphas addressed Jesus in the form of a solemn oath: "I adjure You by the living God that You tell us if You are the Christ, the Son of God" (Mathew 26:63, NKJV).

To this appeal Christ could not remain silent. Every person present felt the penetrating eyes of Jesus as He said, "It is as you said." At last they had what they needed to condemn Him! Caiaphas and the others jumped at His answer, shouting, "Blasphemy! . . . He is deserving of death."

Key Thought: "Conviction mingled with passion led Caiaphas to do as he did. He was furious with himself for believing Christ's words, and instead of rending his heart under a deep sense of truth, and confessing that Jesus was the Messiah, he rent his priestly robes in determined resistance. This act was deeply significant. Little did Caiaphas realize its meaning. In this act, done to influence the judges and secure Christ's condemnation, the high priest had condemned himself. By the law of God he was disqualified for the priesthood. He had pronounced upon himself the death sentence" (*The Desire of Ages,* p. 708).

Today's Lesson: Jesus allowed Himself to be condemned unjustly in order to carry out His mission to save the world from sin.

Judas

The Desire of Ages, Chapter 76.

" 'I have sinned by betraying innocent blood.' And they said, 'What is that to us?' " (Matthew 27:4, NKJV).

If Judas had died before his last journey to Jerusalem, he would have been remembered as a man worthy of a place among the Twelve. Judas had sensed the Savior's drawing power and felt a desire to be changed. He attached Himself to the Master, and Jesus did not repulse Him. The other disciples thought well of Judas and made him their treasurer. Jesus entrusted Judas—as He did the other disciples—with power to heal the sick and to cast out devils.

But even as he associated with Jesus, Judas cultivated a disposition to criticize and accuse. Christ's oft-repeated statement that His kingdom was not of this world offended Judas; he continually advanced the idea that Christ should reign as king. At the miracle of the loaves, it was Judas who suggested that Christ should be forced to become king!

Prior to the week before Calvary Judas had not yet fully hardened his heart. He had contacted the priests about delivering Jesus into their hands, but he had not committed himself. He still had opportunity to repent—especially at the Last Supper, when Jesus made His final appeal of love to him. But Judas crossed the line when he left the upper room.

He didn't think that Jesus would actually permit Himself to be crucified. He thought he could force Jesus' hand by turning Him over to the Jewish leaders.

Key Thought: "Judas now cast himself at the feet of Jesus, acknowledging Him to be the Son of God, and entreating Him to deliver Himself. The Saviour did not reproach His betrayer. He knew that Judas did not repent; his confession was forced from his guilty soul by an awful sense of condemnation and a looking for of judgment, but he felt no deep, heartbreaking grief that he had betrayed the spotless Son of God, and denied the Holy One of Israel. Yet Jesus spoke no word of condemnation" (*The Desire of Ages,* p. 722).

Today's Lesson: Judas continued to disregard the voice of the Holy Spirit until he was unable to recognize sin or to repent of it. The same danger exists for all.

In Pilate's Judgment Hall

The Desire of Ages, Chapter 77.

"When they had gathered together, Pilate said to them, 'Whom do you want me to release to you? Barabbas, or Jesus who is called Christ?' For he knew that because of envy they had delivered Him" (Matthew 27:17, 18, NKJV).

When the Jewish leaders brought Jesus to the Roman governor for sentencing, Pilate was not happy to be aroused from his bed, and he determined to deal quickly and severely with this prisoner. But when he saw Jesus, he paused. He had never before seen a man with such obvious marks of goodness and nobility. Pilate's better nature was awakened.

The Jewish leaders had hoped the governor would sign Christ's death warrant as a favor to them on their great national festival. But he refused to condemn Jesus until he heard a reasonable charge against Him. The Jewish leaders tried to frame their accusations in a way that would justify the death sentence, but Pilate saw through all their deceitful charges. Meanwhile, Jesus said nothing, and Pilate marveled at His eloquent silence. The Holy Spirit was striving with Pilate. He even asked Jesus, "What is truth?" (John 18:38). But he didn't wait for an answer.

Pilate resisted condemning Jesus, but he dreaded the ill will of the Jews. So, when he heard that Jesus was from Galilee, he was happy to send him to Herod, the ruler of that province. Herod questioned Jesus and asked Him to prove by a miracle that He was the Messiah. But through it all, Jesus maintained His profound silence. He would not work a miracle to save Himself the pain and humiliation He must bear as our Substitute.

Key Thought: "Pilate longed to deliver Jesus. But he saw that he could not do this, and yet retain his own position and honor. Rather than lose his worldly power, he chose to sacrifice an innocent life. . . . Conscience and duty point one way, and self-interest points another. The current sets strongly in the wrong direction, and he who compromises with evil is swept away into the thick darkness of guilt" (*The Desire of Ages,* p. 738).

Today's Lesson: Many, like Pilate, allow earthly considerations to prevent them from doing what they know to be right.

Calvary

The Desire of Ages, Chapter 78.

"Pilate answered, 'What I have written, I have written' " (John 19:22, NKJV).

We can scarcely imagine Jesus' last few hours of mental and physical agony—or the public humiliation of the crucifixion. Jesus had had nothing to eat or drink since the Last Supper. His disciples had forsaken Him. He had been insulted and tortured throughout the night. He had endured the farce of a trial—before the Jewish tribunal, the Roman governor, Herod, and Pilate once more.

When Jesus had ridden into Jerusalem on Sunday, He was surrounded by a cheering multitude. Now, even His disciples gave Him a lot of distance. Near the cross, John stood with Jesus' mother, still hoping that He would manifest His power.

As the soldiers roughly nailed His hands and feet to the cross, Jesus made no murmur of complaint, though great drops of sweat stood on his blood-stained face. He prayed, "Father, forgive them; for they know not what they do" (Luke 23:34). But the ignorance of those involved did not remove their guilt, for it was their privilege to know and accept Jesus as their Savior.

Yet, by enduring the cross, Jesus was earning the right to become our Redeemer and our High Priest.

The priestly ridicule must have been particularly hurtful. "He saved others; himself he cannot save" (Matthew 27:42). Exactly right! He could not save Himself and save humanity from sin. He could have come down from the cross, but it is because He would not save Himself that we sinners now have pardon and favor with God.

Key Thought: "Satan with his fierce temptations wrung the heart of Jesus. The Saviour could not see through the portals of the tomb. Hope did not present to Him His coming forth from the grave a conqueror, or tell Him of the Father's acceptance of the sacrifice. He feared that sin was so offensive to God that Their separation was to be eternal. Christ felt the anguish which the sinner will feel when mercy shall no longer plead for the guilty race" (*The Desire of Ages,* p. 753).

Today's Lesson: The cost of our salvation was not just the physical agony of Jesus' crucifixion—terrible as that was—but the separation sin caused between Him and His Father.

"It Is Finished"

The Desire of Ages, Chapter 79.

"So when Jesus had received the sour wine, He said, 'It is finished!' And bowing His head, He gave up His spirit" (John 19:30, NKJV).

To the angels and the inhabitants of unfallen worlds, the cry, "It is finished," had great significance, but even then they did not fully understand the broad implications of the great controversy.

Yet, they did see clearly now Satan's true character and the depth of his rebellion. Now they understood why God had let Satan live so long after His expulsion from heaven. God wanted to provide for the eternal security of His universe, and to do that He must give Satan time to demonstrate the principles that supported his claims against God.

From Jesus' birth, angels and the unfallen worlds had watched the awesome standoff between Satan and Jesus. With intense interest, they watched our Lord in Gethsemane and then on the cross, holding fast to His trust in His heavenly Father. Now Satan's disguise was torn away—the last link between him and the heavenly world was broken.

The angels did not even then understand all that was involved in the great controversy—the principles were to be revealed more fully. For the sake of men and women, Satan's existence must be continued so that humanity, as well as angels, can clearly see the issues.

What are the issues men and women must learn before the controversy can end? That Satan has lied in claiming that God's law cannot be kept. They needed to learn that sinners can be forgiven and empowered to keep that law, that God can transform sinners by imparting His attributes to them, and that this transformation will be the final vindication of God's handling of the sin problem.

Key Thought: "By His life and His death, Christ proved that God's justice did not destroy His mercy, but that sin could be forgiven, and that the law is righteous, and can be perfectly obeyed. Satan's charges were refuted. God had given man unmistakable evidence of His love" (*The Desire of Ages,* p. 762).

Today's Lesson: Jesus' triumph over sin on the cross has settled the issues at stake in the great controversy ever since Satan rebelled against God in heaven.

In Joseph's Tomb

The Desire of Ages, Chapter 80.

"Pilate said to them, 'You have a guard; go your way, make it as secure as you know how.' So they went and made the tomb secure, sealing the stone and setting the guard" (Matthew 27:65, 66, NKJV).

At last Jesus was at rest—on the Sabbath day He had sanctified. The cruel scene enacted on Golgotha had mercifully come to an end. There was no mocking now; the crowd went home in solemn silence. A few weeks later, many of them would be among the thousands who responded to Peter's sermon on Pentecost. The Jewish leaders remained unchanged in their enmity against Jesus; yet, having achieved His death, they were not at peace. They had heard Jesus' unforgettable words from the cross; they had seen the darkness and the earthquake.

The spear thrust didn't cause Jesus' death. He died of a broken heart—broken by mental anguish, killed by the sins of the world. With Jesus' death, the hopes of His disciples perished. But Joseph of Arimathea and Nicodemus, both members of the Sanhedrin, were determined that the body of Jesus should have an honorable burial.

Gently and reverently, they removed Jesus from the cross with their own hands. They placed Him in Joseph's new tomb. Nicodemus provided a costly mixture of myrrh and aloes for His embalming.

But it was a restless Sabbath for the priests and rulers.

Key Thought: "Neither Joseph nor Nicodemus had openly accepted the Saviour while He was living. They knew that such a step would exclude them from the Sanhedrin, and they hoped to protect Him by their influence in its councils. For a time they had seemed to succeed; but the wily priests, seeing their favor to Christ, had thwarted their plans. In their absence Jesus had been condemned and delivered to be crucified. Now that He was dead, they no longer concealed their attachment to Him. While the disciples feared to show themselves openly as His followers, Joseph and Nicodemus came boldly to their aid. The help of these rich and honored men was greatly needed at this time" (*The Desire of Ages,* pp. 773, 774).

Today's Lesson: In the hour of apparent defeat and darkness, God is still working out His eternal purposes.

"The Lord Is Risen"

The Desire of Ages, Chapter 81.

"He is not here; for He is risen, as He said. Come, see the place where the Lord lay" (Matthew 28:6, NKJV).

An earthquake marked the death of Jesus and another marked His resurrection. When Jesus walked from the tomb on Sunday morning, the Roman guards saw the One whom the crowd had mocked and insulted on Friday. They fainted as dead men at the sight. Eventually, they revived enough to stagger into the city and begin telling what they had seen.

Hearing the news, the faces of the priests were as those of the dead. They persuaded the guards with money to forget what they had seen. But many heard the exciting news before the priests could stop the story.

Christ arose from the dead as the first fruits of those who have died. He was the Antitype of the wave sheaf in the sacrificial system; in fact, He was resurrected the very day when the wave sheaf was to be presented in the temple ceremony. So, Christ's resurrection from the dead represented the first fruits of the spiritual harvest to be gathered for the kingdom of God.

The earthquakes also opened the graves of many who had died serving the Lord at the cost of their own lives. They, too, became witnesses of God's power to resurrect the faithful dead. They went into Jerusalem declaring that Christ had risen from the dead and that they also had been raised—what a magnificent witness to the power of God's promises!

Key Thought: "To the believer, death is but a small matter. Christ speaks of it as if it were of little moment. 'If a man keep My saying, he shall never see death,' 'he shall never taste of death.' To the Christian, death is but a sleep, a moment of silence and darkness. The life is hid with Christ in God, and 'when Christ, who is our life, shall appear, then shall ye also appear with Him in glory.' John 8:51, 52; Col. 3:4" (*The Desire of Ages,* p. 787).

Today's Lesson: Christians can have the overwhelming peace of knowing that if they should die today, they would experience only a short "nap" until they would hear the voice of the Lifegiver.

"Why Weepest Thou?"

The Desire of Ages, Chapter 82.

" 'Sir, if You have carried Him away, tell me where You have laid Him, and I will take Him away.' Jesus said to her, 'Mary!' " (John 20:15, 16, NKJV).

The women waited and watched for the hours of the Sabbath to pass. Very early on Sunday they made their way to the tomb, taking precious spices to anoint the Lord's body and wondering who would remove the great stone that sealed His tomb.

The women came from different directions. Mary Magdalene, arriving first and seeing the stone removed, hurried away to tell the disciples. When the other women arrived, they saw a light about the tomb but no body. Then an angel told them the good news of Jesus' resurrection and instructed them to tell the disciples.

Meanwhile, Mary returned with Peter and John, only to find the tomb empty and Jesus' grave clothes neatly folded. Overwhelmed with grief, she mistook Jesus for the gardener. When Jesus called her name, her great grief turned to joy. She knelt to embrace Him, but He raised His hand with the message that He had not ascended to His heavenly Father for approval of what had transpired. He needed to receive confirmation that His sacrifice was accepted.

Christ's first work on earth after His resurrection was to convince His disciples of His undiminished love for them, in spite of their guilt for forsaking Him at the cross.

Key Thought: "Jesus refused to receive the homage of His people until He had the assurance that His sacrifice was accepted by the Father. He ascended to the heavenly courts, and from God Himself heard the assurance that His atonement for the sins of men had been ample, that through His blood all might gain eternal life. The Father ratified the covenant made with Christ, that He would receive repentant and obedient men, and would love them even as He loves His Son. Christ was to complete His work, and fulfill His pledge to 'make a man more precious than fine gold; even a man than the golden wedge of Ophir.' Isa. 13:12" (*The Desire of Ages,* p. 790).

Today's Lesson: Jesus continues to reach out to us with undiminished love, even after we have forsaken Him in our weak moments.

The Walk to Emmaus

The Desire of Ages, Chapter 83.

"What kind of conversation is this that you have with one another as you walk and are sad?"(Luke 24:17, NKJV).

On the afternoon of the resurrection day, two disheartened followers of Jesus were making the eight-mile walk from Jerusalem to Emmaus. They had heard that some of the women had seen Jesus alive, but the news was hard to believe.

Soon a Stranger joined them, but they were too absorbed in their gloomy thoughts to pay much attention to Him. They continued to rehearse the events of the past week, trying to understand the meaning of these events. Jesus longed to comfort them, especially when they were weeping. It was obvious that they had not lost their appreciation for Jesus, whom they still believed to be a "prophet," but they didn't understand the meaning of the Scriptures they were discussing.

Then the Master Teacher said, "O foolish ones, and slow of heart to believe in all that the prophets have spoken! Ought not the Christ to have suffered these things and to enter into His glory?" (Luke 24:25, 26, NKJV). Here Jesus showed the importance of the Old Testament as a witness to His mission. Jesus' miracles are a proof of His divinity, but a stronger proof that He is the world's Redeemer is found in comparing the prophecies of the Old Testament with the history of the New.

Key Thought: "Beginning at Moses, the very Alpha of Bible history, Christ expounded in all the Scriptures the things concerning Himself. Had He first made Himself known to them, their hearts would have been satisfied. In the fullness of their joy they would have hungered for nothing more. But it was necessary for them to understand the witness borne to Him by the types and prophecies of the Old Testament. Upon these their faith must be established. Christ performed no miracle to convince them, but it was His first work to explain the Scriptures. They had looked upon His death as the destruction of all their hopes. Now He showed from the prophets that this was the very strongest evidence for their faith" (*The Desire of Ages,* pp. 796, 799).

Today's Lesson: It is possible to have our heads filled with much information but little understanding.

"Peace Be Unto You"

The Desire of Ages, Chapter 84.

"Why are you troubled? And why do doubts arise in your hearts?" (Luke 24:38, NKJV).

After Jesus revealed His identity to the travelers to Emmaus, they hurried back to Jerusalem, although the hour was late. They knew the eleven disciples would not be asleep until they knew for certain Jesus was alive. They excitedly unfolded their story of walking with Jesus. The disciples recounted what the women had told them. Some still thought it was all too good to be true!

Then Jesus appeared. His first words were, "Peace be unto you." But the disciples were "terrified and affrighted, and supposed that they had seen a spirit" (Luke 24:36, 37). Jesus then showed them His hands and feet and asked if they had something to eat! He reviewed the meaning of His death and resurrection. Hs pointed out more clearly the nature and extent of their work—that they were entrusted with telling the entire world of the salvation available through their Lord. Then Jesus breathed on them the Holy Spirit—symbolizing the fact that without the Holy Spirit this work could not be accomplished.

Thomas was not with the disciples at that first appearance of Jesus. During the week they told him the whole story, but he was determined not to believe. Then Jesus appeared with Thomas present. The Lord's compassion was demonstrated again as He asked Thomas to touch His hands and side. Jesus' kind reproof of Thomas is for us all today: Should everyone follow Thomas' example, no one would believe—for all who receive Christ today must do so through the testimony of others.

Key Thought: "The Holy Spirit is the breath of spiritual life in the soul. The impartation of the Spirit is the impartation of the life of Christ. It imbues the receiver with the attributes of Christ. Only those who are thus taught of God, those who possess the inward working of the Spirit, and in whose life the Christ-life is manifested, are to stand as representative men, to minister in behalf of the church" (*The Desire of Ages,* p. 805).

Today's Lesson: God does not expect us to believe without a basis for our faith, but faith that insists on absolute proof is not real faith.

By the Sea Once More

The Desire of Ages, Chapter 85.

"After these things Jesus showed Himself again to the disciples at the Sea of Tiberias" (John 21:1, NKJV).

Peter, with his old love for fishing, suggested that the disciples catch some fish. They all needed food and clothing, and the proceeds would satisfy their needs. But they caught nothing all night.

On the shore Jesus was watching, unseen by the disciples. As morning broke, the Stranger on the beach told them to cast their nets on the right side of the ship—and immediately, it was filled with fish. Jesus told them to haul in the fish and eat the breakfast He had prepared.

One of the issues that needed to be resolved was Peter's shameful denial of his Lord and thus the confidence the disciples could have in him. Secret sins are to be confessed in secret to God, but open sin requires open confession.

During the meal Jesus said to Peter, "Simon . . . lovest thou me?" (John 21:15). Three times Jesus asked the same question, and three times Peter gave the same reply. Three times Peter had denied Jesus openly, and three times He openly, sincerely confessed His repentance. The first work Jesus gave to Peter was to feed the "lambs"—those young in the faith—a work in which Peter had little experience.

In this interchange the disciples were learning how to deal patiently, sympathetically, and in forgiving love with those who fail in their duties. Without the love of Christ in the heart, the work of the Christian leader is a failure.

Key Thought: "Before his fall, Peter was always speaking unadvisedly, from the impulse of the moment. He was always ready to correct others, and to express his mind, before he had a clear comprehension of himself or of what he had to say. But the converted Peter was very different. He retained his former fervor, but the grace of Christ regulated his zeal. He was no longer impetuous, self-confident, and self-exalted, but calm, self-possessed, and teachable. He could then feed the lambs as well as the sheep of Christ's flock" (*The Desire of Ages,* pp. 812, 815).

Today's Lesson: Even those who fall into great sin can be forgiven and used successfully in God's work.

Go Teach All Nations

The Desire of Ages, Chapter 86.

"All authority has been given to Me in heaven and on earth. Go therefore and make disciples of all the nations, baptizing them in the name of the Father and of the Son and of the Holy Spirit, teaching them to observe all things that I have commanded you; and lo, I am with you always, even to the end of the age"
(Matthew 28:18–20, NKJV).

On a mountain in Galilee, about five hundred believers were gathered, eager to learn all that could be learned from the disciples who had seen Jesus since His resurrection. Suddenly, Jesus appeared and showed Himself to the people. They worshiped Him—but not all. Some still doubted, and so it will always be.

This was the only interview Jesus had with many of the believers after the resurrection. As He spoke to the people, He made it clear that His sacrifice on behalf of men and women was full and complete. The conditions of the atonement had been fulfilled and accepted by the Father. He was now on His way to the throne of God to enter upon His mediatorial work.

Further, He made clear that His followers are to work together with God to restore health to the body as well as to the soul. Human afflictions—physical, as well as spiritual—are caused by violating God's laws.

Key Thought: "The gospel is to be presented, not as a lifeless theory, but as a living force to change the life. God desires that the receivers of His grace shall be witnesses to its power. Those whose course has been most offensive to Him He freely accepts; when they repent, He imparts to them His divine Spirit. . . . He would have His servants bear testimony to the fact that through His grace men may possess Christlikeness of character, and may rejoice in the assurance of His great love. He would have us bear testimony to the fact that He cannot be satisfied until the human race are reclaimed and reinstated in their holy privileges as His sons and daughters" (*The Desire of Ages,* p. 826).

Today's Lesson: The essence of the gospel is the restoration of God's character in men and women.

"To My Father, and Your Father"

The Desire of Ages, Chapter 87.

*"Men of Galilee, why do you stand gazing up into heaven?
This same Jesus who was taken up from you into heaven,
will so come in like manner as you saw Him go into
heaven" (Acts 1:11, NKJV).*

A fter His resurrection Jesus had lingered on earth so His disciples might become familiar with Him in His risen and glorified body. Now the time had come for Him to return to heaven. He led the disciples up the familiar path to the summit of the Mount of Olives.

Jesus paused, and the disciples gathered around Him. Beams of light seemed to radiate from His face as He looked lovingly upon them. He spoke words of tender mercy and stretched out His arms as if assuring them of His protecting care. Then He slowly ascended from among them. Awestricken, the disciples looked with straining eyes for a last glimpse as a cloudy chariot of angels received Him.

Suddenly, like rich music, they heard the angels' promise of Christ's return. When the disciples returned to Jerusalem, the people looked upon them in amazement. Most people thought that they would appear downcast and ashamed because their Leader was dead. Instead, there was only gladness and triumph. They no longer were uncertain about the future. They knew that they had a Friend at the throne of God—a Friend still in human form.

Key Thought: "Christ had ascended to heaven in the form of humanity. The disciples had beheld the cloud receive Him. The same Jesus who had walked and talked and prayed with them; who had broken bread with them; who had been with them in their boats on the lake; and who had that very day toiled with them up the ascent of Olivet,—the same Jesus had now gone to share His Father's throne. And the angels had assured them that the very One whom they had seen go up into heaven, would come again even as He had ascended. He will come 'with clouds; and every eye shall see Him' . . . Rev. 1:7" (*The Desire of Ages,* p. 832).

Today's Lesson: Jesus forever retains His humanity. As our High Priest in heaven, He knows exactly what we each need when we are faced with temptation.

The Beatitudes

Thoughts From the Mount of Blessing, Chapters 1, 2.

"Seeing the multitudes, He went up on a mountain, and when He was seated His disciples came to Him. Then He opened His mouth and taught them"
(Matthew 5:1, 2, NKJV).

In the Sermon on the Mount, Christ opened to men the nature of His spiritual kingdom of love, grace, and righteousness. His subjects are the poor in spirit, the meek, those persecuted for the sake of righteousness. The kingdom of heaven belongs to these. Though not yet fully accomplished, the work has begun in them which will make them worthy of His everlasting kingdom.

Through the desire for self-exaltation we are following Eve's course in Eden. The love of self destroys our peace; we depend on life's conditions for our happiness. But Jesus teaches that happiness comes from righteousness.

Righteousness is holiness—likeness to God—and "God is love" (1 John 4:16). Righteousness is harmony with the law of God, for "all thy commandments are righteousness" (Psalm 119:172), and "love is the fulfilling of the law" (Romans 13:10). Righteousness is love, and love is the light and the life of God. The righteousness of God is embodied in Christ. We receive righteousness by receiving Him.

As we recognize the perfection of our Savior's character, we will want to become completely transformed and renewed in the image of His purity. The more we know of God, the higher will be our ideal of character and the more earnest will be our longing to reflect His likeness. A divine element combines with the human when the soul reaches out after God.

Key Thought: "The divine love glowing in the heart, the Christlike harmony manifested in the life, are as a glimpse of heaven granted to men of the world, that they may appreciate its excellence.

"It is thus that men are led to believe 'the love that God hath to us.' 1 John 4:16. Thus hearts once sinful and corrupt are purified and transformed, to be presented 'faultless before the presence of His glory with exceeding joy.' Jude 24" (*Thoughts From the Mount of Blessing,* pp. 41, 42).

Today's Lesson: God's outline for happiness in this life—as well as in the life to come—is the safest and nicest way to live.

The Spirituality of the Law

Thoughts From the Mount of Blessing, Chapter 3.

***"Do not think that I came to destroy the Law or the
Prophets. I did not come to destroy but to fulfill"
(Matthew 5:17, NKJV).***

W hen Jesus explained the spiritual nature of the law to the people
seated before Him on the mountainside, He was opening to
them the principles of the same law He Himself had proclaimed
centuries before to Israel in flaming fire on Mount Sinai. He assured His
hearers that it was not His purpose to set aside the smallest provision
of the law. The principles of righteousness embedded in the law are
as unchangeable as God's throne. Instead, Jesus came to magnify the
law. He came to "fulfill" the law, meaning to "fill up" the measure of
the law's requirements, giving us an example of perfect conformity to
God's will.

Whenever men and women choose their own way, they place
themselves in controversy with God. They will have no place in the
kingdom of heaven, for they are at war with the very principles of
heaven. Even those who attempt to be commandment keepers may be
in contradiction with God. A legal religion is insufficient to bring the
soul into harmony with God. The hard, rigid orthodoxy of the Pharisees,
destitute of contrition, tenderness, or love, was only a stumbling
block to sinners. The only true faith is that which "worketh by love"
(Galatians 5:6) to purify the soul. It is like leaven that transforms the
character.

Key Thought: "The conditions of eternal life, under grace, are
just what they were in Eden—perfect righteousness, harmony with
God, perfect conformity to the principles of His law. The standard of
character presented in the Old Testament is the same that is presented
in the New Testament. This standard is not one to which we cannot
attain. In every command or injunction that God gives there is a
promise . . . underlying the command. God has made provision that we
may become like unto Him, and He will accomplish this for all who do
not interpose a perverse will and thus frustrate His grace" (*Thoughts
From the Mount of Blessing,* p. 76).

Today's Lesson: God has promised to put His laws into our hearts
and write them on our minds.

The True Motive in Service

Thoughts From the Mount of Blessing, Chapter 4.

"Take heed that you do not do your charitable deeds before men, to be seen by them. Otherwise you have no reward from your Father in heaven" (Matthew 6:1, NKJV).

The principles cherished by the Pharisees are characteristic of the natural inclination of humanity in all ages, and as the Savior showed the contrast between His own spirit and methods and those of the rabbis, His teaching is equally applicable to the people of all time. In the days of Christ, the Pharisees considered worldly honor and prosperity as the rewards of virtue, and they were continually trying to earn God's favor in order to secure these benefits. At the same time they paraded their acts of charity before the people in order to gain a reputation for sanctity and righteousness.

Jesus rebuked this hunger for attention and honor. He taught that real godliness never tries to display itself. By their good works, Christ's followers are to bring glory, not to themselves, but to Him through whose grace and power makes their good works possible.

God never deserts a soul, never gives us up to our own ways, as long as there is hope for our salvation. Our heavenly Father follows us with warnings and assurances of compassion until further opportunities and privileges would be wholly in vain. By resisting the Spirit of God, a person prepares the way for a further resistance when the Spirit comes with mightier power. Thus, he passes on from one stage of resistance to another, until at last the light will fail to impress, and he will cease to respond in any measure to God's Spirit.

Key Thought: "If you will seek the Lord and be converted every day; if you will of your own spiritual choice be free and joyous in God; . . . come wearing the yoke of Christ,—the yoke of obedience and service,—all your murmurings will be stilled, all your difficulties will be removed, all the perplexing problems that now confront you will be solved" (*Thoughts From the Mount of Blessing,* p. 101).

Today's Lesson: Motive is the key to our service for God. When the motive is right, service for Him becomes a pleasure—not a burden.

AUGUST 24

The Lord's Prayer

Thoughts From the Mount of Blessing, Chapter 5.

"It came to pass, as He was praying in a certain place, when He ceased, that one of His disciples said to Him, 'Lord, teach us to pray, as John also taught his disciples' " (Luke 11:1, NKJV).

Jesus gave the Lord's Prayer twice—first to the multitude in the Sermon on the Mount and again, some months later, to the disciples alone. On one occasion the disciples returned to find Jesus absorbed in prayer to His Father. Their hearts were touched, and they asked Him to teach them to pray. They knew He spent long hours in prayer; they knew that this gave Him energy and power to do His work day by day.

In answer to their request, Jesus gave them no new form of prayer. He repeated what He had taught them before. They needed to understand more deeply the instruction He had already given them.

In giving them, and us, a model prayer, Jesus did not intend to restrict us to these exact words. The ideas in the Lord's Prayer are the elements that should be included in every prayer. In every act of life we are to make manifest God's name. The Lord's Prayer calls upon us to possess His character. We cannot hallow His name, we cannot represent Him to the world, unless in our life and character we represent the very life and character of God.

Key Thought: "The last like the first sentence of the Lord's Prayer, points to our Father as above all power and authority and every name that is named. The Saviour beheld the years that stretched out before His disciples, not, as they had dreamed, lying in the sunshine of worldly prosperity and honor, but dark with the tempests of human hatred and satanic wrath. . . . In the prayer that breathes their daily wants, the disciples of Christ were directed to look above all the power and dominion of evil, unto the Lord their God, whose kingdom ruleth over all and who is their Father and everlasting Friend" (*Thoughts From the Mount of Blessing,* p. 120).

Today's Lesson: It is our privilege to come to the Father in prayer at every opportunity; He loves to hear our praise and petitions.

Not Judging, but Doing

Thoughts From the Mount of Blessing, Chapter 6.

"Judge not, that you be not judged" (Matthew 7:1, NKJV).

The effort to earn salvation by one's own works, Jesus pointed out, inevitably leads men and women to pile up human rules as a barrier against sin. As they see their failure to keep the law, they devise yet more regulations in an attempt to force themselves—and others—to obey. In the end, the goal becomes trying to impress God instead of honoring Him by the way we live.

Such a system, with its multitude of rules, will lead us to judge all those who come short of measuring up to the standard we have set. The atmosphere of selfish and narrow criticism stifles the noble and generous emotions and causes us to become self-centered judges and petty spies.

Jesus pointed out another problem in making our own opinions—our own views of duty or interpretations of Scripture—the criteria for others. Those who do so often do not live up to their own ideals. They judge others without being able to see their own failings.

Human beings can judge only on outward appearance; we do not know the secret springs of action or how the Lord may be leading a particular individual. He who is guilty of wrong is often the first to suspect wrong. By condemning another, we are often trying to conceal or excuse the evil of our own hearts.

Key Thought: "Do you desire to become a follower of Christ, yet know not how to begin? Are you in darkness and know not how to find the light? Follow the light you have. Set your heart to obey what you do know of the word of God. . . . As you receive the word in faith, it will give you power to obey. As you give heed to the light you have, greater light will come. You are building on God's word, and your character will be builded after the similitude of the character of Christ" (*Thoughts From the Mount of Blessing,* p. 150).

Today's Lesson: The habit of judging others, criticizing and faultfinding, is an indication that our lives are not right and that we have not experienced God's forgiving grace for ourselves.

"The Sower Went Forth to Sow"

Christ's Object Lessons, Chapters 1, 2.

"He who received seed on the good ground is he who hears the word and understands it, who indeed bears fruit and produces: some a hundredfold, some sixty, some thirty"
(Matthew 13:23, NKJV).

Christ illustrated the nature of the heavenly kingdom with a story of a man sowing seed. He led the minds of His hearers from literal seed being cast into the soil to the gospel seed that is scattered in human hearts and brings men and women back to loyalty to God. Like a sower in the field, Jesus came to scatter the heavenly grain of truth. The same laws that govern earthly seed sowing govern the sowing of the seeds of truth.

God's kingdom is not to prevail by force but by implanting a new principle in the hearts of men and women. The seed is the Word of God, and the essence of that seed is a new way of looking at truth and our responsibilities as God's children. The gospel seed is about the kind of God who is in charge of the universe. This is precisely what Satan has done his best to confuse and misrepresent.

As we search the Scriptures, we are to gain a practical knowledge of the plan of salvation that will restore God's image in our souls and strengthen us against temptation. Receiving the gospel seed in our lives will enable us to work in harmony with Christ' mission of mercy to the world.

Key Thought: "So the sowers have something to do that the seed may not be choked with thorns or perish because of shallowness of soil. At the very outset of the Christian life every believer should be taught its foundation principles. He should be taught that he is not merely to be saved by Christ's sacrifice, but that he is to make the life of Christ his life and the character of Christ his character. Let all be taught that they are to bear burdens and to deny natural inclination. . . . The plowshare of truth will do its work" (*Christ's Object Lessons,* pp. 57, 58).

Today's Lesson: As we search the Scriptures, God is placing seeds in our minds—seeds that will change our characters.

"First the Blade, Then the Ear"

Christ's Object Lessons, Chapter 3.

*"He said, 'The kingdom of God is as if a man should scatter
seed on the ground, and should sleep by night and rise by
day, and the seed should sprout and grow, he himself does
not know how. . . . But when the grain ripens, immediately
he puts in the sickle, because the harvest has come' "
(Mark 4:26–29, NKJV).*

Just as the farmer must prepare the soil for the seed, so the teacher of truth must prepare the soil of the heart. He must sow the seed, but only God's power can produce spiritual life. The germination of the seed represents the beginning of spiritual life, and the development of the plant is a figure of Christian growth. There can be no life without growth—either in nature or in God's kingdom of grace. Plants grow silently and imperceptibly. Spiritual growth is the same. Our spiritual life may be perfect at every stage of growth, yet there will be continuous advancement if God's purpose is being fulfilled. Sanctification is the work of a lifetime.

The farmer's objective in sowing seed and cultivating the growing plants is to produce a bountiful harvest. In the same way, Christ wants to reproduce Himself in the hearts of men and women. The object of the Christian life is to bear fruit—reproducing Christ's character in our lives that we may share Him with others.

Key Thought: " 'When the fruit is brought forth, immediately he putteth in the sickle, because the harvest is come.' Christ is waiting with longing desire for the manifestation of Himself in His church. When the character of Christ shall be perfectly reproduced in His people, then He will come to claim them as His own.

"It is the privilege of every Christian not only to look for but to hasten the coming of our Lord Jesus Christ, (2 Peter 3:12, margin). Were all who profess His name bearing fruit to His glory, how quickly the whole world would be sown with the seed of the gospel" (*Christ's Object Lessons,* p. 69).

Today's Lesson: Spiritual growth is the natural result of having Christ in the heart. If He is living in us, He will reproduce His character in our life.

Tares

Christ's Object Lessons, Chapter 4.

" 'Sir, did you not sow good seed in your field? How then does it have tares?' He said to them, 'An enemy has done this' " (Mathew 13:27, 28, NKJV).

The parable of the tares—or weeds—focuses on the church, not the world, because it is in the church where we are to grow and ripen for God's harvest. The tares represent those within God's church who appear to be His followers but who actually are weeds. Just as weeds often resemble desirable plants and are difficult to detect, so those within the church who profess to be Christ's followers but who are actually the product of Satan's deceptions are often hard to distinguish from genuine Christians.

Christ has plainly taught that those who persist in open sin must be separated from the church, but He has not given us the work of judging character and motive. The parable teaches that we are to let these weeds within the church have sufficient time to demonstrate what they really are. This is the way God has dealt with Satan and the issues of the great controversy. When Satan first challenged God in heaven, the angels did not fully discern his character. God bore long with Satan. Shouldn't we be at least as patient with our fellow church members, allowing them to demonstrate whether they are weeds or good grain?

Jesus Himself will be the Judge. He will decide who are worthy to live with Him forever in heaven. Profession will count for nothing in the end; it is character—whether we are weeds or good grain—that decides our destiny.

Key Thought: "The tares closely resembled the wheat while the blades were green; but when the field was white for the harvest, the worthless weeds bore no likeness to the wheat. . . . Sinners who make a pretension of piety mingle for a time with the true followers of Christ . . . but in the harvest of the world there will be no likeness between good and evil" (*Christ's Object Lessons,* p. 74).

Today's Lesson: The point of this parable is not that we should be judging and condemning others as weeds but that we should look at our own lives in humility and distrust of self.

"Like a Grain of Mustard Seed"

Christ's Object Lessons, Chapter 5.

"For you see your calling, brethren, that not many wise according to the flesh, not many mighty, not many noble, are called. But God has chosen the foolish things of the world to put to shame the wise, and God has chosen the weak things of the world to put to shame the things which are mighty" (1 Corinthians 1:26, 27, NKJV).

Jesus said: "The kingdom of heaven is like a mustard seed, which a man took and sowed in his field, which indeed is the least of all the seeds; but when it is grown it is greater than the herbs and becomes a tree, so that the birds of the air come and nest in its branches" (Matthew 13: 31, 32, NKJV). As Jesus spoke, the people could see mustard plants growing in profusion nearby, much taller than the surrounding grass. Birds were flitting from twig to twig. Yet the seed that produced this large plant was among the smallest of all seeds. Jesus used this fact to illustrate His kingdom. In the beginning it seemed small and insignificant. However, the mighty truths that give it life caused it to grow rapidly; its influence spread throughout the world, drawing men and women into its embrace. Long after the empire of Rome would fade from the world stage, Christ's kingdom would remain—a powerful and influential movement.

Seeds grow by the life-giving power placed within them by the Creator. Their growth does not depend on human power. So it is with Christ's kingdom. It grows by the power of truth and righteousness, counteracting error and sin.

Key Thought: "In this last generation the parable of the mustard seed is to reach a signal and triumphant fulfillment. The little seed will become a tree. The last message of warning and mercy is to go to 'every nation and kindred and tongue' (Rev. 14:6-14), 'to take out of them a people for His name' (Acts 15:14; Rev. 18:1). And the earth shall be lightened with His glory" (*Christ's Object Lessons,* p. 79).

Today's Lesson: For His church in every generation, God has a special truth and a special work. It may begin in a small way, but it will grow with His blessing.

AUGUST 30

Other Lessons From Seed-Sowing

Christ's Object Lessons, Chapter 6.

"We are God's fellow workers; you are God's field, you are God's building" (1 Corinthians 3:9, NKJV).

God has many precious lessons to teach us from the work of seed sowing and the way the plants grow as they develop from the seed. All things in nature operate according to God's laws. We should teach our children to recognize His power working in the things of nature so they will see His hand in spiritual realities, as well. They will be able to have faith in Him and realize His power in their lives as they come to understand the way He provides in nature for the needs of all living things. They will be better able to cooperate with Him in their own lives.

In nature, we can see the cooperation of divine and human effort in the way plants grow. Unless humans sow the seed, there will be no reaping. But without God's divine power in providing the needed sunshine and showers, the seeds will not germinate or grow. It is the same in spiritual things. In the formation of character and every aspect of Christian work, we humans have a part to act, but we must work in harmony with divine power or our efforts will be in vain.

As our children develop, we should be cultivating in them the natural gifts and graces appropriate to each stage of their lives, letting them grow naturally as do the plants in the garden. As we do so, the divine Sower will plant in their souls seeds that will last forever.

Key Thought: "In the laws of God in nature, effect follows cause with unerring certainty. The reaping will testify as to what the sowing has been. The slothful worker is condemned by his work. The harvest bears witness against him. So in spiritual things: the faithfulness of every worker is measured by the results of his work. The character of his work, whether diligent or slothful, is revealed by the harvest. It is thus that his destiny for eternity is decided" (*Christ's Object Lessons,* p. 84).

Today's Lesson: A godly character is not the random result of chance. The seeds sown produce a sure harvest—either for life or death.

Like Unto Leaven

Christ's Object Lessons, Chapter 7.

"To what shall I liken the kingdom of God? It is like leaven, which a woman took and hid in three measures of meal till it was all leavened" (Luke 13:20, 21, NKJV).

Among the Jews leaven was sometimes used as an emblem of sin. At Passover the people were directed to remove all the leaven from their houses as a sign that they were putting away sin from their hearts. Christ warned His disciples, "Beware ye of the leaven of the Pharisees, which is hypocrisy" (Luke 12:1). But in Jesus' parable, leaven is used to illustrate something entirely different—the quickening, permeating power of God's grace in the human life.

In this parable, Jesus wanted to teach that no one has fallen so far from His ideal that they are beyond the working of God's powerful grace. He implants a new principle of spiritual life in everyone who will submit to the Holy Spirit.

Leaven works outward from within when it is mixed with the flour. So it is that God's grace works within the life, transforming it from the inside out. A mere surface change is not enough to bring us into harmony with God. Many people try to reform their lives by correcting this or that bad habit. They think they can change their lives this way, but they are beginning in the wrong place. The place to start is with the heart.

The essence of all righteousness is loyalty to our Redeemer. This will lead us to do right because it is right—because right-doing is pleasing to God.

Key Thought: "The word of God is to have a sanctifying effect on our association with every member of the human family. The leaven of truth will not produce the spirit of rivalry, the love of ambition, the desire to be first. True, heaven-born love is not selfish and changeable. It is not dependent on human praise. . . . He does not love others because they love and please him, because they appreciate his merits, but because they are Christ's purchased possession" (*Christ's Object Lessons,* pp. 101, 102).

Lesson for Today: Like leaven, the grace of God works in us to permeate every aspect of our lives with His divine power.

Hidden Treasure

Christ's Object Lessons, Chapter 8.

"Again, the kingdom of heaven is like treasure hidden in a field, which a man found and hid; and for joy over it he goes and sells all that he has and buys that field"
(Matthew 13:44, NKJV).

The field containing the treasure represents the Holy Scriptures. And the treasure it contains is the gospel. Many know biblical information, but they do not understand the gospel.

God does not conceal His truth from men and women. They make it obscure to themselves by their own course of action. Christ gave the Jewish people abundant evidence that He was the Messiah, but most refused to accept Him, because doing so would require a distinct change in their lives. They rejected the treasure of the gospel—the greatest gift God could give.

Human theories and speculations will never lead to an understanding of God's Word. Those who suppose that they understand philosophy think their explanations are necessary to unlock the treasures of knowledge and to prevent heresies from coming into the church. But it is these very explanations that have introduced false theories and heresies. Men have tried hard to explain what they thought were complicated passages of the Bible, but too often their efforts have only confused the very passages they were trying to make clear.

It takes faith—enlightened by the intellect and controlled by a discerning heart—to recognize and appreciate the heavenly treasure. This faith is inseparable from repentance and transformation of character. To have faith means to find and accept the gospel treasure, with all the obligations involved. Without the eye of faith, we cannot "see" the gospel treasure.

Key Thought: "If men would be obedient, they would understand the plan of God's government. . . . Human beings would be altogether different from what they now are, for by exploring the mines of truth men would be ennobled. The mystery of redemption, the incarnation of Christ, His atoning sacrifice, would not be as they are now, vague in our minds. They would be not only better understood, but altogether more highly appreciated" (*Christ's Object Lessons,* p. 114).

Today's Lesson: The gospel treasure is available to everyone who is willing to make any sacrifice to possess it. It requires a total surrender of self.

The Pearl

Christ's Object Lessons, Chapter 9.

"The kingdom of heaven is like a merchant seeking beautiful pearls, who, when he had found one pearl of great price, went and sold all that he had and bought it" (Matthew 13:45, 46, NKJV).

Christ Himself is the pearl of great price. All the fullness of divinity is concentrated in Him. His righteousness, like a pure, white pearl, has no defect or stain. In Christ, we find everything that satisfies the needs and longings of the human soul—for this world and the next. Our Redeemer is like a pearl so precious that nothing else can compare with it at all.

In the parable, the pearl is not pictured as a gift. The merchant bought it, spending everything he possessed. In one sense, Jesus is a gift to us from heaven. But in another sense, He costs us everything we have and are. We must give ourselves to Him without reserve—soul, body, and spirit—to live a life of willing obedience to His requirements. It's true that we can never earn salvation, but we are to seek it earnestly and be willing to abandon anything in order to obtain it.

Some seem to be always seeking for the heavenly pearl but never find it. They do not make an entire surrender of their wrong habits. They do not die to self that Christ may live in them. They have not overcome unholy ambition and their love for worldly attractions. They seem to be always drawing near—almost Christians, yet not fully Christians—but never entering the kingdom of heaven. "Almost saved" means to be wholly lost.

Key Thought: "[At Pentecost] the Spirit of Christ animated the whole congregation; for they had found the pearl of great price.

"These scenes are to be repeated, and with greater power. . . . Christ is again to be revealed in His fulness by the Holy Spirit's power. Men will discern the value of the precious pearl, and with the apostle Paul they will say, 'What things were gain to me, those I counted loss for Christ. . . .' Phil. 3:7, 8" (*Christ's Object Lessons,* p. 121).

Today's Lesson: The gospel of Christ is a blessing that everyone may possess—the poorest, as well as the richest.

The Net

Christ's Object Lessons, Chapter 10.

"Again, the kingdom of heaven is like a dragnet that was cast into the sea and gathered some of every kind, which, when it was full, they drew to shore; and they sat down and gathered the good into vessels, but threw the bad away. So it will be at the end of the age. The angels will come forth, separate the wicked from among the just, and cast them into the furnace of fire" (Matthew 13:47–50, NKJV).

Just as a net gathers both desirable and undesirable fish, so the preaching of the gospel gathers all kinds of people into the church. The world is quick to point to the sins and mistakes evident in the lives of some who profess to be Christians. The world criticizes the church because of the inconsistent lives of some of its members. Even earnest Christians sometimes stumble over the sins they see in the church, wondering if God, perhaps, excuses such sin. But Jesus' parable demonstrates that although good and bad exist side by side in the church today, the judgment at the end of time will separate the genuine followers of Christ from those who are His in name only. It may not be evident now, but in the judgment it will be painfully clear who are the wicked and who are the righteous.

Both the parable of the tares and the parable of the net plainly teach that there will never be a time when all the wicked will be converted and turn to God. These parables also teach that there is no further probation after the judgment. When the work of the gospel is finished, the separation of the good and the evil will immediately follow, and the destiny of each group is forever fixed.

Key Thought: "God does not desire the destruction of any. . . . Throughout the period of probationary time His Spirit is entreating men to accept the gift of life. It is only those who reject His pleading that will be left to perish. God has declared that sin must be destroyed as an evil ruinous to the universe. Those who cling to sin will perish in its destruction" (*Christ's Object Lessons,* p. 123).

Today's Lesson: Character, not profession, decides our eternal destiny.

"Things New and Old"

Christ's Object Lessons, Chapter 11.

"Then He said to them, 'Therefore every scribe instructed concerning the kingdom of heaven is like a householder who brings out of his treasure things new and old' " (Matthew 13:52, NKJV).

The householder doesn't hoard his treasure; he uses it to bless others. And as he uses it in blessing, the treasure increases. Everyone who has the righteousness of Jesus in his heart will want to share it with others.

The Word of God is the great storehouse of truth. His love and character can also be seen in the book of nature and in the way He deals with us in life. These are the sources of the treasure that we can draw on to bless our own souls and the souls of others. Our understanding of the truths of redemption can be constantly developed as we learn more and more of God's love.

The truth as it is in Jesus can be experienced but never explained. Its height and breadth and depth pass our knowledge. Yet, we can grow in grace and knowledge. We will understand God's love to the same degree that we appreciate His sacrifice for us. As we search God's Word, the grand theme of redemption will open more fully to our minds. As long as time shall last, it will increase in brightness as we behold it, and the more we grasp of God's saving grace, the more we will be able to share its glory with others.

Key Thought: "In every age there is a new development of truth, a message of God to the people of that generation. The old truths are all essential; new truth is not independent of the old, but an unfolding of it. It is only as the old truths are understood that we can comprehend the new. . . . But it is the light which shines in the fresh unfolding of truth that glorifies the old. He who rejects or neglects the new does not really possess the old. For him it loses its vital power and becomes but a lifeless form" (*Christ's Object Lessons,* pp. 127, 128).

Today's Lesson: The theme of redemption will occupy our minds and hearts throughout eternity. There will always be deeper meanings to discover.

Asking to Give

Christ's Object Lessons, Chapter 12.

"The Lord God has given Me the tongue of the learned, that I should know how to speak a word in season to him who is weary. He awakens Me morning by morning, He awakens My ear to hear as the learned"
(Isaiah 50:4, NKJV).

When He fed the multitude and in His sermon spoke about the bread from heaven, Christ was opening to the disciples their work as His representatives. They were to receive the bread of life from His hand and give it to the people. Every blessing they received was not only for themselves; Jesus designed that they should share with others all that they received from Him. He knew how often their faith would be tested. He knew they would often be thrown into unexpected situations and realize how insufficient they were in their own strength. They would find people starving for the bread of life—and would feel how destitute and helpless they were to feed them spiritually. All this would help them realize that they must themselves receive spiritual food in order to have anything to give others. It is the same with God's people today.

We need to come to God in prayer often, asking for His grace—for ourselves so we may bless others. Then we should believe that He will do for us just what He has promised. Jesus has said, "What things soever ye desire, when ye pray, believe that ye receive them, and ye shall have them" (Mark 11:24). In this way we will be prepared to minister to those we meet. It is our privilege to behold the glory and righteousness of God and reflect these blessings to others.

Key Thought: "Let your heart break for the longing it has for God, for the living God. The life of Christ has shown what humanity can do by being partaker of the divine nature. All that Christ received from God we too may have. Then ask and receive. With the persevering faith of Jacob, with the unyielding persistence of Elijah, claim for yourself all that God has promised" (*Christ's Object Lessons,* p. 149).

Today's Lesson: Prayer does not work a change in God; instead, it brings us into harmony with Him.

Two Worshipers

Christ's Object Lessons, Chapter 13.

***"He spoke this parable to some who trusted in themselves
that they were righteous, and despised others"
(Luke 18:9, NKJV).***

The Pharisee went to the temple to worship, not because he felt he was a sinner in need of pardon but because he thought he was righteous and wanted people to see his piety.

The publican went to the temple overwhelmed with a sense of guilt. He was thinking only of his need of forgiveness and peace with God. He trusted in God's mercy.

These two individuals represent the two main classes of those who come to worship God: those who are self-righteous and those who recognize their need of a Savior. These two classes have existed ever since Cain and Abel brought their sacrifices to God. Spiritual pride is the downfall of many today. There is nothing so offensive to God or so dangerous to our eternal salvation as pride and self-sufficiency. Of all sins it is the most hopeless, the most incurable.

Those who recognize their need and are spiritually humble, however, will find the Savior ready to lift them up. It is not in Satan's power to overcome a single soul who throws himself on Christ in simple trust. "If we confess our sins, he is faithful and just to forgive us our sins, and to cleanse us from all unrighteousness" (1 John 1:9).

Key Thought: "The life in which the fear of the Lord is cherished will not be a life of sadness and gloom. It is the absence of Christ that makes the countenance sad, and the life a pilgrimage of sighs. Those who are filled with self-esteem and self-love do not feel the need of a living, personal union with Christ. . . . They desire to walk in a path wide enough to take in their own attributes. Their self-love, their love of popularity and love of praise, exclude the Saviour from their hearts. . . . But Christ dwelling in the soul is a wellspring of joy. For all who receive Him, the very keynote of the word of God is rejoicing" (*Christ's Object Lessons,* p. 162).

Today's Lesson: If we are ever to be saved, it will be through God's infinite grace, not through our own goodness.

"Shall Not God Avenge His Own?"

Christ's Object Lessons, Chapter 14.

"Shall God not avenge His own elect who cry out day and night to Him, though He bears long with them? I tell you that He will avenge them speedily. Nevertheless, when the Son of Man comes, will He really find faith on the earth?" (Luke 18:7, 8, NKJV).

In this parable, Christ draws a sharp contrast between the unjust judge and God. The judge yielded to the widow's request merely because she persistently pressed her petition, and he wanted to be free of her. He felt no pity or compassion. The point of Jesus' story is how different is God's attitude toward those who bring their needs to Him. We cannot weary God with our prayers.

Satan is our great adversary. He accuses us before God day and night (see Revelation 12:10). He tries to paint our sins in their worst light. But God has invited us to come to Him when Satan presses our guilt upon us. He promises to rebuke Satan and deliver us. Although we have sinned, Christ has taken the guilt of our sins upon Himself and offers us His own perfect righteousness. We are not left defenseless against Satan. Prayer moves God's omnipotent arm on our behalf.

The ties between heaven and earth are closer and stronger than we realize. Angels move among men and women today just as they did in Bible times. These mighty angels are poised to care for us and cooperate with our efforts to live for God.

Key Thought: "Christ desires nothing so much as to redeem His heritage from the dominion of Satan. But before we are delivered from Satan's power without, we must be delivered from his power within. The Lord permits trials in order that we may be cleansed from earthliness, from selfishness, from harsh, unchristlike traits of character. . . . Often we enter the furnace of trial with our souls darkened with selfishness; but if patient under the crucial test, we shall come forth reflecting the divine character" (*Christ's Object Lessons,* pp. 174, 175).

Today's Lesson: If we surrender our lives to Jesus, we can never be placed in a position for which God has not made provision. He will always respond to us when we turn to Him.

"This Man Receiveth Sinners"

Christ's Object Lessons, Chapter 15.

"Then all the tax collectors and the sinners drew near to Him to hear Him. And the Pharisees and scribes murmured, saying, 'This Man receives sinners and eats with them' " (Luke 15:1, 2, NKJV).

It angered the rabbis that tax collectors and sinners flocked around Jesus and listened to His words with rapt attention. These people never came to the synagogue, and they showed only contempt for the religious leaders. Yet, they enjoyed being with Jesus and took every opportunity to hear Him speak. If Jesus were truly the spiritual teacher He claimed to be, the rabbis argued, He would treat these outcasts with the indifference they deserved. "This Man receives sinners and eats with them," they sneered. They meant it as a criticism, but Jesus accepted it as a compliment. "You're right," He responded, "I do receive sinners!" He then told three parables to illustrate that His mission on earth was to receive sinners.

In the parable of the shepherd, Jesus emphasized that if there had been but one lost sheep, Christ would have died for that one sheep which could not, on its own, find its way back to the fold. God always takes the initiative to find lost sinners.

In the parable of the lost coin, Jesus focused on those who are lost in sin but who have no sense of their condition. God will recover that sin-defaced person and retrace His own image upon the recovering sinner.

The third parable—the story of the lost son—shows us the undying love of the Father for His children who have left him. The Father never stops looking for His lost child. And when the sinner returns, the Father receives him with rejoicing.

Key Thought: "Many souls go down to ruin for want of a hand stretched out to save. These erring ones may appear hard and reckless; but if they had received the same advantages that others have had, they might have revealed far more nobility of soul, and greater talent for usefulness. . . . Angels weep, while human eyes are dry and hearts are closed to pity" (*Christ's Object Lessons,* pp. 191, 192).

Today's Lesson: All the resources of heaven are given to those who are working to save the lost.

"Lost and Is Found"

Christ's Object Lessons, Chapter 16.

"When he was still a great way off, his father saw him and had compassion, and ran and fell on his neck and kissed him" (Luke 15:20, NKJV).

The parable of the prodigal son illustrates the Father's great love for His children. Even those who have known His love—who have been His son or daughter—can allow the tempter to lead them astray. They can leave the Father and go off into the far country of sin to live as they choose. The Father will not prevent them from leaving. But whoever tries to live apart from God is squandering the powers of mind, heart, and soul. He will find himself spiritually bankrupt.

The father in Jesus' story never quit looking for his son to return. In the same way, God never gives up on those who choose to turn away from Him. His love remains unchanged, and He will do everything possible to draw the sinner back home.

In his restless youth the prodigal had looked upon his father as stern and severe. So those who are deceived by Satan look upon God as hard and exacting. They regard His law as a restriction—a burdensome yoke from which they are glad to escape. In his wretchedness, the prodigal son came to himself at last; he saw that he had no one to blame for his destitute condition except himself. All his suffering was his own fault. What a picture of the sinner's condition! It was his father's love that caused him to decide to return home. So, God will draw all those to Him who do not actively refuse His love.

Key Thought: "Arise and go to your Father. He will meet you a great way off. If you take even one step toward Him in repentance, He will hasten to enfold you in His arms of infinite love. . . . The very first reaching out of the heart after God is known to Him. Never a prayer is offered, however faltering, . . . but the Spirit of God goes forth to meet it" (*Christ's Object Lessons,* p. 206).

Today's Lesson: Every sinner who returns, God will cover with the pure robe of Christ's spotless righteousness and will restore Him to the heavenly family.

SEPTEMBER 10

"Spare It This Year Also"

Christ's Object Lessons, Chapter 17.

*"A certain man had a fig tree planted in his vineyard, and
he came seeking fruit on it and found none"*
(Luke 13:6, NKJV).

The parable of the barren fig tree illustrates Christ's mission of mercy to the world, as well as God's justice and His judgment against sin. God didn't send His Son to earth to condemn men and women but that they might be saved by His sacrifice of Himself (see John 3:17). However, the very people who should have been looking for Him rejected Him. God had blessed the Jewish nation with all the advantages He could possibly bestow to make it fruitful and spiritually vibrant, but in spite of all that He had done, Israel was a barren fig tree. It was merely occupying space in His vineyard that a productive tree might fill. Israel was robbing the world of the blessings God intended for it to share with others.

In the parable, nothing would give the owner of the fig tree greater joy than to see it grow and become fruitful. He didn't give up on the tree; he showered it with even greater attention. He resolved to spare it as long as possible. But if the Jewish nation continued to be barren and unresponsive, the time would come when it must be cut down.

The warning was not for Israel alone; it sounds down to us today. How long have we received the Master's gifts? How long has He looked for us to bear fruit in our lives? Are we fruitless trees in the Lord's vineyard? Can others see the fruit of the Holy Spirit in our life? We have received rich blessings from God, and He expects us to be channels of these same blessings to others. We are to bear fruit to His glory.

Key Thought: "The heart that does not respond to divine agencies becomes hardened until it is no longer susceptible to the influence of the Holy Spirit. Then it is that the word is spoken, 'Cut it down; why cumbereth it the ground?' " (*Christ's Object Lessons,* p. 218).

Today's Lesson: In spite of our neglected opportunities to be faithful witnesses for God, He has not cut us down—He continues to spare us.

"Go Into the Highways and Hedges"

Christ's Object Lessons, Chapter 18.

"Then the master said to the servant, 'Go out into the highways and hedges, and compel them to come in, that my house may be filled' " (Luke 14:23, NKJV).

The feast Jesus speaks about in this parable represents the rich blessings God offers us through the gospel. Jesus Himself is the bread of life, the water of life. God has provided the banquet at infinite cost to Himself, and now He invites everyone to come and enjoy the riches of His generosity.

To many, however, worldly possessions, wealth, and pleasure count for more than the gospel. They make excuses for not accepting God's gracious invitation. Their refusal shows their contempt for the Master and the low value they place upon the sacrifice He has made for them. As Jesus' parable shows, God will turn from these who have spurned His invitation and find others who will be grateful for the salvation He offers.

As we share the gospel invitation, we must not wait for individuals to come to us—we must seek them out where they are. Many will accept if we approach them personally in a kind, friendly manner. We don't have to be able to speak eloquently or even have great knowledge of the Scriptures in order to win souls for Christ. Many are longing to hear a simple answer to their question: What must I do to be saved?

God does not force men and women to accept His invitation. He "compels" them to come in only in the sense that He appeals to the heart with urgency.

Key Thought: "To every soul Christ's invitation will be given. The messengers are saying, 'Come; for all things are now ready.' Heavenly angels are still working in co-operation with human agencies. . . . Angels are waiting to bear the tiding to heaven that another lost sinner has been found. The hosts of heaven are waiting, ready to strike their harps and to sing a song of rejoicing that another soul has accepted the invitation to the gospel feast" (*Christ's Object Lessons*, p. 237).

Today's Lesson: We are living in the time when God's last invitation of mercy is being given to the world. This is the message He has entrusted to us.

The Measure of Forgiveness

Christ's Object Lessons, Chapter 19.

"Then Peter came to Him and said, 'Lord, how often shall my brother sin against me, and I forgive him? Up to seven times?' " (Matthew 18:21, NKJV).

Nothing can justify an unforgiving spirit. Those who are unforgiving toward others cannot receive God's pardoning grace for themselves, because they do not understand forgiveness— neither how to forgive nor how to accept forgiveness.

The rabbis taught that one need not forgive a person after the third offense. Peter, thinking to follow Jesus' liberal example, suggested expanding forgiveness to seven offenses. But Christ helped him (and us) to see that we are never to stop forgiving. Not "seven times," Jesus told Peter, "but seventy times seven." Love forgives as often as is necessary. Love doesn't keep count. That is the way God forgives us, and it is the way we should forgive our fellow brothers and sisters. We have received freely from God; let us give freely to others. The king in Jesus' parable asks his servant, "Shouldest not thou also have had compassion on thy fellowservant, even as I had pity on thee?" (Matthew 18:33). We should forgive those who wrong us in just the same way that we would want them to forgive us should the situation be reversed. God's forgiving mercy to us is to be the measure of the mercy we show to others.

Forgiveness does not mean that we regard sin lightly. The fact that God will always forgive us doesn't mean that we have no responsibility to obey His commandments. Those who have been forgiven will be all the more careful to show their gratitude by their obedience.

Key Thought: "We are not forgiven *because* we forgive, but *as* we forgive. The ground of all forgiveness is found in the unmerited love of God, but by our attitude toward others we show whether we have made that love our own. Wherefore Christ says, 'With what judgment ye judge, ye shall be judged; and with what measure ye mete, it shall be measured to you again.' Matt. 7:2" (*Christ's Object Lessons,* p. 251).

Today's Lesson: If we do not forgive others, God cannot forgive us. Not because He will not but because we cannot accept His forgiveness if we don't have a forgiving heart.

Gain That Is Loss

Christ's Object Lessons, Chapter 20.

"God said to him, 'You fool! This night your soul will be required of you; then whose will those things be which you have provided?' So is he who lays up treasures for himself, and is not rich toward God"
(Luke 12:20, 21, NKJV).

Jesus told this parable after a man asked him to settle a dispute he was having with his brother over an inheritance. Jesus could have given a ruling on the issue. He knew what was fair and right. But He also knew the brothers were quarreling because both were covetous. So He replied, in effect, "It is not My work to settle difficulties of this kind. I came to preach the gospel and call attention to eternal values."

Then He told the story of a foolish rich man. In doing so, He wanted to point out the folly of placing our affections on this world and ignoring eternal realities. The rich man in His story had received all his wealth from God. God had caused his crops to flourish and blessed him with bountiful harvests. The rich man was so concerned about caring for his wealth that he gave no thought to God, the Source of all his blessings. He never considered that God had given him riches so that he could help the needy. He could easily have provided for the needs of many. But he closed his heart to the poor and used his great wealth to please himself.

When he died, his wealth was of no value to him, because he had no treasure in heaven.

Key Thought: "This man has lived and planned for self. He sees that the future is abundantly provided for; there is nothing for him now but to treasure and enjoy the fruits of his labors. He regards himself as favored above other men, and takes credit to himself for his wise management. He is honored by his fellow townsmen as a man of good judgment and a prosperous citizen. . . .

"The only thing that would be of value to him now he has not secured" (*Christ's Object Lessons,* p. 258).

Today's Lesson: Faithful stewards will lay up treasure in heaven by blessing others with the earthly treasure God has given them.

SEPTEMBER 14

"A Great Gulf Fixed"

Christ's Object Lessons, Chapter 21.

"Between us and you there is a great gulf fixed, so that those who want to pass from here to you cannot, nor can those from there pass to us" (Luke 16:26, NKJV).

In the parable of the rich man and Lazarus, Christ showed that human beings decide their eternal destiny by the choices they make in this life. God offers His grace to everyone. But if a person chooses to live for self, he cuts himself off from everlasting life. There will be no future probation after death in which he can make different choices. His own decisions have fixed an impassable gulf between himself and God.

It was the duty of the rich man in Jesus' story to care for just such cases as Lazarus, the beggar. God had made this man a steward of His means. So today there are many who are hungry, without clothing, without homes, whom we can help. If we neglect to do so, we incur a burden of guilt that we will have to face someday. Covetousness is a form of idolatry; all selfish indulgence is an offense in God's sight.

This parable has been used to argue that the dead are conscious after death. But in telling this story the way He did, Christ was meeting the people on their own ground. Many who were listening to Him did believe the dead were aware of what was going on. So, Jesus used this prevalent—but mistaken—idea to convey important points: that possession does not determine a person's value and that we cannot change our characters after death.

Key Thought: "To learn of Christ means to receive His grace, which is His character. But those who do not appreciate and utilize the precious opportunities and sacred influences granted them on earth, are not fitted to take part in the pure devotion of heaven. Their characters are not molded according to the divine similitude. By their own neglect they have formed a chasm which nothing can bridge. Between them and the righteous there is a great gulf fixed" (*Christ's Object Lessons,* p. 271).

Today's Lesson: We form our characters during the days of our lives here on earth, and that character determines our eternal destiny.

Saying and Doing

Christ's Object Lessons, Chapter 22.

"Not every one that saith unto me, Lord, Lord, shall enter into the kingdom of heaven; but he that doeth the will of my Father which is in heaven" (Matthew 7:21).

In giving the parable of the father and the two sons, Jesus was teaching that the test of sincerity is not in words but in deeds. In this parable the father represents God, and the vineyard represents the church. The two sons stand for two classes of people. The son who refused to obey, saying, "I will not," represents those who are living in open transgression and make no pretense of following God's will. Yet, many of these later repent and obey God's call. The son who quickly agreed to obey—but did not do so—represents professed Christians whose lives do not match their words.

The test of sincerity comes to every person. Will there be actions or only words? Will our lives give evidence that we are obedient to God's will? Self-righteousness is not true righteousness, and God will accept only sincere service from the heart. When the appeals of the Holy Spirit come, the only safe course is to respond without delay. There is more hope for open sinners than there is for professed Christians who do not live what they claim to believe.

God is our Father in heaven, and He has a father's claim to our faithful service. Jesus is an example of what every son and daughter of God may be. He obeyed His Father while on earth, not in word only but in deed.

Key Thought: "God's great object in the working out of His providences is to try men, to give them opportunity to develop character. Thus He proves whether they are obedient or disobedient to His commands. Good works do not purchase the love of God, but they reveal that we possess that love. If we surrender the will to God, we shall not work in order to earn God's love. His love as a free gift will be received into the soul, and from love to Him we shall delight to obey His commandments" (*Christ's Object Lessons,* p. 283).

Today's Lesson: Actions, not words, are the real test of character and of our love for God.

The Lord's Vineyard

Christ's Object Lessons, Chapter 23.

"There was a certain landowner who planted a vineyard and set a hedge around it, dug a winepress in it and built a tower. And he leased it to vinedressers and went into a far country" (Matthew 21:33, NKJV).

In this parable, Jesus pointed out the rich blessings God had given to the Jewish people. It was His purpose that the Jews would use these advantages to share the knowledge of His truth and His love with the world. They were to give the world an example of faithful obedience to God. As they did this, God would bless them further until they would be the means of enlightening the whole world. He intended to make Israel a praise and a glory among the nations. He gave them every spiritual advantage.

The parable pictures God choosing land from the wilderness and fashioning it into a beautiful vineyard. It pictures the care He lavished upon His vineyard—fencing it and planting it with the most choice vines. He anticipated a rich harvest. But Israel failed to carry out the lofty purpose God envisioned. Jesus showed how the Jewish nation was bringing ruin on itself and forfeiting God's blessings.

The parable of the vineyard applies not just to the Jewish nation; it also has meaning for God's church today. The church is precious in God's eyes. He wants to see His people appreciating His blessings and walking with Him in grateful obedience. Through His people today, God wants to manifest to the world His character and the principles of His kingdom. It is our privilege to be His ambassadors and to be channels of His blessings to a world that needs to understand His love and the importance of His commandments.

Key Thought: "Shall the warnings from God be passed by unheeded? . . . Shall the world's scorn, the pride of reason, conformity to human customs and traditions, hold the professed followers of Christ from service to Him? Will they reject God's word as the Jewish leaders rejected Christ? The result of Israel's sin is before us. Will the church of today take warning?" (*Christ's Object Lessons,* p. 306).

Today's Lesson: Even today, Christ waits to manifest His character and the principles of His kingdom to the world.

Without a Wedding Garment

Christ's Object Lessons, Chapter 24.

"Then he said to his servants, 'The wedding is ready, but those who were invited were not worthy' "
(Matthew 22:8, NKJV).

The parable of the wedding garment is another illustration of the gospel invitation. In this story, Jesus focuses on those who come to enjoy the marriage supper but who are not concerned to honor the king who is providing the feast.

The wedding garment that the king requests each guest to wear represents the righteous character of Christ that each person must possess in order to be a guest at the wedding. The Bible says that the fine linen "is the righteousness of saints" (Revelation 19:8). Only this garment can make us fit to appear in God's presence, and He provides it as the free gift of His grace.

But as the king reviewed his guests, he noticed that one man had not put on the garment He had graciously provided. This represents the judgment, when everyone's true character will be revealed. Not all who profess to be Christians are true disciples. Before the final reward is given, it must be decided who are worthy to share the inheritance of the righteous. This decision must be made prior to the second coming of Christ in the clouds of heaven, for when He comes, His reward is with Him "to give every man according as his work shall be" (Revelation 22:12).

The guest who refused to wear the wedding garment had no excuse. He had rejected the only thing that would fit him for a place at the table. Those who reject the gift of Christ's righteousness are rejecting the only thing that will fit them to sit down with Him at the wedding feast in His kingdom.

Key Thought: "This covering, the robe of His own righteousness, Christ will put upon every repenting, believing soul. . . .

"This robe, woven in the loom of heaven, has in it not one thread of human devising. Christ in His humanity wrought out a perfect character, and this character He offers to impart to us" (*Christ's Object Lessons,* p. 311).

Today's Lesson: Nothing we can do will cover our sins. That is why God offers to clothe us with the robe of Jesus' perfect righteousness.

Talents

Christ's Object Lessons, Chapter 25.

"And to one he gave five talents, to another two, and to another one, to each according to his own ability; and immediately he went on a journey"
(Matthew 25:15, NKJV).

Each person has his or her place in God's eternal plan. To each of us He has committed talents and abilities. The question we should be asking is not *How much have I received?* but *What am I doing with that which I have?* The development of all our powers is the first duty we owe to God and to our fellow human beings. If we are not growing daily in usefulness, we are not fulfilling God's purpose for us. When we take the name of Christ, we pledge to become all that it is possible for us to become under His instruction and blessings. He expects us to cultivate the gifts He has given us to the highest possible degree so that we may do the greatest amount of good we can.

God accepts only those who are determined to aim high—to do their best. He never lowers His standard of righteousness, but He will provide all the help and grace we need to reach the standard.

God gives us talents; we form our characters by the use we make of them. But He requires only that we develop and use what He has given us. He does not expect the one-talent person to do the work of the one with ten talents. But He does expect us to make the most of all the talents He has given.

Key Thought: "Be ambitious, for the Master's glory, to cultivate every grace of character. . . .

"A character formed according to the divine likeness is the only treasure that we can take from this world to the next. Those who are under the instruction of Christ in this world will take every divine attainment with them to the heavenly mansions. And in heaven we are continually to improve. How important, then, is the development of character in this life" (*Christ's Object Lessons,* p. 332).

Today's Lesson: Whatever God asks us to do, we can do in His strength. All His commands come with a promise that He will help us to obey.

"Friends by the Mammon of Unrighteousness"

Christ's Object Lessons, Chapter 26.

"No servant can serve two masters; for either he will hate the one and love the other, or else he will be loyal to the one and despise the other. You cannot serve God and mammon" (Luke 16:13, NKJV).

In Jesus' day, as in ours, men and women were caught up in the pursuit of wealth. Jesus told this story of a shrewd but dishonest servant to teach the lesson that those in the world often pursue their goals more energetically and with more planning than do those who are seeking to advance God's kingdom. "The sons of this world," He said, "are more shrewd in their generation than the sons of light" (Luke 16:8, NKJV). That is, the world displays more wisdom and earnestness in serving self than God's people demonstrate in their service for Him. The Lord has given His people capabilities, influence, and money so they can work with Him in saving souls for His kingdom. But how often these blessings either are left idle or are diverted to our own well being.

Christ calls upon every one to consider—to make an honest reckoning. Put on one side of the scale Jesus—eternal life, truth, heaven, and redeemed souls. Put on the other side every advantage and attraction the world can offer. Weigh the loss of your own soul and the souls of those you might have been instrumental in saving against the reality of eternal life in heaven and the earth made new. Weigh the value of these for time and eternity. "What shall it profit a man, if he shall gain the whole world, and lose his own soul?" (Mark 8:36). Heaven will be precious indeed to those who have rightly valued the blessings of God's kingdom in comparison with the fleeting pleasures of this world.

Key Thought: "The lesson of this parable is for all. Everyone will be held responsible for the grace given him through Christ. Life is too solemn to be absorbed in temporal or earthly matters. The Lord desires that we shall communicate to others that which the eternal and unseen communicates to us" (*Christ's Object Lessons,* p. 373).

Today's Lesson: Salvation and eternal life are infinitely more valuable than anything this world can possibly offer.

"Who Is My Neighbour?"

Christ's Object Lessons, Chapter 27.

" 'Which of these three do you think was neighbor to him who fell among the thieves?' And he said, 'He who showed mercy on him.' Then Jesus said to him, 'Go and do likewise' " (Luke 10:36, 37, NKJV).

A lawyer asked Jesus, "What shall I do to have eternal life?" (see Luke 10:25). In His answer Jesus focused on obeying God's commandments. He always presented the law as a divine whole, declaring that it is impossible to break one commandment and keep the others, for the same principle runs through all of them.

Jesus' answer to the lawyer's second question: Who is my neighbor? (see verse 29), involved a story—the story of the good Samaritan. Here Christ taught that our neighbor is anyone, everyone, who needs our help. Our neighbors are not merely those who belong to the same church we do. A neighbor is not limited to those who belong to our own race, class, color, or nationality. Our neighbor is every soul who has been wounded and bruised by the adversary.

In giving this lesson, Christ presented the principles of the law in a direct, forcible way, showing His Jewish listeners their prejudice and their reluctance to carry out the principles that God had given in His law. His words were so definite and pointed that there could be no rebuttal.

Like the Jews in Jesus' day, many Christians today consider loving their neighbor to be a relatively unimportant issue. But according to this parable, it is extremely important to God. Whether we love our neighbor—and how we show that love—is crucial to our eternal salvation.

Key Thought: "The sanctification of the soul by the working of the Holy Spirit is the implanting of Christ's nature in humanity. Gospel religion is Christ in the life—a living, active principle. It is the grace of Christ revealed in character and wrought out in good works. The principles of the gospel cannot be disconnected from any department of practical life. Every line of Christian experience and labor is to be a representation of the life of Christ" (*Christ's Object Lessons,* p. 384).

Today's Lesson: A right example will do more to benefit the world than all our profession.

The Reward of Grace

Christ's Object Lessons, Chapter 28.

"Take what is yours and go your way. I wish to give to this last man the same as to you. Is it not lawful for me to do what I wish with my own things? Or is your eye evil because I am good?" (Matthew 20:14, 15, NKJV).

Peter heard Jesus tell the young ruler, "If you want to be perfect, sell everything you have and give it all to the poor. Then, follow Me, and you will have treasure in heaven" (see Matthew 19:21). Peter was interested in finding out more about this "treasure in heaven." Coming to Jesus, he pointed out that he and the other disciples had left everything to follow Jesus. What reward would they receive? he wanted to know.

But the very question revealed a selfish motivation for following Jesus. So, Jesus told a parable to illustrate how God deals with His servants—and the spirit He wants them to have as they work for Him. The workers did not all labor equally, but they all received the same wage. The point of the story is that God is equally gracious to all. Salvation is given not as payment for services rendered but as a free gift. It is not how long we have worked for the Master or what we have accomplished that determines our reward. He values the willingness and faithfulness with which we serve Him.

When Christ abides in the soul, when we have the right motivation for serving Him, the thought of reward is not uppermost in our thinking. Yes, we value the rewards He has promised—salvation and all other blessings—but we serve Him from love, and we trust that He will fulfill all His promises as He sees best, giving us everything we need.

Key Thought: "Not in our learning, not in our position, not in our numbers or entrusted talents, not in the will of man, is to be found the secret of success. Feeling our inefficiency we are to contemplate Christ, and through Him . . . the willing and obedient will gain victory after victory" (*Christ's Object Lessons,* p. 404).

Today's Lesson: Without Christ's grace of pardon and His grace of power, our highest achievements are no more than sounding brass.

"To Meet the Bridegroom"

Christ's Object Lessons, Chapter 29.

"While they went to buy, the bridegroom came, and those who were ready went in with him to the wedding; and the door was shut" (Matthew 25:10, NKJV).

As Christ watched a wedding party waiting for the bridegroom, He told His disciples a parable of ten bridesmaids. The story illustrates the experience of His church just before His second coming. Some of the bridesmaids had oil for their lamps, and some did not. These represent two groups within the church awaiting the coming of Jesus. They are called virgins because they profess a pure faith. The lamps represent the Word of God. The psalmist says, "Thy word is a lamp unto my feet, and a light unto my path" (Psalm 119:105). The oil is a symbol of the Holy Spirit. This story also points out the sad fact that the return of Jesus would be delayed.

As the bridesmaids wait for the bridegroom, the time seems long. Their faith is tested. At last, at midnight, a cry is heard, "The bridegroom is coming, go meet Him!" But some who are waiting have no oil in their lamps. They are destitute of the Holy Spirit and can only wander in darkness.

Knowledge of God and His Word is of no use without the quickening power of the Holy Spirit. A theory of truth, unaccompanied by the Holy Spirit, cannot give spiritual life or transform the soul. Without the light given by the Spirit, men and women cannot distinguish truth from error, and they will fall under Satan's powerful temptations.

Key Thought: "The religion of Christ means more than the forgiveness of sin; it means taking away our sins, and filling the vacuum with the graces of the Holy Spirit. . . . It means a heart emptied of self, and blessed with the abiding presence of Christ. . . . The beauty and fragrance of the character of Christ revealed in the life testifies that God has indeed sent His Son into the world to be its Saviour" (*Christ's Object Lessons,* pp. 419, 420).

Today's Lesson: The light that faithful, last-day Christians carry is not head knowledge of Bible truth but transformed lives that attract others to the good news of Christ's return.

God's Purpose for His Church

The Acts of the Apostles, Chapter 1.

*"He hath chosen us in him before the foundation of the
world, that we should be holy and without blame before
him in love. . . . To the praise of the glory of his grace,
wherein he hath made us accepted in the beloved . . . . that
in the dispensation of the fulness of times he might gather
together in one all things in Christ, both which are in
heaven, and which are on earth; even in him"
(Ephesians 1:4–10).*

The church is God's appointed means for the salvation of men and women. It was organized for service, and its mission is to carry the gospel to the world. God had designed the Jewish nation to be a house of prayer for all people (see Isaiah 56:7). Israel's main purpose was to reveal God's character to men and women everywhere. God committed to them His sacred Scriptures. He wanted them to lift up Christ before all nations through the sanctuary service.

But the people of Israel lost sight of their high privileges as God's representatives. They shut themselves away from the world in order to escape temptation. The restrictions God had placed upon their association with idolaters, they used to build up a wall of separation.

All that Israel had failed to do, God now asked the Christian church to fulfill following Jesus' return to heaven. The church, to be successful, was to be God's city of refuge in a revolted world. It is the theater of His grace in which He delights to reveal His power to transform hearts.

Key Thought: "The Saviour turned from them [the Jewish nation] to entrust to others the privileges they had abused and the work they had slighted. God's glory must be revealed, His word established. Christ's kingdom must be set up in the world. The salvation of God must be made known in the cities of the wilderness; and the disciples were called to do the work that the Jewish leaders had failed to do" (*The Acts of the Apostles,* p. 16).

Today's Lesson: God's people today are to allow His grace to transform their hearts so they may unfold His truth of those who are searching for salvation.

The Training of the Twelve

The Acts of the Apostles, Chapter 2.

***"Verily, verily, I say unto you, He that believeth on me,
the works that I do shall he do also; and greater works
than these shall he do; because I go unto my Father"
(John 14:12).***

Jesus did not choose the learning of the Jewish Sanhedrin or the power of Rome to carry on His work. He chose humble men He could train as the leaders of His church. In turn, they were to train others and send them out with the gospel message.

He ordained the twelve disciples as the first step in the organization of the church, and in doing so, He chose feeble agencies through whom His word and Spirit could be dispersed to the world. Their main task was to go forth as His witnesses to declare to the world what they had seen and heard of Him.

One of the important lessons Jesus tried to teach His disciples was that in God's kingdom there are no territorial lines, no caste, no aristocracy, no higher and lower classes. In Him, the wall of partition between Israel and all other nations was broken down (see Ephesians 2:14).

The disciples presented a wide variety of character; they would find unity of feeling, thought, and action only in Christ.

Key Thought: "As Christ's earthly ministry drew to a close, and He realized that He must soon leave His disciples to carry on the work without His personal supervision, He sought to encourage them and to prepare them for the future. He did not deceive them with false hopes. As an open book He read what was to be. He knew He was about to be separated from them, to leave them as sheep among wolves. . . . He knew that for witnessing to Him as the Messiah, some of them would suffer death. And something of this He told them. In speaking of their future, He was plain and definite, that in their coming trial they might remember His words and be strengthened to believe in Him as the Redeemer" (*The Acts of the Apostles,* p. 21).

Today's Lesson: One of the strengths of the church is its diversity. We need to value these differences and gain from them.

The Great Commission

The Acts of the Apostles, Chapter 3.

"Ye shall receive power, after that the Holy Ghost is come upon you: and ye shall be witnesses unto me both in Jerusalem, and in all Judaea, and in Samaria, and unto the uttermost part of the earth" (Acts 1:8).

Before ascending to heaven, Christ gave His disciples their commission. He told them that they were to be the executors of His will, in which He bequeathed to the world the treasures of eternal life. This gospel commission is the great missionary charter of Christ's kingdom and extends to the present day.

The disciples were to carry their work forward in Christ's name. That name contains the vital power by which sinners may be saved. Their faith was to center on Him.

When Christ sent the disciples forth, He plainly set before them the necessity of speaking with the same simplicity with which He had spoken. He did not tell them that their work would be easy. He explained the vast confederacy of evil arrayed against them. But He assured the disciples that they would not be left to fight alone—that He would take upon Himself the responsibility for their success.

He told the disciples that they were to begin their work in Jerusalem, because many there secretly believed Jesus to be the Messiah. And shortly they saw the wisdom of these words, as thousands were converted by the power of the Spirit.

Key Thought: "The Saviour knew that no argument, however logical, would melt hard hearts or break through the crust of worldliness and selfishness. He knew that His disciples must receive the heavenly endowment; that the gospel would be effective only as it was proclaimed by hearts made warm and lips made eloquent by a living knowledge of Him who is the way, the truth, and the life. The work committed to the disciples would require great efficiency; for the tide of evil ran deep and strong against them. A vigilant, determined leader was in command of the forces of darkness, and the followers of Christ could battle for the right only through the help that God, by His Spirit, would give them" (*The Acts of the Apostles,* p. 31).

Today's Lesson: The gospel is still most effectively presented in simplicity and earnestness.

Pentecost

The Acts of the Apostles, Chapter 4.

"When the day of Pentecost was fully come, they were all with one accord in one place" (Acts 2:1).

As the disciples waited for the fulfillment of Christ's promise, they humbled their hearts in true repentance and confessed their unbelief. And they determined that, so far as possible, they would atone for their former unbelief by bravely confessing Jesus before the world. They prayed for the ability to preach and teach effectively. Putting away all their differences and all desire for the supremacy, they came close together in Christian fellowship.

These days of preparation were days of deep heart-searching. The disciples felt their spiritual need and cried to the Lord for the Holy Spirit who was to fit them for the work of saving souls. At Pentecost the Spirit came upon the waiting disciples with a fullness that reached every heart. They began to speak with fluency languages they had not been able to speak before. Now they could freely talk to the many Jews who came from different lands to celebrate the feasts in Jerusalem. From this time on, the language of the disciples was pure, simple, and accurate, whether they spoke in their native tongue or in a foreign language.

The priests and rulers were very angry at this wonderful manifestation. Peter declared that this demonstration of the Spirit was a direct fulfillment of Joel's prophecy (see Joel 2:28–32).

In his sermon, Peter pointedly pointed out the fact that the Jewish people had rejected Christ because they had been deceived by the priests and rulers and that if they waited for these leaders to acknowledge Christ before they dared to do so themselves, they would never accept Him.

Key Thought: "The arguments of the apostles alone, though clear and convincing, would not have removed the prejudice that had withstood so much evidence. But the Holy Spirit sent the arguments home to hearts with divine power. The words of the apostles were as sharp arrows of the Almighty, convicting men of their terrible guilt in rejecting and crucifying the Lord of glory" (*The Acts of the Apostles,* p. 45).

Today's Lesson: Our most persuasive arguments for Christ are never stronger than power of the Holy Spirit who accompanies them to the hearts of our listeners.

The Gift of the Spirit

The Acts of the Apostles, Chapter 5.

"I will pray the Father, and He will give you another Helper, that He may abide with you forever, even the Spirit of truth, whom the world cannot receive, because it neither sees Him nor knows Him; but you know Him, for He dwells with you and will be in you. I will not leave you orphans; I will come to you" (John 14:16–18, NKJV).

The promise of the Holy Spirit is not limited to any age or to any race. From the day of Pentecost in the time of the apostles to the present age, the Comforter has been sent to all who yielded themselves fully to the Lord and to His service. To everyone who has accepted Christ as a personal Savior, the Holy Spirit comes as a counselor, guide, and witness.

Facing great opposition, the disciples were compelled to strive with all their God-given powers to reach the measure of the stature of men and women in Christ Jesus. Daily, they prayed for fresh supplies of grace, that they might reach higher and still higher toward perfection.

Spiritual ecstasy under extraordinary circumstances does not necessarily prove that a person is a genuine Christian. Rapture is not holiness. Holiness is an entire surrender of the will to God. It is living by every word that proceeds from the mouth of God. It is doing His will and relying on Him with unquestioning confidence for all our needs.

The Holy Spirit regenerates us and makes the salvation of Jesus, accomplished for us by His death, effective in our lives.

Key Thought: "There are some who, instead of wisely improving present opportunities, are idly waiting for some special season of spiritual refreshing by which their ability to enlighten others will be greatly increased. They neglect present duties and privileges, and allow their light to burn dim, while they look forward to a time when, without any effort on their part, they will be made the recipients of special blessing, by which they will be transformed and fitted for service" (*The Acts of the Apostles,* p. 54).

Today's Lesson: The latter rain of the Holy Spirit will come only to those who have let the Spirit mature them for the harvest.

At the Temple Gate

The Acts of the Apostles, Chapter 6.

"Silver and gold I do not have, but what I do have I give you: In the name of Jesus Christ of Nazareth, rise up and walk" (Acts 3:6, NKJV).

Peter and John were going up to the temple to worship when they saw at the "Beautiful Gate" a cripple from birth who had longed to see Jesus that he might be healed. He persuaded some friends to bring him daily to the temple, thinking that he would see Jesus—but then he learned that Jesus had been crucified.

As Peter and John passed, this crippled man asked for some money. Peter declared his poverty but offered to share what he had—the mercy and power of Christ. More than that, he took the cripple by his hand and helped him to stand on his feet, free from pain. Onlookers saw what happened, and they made it clear that the cure had been done in the name and through the power of Jesus of Nazareth whom God had raised from the dead.

The healed man held on to Peter for sheer joy, while a crowd quickly gathered. Peter gave another dramatic sermon about the crucified Messiah who had been resurrected. In spite of this miracle, the priests and rulers maintained their persistent malignancy—and they arrested Peter.

The next day, the rulers, elders, and scribes met together for the trial. No longer was Peter impulsive and self-confident as they had known him to be in the past. Instead, he forcefully defended himself—and His Master.

Key Thought: "The wrath of God is not declared against unrepentant sinners merely because of the sins they have committed, but because, when called to repent, they choose to continue in resistance, repeating the sins of the past in defiance of the light given them. If the Jewish leaders had submitted to the convicting power of the Holy Spirit, they would have been pardoned; but they were determined not to yield. In the same way, the sinner, by continued resistance, places himself where the Holy Spirit cannot influence him" (*The Acts of the Apostles,* p. 62).

Today's Lesson: Every decision we make today—good or evil—causes it to become easier to make that same decision tomorrow.

A Warning Against Hypocrisy

The Acts of the Apostles, Chapter 7.

"Then Ananias, hearing these words, fell down and breathed his last. So great fear came upon all those who heard these things" (Acts 5:5, NKJV).

M any of the early believers were immediately cut off from family and friends by zealous and angry Jews, making it necessary to provide them with food and shelter. But the believers "were of one heart and one soul; neither did anyone say that any of things he possessed was his own, but they had all things in common" (Acts 4:32, NKJV).

The conduct of Ananias and Sapphira was in sharp contract to this prevailing benevolence. With the others, these professed disciples had shared the privilege of hearing the gospel; they were present at the dramatic events of Pentecost. Under deep conviction of the Holy Spirit the couple had made a pledge to the Lord to give the proceeds from the sale of certain property to the church. But they yielded to feelings of covetousness, regretting their promise and feeling they had been too hasty. After talking the matter over, they decided not to fulfill their pledge and to hold back a large share of the money for themselves.

God hates hypocrisy and falsehood. Peter was enlightened by the Spirit regarding the fraud, and he confronted Ananias and Sapphira. The exposure resulted in their deaths. In God's wisdom, this confrontation was necessary to guard the young church from becoming demoralized. It was a warning to the Christian church for all time to come to avoid pretense and hypocrisy.

Key Thought: "But the hearts of men become hardened through selfishness, and, like Ananias and Sapphira, they are tempted to withhold part of the price, while pretending to fulfill God's requirements. Many spend money lavishly in self-gratification. Men and women consult their pleasure and gratify their taste, while they bring to God, almost unwillingly, a stinted offering. They forget that God will one day demand a strict account of how His goods have been used, and that He will no more accept the pittance they hand into the treasury than He accepted the offering of Ananias and Sapphira" (*The Acts of the Apostles,* p. 75).

Today's Lesson: God loves a cheerful, willing giver. Promises to God should be kept.

SEPTEMBER 30

Before the Sanhedrin

The Acts of the Apostles, Chapter 8.

"So they departed from the presence of the council, rejoicing that they were counted worthy to suffer shame for His name" (Acts 5:41, NKJV).

The disciples continued to preach in the most difficult place in the world—Jerusalem, where the deepest prejudice and confusion prevailed. Priests and rulers heard with amazement the bold testimony of the disciples, whose work was accompanied by signs and miracles. A great number of believers were joining the young church.

But the priests and rulers, failing to silence the disciples, again moved to imprison them. The disciples answered all the charges with a simple defense: "We ought to obey God rather than men" (Acts 5:29). The disciples turned the tables on their accusers by charging the members of the Sanhedrin with murdering the Messiah!

When the rulers heard this, they were so enraged that they proposed to kill the disciples even as they had done with Jesus. But Gamaliel, "a teacher of the law held in respect" (Acts 5:34), kept a cool head. He warned them that they might be fighting against God, and he counseled that it would be better to release the disciples and wait to see if their little movement would disintegrate or grow.

Key Thought: "What was the strength of those who in the past have suffered persecution for Christ's sake? It was union with God, union with the Holy Spirit, union with Christ. Reproach and persecution have separated many from earthly friends, but never from the love of Christ. Never is the tempest-tried soul more dearly loved by His Saviour than when he is suffering reproach for the truth's sake. 'I will love him,' Christ said, 'and will manifest Myself to him.' John 14:21. When for the truth's sake the believer stands at the bar of earthly tribunals, Christ stands by his side. When he is confined within prison walls, Christ manifests Himself to him and cheers his heart with His love. When he suffers death for Christ's sake, the Saviour says to him, They may kill the body, but they cannot hurt the soul. 'Be of good cheer; I have overcome the world.'. . . John 16:33" (*The Acts of the Apostles,* pp. 85, 86).

Today's Lesson: All opposition to God's work will ultimately fail.

The Seven Deacons

The Acts of the Apostles, Chapter 9.

"Therefore, brethren, seek out from among you seven men of good reputation, full of the Holy Spirit and wisdom, whom we may appoint over this business"
(Acts 6:3, NKJV).

The early church grew rapidly and was made up of many classes of people and different nationalities. Early on, some Greek-speaking Jewish church members complained against the Hebrew-speaking Jewish members, claiming that their widows were being neglected in the daily distribution of food.

The apostles wisely realized that the twelve of them could not properly care for all the issues arising in the growing membership. So, they took the important step of delegating some of the burdens of leadership to others. Calling the church together, they outlined a plan of electing deacons to assume various duties in order to free the apostles for the work of preaching the gospel. These deacons would oversee special lines of work such as determining individual needs, as well as caring for the general financial well-being of the church.

The beneficial results of this far-reaching decision were immediate— "The word of God spread, and the number of the disciples multiplied greatly in Jerusalem, and a great many of the priests were obedient to the faith" (Acts 6:7, NKJV). This growth was due to the apostles being able to spend more time preaching—and also to the zeal and good judgment shown by the seven deacons who were selected.

Key Thought: " 'God is not the author of confusion, but of peace, as in all churches of the saints.' 1 Corinthians 14:33. He requires that order and system be observed in the conduct of church affairs today no less than in the days of old. He desires His work to be carried forward with thoroughness and exactness so that He may place upon it the seal of His approval. Christian is to be united with Christian, church with church, the human instrumentality co-operating with the divine, every agency subordinate to the Holy Spirit, and all combined in giving to the world the good tidings of the grace of God" (*The Acts of the Apostles,* p. 96).

Today's Lesson: Various gifts are required for the well-being of a local church. No group or individual has all the answers or leadership abilities.

October 2

The First Christian Martyr

The Acts of the Apostles, Chapter 10.

"And Stephen, full of faith and power, did great wonders and signs among the people" (Acts 6:8, NKJV).

Stephen was a man of piety and faith. He was a student of the prophecies and learned in the law. He ably defended gospel truths and defeated his opponents with his arguments.

He was soon brought to trial before the Sanhedrin. Jewish scholars from surrounding countries were summoned to refute his arguments; among them was Saul of Tarsus. Because the priests and rulers could not discredit Stephen's doctrinal positions, they brought in false accusers who told lies about him.

As Stephen faced his judges, his face shone with a holy radiance. He began his defense against the lying charges against him with a clear, thrilling voice, holding the assembly spellbound. He rehearsed the history of God's chosen people, demonstrating his own loyalty to God and to the Jewish faith. When He reached the coming of the Messiah and connected Jesus with this event, the priest pretended to be filled with horror and tore his robe. The Sanhedrin was in a tumult, and Stephen knew he was giving his last testimony. He concluded abruptly, turning on his infuriated judges with a scathing indictment of what they had done to Jesus.

In satanic rage, his persecutors grabbed him and "cast him out of the city" (Acts 7:58), where they stoned him to death. But his death made a profound impression on Saul, who was to figure largely in the early church's subsequent history.

Key Thought: "After the death of Stephen, Saul was elected a member of the Sanhedrin council in consideration of the part he had acted on that occasion. . . . But soon this relentless persecutor was to be employed in building up the church that he was now tearing down. A Mightier than Satan had chosen Saul to take the place of the martyred Stephen, to preach and suffer for His name, and to spread far and wide the tidings of salvation through His blood" (*The Acts of the Apostles,* p. 102).

Today's Lesson: In the last days, individuals will stand before tribunals as did Stephen to give an answer for their faith. God will be with them as He was with Stephen.

290

The Gospel in Samaria

The Acts of the Apostles, Chapter 11.

"*Then Philip went down to the city of Samaria and preached Christ to them" (Acts 8:5, NKJV).*

A fter the death of Stephen, persecution against the Christians arose so relentlessly in Jerusalem that many fled to locations scattered throughout Judea and Samaria. During this perilous time, Nicodemus publicly expressed his faith in the crucified Savior. He and Joseph of Arimathea came out openly for the new Christian faith and shared their great wealth and influence to help sustain the persecuted church. Many who had shown Nicodemus great respect when he was wealthy now scorned and persecuted him when he became a poor man—but he never faltered in the defense of his new faith.

When the Jerusalem Christians were scattered by persecution, they went forth filled with missionary zeal. Philip, one of the seven deacons, went to Samaria. He was a persuasive, eloquent preacher. The "multitudes with one accord heeded the things spoken by Philip, hearing and seeing the miracles which he did" (Acts 8:6, NKJV).

While Philip was in Samaria, a heavenly messenger told him to go down the south road from Jerusalem to Gaza. There he found an Ethiopian of great authority who worked directly for his queen. Philip presented the gospel to him as they rode together in his chariot— and baptized him. This man would give the light he had received to others.

The same Spirit still guides God's faithful messengers to individuals who are ready to receive the gospel. From faith to faith, the good news goes from generation to generation.

Key Thought: "This Ethiopian represented a large class who need to be taught by such missionaries as Philip—men who will hear the voice of God and go where He sends them. There are many who are reading the Scriptures who cannot understand their true import. All over the world men and women are looking wistfully to heaven. Prayers and tears and inquiries go up from souls longing for light, for grace, for the Holy Spirit. Many are on the verge of the kingdom, waiting only to be gathered in" (*The Acts of the Apostles,* p. 109).

Today's Lesson: In God's providence, all things work together to accomplish His purposes—even persecution. The church flourishes under difficult conditions.

From Persecutor to Disciple

The Acts of the Apostles, Chapter 12.

" 'Lord, what do You want me to do?' And the Lord said to him, 'Arise and go into the city, and you will be told what you must do' " (Acts 9:6, NKJV).

Saul was a Jew who was also a Roman citizen by birth. He had been educated under eminent rabbis in Jerusalem. During Stephen's trial and conviction, he had taken a prominent role.

When persecution came to the Jerusalem Christians, they scattered and made converts in other cities. The Jews pursued their attacks against these far-flung Christians, as well. They sent Saul to Damascus to help stamp out this troublesome sect by arresting Christians and bringing them back to Jerusalem for trial.

Shortly before noon, on the outskirts of Damascus, a voice and a bright light stopped Saul in his tracks. Blinded and bewildered, he fell to the ground, only to hear, "Saul, Saul, why persecutest thou Me?"

In a flash, he realized that by persecuting Christ's followers, he had been doing Satan's work. He now saw the truthfulness of the Christian claims. He recalled Stephen's words in all their clarity.

After the light faded, his companions led Saul, still unable to see, into Damascus. The Christians in the city were afraid this was all a ruse to learn where they were hiding. They refused to have anything to do with their persecutor. Saul spent the time piecing together the prophecies in the Old Testament referring to the Messiah and asking Jesus for forgiveness for his sins.

At last, an angel sent Ananias to welcome Paul into the Christian church!

Key Thought: "Many have an idea that they are responsible to Christ alone for their light and experience, independent of His recognized followers on earth. Jesus is the friend of sinners, and His heart is touched with their woe. He has all power, both in heaven and on earth; but He respects the means that He has ordained for the enlightenment and salvation of men; He directs sinners to the church, which He has made a channel of light to the world" (*The Acts of the Apostles,* p. 122).

Today's Lesson: In the last days, some of the church's greatest enemies will be converted and become its most staunch defenders.

Days of Preparation

The Acts of the Apostles, Chapter 13.

"Saul increased all the more in strength and confounded the Jews who dwelt in Damascus, proving that this Jesus is the Christ" (Acts 9:22, NKJV).

The news of Saul's conversion came as a great surprise to the Jews. Courageous, independent, persevering—Saul's talents would have enabled him to serve the Jewish nation in almost any capacity. He could reason with extraordinary clearness, and his withering sarcasm could place an opponent in an unpleasant position. But now the Jewish leaders saw this young man of unusual promise united with their enemies.

As Paul continued to preach Christ, the admiration of his former friends swiftly turned to intense hatred. Paul left for a safe retreat in Arabia. Here he had time to reflect further on his new course. Jesus communed with him and established him in his new faith. Here Paul saw more clearly the meaning of his call "to be an apostle of Jesus Christ through the will of God" (1 Corinthians 1:1, NKJV).

After his time in Arabia, Paul returned to Damascus and continued preaching Christianity with vigor. The Jews decided to kill him. Escaping from Damascus, Paul went to Jerusalem to meet Peter, but he found that the Christians there were still afraid of him. Barnabas vouched for Saul's sincerity, but he soon had to flee for his life once more.

Key Thought: "A general slain in battle is lost to his army, but his death gives no additional strength to the enemy. But when a man of prominence joins the opposing force, not only are his services lost, but those to whom he joins himself gain a decided advantage. Saul of Tarsus, on his way to Damascus, might easily have been struck dead by the Lord, and much strength would have been withdrawn from the persecuting power. But God in His providence not only spared Saul's life, but converted him, thus transferring a champion from the side of the enemy to the side of Christ. An eloquent speaker and a severe critic, Paul, with his stern purpose and undaunted courage, possessed the very qualifications needed in the early church" (*The Acts of the Apostles,* p. 124).

Today's Lesson: The experience of Paul teaches us that it is not always wise to seek confrontation.

A Seeker for Truth

The Acts of the Apostles, Chapter 14.

***"There was a certain man in Caesarea called Cornelius,
a centurion of what was called the Italian Regiment,
a devout man and one who feared God with all his
household, who gave alms generously to the people, and
prayed to God always" (Acts10:1, 2, NKJV).***

While at Joppa, Peter was called by God to take the gospel to Cornelius, a Roman centurion. Through his contacts with the Jews, Cornelius had already gained a knowledge of God and worshiped Him sincerely. He was looking for the Messiah and was open to more light.

An angel could have told Cornelius the story of Jesus, but it was God's plan that Peter—someone subject to the same human weaknesses as was Cornelius—should be the one to bring the gospel to this Roman soldier of wealth and noble birth.

God was gently opening a new phase of His work; the young Christian church was to include Gentiles, as well as Jews. This would require a decided change in the thinking of men like Peter who still harbored deep prejudices against Gentiles. The remarkable conversion of Cornelius and his household was the first fruits of a harvest to be gathered in as Jews and Gentiles found room for each other in the Christian church.

Key Thought: "The greatest men of this earth are not beyond the power of a wonder-working God. If those who are workers together with Him will be men of opportunity, doing their duty bravely and faithfully, God will convert men who occupy responsible positions, men of intellect and influence. Through the power of the Holy Spirit many will accept the divine principles. Converted to the truth, they will become agencies in the hand of God to communicate the light. They will have a special burden for other souls of this neglected class. Time and money will be consecrated to the work of the Lord, and new efficiency and power will be added to the church " (*The Acts of the Apostles,* p. 140).

Today's Lesson: Prejudice of various kinds is still a problem in God's church some two thousand years after God cautioned Peter that no one is "unclean." We need to learn that God is no respecter of persons.

Delivered From Prison

The Acts of the Apostles, Chapter 15.

"Now about that time Herod the king stretched out his hand to harass some from the church. Then he killed James the brother of John with the sword"
(Acts 12:1, 2, NKJV).

Herod Agrippa, tetrarch of Galilee, was eager to gain the favor of the Jews. He had James, the brother of John, thrown into prison and then beheaded—as another Herod had done to John the Baptist. He then imprisoned Peter, which pleased many of the Jews, who urged him to execute Peter publicly. But Herod delayed executing Peter until after Passover.

Herod used double caution in guarding Peter, binding him with chains that were fastened to the wrists of two soldiers. The night before his scheduled execution, Peter was sleeping. An angel awakened him, released him from his chains, and led him past the sleeping guards. The angel took Peter through three gates out into the street, where he left the apostle in a daze. When he came to himself, he hurried to the house where the Christian leaders were assembled.

After telling his friends of his miraculous deliverance, Peter went to other Christian homes to let them know his good news.

When Herod learned of Peter's escape, he knew that no human being was responsible. He realized that he had set himself in bold defiance against God.

Key Thought: "The principalities and powers of heaven are watching the warfare which, under apparently discouraging circumstances, God's servants are carrying on. New conquests are being achieved, new honors won, as the Christians, rallying round the banner of their Redeemer, go forth to fight the good fight of faith. All the heavenly angels are at the service of the humble, believing people of God; and as the Lord's army of workers here below sing their songs of praise, the choir above join with them in ascribing praise to God and to His Son.

"We need to understand better than we do the mission of the angels. It would be well to remember that every true child of God has the co-operation of heavenly beings" (*The Acts of the Apostles,* p. 154).

Today's Lesson: Heaven and earth are much closer than we usually realize. Angels surround us as we go about God's work.

The Gospel Message in Antioch

The Acts of the Apostles, Chapter 16.

"The hand of the Lord was with them, and a great number believed and turned to the Lord. Then news of these things came to the ears of the church in Jerusalem, and they sent out Barnabas to go as far as Antioch"
(Acts 11:21, 22, NKJV).

Until this time, the disciples had largely confined their work to the Hebrew and Greek Jews, colonies of whom could be found in nearly all the cities of the world. One of those cities was Antioch, a commercial center in Syria, where Barnabas was laboring with success. Sensing that Providence would bless an even greater advance, he went to Tarsus to seek Paul's help. The two men worked well together. Paul's learning and zeal exerted a powerful influence in Antioch, and the Holy Spirit made his preaching effective.

The followers of Jesus were first called "Christians" in Antioch—because Christ was the main theme of their preaching and teaching. And it was from Antioch that the church sent forth Paul and Barnabas as ordained missionaries to the pagan world. The two men were always mindful of their ties and responsibilities to the other church leaders.

Key Thought: "God had abundantly blessed the labors of Paul and Barnabas during the year they remained with the believers in Antioch. But neither of them had as yet been formally ordained to the gospel ministry. They had now reached a point in their Christian experience when God was about to entrust them with the carrying forward of a difficult missionary enterprise, in the prosecution of which they would need every advantage that could be obtained through the agency of the church. . . .

"Before being sent forth as missionaries to the heathen world, these apostles were solemnly dedicated to God by fasting and prayer and the laying on of hands. Thus they were authorized by the church, not only to teach the truth, but to perform the rite of baptism and to organize churches, being invested with full ecclesiastical authority" (*The Acts of the Apostles,* pp. 160, 161).

Today's Lesson: It is important that there be room for both individual initiative and the organized ministry of the whole church, if God's work is to move forward in harmony.

Heralds of the Gospel

The Acts of the Apostles, Chapter 17.

*"When the Jews saw the multitudes, they were filled with
envy; and contradicting and blaspheming, they opposed
the things spoken by Paul. Then Paul and Barnabas grew
bold and said, 'It was necessary that the word of God
should be spoken to you first; but since you reject it, and
judge yourselves unworthy of everlasting life, behold, we
turn to the Gentiles' "
(Acts 13:45, 46, NKJV).*

After their ordination in Antioch, Paul, Barnabas, and Mark, a relative of Barnabas, left for Cyprus. There, Sergius Paulus, the deputy of the country, wanted to hear their message, but Elymas, a sorcerer, tried to prevent the meeting. Paul rebuked Elymas as a child of the devil and told him that he would be temporarily blind. This greatly impressed Paulus and convinced him of the truthfulness of Paul's message.

The disciples continued on to Pamphylia, in what today is southern Turkey, where they were beset with many dangers. Here young Mark, overwhelmed with discouragement and unused to hardships, refused to go further and returned to Jerusalem. This caused Paul to judge Mark unfavorably, although Barnabas excused him because of his inexperience. In later years, Paul was reconciled to Mark after he had developed into a valuable worker.

Their next stop was Antioch in Pisidia, where they spoke in the Jewish synagogue on the Sabbath. Paul reviewed Jewish history, speaking plainly about how the religious leaders in Jerusalem had rejected Jesus as the Messiah. He proclaimed boldly the good news of repentance and the remission of sin through Jesus, the Savior.

Key Thought: "In turning to the Gentiles in Antioch of Pisidia, Paul and Barnabas did not cease laboring for the Jews elsewhere. . . . Later, . . . Paul and his companions in labor preached the gospel to both Jews and Gentiles. But their chief energies were henceforth directed toward the building up of the kingdom of God in heathen territory, among peoples who had but little or no knowledge of the true God and of His Son" (*The Acts of the Apostles,* pp. 174, 175).

Today's Lesson: There is a time for declaring unpopular truths and a time to emphasize common ground. God will help us know the right time for each.

Preaching Among the Heathen

The Acts of the Apostles, Chapter 18.

***"The unbelieving Jews stirred up the Gentiles and
poisoned their minds against the brethren"
(Acts 14:2, NKJV).***

In Iconium the unbelieving Jews made the apostles' work more
difficult. Because of the lies these enemies told, Paul and Barnabas
were repeatedly brought before the authorities, but the magistrates
could see that their teachings tended to make men virtuous, law-abiding
citizens and that the morals and order of the city would improve if
the truths taught by the apostles were accepted. Nevertheless, false
charges continued to make their work difficult, and their friends
eventually had to help the apostles escape for their lives.

Going on to Lystra and Derbe, towns inhabited largely by a pagan,
superstitious people, Paul changed his methods. There was no Jewish
synagogue in Lystra, so Paul and Barnabas gathered near a temple
dedicated to Jupiter and explained the simple truths of gospel. They
first talked about God as the Creator and His visible creation. Then
through these works, they led the people's minds to consider the great
Ruler of the universe.

Paul healed a crippled man in Lystra, and when the people saw the
miracle, they assumed that the apostles were gods who had "come down
to us in the likeness of men" (Acts 14:11, NKJV). Their enthusiasm only
increased when Paul and Barnabas resolutely denied being divine. But
their adoration turned to fury as the apostles continued to refuse their
worship. They ended up stoning Paul and leaving him for dead!

Timothy was converted at Lystra, so the apostles' time there was
not spent in vain.

Key Thought: "When men of promise and ability were converted,
as in the case of Timothy, Paul and Barnabas sought earnestly to show
them the necessity of laboring in the vineyard. And when the apostles
left for another place, the faith of these men did not fail, but rather
increased. . . . This careful training of new converts was an important
factor in the remarkable success that attended Paul and Barnabas as
they preached the gospel in heathen lands" (*The Acts of the Apostles,*
pp. 186, 187).

Today's Lesson: The Lord has promised to be with us wherever
we go as we carry His message to men and women everywhere.

Jew and Gentile

The Acts of the Apostles, Chapter 19.

"Why do you test God by putting a yoke on the neck of the disciples which neither our fathers nor we were able to bear?" (Acts 15:10, NKJV).

W hen Paul and Barnabas arrived back in Antioch following their first missionary journey, some Jewish Christians from Jerusalem introduced a question that soon led to controversy in the young church. In order to be saved, must the Gentile converts be circumcised and keep the entire ceremonial law (see Acts 15:5)? On one side of the question were Paul and Barnabas—on the other were the Jewish believers from Jerusalem.

The "Jerusalem party" was slow to see that all the sacrificial offerings of the Old Testament had prefigured the death of Jesus and were no longer significant this side of the cross. The Antioch church sent Paul, Barnabas, and other responsible men to Jerusalem, insisting all controversy was to cease until a general council of the church should make a final decision.

After much dispute in the council, Peter reminded the members that the Holy Spirit had already decided the matter when Cornelius had been converted. The Holy Spirit had descended with equal power upon both the uncircumcised Gentiles and the circumcised Jews.

James, the brother of Jesus, announced the council's decision: The Gentiles were to abstain from fornication and from eating meat offered to idols or animals that had been strangled (thus not having the blood drained properly). Anyone teaching the necessity of Gentile believers being circumcised would be going against the decision of the church.

Key Thought: "In his ministry, Paul was often compelled to stand alone. He was specially taught of God and dared make no concessions that would involve principle. At times the burden was heavy, but Paul stood firm for the right. He realized that the church must never be brought under the control of human power. The traditions and maxims of men must not take the place of revealed truth. The advance of the gospel message must not be hindered by the prejudices and preferences of men, whatever might be their position in the church" (*The Acts of the Apostles,* p. 199).

Today's Lesson: There is wisdom in a multitude of counselors. God wants His church to move forward in unity.

Exalting the Cross

The Acts of the Apostles, Chapter 20.

***"Then he [Paul] came to Derbe and Lystra. And behold, a
certain disciple was there, named Timothy, the son of a
certain Jewish woman who believed, but his father was
Greek. He was well spoken of by the brethren who were at
Lystra and Iconium" (Acts 16:1, 2, NKJV).***

From a child, Timothy had been raised to know the Scriptures. The
faith of his mother and his grandmother was to him a constant
reminder of the importance of following God's will. The spiritual
lessons he had received from them kept him pure in speech and
unsullied by the evil influences with which he was surrounded. Because
Paul saw that Timothy was faithful, steadfast, and true, he chose this
young man as a companion in labor and missionary travel. Though a
mere youth, Timothy carried out his responsibilities with Paul with
Christian meekness and true faith.

In fact, Paul loved Timothy as his "own son in the faith" (1 Timothy
1:2). As they traveled, Paul carefully taught him how to do successful
work. Watching Paul, Timothy learned not to move from impulse
but to exercise consideration and calm thought in all his labors for
Christ.

Paul felt a deep responsibility for those converted by the Holy
Spirit under his ministry. He felt that even his own salvation might be
imperiled if he should fail to fulfill his duty. He knew that preaching
alone would not be sufficient to educate the believers to hold fast to
the word of life—they must be taught how to grow in Christ. Truth that
is not lived, that is not imparted, loses its life-giving power, its healing
virtue.

Key Thought: "As the lessons of the Bible are wrought into the
daily life, they have a deep and lasting influence upon the character.
These lessons Timothy learned and practiced. He had no specially
brilliant talents, but his work was valuable because he used his God-
given abilities in the Master's service. His knowledge of experimental
piety distinguished him from other believers and gave him influence"
(*The Acts of the Apostles,* p. 205).

Today's Lesson: The lessons Paul taught Timothy are the lessons
we all should be learning if we expect to grow in grace as God wants
us to do.

In the Regions Beyond

The Acts of the Apostles, Chapter 21.

"A vision appeared to Paul in the night. A man of Macedonia stood and pleaded with him, saying, 'Come over to Macedonia and help us' " (Acts 16:9, NKJV).

The time had come for the gospel to be proclaimed beyond the confines of Asia Minor (modern Turkey). The Macedonian call was imperative, admitting of no delay, and Paul's group—including Silas, Timothy, and Luke—responded immediately.

Their first stop was Philippi. On the Sabbath they went to the riverside, where a group of women held a prayer meeting. There they met Lydia, a businesswoman who worshiped God. She responded quickly to Paul's message and asked him to baptize her and her household.

In Philippi they also met a slave girl, who told the future with Satan's help. She followed Paul and his companions, announcing them to be the servants of the most high God. After several days, Paul commanded the evil spirit to leave her. This angered her owners, who had made money from her fortune-telling. Soon Paul and Silas were in prison under heavy guard.

But God had not forgotten His servants. An earthquake opened the prison doors; chains and fetters fell from the prisoners. The jailer, recognizing that he would pay with his own life if all the prisoners escaped, drew his sword to commit suicide. Paul stopped him, assuring him that the prisoners were all present. The jailor put together everything he had seen and heard of Paul and his party and realized he needed the salvation Paul was preaching. He asked Paul to show him the way of life that kept the apostle so calm amidst calamity. All this led to the first Christian church being established in Philippi.

Key Thought: "Paul's labors at Philippi resulted in the establishment of a church whose membership steadily increased. His zeal and devotion, and, above all, his willingness to suffer for Christ's sake, exerted a deep and lasting influence upon the converts. They prized the precious truths for which the apostles had sacrificed so much, and gave themselves with wholehearted devotion to the cause of their Redeemer" (*The Acts of the Apostles,* p. 218).

Today's Lesson: God has a solution to every difficulty in which we may find ourselves.

Thessalonica

The Acts of the Apostles, Chapter 22.

"Some of them were persuaded; and a great multitude of the devout Greeks, and not a few of the leading women, joined Paul and Silas" (Acts 17:4, NKJV).

After leaving Philippi, Paul and Silas traveled to Thessalonica, where there was a large Jewish congregation. As he usually did with Jewish audiences, Paul appealed to the Old Testament Scriptures concerning the Messiah and how those prophecies had been fulfilled in the life and death of Jesus. He told them of Jesus' resurrection from the dead. Explaining the Old Testament prophecies referring the Jesus as the Messiah was the same method the Master had used with the disciples on the road to Emmaus.

Paul told the Thessalonian Jews about his former zeal for the ceremonial law and of his wonderful experience outside Damascus. Before his conversion he had been confident in a hereditary piety, a false hope. He had trusted in forms and ceremonies. His zeal for the law had been disconnected from a faith in God and was of no effect. He had boasted of being blameless in performing the deeds of the law, but he had refused the One who gave the law its value. With holy boldness, Paul proclaimed the gospel, showing the true meaning of the rites and ceremonies connected with the tabernacle service and explaining how they are fulfilled in the Lord's earthly and heavenly ministries.

Key Thought: "Those who today teach unpopular truths need not be discouraged if at times they meet with no more favorable reception, even from those who claim to be Christians, than did Paul and his fellow workers. . . . The messengers of the cross must arm themselves with watchfulness and prayer, and move forward with faith and courage, working always in the name of Jesus. They must exalt Christ as man's mediator in the heavenly sanctuary, the One in whom all the sacrifices of the Old Testament dispensation centered, and through whose atoning sacrifice the transgressors of God's law may find peace and pardon" (*The Acts of the Apostles,* p. 230).

Today's Lesson: One of the most effective ways to witness for Jesus is to recount the way He has led us personally in the past—the victories He has made possible and the forgiveness He has provided.

Berea and Athens

The Acts of the Apostles, Chapter 23.

"These were more fair-minded than those in Thessalonica, in that they received the word with all readiness, and searched the Scriptures daily to find out whether these things were so. Therefore many of them believed, and also not a few of the Greeks, prominent women as well as men" (Acts 17:11, 12, NKJV).

The unprejudiced Bereans were willing to investigate the Bible, not from an idle curiosity but in order to learn what had been written concerning the Messiah. All will be judged, not by their sins but according to the light they have received. The unbelieving Jews of Thessalonica, filled with jealousy and hatred of the apostles, followed them to Berea and aroused the excitable passions of the lower classes. Thus persecution followed the apostles from city to city.

At Athens, the metropolis of paganism, a city famous for intelligence and culture, Paul was stirred with jealousy for God, whom he saw dishonored on every side. As he saw the magnificence of Athens and its culture, he realized its seductive power over those who loved art and science. Paul was oppressed by a feeling of isolation; he longed for the sympathy and fellowship of his companions (see 1 Thessalonians 3:1).

Paul's intellectual power commanded the respect of the learned in Athens, while his earnest, logical reasoning and the power of his oratory held the attention of all in the audience.

Key Thought: "Paul's words contain a treasure of knowledge for the church. He was in a position where he might easily have said that which would have irritated his proud listeners and brought himself into difficulty. Had his oration been a direct attack upon their gods and the great men of the city, he would have been in danger of meeting the fate of Socrates. But with a tact born of divine love, he carefully drew their minds away from heathen deities, by revealing to them the true God, who was to them unknown" (*The Acts of the Apostles,* p. 241).

Today's Lesson: The careful worker for God will adapt the presentation of the gospel message to fit the needs of the audience he or she is addressing. The message may stay the same, but the method of presenting it can vary.

OCTOBER 16

Corinth

The Acts of the Apostles, Chapter 24.

"He reasoned in the synagogue every Sabbath, and persuaded both Jews and Greeks" (Acts 18:4, NKJV).

Corinth was a great commercial center and one of the leading cities of the world. It was also a city almost wholly given up to idolatry. Paul recognized the monumental obstacles to proclaiming the gospel in such a place. Besides its idolatry, Corinth was proverbial—even among the pagans—for its gross immorality.

Once again, Paul adapted the method of his presentation to his hearers. In Athens, the world capital of the intellect, he had met logic with logic, science with science, philosophy with philosophy. But he knew that approach would not capture the attention of the careless and indifferent in Corinth. Thus, He determined to avoid elaborate arguments and focus on "Jesus Christ, and Him crucified" (1 Corinthians 2:2).

He talked about the lowly origin of Jesus, reared in Nazareth, also a town known for its wickedness. He preached the Cross, knowing the subject was a stumbling block to Jews and foolishness to the pagans (see 1 Corinthians 1:23). But to Paul, the Cross was the one object of supreme interest. He knew by personal experience that when a sinner once beholds the love of the Father, as seen in the sacrifice of His Son, a change of heart takes place and, henceforth, Christ is all in all. If Paul's enthusiasm ever wavered, one glance at the Cross was enough to cause him to press forward with renewed energy.

But the Jews of Corinth closed their eyes to the evidence Paul presented so clearly. Though the apostle had a measure of success in Corinth, he doubted the wisdom of trying to build up a church from the material he found there.

Key Thought: "Paul was an eloquent speaker. Before his conversion he had often sought to impress his hearers by flights of oratory. But now he set all this aside. . . . The immediate needs, the present trials, of struggling souls—these must be met with sound, practical instruction in the fundamental principles of Christianity" (*The Acts of the Apostles,* pp. 251, 252).

Today's Lesson: For us, as for Paul, the Cross must be the central focus of what Jesus means to us.

The Thessalonian Letters

The Acts of the Apostles, Chapter 25.

"Our gospel did not come to you in word only, but also in power, and in the Holy Spirit and in much assurance, as you know what kind of men we were among you for your sake. And You became followers of us and of the Lord, having received the word in much affliction, with joy of the Holy Spirit, so that you became examples to all in Macedonia and Achaia who believe"
(1 Thessalonians 1:5–7, NKJV).

Silas and Timothy rejoined Paul in Corinth and brought him a good report of those who had accepted the truth during their first visit to Thessalonica. Through the grace of Christ, a marvelous transformation had taken place in their lives, and the word of the Lord, as presented by them, was accompanied with power. Hearts were won by the truths they presented. Paul longed to visit them in person, but since this was impossible, he wrote to them.

In his first letter to the Thessalonian Christians, Paul tried to instruct them regarding the true state of those who had died. He spoke of them as being asleep (see 1 Thessalonians 4:13–18). Paul had told the believers these things before, but at that time their minds had been striving to grasp doctrines that seemed new and strange. It is not surprising that some points had not been vividly impressed on their minds. Now they rejoiced in the knowledge that their believing friends who had died would be raised from the grave.

Key Thought: "The Thessalonians had eagerly grasped the idea that Christ was coming to change the faithful who were alive, and to take them to Himself. They had carefully guarded the lives of their friends, lest they should die and lose the blessing which they looked forward to receiving at the coming of their Lord. But one after another their loved ones had been taken from them, and with anguish the Thessalonians had looked for the last time upon the faces of their dead, hardly daring to hope to meet them in a future life" (*The Acts of the Apostles,* p. 258).

Today's Lesson: The truth about the resurrection removes the fear and hopelessness that surrounds death. In Jesus, the righteous dead will live again.

OCTOBER 18

Apollos at Corinth

The Acts of the Apostles, Chapter 26.

"Now a certain Jew named Apollos, born at Alexandria, an eloquent man and mighty in the Scriptures, came to Ephesus. This man had been instructed in the way of the Lord; and being fervent in spirit, he spoke and taught accurately the things of the Lord, though he knew only the baptism of John" (Acts 18:24, 25, NKJV).

After leaving Corinth, Paul stopped off briefly in Ephesus before continuing to Jerusalem to attend an approaching festival. At the same time, Apollos came to Ephesus and began to speak boldly in the synagogue (see Acts 18:26).

Later, after receiving further instruction in the gospel from Aquila and Priscilla, Apollos went on to Corinth, where, in public labor and from house to house, "he mightily convinced the Jews, . . . shewing by the scriptures that Jesus was Christ" (Acts 18:28). Paul had planted the seed of truth in Corinth; Apollos now watered it. But soon some church members began to compare the two men, and a party spirit began to hinder the progress of the gospel.

During the time that Paul spent in Corinth, he purposely had presented the gospel in its simplicity—adapting his manner of teaching to the condition of the church. But jealousy and accusations had shut off many of the Corinthian believers against the full working of the Holy Spirit.

Key Thought: "It was Paul who had first preached the gospel in Corinth, and who had organized the church there. . . . Later, by God's direction, other workers were brought in, to stand in their lot and place. The seed sown must be watered, and this Apollos was to do. He followed Paul in his work, to give further instruction, and to help the seed sown to develop. . . . Those who plant and those who water do not cause the growth of the seed; they work under God, as His appointed agencies, co-operating with Him in His work. To the Master Worker belongs the honor and glory that comes with success" (*The Acts of the Apostles,* p. 274).

Today's Lesson: One minister seldom has all the qualifications necessary to address adequately all the needs of a particular church. God gives each person different gifts.

Ephesus

The Acts of the Apostles, Chapter 27.

"It happened, while Apollos was at Corinth, that Paul, having passed through the upper regions, came to Ephesus" (Acts 19:1, NKJV).

Ephesus, the capital of the Roman province of Asia, was a great commercial center, its harbor crowded with shipping from around the world. When he arrived in the city, Paul found twelve men who, like Apollos, had been disciples of John the Baptist and had some knowledge about Christ's mission. But these men knew nothing of the Holy Spirit.

Paul set before them the great truths that are the foundation of the Christian's hope. He told them of Christ's life on earth and His shameful death and how His resurrection sealed the truth of His lifework. He told them also of Christ's promise of the Holy Spirit, through whose power signs and wonders would be performed and lives transformed.

The twelve men listened with gratitude, and God honored them with the baptism of the Holy Spirit, enabling them to speak the language of other nations and to prophesy. They were now qualified to labor as missionaries throughout Asia Minor.

Many today are as ignorant of the Holy Spirit's work on the heart as were these Ephesian believers, yet no truth is more clearly taught in the Bible. Like sap ascending from the root and diffused to the branches, so the Holy Spirit pervades the soul, renews the motives and affections, and brings even the thoughts into obedience to the will of God.

Key Thought: "Could the veil be lifted from before our eyes, we should see evil angels employing all their arts to deceive and to destroy. Wherever an influence is exerted to cause men to forget God, there Satan is exercising his bewitching power. When men yield to his influence, ere they are aware the mind is bewildered and the soul polluted. The apostle's admonition to the Ephesian church should be heeded by the people of God today: 'Have no fellowship with the unfruitful works of darkness, but rather reprove them.' Ephesians 5:11" (*The Acts of the Apostles,* p. 290).

Today's Lesson: The promise of the Holy Spirit is for today as much as it was for New Testament times. We may experience the Spirit's power in our lives.

Days of Toil and Trial

The Acts of the Apostles, Chapter 28.

" 'We are in danger of being called in question for today's uproar, there being no reason which we may give to account for this disorderly gathering.' And when he had said these things, he dismissed the assembly. After the uproar had ceased, Paul called the disciples to him, embraced them, and departed to go to Macedonia" *(Acts 19:40–20:1, NKJV).*

For more than three years, Ephesus had been the center of Paul's work. Now he was planning another missionary journey—this time to Rome (see Acts 19:21). Paul's departure from Ephesus was hastened by an event that occurred during the annual festival honoring the goddess Diana. This gala season was always a trying time for the new believers. Paul's missionary labors had made a serious impact on the pagan worship of Diana, and attendance at the festival had fallen off considerably. The priests of Diana were fearful and angry. Those who manufactured and sold small silver images of Diana were also upset, because their trade was diminishing. These priests and artisans aroused the passions of the people against Paul and incited a riot. The city authorities moved quickly to seize Paul and his companions.

Paul's natural inclination was to defend the truth before the raging multitude, but his friends overruled this decision, knowing the extreme danger he would be in. The tumult constantly increased, and for two hours the people chanted, "Great is Diana of the Ephesians" (Acts 19:28). The income of pagan priests and of the metal workers was at stake.

Finally the chanting stopped from their sheer exhaustion, and the city recorder was able to speak some calming words before he dismissed the crowd.

Key Thought: "Amidst the constant storm of opposition, the clamor of enemies, and the desertion of friends the intrepid apostle almost lost heart. But he looked back to Calvary and with new ardor pressed on to spread the knowledge of the Crucified. He was but treading the blood-stained path that Christ had trodden before him. He sought no discharge from the warfare till he should lay off his armor at the feet of his Redeemer" (*The Acts of the Apostles,* p. 297).

Today's Lesson: When unexpected problems arise, God always has someone prepared to deal with the situation.

A Message of Warning and Entreaty

The Acts of the Apostles, Chapter 29.

"Now I plead with you, brethren, by the name of our Lord Jesus Christ, that you all speak the same thing, and that there be no divisions among you, but that you be perfectly joined together in the same mind and in the same judgment" (1 Corinthians 1:10, NKJV).

Paul's first letter to the Corinthians was written during the latter part of his stay at Ephesus. Before accepting into church fellowship those who made a profession of Christianity, Paul was careful to give them special instruction regarding the privileges and duties of the Christian believer.

The apostle had a keen sense of the conflict that every soul must wage with evil. He pled with new converts to make an entire surrender to God, because he knew that without full surrender, sin is not forsaken—the appetites and passions still strive for the mastery, and temptations confuse the conscience. When Paul was with them, these influences had little power over them, but after his departure, unfavorable conditions arose. Little by little many of the new believers became careless, allowing natural inclinations to control them.

Hearing that troubles were serious in the Corinthian church, Paul knew that his worst fears were realized. But he also knew that the church members would not profit by his visit, so he sent Titus to prepare the way and then wrote his first letter to them. With remarkable clarity he laid down general principles that would lead them to a higher spiritual plane.

Key Thought: "The Corinthian believers needed a deeper experience in the things of God. They did not know fully what it meant to behold His glory and to be changed from character to character. They had seen but the first rays of the early dawn of that glory. Paul's desire for them was that they might be filled with all the fullness of God, following on to know Him whose going forth is prepared as the morning, and continuing to learn of Him until they should come into the full noontide of a perfect gospel faith" (*The Acts of the Apostles,* pp. 307, 308).

Today's Lesson: Being forgiven is only the beginning of our Christian walk; the purpose of the gospel is growth in grace.

Called to Reach a Higher Standard

The Acts of the Apostles, Chapter 30.

"Do you not know that those who run in a race all run, but one receives the prize? Run in such a way that you may obtain it. And everyone who competes for the prize is temperate in all things. Now they do it to obtain a perishable crown, but we for an imperishable crown" (*1 Corinthians 9:24, 25, NKJV*).

In his first letter to the believers at Corinth, Paul makes a striking comparison between the Christian life and the celebrated foot races held at stated intervals near Corinth. These contests were governed by strict regulations, and Paul emphasizes the preparation necessary for success—the careful discipline, the abstemious diet, the necessity for temperance. Harmful indulgence of appetite or any other gratification that would lower mental or physical vigor was strictly forbidden during the training period. Never should the runner—or the Christian—allow his attention to be diverted by amusements, luxuries, or ease. All his habits and passions must be brought under the strictest discipline. Reason, enlightened by the teaching of God's Word and guided by His Spirit, must hold the reins of power.

And after all this, the Christian must put forth the utmost exertion in order to gain the victory. As with the runner, the Christian will press forward with even more zeal and determination the closer he comes to the finish line. Only one athlete could win the prize in the Corinthian race. But every Christian who is earnest and persevering may win the crown of eternal life.

Key Thought: "The apostle's words of warning to the Corinthian church are applicable to all time and are especially adapted to our day. By idolatry he meant not only the worship of idols, but self-serving, love of ease, the gratification of appetite and passion. A mere profession of faith in Christ, a boastful knowledge of the truth, does not make a man a Christian. A religion that seeks only to gratify the eye, the ear, and the taste, or that sanctions self-indulgence, is not the religion of Christ" (*The Acts of the Apostles,* p. 317).

Today's Lesson: The Christian life requires determination and effort, but everyone may cross the finish line a winner, by the grace of God.

The Message Heeded

The Acts of the Apostles, Chapter 31.

"Therefore, if anyone is in Christ, he is a new creation; old things have passed away; behold, all things have become new" (2 Corinthians 5:17, NKJV).

From Ephesus, Paul set out on another missionary tour into the area of his earlier labors in Greece. The condition of the Corinthian church still weighed heavily on his heart. Then he met Titus again and learned that a wonderful change had taken place in the lives of the Corinthian believers. Many had accepted the instruction in his first letter and had repented of their sins. Filled with joy, the apostle sent a second letter, expressing his gladness of heart because of the good work carried out in them.

Paul was always concerned about the churches he had raised up. False teachers often tried to destroy his influence among the believers. But now it seemed that his burden for Corinth had been removed, and Paul ascribed to God all the praise for this transformation of heart and life in the believers there.

Some had accused Paul of boasting in his first letter to Corinth. In his second letter, he pointed out that the only recommendation he needed was those Corinthian believers who had been led from the worship of idols to the faith of the gospel. The evidence of his apostleship was written upon the hearts of the converted and confirmed by their renewed lives.

Key Thought: "In the contemplation of Christ we linger on the shore of a love that is measureless. . . . We consider His life on earth, His sacrifice for us, His work in heaven as our advocate, and the mansions He is preparing for those who love Him, and we can only exclaim, O the height and depth of the love of Christ! . . . .

"It was on the earth that the love of God was revealed through Christ. It is on the earth that His children are to reflect this love through blameless lives. Thus sinners will be led to the cross to behold the Lamb of God" (*The Acts of the Apostles,* pp. 333, 334).

Today's Lesson: When troubles press in from without and within, we can renew our vision and strength by reflecting on the marvelous love of Christ.

A Liberal Church

The Acts of the Apostles, Chapter 32.

"If we have sown spiritual things for you, is it a great thing if we reap your material things? If others are partakers of this right over you, are we not even more? Nevertheless we have not used this right, but endure all things lest we hinder the gospel of Christ. Do you not know that those who minister the holy things eat of the things of the temple. . . ? Even so the Lord has commanded that those who preach the gospel should live from the gospel" (1 Corinthians 9:11–14, NKJV).

The tithe was but a part of God's plan for the support of His work. His plan includes numerous other gifts and offerings. By this system of benevolence the Lord taught the Israelites that He must be placed first in all things. And God does not intend that Christians, whose privileges far exceed those of the Jewish nation, should give less freely than they gave.

If professing Christians would faithfully bring to God their tithes and offerings, His treasury would be full, and there would be no need for other fund-raising activities to support the work of the gospel.

Too many Christians are inclined to spend money for self-indulgence—spending freely, even extravagantly, on clothes, homes, pleasure, and luxuries of all kinds. Those whose hearts are aglow with the love of Christ will consider it a pleasure to generously advance the work of God with their financial resources. Freely we have received; freely should we give.

Key Thought: "The willingness to sacrifice on the part of the Macedonian believers came as a result of wholehearted consecration. Moved by the Spirit of God, they 'first gave their own selves to the Lord' (2 Corinthians 8:5), then they were willing to give freely of their means for the support of the gospel. . . . In their simplicity and integrity, and in their love for the brethren, they gladly denied self, and thus abounded in the fruit of benevolence" (*The Acts of the Apostles,* pp. 343, 344).

Today's Lesson: It is a spiritual and psychological principle that where our treasure is, there will our heart be also. And the reverse is true also: Where our hearts are, there will our treasure be, as well.

OCTOBER 25

Laboring Under Difficulties

The Acts of the Apostles, Chapter 33.

"I have coveted no one's silver or gold or apparel. Yes, you yourselves know that these hands have provided for my necessities, and for those who were with me. I have shown you in every way, by laboring like this, that you must support the weak. And remember the words of the Lord Jesus, that He said, 'It is more blessed to give than to receive' " (Acts 20:33–35, NKJV).

A t times, when Paul had used all his means in furthering the cause of Christ, he resorted to working with his hands to gain a living. Especially was this the case when he preached the gospel in places where his motives might be misunderstood (see 2 Thessalonians 3:8, 9).

In every age Satan has tried to hinder the work of God by introducing a spirit of fanaticism. Misguided persons have taught that to gain true holiness, one must bring the mind above all earthly considerations—including manual labor. Some have even taught that it is a sin to work, that Christians should devote their lives wholly to spiritual things and take no thought concerning their temporal welfare. Paul's example is a solid rebuke to such extreme views.

Sometimes local churches provided funds to help support Paul; the apostle noted in his second Corinthian letter, for example, that Silas and Timothy brought funds from the churches in Macedonia (see 2 Corinthians 11:7–10).

Key Thought: "There is a large field open before the self-supporting gospel worker. Many may gain valuable experiences in ministry while toiling a portion of the time at some form of manual labor, and by this method strong workers may be developed for important service in needy fields.

"The self-sacrificing servant of God who labors untiringly in word and doctrine, carries on his heart a heavy burden. He does not measure his work by hours. . . . From heaven he received his commission, and to heaven he looks for his recompense when the work entrusted to him is done" (*The Acts of the Apostles,* pp. 355, 356).

Today's Lesson: God's blessings will rest on us as we each live by the law of self-denial and carry out the part He has for us in the work of proclaiming the gospel to the world.

OCTOBER 26

A Consecrated Ministry

The Acts of the Apostles, Chapter 34.

"Our light affliction, which is but for a moment, worketh for us a far more exceeding and eternal weight of glory; while we look not at the things which are seen, but at the things which are not seen" (2 Corinthians 4:17, 18).

Jesus gave us the example of what it means to minister. His whole life was a demonstration of the law of unselfish service, and those who follow Him will minister as He did, not looking for their own ease or convenience.

Relying on the power of Jesus, His followers will be able to present the gospel message with force. They will lean more and more on Jesus' strength and rely less and less on their own. Time spent with God will give an influence to their lives even greater than the impact of their preaching.

Satan's temptations are most successful against those who are depressed and discouraged. It was when Paul felt that the heavens were as brass over his head that he trusted most fully in God. He realized that his high calling required his best energies, and he devoted himself entirely to God's work. He is an example to ministers today. Our best powers belong to God, and we should not let anything divert us from the work he has called us to do for Him.

Key Thought: "Some who have labored in the ministry have failed of attaining success because they have not given their undivided interest to the Lord's work. Ministers should have no engrossing interests aside from the great work of leading souls to the Saviour. The fishermen whom Christ called, straightway left their nets and followed Him. Ministers cannot do acceptable work for God and at the same time carry the burden of large personal business enterprises. Such a division of interest dims their spiritual perception. The mind and heart are occupied with earthly things, and the service of Christ takes a second place. They seek to shape their work for God by their circumstances, instead of shaping circumstances to meet the demands of God" (*The Acts of the Apostles,* p. 365).

Today's Lesson: God is looking for complete consecration from each of us—minister or layperson. We are to give Him our best.

Salvation to the Jews

The Acts of the Apostles, Chapter 35.

"My heart's desire and prayer to God for Israel is, that they might be saved" (Romans 10:1).

During his time in Corinth, Paul thought about traveling to Rome, where a Christian church had already been established. To prepare the way for his arrival, he sent the believers in Rome a letter setting forth the great principles of the gospel. In this letter, Paul presented the doctrine of justification by faith in Christ clearly and powerfully. Ever since, it has stood as a beacon to guide repentant sinners into the fullness of salvation and righteousness.

Paul freely expressed his burden for the Jews in this letter. The Jews were God's chosen people, through whom He had intended to bless the entire world. Even though Israel rejected His Son, God did not reject Israel.

Paul compared the remnant in Israel to a noble olive tree, some of whose branches had been broken off. He compared the Gentiles to branches from a wild olive tree that had been grafted onto the parent stock. Through unbelief and the rejection of God's purpose, Israel as a nation had lost its connection with God. But He was creating a reunited Israel made up of Jewish branches and Gentile branches so that "all Israel shall be saved" (Romans 11:26).

Key Thought: "In the closing proclamation of the gospel, when special work is to be done for classes of people hitherto neglected, God expects His messengers to take particular interest in the Jewish people whom they find in all parts of the earth. As the Old Testament Scriptures are blended with the New in an explanation of Jehovah's eternal purpose, this will be to many of the Jews as the dawn of a new creation, the resurrection of the soul. As they see the Christ of the gospel dispensation portrayed in the pages of the Old Testament Scriptures, and perceive how clearly the New Testament explains the Old, their slumbering faculties will be aroused, and they will recognize Christ as the Saviour of the world. Many will by faith receive Christ as their Redeemer" (*The Acts of the Apostles,* p. 381).

Today's Lesson: Spiritual Israel—God's family around the world today—is made up of all nations and peoples.

Apostasy in Galatia

The Acts of the Apostles, Chapter 36.

"I marvel that you are turning away so soon from Him who called you in the grace of Christ, to a different gospel, which is not another; but there are some who trouble you and want to pervert the gospel of Christ"
(Galatians 1:6, 7, NKJV).

False teachers who had arisen among the believers in Jerusalem were causing division, heresy, and controversy in the Christian church at Galatia. These teachers were ignoring the decision of the general church council and insisting that Gentile converts must be circumcised and observe the other regulations of the Jewish ceremonial law. Paul met this crisis head on in his letter to the Galatian Christians.

He unapologetically denounced the errors these teachers were introducing in the church—errors that were taking the place of the pure gospel message. He urged the believers to come back to their former faith in the gospel and told them that if they took up the obsolete ceremonies of Judaism they would be turning their backs on Christ, the foundation of their faith.

Paul pointed out that these false teachers were hypocrites and that their religion was made up of observing ceremonies by which they expected to gain God's favor. They had no use for a gospel that called for obedience to God's Word.

Key Thought: "It is Satan's studied effort to divert minds from the hope of salvation through faith in Christ and obedience to the law of God. In every age the archenemy adapts his temptations to the prejudices or inclinations of those whom he is seeking to deceive. In apostolic times he led the Jews to exalt the ceremonial law and reject Christ; at the present time he induces many professing Christians, under pretense of honoring Christ, to cast contempt on the moral law and to teach that its precepts may be transgressed with impunity. It is the duty of every servant of God to withstand firmly and decidedly these perverters of the faith and by the word of truth fearlessly to expose their errors" (*The Acts of the Apostles,* p. 387).

Today's Lesson: Anything that takes our eyes off Jesus and His righteousness and places them on us and our performance is contrary to the true gospel.

Paul's Last Journey to Jerusalem

The Acts of the Apostles, Chapter 37.

"When we heard these things, both we and those from that place pleaded with him [Paul] not to go up to Jerusalem" (Acts 21:12, NKJV).

Paul wanted to reach Jerusalem before the Passover so that he could meet with Jews who would be coming from all over the world to attend the feast. He also wanted to bring the large offering that the Gentile churches had raised to help their poor brothers and sisters in Judea.

Before boarding the ship he learned of a plot by the Jews to take his life. So, he decided to take a longer route around Macedonia. He caught up with his companions at Troas.

On the last night before Paul's party left Troas, a large group assembled in a third-floor room to hear a final message from their beloved teacher. Paul preached until midnight, and young Eutychus, sitting in a window, fell asleep and plunged to his death. But Paul prayed to God to restore his life. Then turning to the onlookers, he said, "Do not trouble yourselves, for his life is in him" (Acts 20:10, NKJV). The worship service then continued until dawn.

The next day at Miletus, thirty miles from Ephesus, Paul met with the church leaders from that city and gave them advice on various matters. Both Paul and the leaders knew they would never see each other again. He warned them of troubling times ahead, when false teachers, arising from within the church itself, would speak "perverse things" (Acts 20:30, NKJV).

Key Thought: "He [Paul] could not count upon the sympathy and support of even his own brethren in the faith. The unconverted Jews who had followed so closely upon his track, had not been slow to circulate the most unfavorable reports at Jerusalem, both personally and by letter, concerning him and his work; and some, even of the apostles and elders, had received these reports as truth, making no attempt to contradict them, and manifesting no desire to harmonize with him" (*The Acts of the Apostles,* p. 398).

Today's Lesson: Paul's prediction that voices would arise from within the church to present false teachings and lead people astray has been fulfilled through each age of the church—and continues still.

OCTOBER 30

Paul a Prisoner

The Acts of the Apostles, Chapter 38.

" 'I am a Jew from Tarsus, in Cilicia, a citizen of no mean city; and I implore you, permit me to speak to the people.' So when he had given him permission, Paul stood on the stairs and motioned with his hand to the people. And when there was a great silence, he spoke to them in the Hebrew language" (Acts 21:39, 40, NKJV).

In Jerusalem, Paul and his companions formally presented to the church leaders the offering for the Jewish poor that the Gentile churches had sent. This generous offering, freely given, did much to validate the loyalty of Gentile Christians to the organized church everywhere.

However, certain leaders who had previously supported Paul's outreach to the Gentiles now felt threatened by the rapid growth of Gentiles within the Christian church. They pressured Paul to show his loyalty to the Jewish leadership by conforming more closely to their concerns. Throughout his ministry, Paul had looked to God for direct guidance. At the same time, he had been very careful to labor in harmony with the decisions of the general council at Jerusalem.

Paul found comfort in the knowledge that he had done his duty in encouraging a spirit of loyalty, generosity, and brotherly love in his converts—as revealed in their generous offering for their Jewish brothers and sisters. This was a golden opportunity for all the church leaders to confess frankly that God had worked mightily through Paul. Instead, many felt that Paul was largely responsible for the difficulties between Jewish and Gentile Christians. They proposed a compromise, and Paul agreed for the sake of unity. But their suggestion led to his imprisonment.

Key Thought: "Had the leaders in the church fully surrendered their feeling of bitterness toward the apostle, and accepted him as one specially called of God to bear the gospel to the Gentiles, the Lord would have spared him to them. God had not ordained that Paul's labors should so soon end, but He did not work a miracle to counteract the train of circumstances to which the course of the leaders in the church at Jerusalem had given rise" (*The Acts of the Apostles,* p. 417).

Today's Lesson: Compromises for the sake of peace rarely turn out well.

The Trial at Caesarea

The Acts of the Apostles, Chapter 39.

"Meanwhile he [Felix] also hoped that money would be given him by Paul, that he might release him. Therefore he sent for him more often and conversed with him. But after two years Porcius Festus succeeded Felix; and Felix, wanting to do the Jews a favor, left Paul bound"
(Acts 24:26, 27, NKJV).

Five days after Paul arrived in chains at Caesarea, he was brought before Felix, the Roman governor. His Jewish opponents from Jerusalem were present as well to press their charges against him as a threat to the peace of the empire. They brought a web of false stories against Paul. Felix had already read the charges against Paul and knew that the Jews' accusations were unsubstantiated. So, he gave Paul opportunity to answer his accusers, which Paul was happy to do. The candor and sincerity with which the apostle spoke impressed Felix, but he held back from releasing Paul for fear of offending the Jews.

Later Felix and his wife, Drusilla, requested a private interview with Paul. Paul presented before them God's righteousness and justice. He showed them their duty to obey God's law, living a life of sobriety, keeping their passions under the control of reason, and preserving their physical and mental powers.

Above all, Paul directed their minds to the one great Sacrifice for sin. Only by faith in Christ can the sinner be cleansed from guilt and be enabled to obey the law of his Maker.

Key Thought: "Paul dwelt especially upon the far-reaching claims of God's law. He showed how it extends to the deep secrets of man's moral nature and throws a flood of light upon that which has been concealed from the sight and knowledge of men. . . . The law searches his thoughts, motives, and purposes. The dark passions that lie hidden from the sight of men, the jealousy, hatred, lust, and ambition, the evil deeds meditated upon in the dark recesses of the soul, yet never executed for want of opportunity—all these God's law condemns" (*The Acts of the Apostles,* p. 424).

Today's Lesson: There is a time to speak truth to power. Paul's fearless presentation of truth to the Roman ruler is a model of Christian witness.

Paul Appeals to Caesar

The Acts of the Apostles, Chapter 40.

"Then Festus, when he had conferred with the council, answered, 'You have appealed to Caesar? To Caesar you shall go!' " (Acts 25:12, NKJV).

Paul's Jewish opponents did not want him to go to Rome. They wanted Festus to release Paul to their jurisdiction and send him to Jerusalem. They planned to kill him on the way there. But Paul had appealed to Caesar, and God strengthened Festus in his determination to send Paul to Rome. The apostle would rather trust the justice of a pagan Roman court than endure the suspense of trial and further imprisonment in Caesarea surrounded by the malignant Jews.

Satan was working through the Jewish leaders to try to cripple the work of the gospel. He has continued the same oppression and persecution against God's faithful messengers throughout the centuries since Paul's day. He follows the same course today, and the opposition will grow only stronger as the end draws nearer. In the future, God's faithful servants will encounter the same hardness of heart, the same cruel determination, the same unyielding hatred Paul had to endure. As the end approaches, it will require the firmest truth, the most heroic purpose, to hold fast the faith once delivered to the saints.

Key Thought: "God desires His people to prepare for the soon-coming crisis. Prepared or unprepared, they must all meet it; and those only who have brought their lives into conformity to the divine standard, will stand firm at that time of test and trial. When secular rulers unite with ministers of religion to dictate in matters of conscience, then it will be seen who really fear and serve God. When the darkness is deepest, the light of a godlike character will shine the brightest. When every other trust fails, then it will be seen who have an abiding trust in Jehovah. And while the enemies of truth are on every side, watching the Lord's servants for evil, God will watch over them for good. He will be to them as the shadow of a great rock in a weary land" (*The Acts of the Apostles,* pp. 431, 432).

Today's Lesson: Through all of Satan's attacks, we can be certain that God will give us strength to stand firm.

"Almost Thou Persuadest Me"

The Acts of the Apostles, Chapter 41

" 'King Agrippa, do you believe the prophets? I know that you do believe.' Then Agrippa said to Paul, 'You almost persuade me to become a Christian.' And Paul said, 'I would to God that not only you, but also all who hear me today, might become both almost and altogether such as I am, except for these chains' " (Acts 26:27–29, NKJV).

While Festus waited for a suitable ship to take Paul to Rome, King Agrippa—the last of the Herods—and his wife, Bernice, came to pay their respects to Festus. Festus told Agrippa about his interesting prisoner, outlining the circumstances that had led to Paul's appeal to Caesar. Agrippa became interested and wanted to hear Paul for himself.

Paul stood manacled before the assembled company. What a contrast—earthly pomp and the power of heavenly simplicity! Festus himself eloquently presented Paul to King Agrippa in words that were not at all what the Jewish leaders wanted him to say.

Paul was not intimidated by the lavish splendor of the court or the power of those who had gathered. Graciously, he acknowledged that Agrippa was well acquainted with Jewish beliefs and would give him a fair hearing. Paul then related his life's story—including his remarkable conversion to Jesus Christ. He showed how the Old Testament had foretold the coming Messiah and how Jesus met every specification of the prophecies. Agrippa seemed spellbound. "Almost thou persuadeth me," he admitted.

Key Thought: "Festus, Agrippa, and Bernice . . . had that day heard the offer of salvation through the name of Christ. One, at least, had been almost persuaded to accept the grace and pardon offered. But Agrippa put aside the proffered mercy, refusing to accept the cross of a crucified Redeemer. . . .

"As the assembly dispersed, they talked among themselves, saying, 'This man doeth nothing worthy of death or of bonds.'. . .

'This man,' he [Agrippa] said to Festus, 'might have been set at liberty, if he had not appealed unto Caesar' " (*The Acts of the Apostles,* p. 438).

Today's Lesson: In the last days, God's people will have the opportunity to share their faith with those in the world's highest positions of authority.

The Voyage and Shipwreck

The Acts of the Apostles, Chapter 42.

"Paul said to the centurion and the soldiers, 'Unless these men stay in the ship, you cannot be saved' "
(Acts 27:31, NKJV).

Two thousand years ago, traveling by sea was filled with hardship and peril. Mariners directed their course largely by the position of the sun and stars, and during a portion of the year safe navigation was almost impossible.

Paul, in feeble health, was bound in chains for the journey. One concession made the trip easier—Luke and Aristarchus were permitted to travel with him. The voyage began well, although winter was approaching rapidly. The party left Fair Havens with a soft south wind, but soon a ferocious gale arose, and the ship was in great danger. Worse was soon to come.

The ship began to leak heavily, and the sailors threw most of the cargo overboard to lighten the ship. During a lull in the storm, Paul stood on the deck and shouted to the crew that an angel had assured him that everyone on board would be spared—that they would be cast onto an island. Hope revived among the passengers and crew at his words.

That night they realized they were approaching land of some kind. The most critical moment was before them, and the roar of the breakers was frightful. The ship broke apart, but everyone managed to reach shore safely. Not one was missing.

Key Thought: "For fourteen days they drifted under a sunless and starless heaven. The apostle, though himself suffering physically, had words of hope for the darkest hour, a helping hand in every emergency. He grasped by faith the arm of Infinite Power, and his heart was stayed upon God. He had no fears for himself; he knew that God would preserve him to witness at Rome for the truth of Christ. But his heart yearned with pity for the poor souls around him, sinful, degraded, and unprepared to die. As he earnestly pleaded with God to spare their lives, it was revealed to him that his prayer was granted" (*The Acts of the Apostles,* p. 442).

Today's Lesson: In times of life's greatest stress, we may calmly trust in the Lord and not have to depend on our own efforts or understanding.

NOVEMBER 4

In Rome

The Acts of the Apostles, Chapter 43.

**"When the brethren heard about us, they came to meet
us as far as Appii Forum and Three Inns. When Paul saw
them, he thanked God and took courage"
(Acts 28:15, NKJV).**

Since receiving Paul's letter, the Christians in Italy had looked
forward eagerly to his visit. They had not expected to see him
arrive as a prisoner, but his sufferings only endeared him to them
the more.

Entering Rome, Paul and the other prisoners reached Appii Forum.
The busy thoroughfare was filled with its usual crowds. Suddenly a cry
of joy was heard, and a man raced toward Paul and fell upon his neck
with tears of rejoicing. Many times this was repeated as his converts
recognized him. Each time, everything came to a standstill, but the
soldiers permitted it, for they had learned to respect Paul, who had
saved their lives on their sea journey. Paul's experience had been a
succession of trials, suffering, and disappointment, but in that hour
he felt amply repaid.

The centurion gave such a good report about Paul when he turned
over his prisoner that the chief captain of the emperor's guard did not
throw Paul into prison; he put him under house arrest, but Paul was
still chained to a soldier. Though a prisoner, Paul continued to write
letters to the churches and send out workers.

Key Thought: "While apparently cut off from active labor, Paul
exerted a wider and more lasting influence than if he had been free
to travel among the churches as in former years. As a prisoner of the
Lord, he had a firmer hold upon the affections of his brethren; and his
words, written by one under bonds for the sake of Christ, commanded
greater attention and respect than they did when he was personally
with them. Not until Paul was removed from them, did the believers
realize how heavy were the burdens he had borne in their behalf. . . . And
as they learned of his courage and faith during his long imprisonment
they were stimulated to greater fidelity and zeal in the cause of Christ"
(*The Acts of the Apostles,* p. 454).

Today's Lesson: In whatever circumstances we find ourselves, we
can do God's work and follow His plan for our lives.

Caesar's Household

The Acts of the Apostles, Chapter 44.

"Then Paul dwelt two whole years in his own rented house, and received all who came to him, preaching the kingdom of God and teaching the things which concern the Lord Jesus Christ with all confidence, no one forbidding him" (Acts 28:30, 31, NKJV).

In the early days of the church, the leading figures of the world either were unaware of the humble Jesus or regarded Him with hatred or derision. Now, in the metropolis of the world, those in the imperial halls of the Roman Empire were hearing the gospel. Nero seemed to have obliterated from his soul the last traces of the divine influence, but even in Nero's household, trophies were won for the cross. These were not Christians secretly, but openly.

As much as his sermons, Paul's chains won the attention of the court to Christianity. His patience and cheerfulness during his long and unjust imprisonment, his courage and faith, were a continual witness to His Lord. In his letter to the Philippian Christians Paul told them of converts won in Rome. He was able to say, "My bonds in Christ are manifest in all the palace, and in all other places" (Philippians 1:13). Among those who sent greetings to the Philippian Christians, Paul mentions especially those "that are of Caesar's household" (Philippians 4:22).

Patience as well as courage has its victories. By meekness under trial, no less than boldness in enterprise, men and women may be won to Christ.

Key Thought: "Not in freedom from trial, but in the midst of it, is Christian character developed. Exposure to rebuffs and opposition leads the follower of Christ to greater watchfulness and more earnest prayer to the mighty Helper. Severe trial endured by the grace of God develops patience, vigilance, fortitude, and a deep and abiding trust in God. It is the triumph of the Christian faith that it enables its follower to suffer and be strong; to submit, and thus to conquer; to be killed all the day long, and yet to live; to bear the cross, and thus to win the crown of glory" (*The Acts of the Apostles,* pp. 467, 468).

Today's Lesson: Our lives are a sermon in deeds—one that often speaks louder than any spoken witness.

Written From Rome

The Acts of the Apostles, Chapter 45.

"If then you were raised with Christ, seek those things which are above, where Christ is, sitting at the right hand of God. Set your mind on things above, not on things on the earth, for you died, and your life is hidden with Christ in God" (Colossians 3:1–3, NKJV).

Paul was constantly concerned for the well-being of the churches he had helped establish in Asia Minor. From his Roman prison he wrote letters to the Ephesian, Colossian, and Philippian believers. His primary fear was that these church members would not get the whole picture of what it means to be followers of Christ.

In many ways Paul emphasized that Christianity is more than knowing historical facts about the life and death of Jesus—that God expects new, transformed lives following the example of Jesus. In Ephesians 4:24, for example, he explained that the church was organized not merely to transmit information about Jesus but to help believers find unity in Jesus—to mature in their understanding of Him so that they would not be tossed around by every wind of doctrine. They are to mature, learning how to speak the truth in love, living the truth as it is in Jesus, not merely having the gospel in their heads but in their hearts.

In Philippians 2, Paul eloquently described how Jesus became a human being like the rest of us, to give us an example of humble self-sacrifice.

Key Thought: "The work of gaining salvation is one of copartnership, a joint operation. There is to be co-operation between God and the repentant sinner. This is necessary for the formation of right principles in the character. Man is to make earnest efforts to overcome that which hinders him from attaining to perfection. But he is wholly dependent upon God for success. Human effort of itself is not sufficient. . . . Resistance of temptation must come from man, who must draw his power from God. On the one side there is infinite wisdom, compassion, and power; on the other, weakness, sinfulness, absolute helplessness" (*The Acts of the Apostles,* p. 482).

Lesson for Today: As followers of Jesus, we must be serious about allowing Him to transform us into persons He can trust with eternal life.

At Liberty

The Acts of the Apostles, Chapter 46.

"At my first defense no one stood with me, but all forsook me. May it not be charged against them. But the Lord stood with me and strengthened me, so that the message might be preached fully through me, and that all the Gentiles might hear. And I was delivered out of the mouth of the lion" (2 Timothy 4:16, 17, NKJV).

Even in prison, Paul's influence had been expanding. Now, clouds were gathering that threatened not only his own safety but also the prosperity of the church.

Paul's Jewish opponents became even more active in their efforts against him. Nero's second wife was openly hostile to Christianity. The relative freedom of "house arrest" Paul had enjoyed for two years changed. His former guard, a man of integrity, was replaced by one who gave Paul no special favors. Nero's life went from bad to worse. He murdered his own mother and his first wife. But no matter how depraved Nero became, he still was the absolute ruler of the civilized world—even worshiped as a god! However, in a way that God alone could devise, Nero, a man totally without moral integrity of any kind, declared Paul innocent and released him!

Had Paul's trial been delayed further, he doubtless would have perished in the awful persecution of Christians carried out by Nero. The jury is still out as to who was actually responsible for the fire that destroyed half of the city of Rome. Initially, Nero was blamed, but he turned the accusation against the Christians. His cruel device worked, and thousands of new believers in Christ were killed.

Paul was spared this terrible persecution; he had left Rome, soon after his release, to visit churches in Asia Minor.

Key Thought: "God did shield His servant. At Paul's examination the charges against him were not sustained, and, contrary to the general expectation, and with a regard for justice wholly at variance with his character, Nero declared the prisoner guiltless. Paul's bonds were removed; he was again a free man" (*The Acts of the Apostles,* p. 486, 487).

Lesson For Today: God takes a personal interest in His people. He sometimes delivers in miraculous ways, but no matter the outcome, He is always present to sustain.

The Final Arrest

The Acts of the Apostles, Chapter 47.

"The Lord give mercy unto the house of Onesiphorus; for he oft refreshed me, and was not ashamed of my chain: But, when he was in Rome, he sought me out very diligently, and found me. The Lord grant unto him that he may find mercy of the Lord in that day" (2 Timothy 1:16–18).

Paul's work among the churches after his acquittal at Rome did not escape the eyes of his enemies. Since Nero's persecution of the Christians in Rome, believers everywhere were under imperial sanction. The Jews conceived the idea of charging Paul with the crime of burning Rome. No one could possibly believe such an accusation, but even a hint of plausibility would seal his doom. Through their evil efforts, Paul was again arrested and hurried to his final imprisonment.

When he arrived in the city again, Paul discovered that few Christians remained in Rome. Most had been killed or fled. Those who were left were greatly depressed and intimidated.

Upon his arrival, Paul was thrown into a gloomy dungeon and regarded with general hatred. His few remaining friends, who had steadfastly shared in his burdens, began to leave, as well—first Phygellus and Hermogenes, then Demas. Paul sent Crescens to the churches in Galatia, Titus to Dalmatia, Tychicus to Ephesus. Writing to Timothy of this experience, Paul said wistfully, "Only Luke is with me" (2 Timothy 4:11). Paul, weary now with age and toil, needed the services of Luke, his physician and faithful friend. Luke made it possible for Paul to continue communicating with the world outside his prison.

In these trying hours, Paul was cheered by frequent visits from Onesiphorus. Onesiphorus knew that Paul was in chains for the truth's sake, while he himself went free. He spared no efforts to make Paul's life as comfortable as possible.

Key Thought: "The desire for love and sympathy is implanted in the heart by God Himself. Christ, in His hour of agony in Gethsemane, longed for the sympathy of His disciples. And Paul, though apparently indifferent to hardship and suffering, yearned for sympathy and companionship" (*The Acts of the Apostles,* p. 491).

Today's Lesson: We can be a source of encouragement and strength to those who are carrying heavy burdens.

Paul Before Nero

The Acts of the Apostles, Chapter 48.

***"Let us hold fast the confession of our hope without
wavering, for He who promised is faithful"
(Hebrews 10:23, NKJV).***

A mong the Romans it was customary to allow an accused person
to employ an advocate to plead on his behalf before courts of
justice. But when Paul was summoned before Nero, no man
ventured to act as his advocate; no friend was at hand even to preserve
a record of the trial or of the arguments he urged in his own defense.
Among the Christians at Rome, not one person came forward to stand
by the aged apostle in that trying hour.

Imagine the picture! Paul—a tower of integrity and truth—standing
before Nero, the haughty, debauched monarch. Nero stood unrivaled
in earthly power and authority. His name made the world tremble.
His frown was more to be dreaded than the plague. Paul, the aged
warrior of the Lord, stood before the arrogant emperor without money,
without friends, without legal counsel—but his heart was at peace with
God. A comparison between the trial of Jesus and the trial of Paul
is dramatically obvious. The crowd in Paul's Roman courtroom was
much like the crowd surrounding Jesus and Pilate.

New accusations that Paul had instigated the burning of Rome
were added to the old charges of sedition and heresy. Paul preserved
his unbroken serenity. Judges and people looked at him in surprise.
When he was permitted to speak on his own behalf, all listened with
eager interest. Light shone for many who afterward followed it.

Key Thought: "For a moment, heaven was opened to the guilty
and hardened Nero, and its peace and purity seemed desirable.
That moment the invitation of mercy was extended even to him. But
only for a moment was the thought of pardon welcomed. Then the
command was issued that Paul be taken back to his dungeon; and as
the door closed upon the messenger of God, the door of repentance
closed forever against the emperor of Rome" (*The Acts of the Apostles,*
p. 496).

Today's Lesson: God has promised to be with those who are
called upon to witness for Him before courts and rulers. He will give
us words for the occasion, as He did for Paul.

Paul's Last Letter

The Acts of the Apostles, Chapter 49.

"I am already being poured out as a drink offering, and the time of my departure is at hand. I have fought the good fight, I have finished the race, I have kept the faith. Finally, there is laid up for me the crown of righteousness, which the Lord, the righteous Judge, will give to me on that Day, and not to me only but also to all who have loved His appearing" (2 Timothy 4:6–8, NKJV).

Going back to his dark dungeon after proclaiming the wonderful story of a crucified and risen Savior, Paul knew that the seed he had planted would grow into many new believers in the city of Rome. But he also knew that his days were surely numbered—and he thought of young Timothy in Ephesus.

Paul and Timothy were bound together by an unusually deep and strong affection—that of a faithful son ever grateful for his honored father. And Paul longed to see Timothy again. Even under the most favorable circumstances, several months must pass before Timothy could reach Rome from Ephesus. Knowing this, Paul wrote his young friend a letter—his last testimony—knowing he might not be spared to tell Timothy these things in person.

Paul emphasized that the true minister will not shun hardship or responsibility. He will commit the knowledge he has received from God to faithful men, who in their turn will teach others. Paul also warned Timothy against false teachers. Paul's life was a demonstration of the truths he taught. This was his power.

Key Thought: "What the church needs in these days of peril is an army of workers who, like Paul, have educated themselves for usefulness, who have a deep experience in the things of God, and who are filled with earnestness and zeal. Sanctified, self-sacrificing men are needed; men who will not shun trial and responsibility; men who are brave and true; men in whose hearts Christ is formed 'the hope of glory,' and who with lips touched with holy fire will 'preach the word' " (*The Acts of the Apostles,* p. 507).

Today's Lesson: There is a crown of righteousness reserved for each one who, like Paul, finishes life's race having kept the faith.

Condemned to Die

The Acts of the Apostles, Chapter 50.

"I know whom I have believed, and am persuaded that He is able to keep that which I have committed unto him against that day" (2 Timothy 1:12).

Paul was taken privately to the place of execution. Few spectators were allowed to be present. His persecutors feared that the scenes of his death would win converts to Christianity. But even the hardened soldiers who were assigned the grim task were amazed at his cheerfulness. Paul's spirit of forgiveness and his unwavering confidence in Christ till the very end moved some of these soldiers to accept Jesus as their Savior.

It was not in Paul to face death with such peace. The presence of the Holy Spirit filled his soul. He understood Isaiah's declaration, "Thou wilt keep him in perfect peace, whose mind is stayed on thee: because he trusteth in thee" (Isaiah 26:3).

Paul's life exemplified the truths he proclaimed, and this gave convincing power to his preaching. Here lies the power of truth for all of God's people. The unstudied, unconscious influence of a holy life is the most convincing sermon that can be given. Arguments, even when unanswerable, may provoke only opposition, but a godly example has a power that it is impossible wholly to resist.

Key Thought: "No faithful hand recorded for the generations to come the last scenes in the life of this holy man, but Inspiration has preserved for us his dying testimony. Like a trumpet peal his voice has rung out through all the ages since, nerving with his own courage thousands of witnesses for Christ and wakening in thousands of sorrow-stricken hearts the echo of his own triumphant joy: 'I am now ready to be offered, and the time of my departure is at hand. I have fought a good fight, I have finished my course, I have kept the faith: henceforth there is laid up for me a crown of righteousness, which the Lord, the righteous Judge, shall give me at that day: and not to me only, but unto all them also that love His appearing.' 2 Timothy 4:6-8" (*The Acts of the Apostles,* p. 513).

Today's Lesson: Our lives preach the gospel in far stronger terms than we can do with our words.

A Faithful Undershepherd

The Acts of the Apostles, Chapter 51.

"Blessed be the God and Father of our Lord Jesus Christ, who according to His abundant mercy has begotten us again to a living hope through the resurrection of Jesus Christ from the dead, to an inheritance incorruptible and undefiled and that does not fade away, reserved in heaven for you" (1 Peter 1:3, 4, NKJV).

During the years of ministry that followed Pentecost, Peter was among those who put forth untiring efforts to reach the Jews who came to Jerusalem to worship at the time of the annual festivals. As the early Christian church grew, Peter's talents proved of untold value. His responsibility was twofold: He bore positive witness concerning the Messiah before unbelievers and, at the same time, he did a special work for believers, strengthening them in the faith of Jesus.

Peter had to learn that love for Christ is not a fitful feeling but a living principle to be made manifest as an abiding power in the heart. If the character and deportment of the shepherd is an exemplification of the truth he advocates, the Lord will set the seal of His approval to the work. The shepherd and the flock will become one, united by their common hope in Christ.

Peter's words were written for the instruction of believers in every age, and they have a special significance for those who live at the end of time. Those who would not fall victim to Satan's devices must guard well the avenues of the soul; they must avoid reading, seeing, or hearing that which will suggest impure thoughts.

Peter wrote at a time of special trial to the church. Many had already become participants in Christ's sufferings, and soon the church was to undergo a period of even greater persecution.

Key Thought: "[Peter's] letters bear the impress of having been written by one in whom the sufferings of Christ and also His consolation had been made to abound; one whose entire being had been transformed by grace, and whose hope of eternal life was sure and steadfast" (*The Acts of the Apostles,* p. 517).

Today's Lesson: It is no less important today to guard every avenue to the soul than it was when Peter wrote his counsel to the early Christians.

Steadfast Unto the End

The Acts of the Apostles, Chapter 52.

"Since all these things will be dissolved, what manner of persons ought you to be in holy conduct and godliness, looking for and hastening the coming of the day of God, because of which the heavens will be dissolved being on fire, and the elements will melt with fervent heat?"
(2 Peter 3:11, 12, NKJV).

In his second letter, Peter sets forth the divine plan for the development of character (see 2 Peter 1:5–11). Faith, virtue, knowledge, temperance, patience, godliness, brotherly kindness, and love are the rounds of a spiritual ladder. Christ's ideal for us is that we will progress from rung to rung, adding virtue to virtue. Peter reminds us that by climbing this ladder we are laying hold of the power of Christ. We may claim His unfailing promises.

No one needs to feel he or she cannot attain a perfect Christian character. By the sacrifice of Christ, provision has been made for us to receive everything we need for a life of godliness. God holds before us the high standard of character perfection. He places before us the example of Jesus' character. While on earth, Jesus perfected a life of constant resistance to sin, and now He offers to make this experience possible for us. Christ's example is God's assurance to us that we, too, may obtain complete victory.

Key Thought: "Peter, as a Jew and a foreigner, was condemned to be scourged and crucified. In prospect of this fearful death, the apostle remembered his great sin in denying Jesus in the hour of His trial. Once so unready to acknowledge the cross, he now counted it a joy to yield up his life for the gospel, feeling only that, for him who had denied his Lord, to die in the same manner as his Master died was too great an honor. . . . As a last favor he entreated his executioners that he might be nailed to the cross with his head downward. The request was granted, and in this manner died the great apostle Peter" (*The Acts of the Apostles,* pp. 537, 538).

Today's Lesson: By God's grace, we may climb higher on Peter's ladder of character development each day, adding virtue after virtue to our Christian experience.

John the Beloved

The Acts of the Apostles, Chapter 53.

"Beloved, now we are children of God; and it has not yet been revealed what we shall be, but we know that when He is revealed, we shall be like Him, for we shall see Him as He is. And everyone who has this hope in Him purifies himself, just as He is pure" (1 John 3:2, 3, NKJV).

John is distinguished above the other apostles as "the disciple whom Jesus loved" (John 21:20). He was one of the three permitted to witness Christ's glory on the mount of transfiguration and Christ's agony in Gethsemane. And in His last hours on the cross, the Lord committed His mother to John's care.

But John did not naturally possess a loving character. He was proud, self-assertive, and ambitious for honor. He and his brother were called "sons of thunder." But underneath all this Jesus discerned the ardent, sincere, loving heart. He enabled John to overcome his self-seeking ambitions.

When the mother of John and James asked Jesus for special favors for her two sons when He set up His kingdom, Jesus told her that position in God's kingdom is not gained by favoritism—it is the result of character. And character is the result of conquering self through the grace of our Lord Jesus Christ.

Key Thought: "The depth and fervor of John's affection for his Master was not the cause of Christ's love for him, but the effect of that love. John desired to become like Jesus, and under the transforming influence of the love of Christ he did become meek and lowly. Self was hid in Jesus. Above all his companions, John yielded himself to the power of that wondrous life. He says, 'The life was manifested, and we have seen it.' 'And of His fullness have all we received, and grace for grace.' 1 John 1:2; John 1:16. John knew the Saviour by an experimental knowledge. . . . When he testified of the Saviour's grace, his simple language was eloquent with the love that pervaded his whole being" (*The Acts of the Apostles,* pp. 544, 545).

Today's Lesson: The battle against self is the most difficult battle we face, but God has promised to give us His grace so we will prevail.

A Faithful Witness

The Acts of the Apostles, Chapter 54.

"That which was from the beginning, which we have heard, which we have seen with our eyes, which we have looked upon, and our hands have handled, concerning the Word of life—the life was manifested, and we have seen, and bear witness, and declare to you that eternal life which was with the Father and was manifested to us—that which we have seen and heard we declare to you, that you also may have fellowship with us; and truly our fellowship is with the Father and with His Son Jesus Christ. And these things we write to you that your joy may be full" (1 John 1:1–4, NKJV).

John was a powerful preacher—fervent and deeply in earnest. In beautiful language and with a musical voice he told of the words and works of Christ, speaking in a way that impressed the hearts of those who heard him. The simplicity of his words, the sublime power of the truths he uttered, and the fervor that characterized his teachings gave him access to all classes.

The apostle's life was in harmony with his teaching. Jesus had bidden His disciples to love one another as He had loved them. When Jesus first spoke those words, the disciples could not understand them, but after they had witnessed the sufferings of Christ, after His crucifixion and resurrection and ascension to heaven, they had a clearer concept of God's love and of the nature of the love He wanted them to have for one another.

But gradually a change came. The believers began to look for defects in others. They became more strict in regard to outward ceremonies, more particular about the theory than the practice of the faith.

Key Thought: "As a witness for Christ, John entered into no controversy, no wearisome contention. He declared what he knew, what he had seen and heard.... His testimony in regard to the Saviour's life and death was clear and forcible. Out of the abundance of a heart overflowing with love for the Saviour he spoke; and no power could stay his words" (*The Acts of the Apostles,* p. 555).

Today's Lesson: Love is to be a governing principle of the Christian life, not an occasional impulse.

Transformed by Grace

The Acts of the Apostles, Chapter 55.

"This is the will of God, even your sanctification"
(1 Thessalonians 4:3).

John was an example of true sanctification. He yielded his resentful, ambitious temper to the molding power of Christ. Our sanctification is God's object in all His dealings with us. He gave His son to die for us that we might be sanctified through obedience. True sanctification comes as a result of the operation of the principle of love, but this happens only as we learn the meaning of self-sacrifice. The cross of Christ is the central pillar on which hangs the "far more exceeding and eternal weight of glory" (2 Corinthians 4:17).

John did not teach that salvation was to be earned by obedience; he taught that obedience is the natural fruit of faith and love. The sanctified heart is in complete harmony with the principles of God's law.

Many who are striving to obey God's commandments nevertheless have little peace or joy. This is because they have failed to exercise faith. The Lord wants all of His sons and daughters to be happy, peaceful, and obedient. And through faith in Him, every deficiency of character may be supplied, every sin cleansed, and every excellence developed.

Sanctification is God's will for us. But it must be our desire, as well.

Key Thought: "Sanctification is not the work of a moment, an hour, a day, but of a lifetime. It is not gained by a happy flight of feeling, but is the result of constantly dying to sin, and constantly living for Christ. Wrongs cannot be righted nor reformations wrought in the character by feeble, intermittent efforts. It is only by long, persevering effort, sore discipline, and stern conflict, that we shall overcome. We know not one day how strong will be our conflict the next. So long as Satan reigns, we shall have self to subdue, besetting sins to overcome; so long as life shall last, there will be no stopping place, no point which we can reach and say, I have fully attained. Sanctification is the result of lifelong obedience" (*The Acts of the Apostles,* pp. 560, 561).

Today's Lesson: If we are to grow in Christ, we must be serious about relying on Him to overcome sin in our lives.

Patmos

The Acts of the Apostles, Chapter 56.

***"I, John, both your brother and companion in the
tribulation, and in the kingdom and patience of Jesus
Christ, was on the island that is called Patmos for the
word of God and for the testimony of Jesus Christ"
(Revelation 1:9, NKJV).***

More than fifty years had passed since the organization of the
Christian church. During that time, wherever the gospel
message was preached, it had been constantly opposed—from
the emperor in Rome to the Jewish religious leaders. But through it
all, John had remained a mighty pillar strengthening fellow church
members.

The Jewish rulers were filled with bitter hatred against aged John.
They declared that their efforts against the Christians would be
unsuccessful as long as John's testimony kept ringing in the ears of
the people—and thus his voice had to be silenced!

Finally, John was summoned to Rome, where he met the same
kind of false witnesses Paul and Peter had to face. His hearers were
astonished at his wisdom and eloquence. Emperor Domitian, filled
with rage, had John cast into a cauldron of boiling oil. But the Lord of
the three Hebrews on the plain of Dura spared John's life. Domitian
was furious and banned John to the penal colony on the isle of Patmos.
His enemies thought that his influence would no longer be felt and
that he would surely die soon on Patmos of hardship and distress.
How wrong they were!

Key Thought: "The history of John affords a striking illustration
of the way in which God can use aged workers. When John was exiled
to the Isle of Patmos, there were many who thought him to be past
service, an old and broken reed, ready to fall at any time. But the Lord
saw fit to use him still. Though banished from the scenes of his former
labor, he did not cease to bear witness to the truth. . . . And it was
after John had grown old in the service of his Lord that he received
more communications from heaven than he had received during all
the former years of his life" (*The Acts of the Apostles,* pp. 572, 573).

Today's Lesson: We may experience our own "Patmos," but God
continues to have a purpose for our life.

The Revelation

The Acts of the Apostles, Chapter 57.

"These are the ones who follow the Lamb wherever He goes. These were redeemed from among men, being firstfruits to God and to the Lamb. And in their mouth was found no guile, for they are without fault before the throne of God" (Revelation 14:4, 5, NKJV).

Fifty years after Jesus returned to heaven, the gospel had been carried to men and women throughout most of the inhabited world. The zeal manifested at this time by the followers of Jesus has been recorded by John in Revelation for the encouragement of believers in every age.

Through John, Jesus used the church at Ephesus as a symbol of the entire Christian church in the apostolic period. These early believers were fervent in sharing the gospel, but after a time their zeal began to fade. Coldness crept into the church. Some forgot the wonderful manner in which they had received the truth. In their desire for something novel and startling, they attempted to introduce new doctrines that would be more pleasing to new converts but that were not in harmony with the fundamental principles of the gospel. At this critical time, John was sentenced to Patmos.

The visions Jesus gave John on Patmos were exactly the guidance and comfort that the first-century church needed. And they have been instructive for the church ever since. Deep things of God are portrayed in the book of Revelation. Its messages are addressed to those living in the last day days of this earth's history, as well as being applicable to Christians living in John's day.

Revelation is the complement of the book of Daniel. One is a prophecy; the other, a revelation.

Key Thought: "Christ's true disciples follow Him through sore conflicts, enduring self-denial and experiencing bitter disappointment; but this teaches them the guilt and woe of sin, and they are led to look upon it with abhorrence. Partakers of Christ's sufferings, they are destined to be partakers of His glory. In holy vision the prophet saw the ultimate triumph of God's remnant church" (*The Acts of the Apostles,* p. 590).

Today's Lesson: God has given us detailed information about the last days that will enable us to stand firm for Him through all the difficulties that lie ahead.

The Gospel Triumphant

The Acts of the Apostles, Chapter 58.

"I beheld, and, lo, a great multitude, which no man could number, of all nations, and kindreds, and people, and tongues, stood before the throne, and before the Lamb, clothed with white robes, and palms in their hands; and cried with a loud voice, saying, Salvation to our God which sitteth upon the throne, and unto the Lamb" *(Revelation 7:9, 10).*

More than nineteen hundred years have passed since the apostles rested from their labors, but the history of their toils for Christ is still one of the most precious treasures of the church. They carried the gospel to every nation in a single generation.

Any attack made upon the gospel was like a deep wound to their own souls, and they battled for the cause of Christ with every power of their being. Their understanding of truth and their power to withstand opposition were proportionate to their obedience to God's will.

Paul and the other apostles, and all the righteous ones who have lived since, have acted their part in building the temple. But the structure is not yet complete. We who are living in these last days have a part to do. We are to bring to the foundation material that will stand the test of fire. The Christian who faithfully presents the Word of life, leading men and women into the way of holiness and peace, is bringing to the foundation material that will endure, and in the kingdom of God he will be honored as a wise builder. It is the privilege of every Christian, not only to look for but to hasten the coming of the Savior.

Key Thought: "Christ has given to the church a sacred charge. Every member should be a channel through which God can communicate to the world the treasures of His grace, the unsearchable riches of Christ. There is nothing that the Saviour desires so much as agents who will represent to the world His Spirit and His character. . . . All heaven is waiting for men and women through whom God can reveal the power of Christianity" (*The Acts of the Apostles,* p. 600).

Today's Lesson: What a solemn responsibility to know that our actions can either hasten or delay Christ's coming!

The Destruction of Jerusalem

The Great Controversy, Chapter 1.

"Now as He drew near, He saw the city and wept over it, saying, 'If you had known, even you, especially in this your day, the things that make for your peace!. . . . For the days will come upon you when your enemies will build an embankment around you, surround you and . . . level you, and your children . . . will not leave in you one stone upon another, because you did not know the time of your visitation' " (Luke 19:41–44, NKJV).

Jesus wept, not for Himself, but for the doomed thousands in Jerusalem. Had Israel as a nation preserved her allegiance to God—had the people not rejected Jesus—Jerusalem would have stood forever, the chosen of God.

For three years the Lord of light and glory had gone in and out among His people. The waves of mercy, beaten back by those stubborn hearts, returned in a stronger tide of pitying, inexpressible love. But Israel had turned from her best Friend and only Helper.

When God withdrew His protection from the Jews and removed His restraining power from Satan and his angels, the nation was left to the control of the leader she had chosen. Terrible were the calamities that fell upon Jerusalem when Titus began his siege. Yet, not one Christian perished in the destruction of Jerusalem.

Jerusalem's end foreshadows the events at the end of the world when probation closes and God leaves those who have rejected His mercy to reap what they have sown. Then there will be no protection from Satan's cruelty.

Key Thought: "The world is no more ready to credit the message for this time than were the Jews to receive the Saviour's warning concerning Jerusalem. Come when it may, the day of God will come unawares to the ungodly. When life is going on in its unvarying round; when men are absorbed in pleasure, in business, in traffic, in money-making; when religious leaders are magnifying the world's progress and enlightenment, and the people are lulled in a false security—then, as the midnight thief steals within the unguarded dwelling, so shall sudden destruction come upon the careless and ungodly, 'and they shall not escape' " (*The Great Controversy,* p. 38).

Today's Lesson: Our only safety is in Christ.

Persecution in the First Centuries

The Great Controversy, Chapter 2.

"Be thou faithful unto death, and I will give thee a crown of life" (Revelation 2:10).

We will never know how many millions of faithful Christians sealed their testimony with their blood. Under the fiercest persecution, these witnesses for Jesus kept their faith unsullied. With words of faith, patience, and hope, they encouraged one another to endure privation and distress. Trials and persecution only brought them nearer to their rest and their eternal reward.

By defeat, they conquered. God's workmen were slain, but His work went steadily forward nonetheless. Early church leader Tertullian said to pagan rulers, You may "kill us, torture us, condemn us. . . . Your injustice is the proof that we are innocent. . . . The oftener we are mown down by you, the more in number we grow; the blood of Christians is seed."

In addition to open persecution, Satan was busy planting his banner within the Christian church. He endeavored to gain by trickery and deceit what he had failed to secure by force. Persecutions ceased, and in their stead were substituted the dangerous allurements of temporal prosperity and worldly honor.

Key Thought: "The apostle Paul declares that 'all that will live godly in Christ Jesus shall suffer persecution.' 2 Timothy 3:12. Why is it, then, that persecution seems in a great degree to slumber? The only reason is that the church has conformed to the world's standard and therefore awakens no opposition. The religion which is current in our day is not of the pure and holy character that marked the Christian faith in the days of Christ and His apostles. It is only because of the spirit of compromise with sin, because the great truths of the word of God are so indifferently regarded, because there is so little vital godliness in the church, that Christianity is apparently so popular with the world. Let there be a revival of the faith and power of the early church, and the spirit of persecution will be revived, and the fires of persecution will be rekindled" (*The Great Controversy,* p. 48).

Today's Lesson: Popularity is dangerous to the Christian church; it usually signals that the church has allow the world to make inroads into its teachings and operations.

An Era of Spiritual Darkness

The Great Controversy, Chapter 3.

**"Let no one deceive you by any means; for that Day will
not come unless the falling away comes first, and the
man of sin is revealed, the son of perdition, who opposes
and exalts himself above all that is called God or that is
worshiped, so that he sits as God in the temple of God,
showing himself that he is God. . . . For the mystery of
lawlessness is already at work"
(2 Thessalonians 2:3, 4, 7, NKJV).**

Even in his day Paul saw errors creeping into the young church
that would prepare the way for the development of the papacy.
Little by little, in stealth and silence, and then more openly, the
mystery of iniquity did its deceptive work through incorporating pagan
practices into the church.

With the conversion of Constantine to Christianity in the early part
of the fourth century, the world walked into the church—and paganism
triumphed. As the church moved farther from the apostolic era, it
became more difficult to maintain the pure gospel. The gigantic system
of false religion that resulted is a masterpiece of Satan's power.

The bishop of Rome became the visible head of the universal church
and assumed the names and presumed the power of God Himself. The
Bible was to be interpreted only by church leaders. The seventh-day
Sabbath was replaced by Sunday. Faith was transferred from Jesus
to the pope of Rome. People were taught to look to the priest as their
mediator and to trust to prescribed works of their own to atone for sin.

These were days of peril for true believers, and faithful standard-
bearers were few.

Key Thought: "The advancing centuries witnessed a constant
increase of error in the doctrines put forth from Rome. Even before
the establishment of the papacy the teachings of heathen philosophers
had received attention and exerted an influence in the church. Many
who professed conversion still clung to the tenets of their pagan
philosophy, and not only continued its study themselves, but urged
it upon others as a means of extending their influence among the
heathen. Serious errors were thus introduced into the Christian faith"
(*The Great Controversy,* p. 58).

Today's Lesson: We still need to be careful that false teachings
are not accepted within God's church.

The Waldenses

The Great Controversy, Chapter 4.

"Hold fast what you have till I come"
(Revelation 2:25, NKJV).

The light of truth could not be wholly extinguished even by the gloom that settled upon the earth during the long period of papal supremacy. In every age witnesses for God held to the Bible as the only rule of life and hallowed the true Sabbath. They were branded as heretics; their characters maligned; their writings suppressed, misrepresented, or mutilated. Few traces of their existence can be found, except in the accusations of their persecutors.

The Waldenses were among the foremost of those who resisted the encroachments of papal power. For centuries the churches of the Piedmont in Italy maintained their independence from Rome, but the time came at last when the Vatican insisted upon their submission.

The Bible truths which for many centuries were held and taught by the Waldensian Christians were in marked contrast to the false doctrines put forth from Rome.

Among the leading causes that had led to the separation of the true church from Rome was the hatred of the latter toward the Bible Sabbath. The Waldenses were among the first Europeans to obtain a translation of the Holy Scriptures in their own native tongue. Here the light of truth was kept burning for a thousand years amid the darkness of the Middle Ages.

Key Thought: "The persecutions visited for many centuries upon this God-fearing people were endured by them with a patience and constancy that honored their Redeemer. Notwithstanding the crusades against them, and the inhuman butchery to which they were subjected, they continued to send out their missionaries to scatter the precious truth. They were hunted to death; yet their blood watered the seed sown, and it failed not of yielding fruit. . . . Scattered over many lands, they planted the seeds of the Reformation that began in the time of Wycliffe, grew broad and deep in the days of Luther, and is to be carried forward to the close of time by those who also are willing to suffer all things for 'the word of God, and for the testimony of Jesus Christ' " (*The Great Controversy*, p. 78).

Today's Lesson: It takes courage and ingenuity to keep the truth alive amid fierce persecution.

NOVEMBER 24

John Wycliffe

The Great Controversy, Chapter 5.

***"He who overcomes, and keeps My works until the end, to
him I will give power over the nations"
(Revelation 2:26, NKJV).***

Before the Reformation, few copies of the Bible existed. Except
among the Waldenses, the Word of God had for ages been locked
up in languages known only to the learned. In the fourteenth
century John Wycliffe arose in England as the "morning star of the
Reformation" and became the herald of reform, not for England alone
but for all Christendom.

Wycliffe, broadly educated, was noted for his remarkable talents,
fervent piety, and sound scholarship. The power of his genius and the
extent of his knowledge commanded the respect of both friends and
foes. Like other reformers, Wycliffe did not foresee at first where his
course would lead him. But the more he realized the errors of the papacy,
the more earnestly he accused the priesthood of having banished the
Scriptures and demanded that the Bible be restored to the people.

He also attacked the influence of the swarm of begging friars who
drained the resources of the people and brought useful labor into
contempt. These friars had the authority to grant absolution, hear
confessions, and grant pardons. Wycliffe became so popular that the
pope issued decrees to Wycliffe's university, the king of England, and
to English church leaders, demanding they silence Wycliffe.

The reformer's greatest work was the translation of the Bible
into the English language—the first English translation ever made.
Wycliffe taught the distinctive doctrines of Protestantism—salvation
through faith in Christ alone and the Bible as the only infallible rule of
faith and practice. Nearly half the people in England came to accept
Wycliffe's teachings.

Key Thought: "It was through the writings of Wycliffe that John
Huss, of Bohemia, was led to renounce many of the errors of Romanism
and to enter upon the work of reform. Thus in these two countries, so
widely separated, the seed of truth was sown. From Bohemia the work
extended to other lands. The minds of men were directed to the long-
forgotten word of God. A divine hand was preparing the way for the
Great Reformation" (*The Great Controversy,* p. 96).

Today's Lesson: God uses the brightest minds available, if they
are fully committed to biblical truth.

Huss and Jerome

The Great Controversy, Chapter 6.

"We can do nothing against the truth, but for the truth" (2 Corinthians 13:8).

Before the days of Huss, some men in Bohemia condemned openly the corruption in the church. Church leaders were alarmed and eventually decreed that all who departed from Catholic control should be burned.

During this difficult time, John Huss was accepted into the university in Prague as a charity student. He distinguished himself both for his scholarship and his winning disposition. After a few years, he became rector of the university, and his name was well known throughout Europe.

Jerome, another scholar who was a citizen of Prague, returned from England with the writings of Wycliffe. Huss read Wycliffe with great interest, although he did not immediately and publicly embrace these great truths. But others in Bohemia were fanning the gospel flame, which drew the attention of the pope. He placed the city of Prague under an "interdict," meaning that all church services and other religious rites were suspended—marriages could not take place, nor could religious burials. All this put Prague in a turmoil, and the blame was directed toward Huss. He left the city, turning over and over in his mind the biblical truths that were pressing upon his conscience.

As events unfolded, Huss was to witness on a wider stage, and eventually he was burned to death as a martyr to God's truth. So, too, was Jerome. Through weakness, Jerome first repudiated his Protestant beliefs, but later he stood boldly for God's truth and suffered the same fate as Huss. The death of these faithful servants of God only spread the truth more widely.

Key Thought: "God permitted great light to shine upon the minds of these chosen men, revealing to them many of the errors of Rome; but they did not receive all the light that was to be given to the world. . . . Therefore He revealed it to the leaders little by little, as it could be received by the people. From century to century, other faithful workers were to follow, to lead the people on still further in the path of reform" (*The Great Controversy,* p. 103.

Today's Lesson: Brave men and women have given their lives in defense of God's truth to make possible the liberties we enjoy today.

NOVEMBER 26

Luther's Separation From Rome

The Great Controversy, Chapter 7.

**"In it the righteousness of God is revealed from faith
to faith; as it is written, 'The just shall live by faith' "
(Romans 1:17, NKJV).**

Through Martin Luther God accomplished a great work for the reformation of the church and the enlightenment of the world. While a student at the University of Erfurt, Luther discovered a Latin Bible—the first Bible he had ever seen.

Wanting to be free from the world and its sins, Luther entered the monastery to study and find peace with God and freedom from a sense of his guilt—but in vain. Staupitz, Luther's superior, urged Luther to look away from himself and fasten his faith on the pardoning Savior. Luther discovered faith! Soon he was called to be a professor in the University of Wittenberg where his lectures drew captivated hearers—and where he was awarded the degree of Doctor of Divinity. No longer a mere monk, he was now an authorized herald of the Bible and on a collision course with his own church. The world has never been the same.

Key Thought: "Opposition is the lot of all whom God employs to present truths specially applicable to their time. There was a present truth in the days of Luther,—a truth at that time of special importance; there is a present truth for the church today. . . . He who does all things according to the counsel of His will has been pleased to place men under various circumstances and to enjoin upon them duties peculiar to the times in which they live and the conditions under which they are placed. If they would prize the light given them, broader views of truth would be opened before them. But truth is no more desired by the majority today than it was by the papists who opposed Luther. . . . The great controversy between truth and error, between Christ and Satan, is to increase in intensity to the close of this world's history" (*The Great Controversy,* pp. 143, 144).

Today's Lesson: The issues that disturbed Luther's heart and caused him to search the Bible for answers—how to have peace with God and forgiveness of sin—are still the most important issues facing human beings today.

Luther Before the Diet

The Great Controversy, Chapter 8.

"Therefore whoever confesses Me before men, him I will also confess before My Father who is in heaven. But whoever denies Me before men, him I will also deny before My Father who is in heaven" (Matthew 10:32, 33, NKJV).

A national council (called a "Diet") to be convened at Worms had many political questions to decide, but the object of deepest interest to everyone was the examination of the Saxon reformer, Martin Luther.

Papal legates were alarmed at the idea of Luther publicly explaining his ideas. They hastily arranged for the pope to excommunicate Luther, thus preventing him from speaking in person at the Diet. They preferred to condemn him and his teachings without Luther being present. But God overruled events so that the reformer would be able to defend his teachings before this important assembly. The emperor himself issued Luther a safe conduct to attend the Diet, and he was requested to come and defend his convictions before the assembly.

With his mind stayed on God, Luther ably addressed the gathered political and religious leaders, setting forth God's truth and drawing from the Bible the appropriate texts to sustain his positions.

The religious leaders insisted he repudiate his doctrines that contradicted church positions. Luther's courageous answer was, "Unless I am persuaded by means of the passages I have quoted, and unless they thus render my conscience bound by the word of God, *I cannot and I will not retract,* for it is unsafe for a Christian to speak against his conscience. Here I stand, I can do no other; may God help me. Amen."

Key Thought: "Had the Reformer yielded a single point, Satan and his hosts would have gained the victory. But his unwavering firmness was the means of emancipating the church, and beginning a new and better era. The influence of this one man, who dared to think and act for himself in religious matters, was to affect the church and the world, not only in his own time, but in all future generations" (*The Great Controversy,* p. 166).

Today's Lesson: Our only safe course is to follow the leading of the Spirit as He impresses the truths of God's Word upon our hearts and helps us understand their meaning.

The Swiss Reformer

The Great Controversy, Chapter 9.

"Endure hardship as a good soldier of Jesus Christ" (2 Timothy 2:3, NKJV).

A few weeks after the birth of Luther in a miner's cabin in Germany, Ulric Zwingle was born in a herdsman's cottage among the Alps. Zwingle's childhood surroundings amid scenes of natural beauty and grandeur impressed his mind with God's power and majesty and prepared him for his future mission. Both the Dominicans and the Franciscans tried to get this talented young scholar to join their ranks. But Zwingle's father resisted both and sent his son to Basel to study ancient languages. In Basel, Zwingle discovered the Bible and learned from it that Jesus' death is the sinner's only means of salvation.

Ordained as a priest, Zwingle determined that the Bible must be its own interpreter and should not be overruled by any preconceived theory or doctrine. Zwingle's ideas and the doctrines he preached did not come from Luther—they grew out of Zwingle's own study of God's Word. To many, his teachings were unwelcome. They didn't want to believe that their weary visits to sacred shrines were in vain; it was easier for them to trust their salvation to priests and the pope than to seek for God on their own.

Zwingle was called to serve at the cathedral in Zurich, where he began a series of sermons on Matthew's gospel to which many people flocked. Soon opposition arose from the monks, who were offering pardon for money. But Zwingle continued, little by little, to open the truth to his hearers.

Key Thought: "At the time when God is preparing to break the shackles of ignorance and superstition, then it is that Satan works with greatest power to enshroud men in darkness and to bind their fetters still more firmly. As men were rising up in different lands to present to the people forgiveness and justification through the blood of Christ, Rome proceeded with renewed energy to open her market throughout Christendom, offering pardon for money" (*The Great Controversy,* p. 178).

Today's Lesson: Human beings may try to suppress the truths of God's Word and prevent them from being presented widely, but God will raise up men and women who will give His message to the world just when it is most needed.

Progress of Reform in Germany

The Great Controversy, Chapter 10.

"The entrance of thy words giveth light; it giveth understanding unto the simple" (Psalm 119:130).

After Luther left Worms, he was kidnapped by friends and hurried to the Wartburg Castle to protect him from the papal forces that were planning to capture him after his safe conduct expired. Few people knew where he was. There, he translated the New Testament into the German language.

But Satan was busy, as well. A few deeply religious men who imagined that they had received special revelations from God were persuaded by Satan that they were to continue the great work that Luther had begun before he disappeared. These enthusiasts, however, had rejected the primary principle of the Reformation—that the Word of God is the all-sufficient rule of faith and practice. They looked to their own feelings and impressions.

In the midst of this crisis, Luther left Wartburg for his home in Wittenburg, where the confusion was greatest. He pled with the people to let clear, biblical teachings—not force—overcome this misguided religious fervor. To do otherwise, he argued, would destroy liberty, the very essence of faith. After a week of preaching, Luther broke the spell of fanatical excitement.

Several years later, however, fanaticism again erupted with more terrible results under Thomas Munzer. The cry of these fanatics was that the Bible was a dead letter and that the Spirit was their leader. In response, Luther pointed individuals to the German Bible and his books, which were being sold by large numbers throughout Germany.

Key Thought: "The study of the Scriptures was working a mighty change in the minds and hearts of the people. . . . A superstitious observance of forms had been scrupulously maintained; but in all their service the heart and intellect had had little part. The preaching of Luther, setting forth the plain truths of God's word, and then the word itself, placed in the hands of the common people, had aroused their dormant powers, not only purifying and ennobling the spiritual nature, but imparting new strength and vigor to the intellect " (*The Great Controversy,* p. 195).

Today's Lesson: Both human reason and subjective impressions can be overcome only by clear biblical principles and the guidance of the Holy Spirit.

Protest of the Princes

The Great Controversy, Chapter 11.

"I will speak of Your testimonies also before kings, and will not be ashamed" (Psalms 119:46, NKJV).

The Diet of Spires in 1526 had given each German state full liberty in religious matters until the meeting of a general council. Emperor Charles V called a second meeting to convene at Spires in 1529 for the purpose of crushing this "heresy" of religious liberty.

Granting liberty of conscience had given rise to numerous political and religious disorders, and the papal forces blamed such troubles on the reformers. Luther was still under the ban imposed by the edict of Worms and could not attend the Diet in Spires, but Duke John of Saxony displayed great courage to support him at that meeting. The assembly ended with a compromise—the German states that had already declared their support for the Reformation could remain so, but no further conversions would be permitted in the remaining states.

The "Reformation princes" objected to this papal coercion of liberty and conscience, leading Charles V to invoke a general council in 1530 at Augsburg finally to silence the Protestants. Luther, Melanchthon, and their associates were asked to prepare a statement of beliefs, to which the brave princes signed their names. The day on which this statement was presented has been called the greatest day of the Reformation and one of the most glorious in the history of Christianity. One of its clearest provisions was that in religious matters the conscience must be free.

By word and example, Luther demonstrated that the power of the Reformation lay in the secret place of prayer, where God gave courage and grace to maintain the truth.

Key Thought: " 'All that the Lutherans have said is true; we cannot deny it,' declared a papist bishop. 'Can you refute by sound reasons the Confession made by the elector and his allies?' asked another of Dr. Eck. 'With the writings of the apostles and prophets—no!' was the reply; 'but with those of the Fathers and of the councils—yes!' 'I understand,' responded the questioner. 'The Lutherans, according to you, are in Scripture, and we are outside' " (*The Great Controversy,* p. 208).

Today's Lesson: In spite of all human and Satanic opposition, God's truth will prevail in the end.

The French Reformation

The Great Controversy, Chapter 12.

"God hath chosen the weak things of the world to confound the things which are mighty" (1 Corinthians 1:27).

The triumph of the Reformation in Germany was followed by years of conflict and darkness. In Switzerland, dark days also came. Zwingle was killed at Cappel in a civil war. Attacked on all sides, the Reformation seemed doomed.

In France, before the name of Luther was heard, light was breaking on Lefevre, an aged man of extensive learning and a professor in the University of Paris. In 1512, he declared his confidence that God alone gives us righteousness by grace and that man's duty is to reflect that grace within. Among his able students was William Farel, who joyfully accepted the basic truths of the Reformation. Lefevre undertook the translation of the New Testament into French, which was published under the authority of the Bishop of Meaux. This publication aroused great interest and infuriated papal authorities. Many converts to Protestantism were burned at the stake.

In one of the schools of Paris, John Calvin, a thoughtful man with a powerful mind, by chance witnessed the burning of a Protestant. He saw on the victim's face a peace and courage that Calvin, himself, woefully lacked with all his learning. He turned rigorously to the Bible, and a new world opened for him. Throughout France, persecution raged, and the cruelest executions were widespread.

Calvin went to Geneva, a city that had embraced Protestantism, and established himself there.

Key Thought: "For nearly thirty years Calvin labored at Geneva, first to establish there a church adhering to the morality of the Bible, and then for the advancement of the Reformation throughout Europe. His course as a public leader was not faultless, nor were his doctrines free from error. But he was instrumental in promulgating truths that were of special importance in his time, in maintaining the principles of Protestantism against the fast-returning tide of popery, and in promoting in the reformed churches simplicity and purity of life, in place of the pride and corruption fostered under the Romish teaching" (*The Great Controversy,* p. 236).

Today's Lesson: Truth captures both the bold and the cautious, men of action and men of learning, but regardless of temperament, God has a special duty for each.

The Netherlands and Scandinavia

The Great Controversy, Chapter 13.

"My doctrine is not mine, but his that sent me" (John 7:16).

Luther's teachings found congenial soil in Holland. Menno Simons, an educated priest, had never read the Bible, thinking it would be heresy to do so. But as he ventured into the New Testament, its influence, along with the writings of Luther, caused him to accept the reformed faith.

For twenty-five years Simons and his wife traveled throughout the Netherlands and northern Germany to spread the gospel, enduring great hardships and frequently risking their lives. Nowhere were the reformed doctrines more widely received than in the Netherlands, and in few countries did the Protestant converts endure more terrible persecution. To read the Bible, to preach it or to hear it preached or even to speak about its teachings, was to incur the death penalty.

Tausen, the "Reformer of Denmark," was so gifted intellectually that he was allowed to choose where he would attend university—as long as he did not go to Wittenberg, the center of Lutheranism. He chose to be educated in Cologne, and there he discovered Luther's writings anyway. Returning to his cloister in Denmark, he shared his belief in the gospel with his fellow monks and persuaded many of them to accept Luther's teachings. Not long afterward, the New Testament was translated into the Danish language, and the people thronged the church whenever Tausen taught.

Key Thought: "Steadily and surely the darkness of ignorance and superstition was dispelled by the blessed light of the gospel. . . . Sweden became one of the bulwarks of Protestantism. A century later, at a time of sorest peril, this small and hitherto feeble nation—the only one in Europe that dared lend a helping hand—came to the deliverance of Germany in the terrible struggle of the Thirty Years' War. . . . It was the armies of Sweden that enabled Germany to turn the tide of popish success, to win toleration for the Protestants, . . . and to restore liberty of conscience to those countries that had accepted the Reformation" (*The Great Controversy*, p. 244).

Today's Lesson: Many in past ages were willing to give up everything—including their lives—that the light of the gospel could shine ever brighter on our path today.

Later English Reformers

The Great Controversy, Chapter 14.

"In him [Jesus] was life; and the life was the light of men. . . . That was the true Light, which lighteth every man that cometh into the world" (John 1:4, 9).

While Luther was translating the Bible into German, Tyndale was doing the same for the English language. Wycliffe's earlier English Bible had been translated from the Latin text, which contained many errors. Tyndale used the recent Greek text of Erasmus for the New Testament. He knew that Christians must be able to read God's Word in their native language in order to grow spiritually. Reprimanded by Catholic scholars, Tyndale said, "If God spare my life, ere many years I will cause a boy that driveth the plow to know more of the Scripture than you do." After a harrowing life, hounded on two continents, Tyndale died a martyr's death.

Other great English leaders of the Reformation, including Latimer, Barnes, Frith, Ridley, and Cranmer, were highly esteemed for their learning and piety. They withdrew from Catholicism and willingly witnessed for their faith with their lives.

John Knox turned away from the traditions of the established church to become the father of the Scottish Presbyterians, preaching fearlessly even to the Queen of England.

When Protestantism was established as the national religion of England, the great principle of religious liberty was not yet fully understood. Instead of the pope, the monarch became the head of the established church. For hundreds of years, dissenters in England suffered persecution, many of whom fled to America.

A century later, Whitefield and the Wesleys appeared as light-bearers for God. The Wesleys were instrumental in founding Methodism.

Key Thought: "At the close of his [Wesley's] long life of more than fourscore years—above half a century spent in itinerant ministry—his avowed adherents numbered more than half a million souls. . . . His life presents a lesson of priceless worth to every Christian. Would that the faith and humility, the untiring zeal, self-sacrifice, and devotion of this servant of Christ might be reflected in the churches of today! " (*The Great Controversy,* p. 264).

Today's Lesson: We should often review the lives of God's giants of faith from earlier years and learn from their experiences.

The Bible and the French Revolution

The Great Controversy, Chapter 15.

"This is the condemnation, that light is come into the world, and men loved darkness rather than light" (John 3:19).

For centuries, light and darkness struggled in France, but eventually the light of Bible knowledge was almost wholly excluded. The nation was left to reap the results of what happens when the Spirit of God is rejected and evil is permitted to come to maturity. Revelation 11 foretold these awful results, especially focusing on the licentiousness and atheism of France during the revolution. During the revolution, the legislative assembly of France proclaimed by decree that God does not exist—the only nation in the world to have done so. The St. Bartholomew Massacre, in which seventy thousand of the very flower of the nation perished for their religious faith, is just one example of how "our Lord was crucified" again as predicted in Revelation 11:8.

In France, the church began what atheism completed. Historians have charged the French church with responsibility for the horrors of the Revolution. Rome had misrepresented the character of God and perverted His requirements. In reaction, men and women rejected both the Bible and its Author, wanting nothing to do with religion. Blasphemy and incredible wickedness were openly displayed; the greatest sinners were highly praised. Voltaire and his associates cast aside the Bible altogether and spread the poison of infidelity.

Key Thought: "All this was as Satan would have it. . . . His policy is deception from first to last, and his steadfast purpose is to bring woe and wretchedness upon men, to deface and defile the workmanship of God, to mar the divine purposes of benevolence and love, and thus cause grief in heaven. Then by his deceptive arts he blinds the minds of men, and leads them to throw back the blame of his work upon God, as if all this misery were the result of the Creator's plan. In like manner, when those who have been degraded and brutalized through his cruel power achieve their freedom, he urges them on to excesses and atrocities" (*The Great Controversy,* pp. 284, 285).

Today's Lesson: The great controversy is revealed in events such as the French Revolution—a foretaste of the time of the seven last plagues.

The Pilgrim Fathers

The Great Controversy, Chapter 16.

"Then I saw another beast coming up out of the earth, and he had two horns like a lamb and spoke like a dragon" (Revelation 13:11, NKJV).

The English Reformers, while renouncing the doctrines of Rome, had retained many of its forms of worship. They argued that these were not intrinsically evil and were not expressly forbidden in the Bible. But others, called "Puritans," looked upon these customs as badges of the religious slavery from which they had been delivered.

At the beginning of the seventeenth century, the new English king declared that the Puritans must conform or be harried out of the land. Some sought refuge in Holland, leaving homes, goods, and their means of livelihood. They considered themselves to be pilgrims, strangers in a strange land.

Some of these pilgrims left Holland to find a home in America. Liberty of conscience inspired them to brave the perils of a long sea journey and the dangers of the wilderness in a foreign land. But they did not yet fully understand their own principle of freedom of conscience. Eleven years after the Pilgrims planted their first colony in America, Roger Williams arrived with a deeper understanding of freedom—the first person in modern Christianity to establish civil government on the doctrine of liberty of conscience.

Key Thought: "The great principle so nobly advocated by Robinson and Roger Williams, that truth is progressive, that Christians should stand ready to accept all the light which may shine from God's holy word, was lost sight of by their descendants. The Protestant churches of America,—and those of Europe as well,—so highly favored in receiving the blessings of the Reformation, failed to press forward in the path of reform. . . . Therefore religion again degenerated into formalism; and errors and superstitions which would have been cast aside had the church continued to walk in the light of God's word, were retained and cherished. Thus the spirit inspired by the Reformation gradually died out, until there was almost as great need of reform in the Protestant churches as in the Roman Church in the time of Luther" (*The Great Controversy,* pp. 297, 298).

Today's Lesson: Truth builds upon truth. In every age, God has present truth for that generation.

Heralds of the Morning

The Great Controversy, Chapter 17.

"I am the light of the world: he that followeth me shall not walk in darkness, but shall have the light of life" (John 8:12).

One of the most important truths revealed in the Bible is that of Christ's second coming to complete the great work of redemption; it is the glorious keynote of God's Word. Holy men in Scripture from Enoch, Job, Isaiah, and Habakkuk, to the apostles, have depicted the wonderful drama of our Lord's return. Through the centuries, the Waldenses, Wycliffe, Luther, Calvin, and the Puritans cried out, "Hasten, O Lord, this blessed day!"

Prophecy not only foretells the manner and object of Christ's return but outlines the signs by which we can know when it is near. Jesus said that signs involving the heavens—the sun, moon, and stars—would herald His return. Likewise, there would be signs on earth, such as an increasing intensity and frequency of earthquakes, famines, pestilences, and wars, that would tell men and women that the last days had come. Jesus warned us, "When these things begin to come to pass, then look up, and lift up your heads; for your redemption draweth nigh" (Luke 21:28). There is no reason not to discern the signs of Jesus' return.

But as the spirit of humility and devotion in the church gave place to pride and formalism, so love for Christ and faith in His coming grew cold, as well. Backsliding churches closed their eyes to the signs of the time.

Key Thought: "Unless the church will follow on in His opening providence, accepting every ray of light, performing every duty which may be revealed, religion will inevitably degenerate into the observance of forms, and the spirit of vital godliness will disappear. This truth has been repeatedly illustrated in the history of the church. . . . Obedience requires a sacrifice and involves a cross; and this is why so many of the professed followers of Christ refused to receive the light from heaven, and, like the Jews of old, knew not the time of their visitation" (*The Great Controversy*, p. 316).

Today's Lesson: It is vital that we understand our place in God's divine scheme of events so we may be prepared for Jesus' return.

An American Reformer

The Great Controversy, Chapter 18.

"Unto two thousand and three hundred days; then shall the sanctuary be cleansed" (Daniel 8:14).

God chose William Miller, an honest-hearted New York farmer, to lead out in the proclamation of Christ's second coming. Miller's love of study and his habit of careful thought and close criticism made him a man of sound judgment and comprehensive views. He reasoned that if the Bible is a revelation from God, it must be consistent with itself and that God gave it to us for our instruction.

Miller accepted the idea that the way in which the prophecies had been fulfilled in the past was a criterion by which to judge the fulfillment of prophecies yet future. He became satisfied that the popular view of Christ's spiritual reign—a temporal millennium on earth before the end of the world—was not sustained by the Bible. He saw clearly that the righteous dead will be raised to life and the righteous living will be changed to immortality when Jesus returns. At the same time, Miller could see that the biblical signs of the end of the world corresponded to what was happening in his day. The prophecy that seemed most clearly to reveal the *time* of the Second Advent was that of Daniel 8:14.

Miller began to present his views in private. Only when others urged him to preach these things himself did Miller reluctantly consent to present his views in public. A large number of ministers in many churches approved his views and gave him their support. Although he drew assemblies of intelligent and attentive hearers, Miller's name was seldom mentioned by the religious press except by way of ridicule or denunciation.

Key Thought: "In view of the testimony of Inspiration, how dare men teach that the Revelation is a mystery beyond the reach of human understanding? It is a mystery revealed, a book opened. The study of the Revelation directs the mind to the prophecies of Daniel, and both present most important instruction, given of God to men, concerning events to take place at the close of this world's history" (*The Great Controversy*, p. 341).

Today's Lesson: It takes courage to go against conventional wisdom and to stand up publicly for one's beliefs.

DECEMBER 8

Light Through Darkness

The Great Controversy, Chapter 19.

"Beginning at Moses and all the Prophets, He expounded to them in all the Scriptures the things concerning Himself" (Luke 24:27, NKJV).

From age to age, God's work presents a striking similarity in every great reformation. But no human being, however honored of Heaven, has ever reached a full understanding of the great plan of redemption—or even a perfect appreciation of the divine purpose in the work for his own time. God unfolds further meaning as His people need it.

The first time He came to earth, Christ arrived at the exact time and in the very manner foretold by prophecy. The "time is fulfilled" had been the prophets' message, and they were correct. The "kingdom of God" they proclaimed was established by the death of Christ; it was not a kingdom marked by earthly rule. When Christ walked with the two disciples toward Emmaus, He explained all this and helped them set the course for the unfolding of truth as it relates to His second coming. They misunderstood the meaning of the prophecies concerning the establishment of His kingdom.

In other words, the experience of the disciples who preached the "gospel of the kingdom" at the first advent of Christ had its counterpart in the experience of those who proclaimed the message of His second coming. Again, they misunderstood the event to which the prophecy referred. But God overruled the 1844 disappointment, bringing good out of their misapprehension of the message they gave.

Key Thought: "With these believers, as with the first disciples, that which in the hour of trial seemed dark to their understanding would afterward be made plain. When they should see the 'end of the Lord' they would know that, notwithstanding the trial resulting from their errors, His purposes of love toward them had been steadily fulfilling. They would learn by a blessed experience that He is 'very pitiful, and of tender mercy;' that all His paths 'are mercy and truth unto such as keep His covenant and His testimonies' " (*The Great Controversy*, p. 354).

Today's Lesson: We need to keep our eyes today on the big picture of the great controversy, knowing that the prophecies of Jesus' return will be fulfilled when He sees the time has come.

A Great Religious Awakening

The Great Controversy, Chapter 20.

"Then I saw another angel flying in the midst of heaven, having the everlasting gospel to preach to those who dwell on the earth—to every nation, tribe, tongue, and people" (Revelation 14:6, NKJV).

A great religious awakening under the proclamation of Christ's soon coming is foretold in the prophecy of the first angel's message of Revelation 14. No such message had ever been given in past ages—the hour of judgment *had now come.*

Like the great Reformation of the sixteenth century, the Advent Movement appeared in different countries at the same time. In 1821, three years after Miller had arrived at his understanding of the prophecies pointing to the time of judgment, Joseph Wolff, "the missionary to the world," traveled extensively from 1821 to 1845 in Egypt, Ethiopia, Palestine, Syria, Persia, and the United States, preaching the Second Coming and distributing the Bible in various languages.

In South America, Lacunza published his views on Christ's near return under the name "Rabbi Ben-Ezra, and in 1825 his book was translated into English. Bengel was a celebrated biblical scholar. The light about Christ's second coming broke on his mind after he heard a sermon on Revelation 21. His writings spread throughout the Christian world.

At Geneva, Switzerland, Gaussen, a well-known and beloved scholar and preacher in the French world, published his lessons on the nearness of Christ's advent—first to children and then, after awakening a great interest, to their parents.

In Scandinavia, though the state church opposed the widespread interest in the advent message, little children miraculously preached Jesus' soon coming.

Key Thought: "The time of expectation passed, and Christ did not appear for the deliverance of His people. Those who with sincere faith and love had looked for their Saviour, experienced a bitter disappointment. Yet the purposes of God were being accomplished; He was testing the hearts of those professed to be waiting for His appearing. There were among them many who had been actuated by no higher motive than fear. Their profession of faith had not affected their hearts or their lives" (*The Great Controversy,* p. 374).

Today's Lesson: At crucial points in His plan, God raises up individuals to give His special message to the world.

A Warning Rejected

The Great Controversy, Chapter 21.

**"Come out of her, my people, lest you share in her sins,
and lest you receive of her plagues"
(Revelation 18:4, NKJV).**

William Miller and his associates had one purpose in mind—to prepare a people for the return of Jesus. They made no attempt to convert anyone to a denomination or particular church. But in the summer of 1844 about fifty thousand individuals withdrew from the Christian churches. At the same time, evidence of a sudden declension in spiritual life existed everywhere in the churches of the United States—a fact noted by both the press and the pulpit.

Spiritual darkness is not due to the arbitrary withdrawal of God's grace but to the neglect or rejection of divine light on man's part. Men and women who deliberately stifle convictions of duty will finally lose the power to distinguish between truth and error.

In refusing the message of the first angel of Revelation 14:6, 7, which would have corrected the evils that separated them from God, men and women were suffering the spiritual death that seemed to distinguish the churches in 1844.

The call to come out of Babylon given in Revelation 18:4 emphasizes the truth that many of God's people must still be in Babylon. The term *Babylon*—confusion—may appropriately be applied to these churches, all professing to derive their doctrines from the Bible, yet divided into almost innumerable denominations with widely conflicting creeds and theories.

Key Thought: "Notwithstanding the spiritual darkness and alienation from God that exist in the churches which constitute Babylon, the great body of Christ's true followers are still to be found in their communion. There are many of these who have never seen the special truths for this time. Not a few are dissatisfied with their present condition and are longing for clearer light. . . . The time will come when those who love God supremely can no longer remain in connection with such as are 'lovers of pleasures more than lovers of God; having a form of godliness, but denying the power thereof' " (*The Great Controversy*, p. 390).

Today's Lesson: God is calling men and women out of the confusion of contemporary Christianity to stand upon His Word and look for Jesus' return.

Prophecies Fulfilled

The Great Controversy, Chapter 22.

"Cast not away therefore your confidence, which hath great recompense of reward. For ye have need of patience, that, after ye have done the will of God, ye might received the promise" (Hebrews 10:35, 36).

When the time passed in the spring of 1844 when the Lord's coming was first expected, those who had looked in faith for His appearing were doubtful and uncertain for a time. The Bible evidence for their position seemed clear and conclusive. The special blessing of the Lord, both in the conversion of sinners and in the revival of spiritual life among Christians, had testified that the message was of God.

In the summer of 1844—midway between the time when it had been first thought that the 2,300 days would end and the autumn of the same year—the message was proclaimed in the very words of Scripture, "Behold, the Bridegroom cometh" (Matthew 25:6). This new light was based on the discovery that the decree of Artaxerxes for the restoration of Jerusalem (which formed the starting point for the 2,300-year prophecy) went into effect in the *autumn* of the year 457 B.C., not at the *beginning* of that year. Hence, the 2,300 years would end in the autumn of 1844.

The Advent Movement took on fresh life and swept over the land like a tidal wave. But again, the movement was destined for disappointment.

Key Thought: "That this admonition is addressed to the church in the last days is evident from the words pointing to the nearness of the Lord's coming: 'For yet a little while, and He that shall come will come and will not tarry.' And it is plainly implied that there would be a seeming delay and that the Lord would appear to tarry. . . . As the bright light of the 'midnight cry' had shone upon their pathway, and they had seen the prophecies unsealed and the rapidly fulfilling signs telling that the coming of Christ was near, they had walked, as it were, by sight. But now, bowed down by disappointed hopes, they could stand only by faith in God and in His word" (*The Great Controversy,* p. 408).

Today's Lesson: We need such a confidence in God that no disappointment, no matter how severe, can destroy our faith in His leading.

What Is the Sanctuary?

The Great Controversy, Chapter 23.

"Then the temple of God was opened in heaven, and the ark of His covenant was seen in His temple. And there were lightnings, noises, thunderings, an earthquake, and great hail" (Revelation 11:19, NKJV).

The scripture above all others that had been the foundation of the advent faith in 1844 was the declaration, "Unto two thousand and three hundred days; then shall the sanctuary be cleansed" (Daniel 8:14). However, in common with the rest of the Christian world, Adventists then believed that the earth, or some portion of it, was the sanctuary.

After their disappointment in 1844, believers knew that the Bible could not fail—but where was the mistake? Some solved the problem by denying that the 2,300 days ended in 1844.

Others, believing that God had led His people in the great Advent Movement, studied further and discovered that the Bible never refers to the earth as God's sanctuary. They found that the Bible fully explains the sanctuary subject. They saw that the sanctuary to which Paul refers in Hebrews 9 is first the earthly sanctuary of the Old Testament and second, the sanctuary in heaven—the great original.

But what is the "cleansing of the sanctuary?" The cleansing, both in the symbolic and in the real service, must be accomplished with blood. The earthly sanctuary is cleansed with the blood of animals, and the heavenly sanctuary is cleansed with the blood of Christ.

Key Thought: "For eighteen centuries this work of ministration continued in the first apartment of the sanctuary. . . . As in the typical service there was a work of atonement at the close of the year, so before Christ's work for the redemption of men is completed there is a work of atonement for the removal of sin from the sanctuary. This is the service which began when the 2300 days ended. At that time, as foretold by Daniel the prophet, our High Priest entered the most holy, to perform the last division of His solemn work—to cleanse the sanctuary" (*The Great Controversy,* p. 421).

Today's Lesson: There is a sanctuary in heaven—the great original reality which served as the pattern for the sanctuary on earth—in which Jesus functions as our great High Priest.

In the Holy of Holies

The Great Controversy, Chapter 24.

***"The Lord, whom ye seek, shall suddenly come to his
temple, even the messenger of the covenant, whom ye
delight in: behold, he shall come, saith the Lord of hosts"
(Malachi 3:1).***

The subject of the sanctuary was the key that unlocked the mystery
of the disappointment of 1844 to the puzzled, confused believers.
It opened to view a complete system of truth, connected and
harmonious, showing that God's hand had directed the great Advent
Movement. Light from the sanctuary illuminated the past, the present,
and the future. The mistake in 1844, they realized, had not been in the
reckoning of the prophetic periods but in the event to take place at the
end of the 2,300 years.

Christ had come, not to the earth as they expected, but to the
Most Holy Place of the heavenly sanctuary, as foreshadowed in the
earthly symbol. The people in 1844 were not yet ready to meet their
Lord. A work of preparation needed to be accomplished for them. As
they followed their High Priest in His ministry in the sanctuary in
heaven, new duties would be revealed. Another message of warning
and instruction was to be given to the church. When this work of
preparation was accomplished, the followers of Christ would be ready
for His appearing.

This work of character examination is the closing work in the
sanctuary service.

Key Thought: "Those who are living upon the earth when the
intercession of Christ shall cease in the sanctuary above are to stand in
the sight of a holy God without a mediator. Their robes must be spotless,
their characters must be purified from sin by the blood of sprinkling.
Through the grace of God and their own diligent effort they must be
conquerors in the battle with evil. While the investigative judgment
is going forward in heaven, while the sins of penitent believers are
being removed from the sanctuary, there is to be a special work of
purification, of putting away of sin, among God's people upon earth.
This work is more clearly presented in the messages of Revelation 14"
(*The Great Controversy,* p. 425).

Today's Lesson: The most important question the universe faces
is whether God's people can be trusted with eternal life.

DECEMBER 14

God's Law Immutable

The Great Controversy, Chapter 25.

"The temple of God was opened in heaven, and there was seen in his temple the ark of his testament"
(Revelation 11:19).

The announcement that the temple of God was opened in heaven and the ark of His testament was seen points to the opening of the Most Holy Place of the heavenly sanctuary in 1844 as Christ entered there to perform the closing work of the atonement. Those who by faith followed their great High Priest into the inner room of the sanctuary in heaven beheld there the ark of His testament. As they studied the subject of the sanctuary, they had come to understand the Savior's change of ministry, and they saw that He was now officiating before the ark of God, pleading His blood on behalf of sinners.

The law of God in the sanctuary in heaven is the great original, of which the commandments inscribed upon the tables of stone were an unerring transcript. The Spirit of God impressed the hearts of those Bible students in the 1840s, and they recognized that the truth concerning the heavenly sanctuary involved acknowledging the claims of God's law and the obligation of the seventh-day Sabbath of the fourth commandment. Here was the secret of the bitter and determined opposition to the harmonious exposition of the Scriptures that revealed the ministry of Christ in the heavenly sanctuary. The human heart does not want to be subject to the law of God.

These truths are presented in Revelation 14:20. Describing God's people at the end of time, John records, "Here are they that keep the commandments of God, and the faith of Jesus" (Revelation 14:12). The law will be the standard of character in the judgment.

Key Thought: "When the leading churches of the United States, uniting upon such points of doctrine as are held by them in common, shall influence the state to enforce their decrees and to sustain their institutions, then Protestant America will have formed an image of the Roman hierarchy, and the infliction of civil penalties upon dissenters will inevitably result" (*The Great Controversy*, p. 445).

Today's Lesson: Faith and obedience are inextricably linked in the service of the sanctuary in heaven, just as they must be in the Christian's experience.

A Work of Reform

The Great Controversy, Chapter 26.

"Every one that doeth evil hateth the light, neither cometh to the light, lest his deeds should be reproved" (John 3:20).

Hallowed by the Creator's rest and blessing, the Sabbath was kept by Adam in his innocence in Eden. From that day to the present, the knowledge of God's law has been preserved in the earth, and the Sabbath of the fourth commandment has been kept by God's people.

Those who received the light concerning the sanctuary and the unchanging nature of the law of God were filled with joy and wonder as they saw the beauty and harmony of the system of truth that opened to their understanding. But truths that would place them at variance with the world were not welcome to many who claimed to be followers of Christ. Those who did not search the Scriptures for themselves were content to accept conclusions in accordance with their desires. The majority of Miller's followers rejected the truths concerning the sanctuary and the law of God, and many also renounced their faith in the Advent Movement.

The history of ancient Israel is a striking illustration of the past experience of the Adventist body. Had the Israelites kept trusting God, who led them out of Egypt, they would have gone directly into the Promised Land. It was not God's will that Israel should wander forty years in the wilderness. In the same way, it was not God's will that Christ's coming should be so long delayed.

Key Thought: The great obstacle both to the acceptance and to the promulgation of truth is the fact that it involves inconvenience and reproach. This is the only argument against the truth which its advocates have never been able to refute. But this does not deter the true followers of Christ. These do not wait for truth to become popular. . . .

"Whatever may be their profession, it is only those who are world servers at heart that act from policy rather than principle in religious things. We should choose the right because it is right, and leave consequences with God" (*The Great Controversy*, p. 460).

Today's Lesson: The majority have always chosen the path of least resistance, preferring to please self rather than God.

DECEMBER 16

Modern Revivals

The Great Controversy, Chapter 27.

"Sanctify them by Your truth. Your word is truth. As You sent Me into the world, I also have sent them into the world. And for their sakes I sanctify Myself, that they also may be sanctified by the truth" *(John 17:17–19, NKJV).*

In the past, true revivals were characterized by people who didn't shrink from self-denial and sacrifice. In many modern revivals, there is a sad lack of genuine repentance that results in reformation. There may be many additions to the church, but little increase in real spiritual life.

Popular revivals are too often based on appealing to the imagination, exciting the emotions, or by gratifying the love for startling innovations. Converts thus gained to the church have little desire to listen to Bible truth—little interest in the testimony of prophets and apostles. Unless a religious service has a sensational character, it has no attractions for them. A message that appeals to unimpassioned reason awakens no response. They pay little attention to the plain warnings of God's Word dealing directly with their eternal interests.

Genuine revival bears fruit in the life. True sanctification is a Bible teaching. Those who follow Christ are to become like Him. By His grace, they are to form characters in harmony with the principles of His holy law. This work can be accomplished only by faith in Christ and by the indwelling power of the Holy Spirit. In true spiritual revivals, justification and sanctification work together to reconcile men and women to God by bringing them into harmony with the principles of God's will.

Key Thought: "It is by beholding that we become changed. And as those sacred precepts in which God has opened to men the perfection and holiness of His character are neglected, and the minds of the people are attracted to human teachings and theories, what marvel that there has followed a decline of living piety in the church. Saith the Lord: 'They have forsaken Me the fountain of living waters, and hewed them out cisterns, broken cisterns, that can hold no water.' Jeremiah 2:13" (*The Great Controversy,* p. 478).

Today's Lesson: We need daily to seek God's grace that both pardons and empowers, so that we can become increasingly in harmony with the principles of God's law.

Facing Life's Record

The Great Controversy, Chapter 28.

"Another book was opened, which is the Book of Life. And the dead were judged according to their works, by the things which were written in the books"
(Revelation 20:12, NKJV).

In Daniel 7 the prophet saw the solemn day when the Judge of all the earth will review the lives and characters of human beings in the presence of the holy angels. The book of life contains the names of everyone who has entered the service of God. The work of the investigative judgment and the blotting out of sins is to be accomplished before the second advent of our Lord.

Satan invents unnumbered schemes to occupy our minds, that we may not dwell upon the very work with which we ought to be best acquainted. The deceiver hates the great truths that bring to view an atoning sacrifice and an all-powerful Mediator. He knows that success for him depends on diverting our minds from Jesus and His truth. If the Savior's mediation for us in the sanctuary in heaven is to be of value to us, we must allow nothing to interfere with the work of becoming like Jesus. To this end we should devote our best energies and efforts.

God's people need clearly to understand the subject of the sanctuary and the investigative judgment. Otherwise, they will not be able to exercise the faith needed at this time or to fulfill the place God has for them in His plan. Christ's intercession on our behalf in the sanctuary in heaven is as essential to the plan of salvation as was His death on the cross.

Key Thought: "All who have truly repented of sin, and by faith claimed the blood of Christ as their atoning sacrifice, have had pardon entered against their names in the books of heaven; as they have become partakers of the righteousness of Christ, and their characters are found to be in harmony with the law of God, their sins will be blotted out, and they themselves will be accounted worthy of eternal life" (*The Great Controversy*, p. 483).

Today's Lesson: Our knowledge of what Christ is doing for us in the heavenly sanctuary today needs to be in our hearts, as well as in our heads.

DECEMBER 18

The Origin of Evil

The Great Controversy, Chapter 29.

***"You were perfect in your ways from the day you were
created, till iniquity was found in you"
(Ezekiel 28:15, NKJV).***

For many, the origin of sin and the reason for its existence are a source of perplexity. They see evil, with its terrible results, and they question how all this can exist under the sovereignty of a God who is infinite in wisdom, power, and love. They can find no explanation of this mystery. And in their uncertainty and doubt they are blind to truths plainly revealed in God's Word.

It is impossible to explain the origin of sin so as to give a reason for it. Sin is unreasonable, because it is the outworking of a principle at war with the great principle of love. Before evil existed, there was peace and joy throughout the universe, based on the freedom of will that God gave to all His intelligent creation.

But Lucifer, the created being closest to God, chose to pervert this freedom. Little by little, Lucifer began to indulge a desire for self-exaltation born of pride. He diffused his own spirit of discontent among the angels.

In His great wisdom, God permitted Lucifer to continue his deceit and misrepresentations until his rebellious spirit ripened into open revolt. Lucifer's own work must condemn him.

Key Thought: "The whole universe will have become witnesses to the nature and results of sin. And its utter extermination, which in the beginning would have brought fear to angels and dishonor to God, will now vindicate His love and establish His honor before the universe of beings who delight to do His will, and in whose heart is His law. Never will evil again be manifest. Says the word of God: 'Affliction shall not rise up the second time.' Nahum 1:9. The law of God, which Satan has reproached as the yoke of bondage, will be honored as the law of liberty. A tested and proved creation will never again be turned from allegiance to Him whose character has been fully manifested before them as fathomless love and infinite wisdom" (*The Great Controversy,* p. 504).

Today's Lesson: God wants us to obey Him because we love Him. That is why He gave us the ability to choose.

Enmity Between Man and Satan

The Great Controversy, Chapter 30.

"I will put enmity between you and the woman, and between your seed and her Seed; He shall bruise your head, and you shall bruise His heel" (Genesis 3:15, NKJV).

The grace that Christ puts in the human mind creates in men and women enmity against Satan. In ourselves, apart from Christ, we are naturally in harmony with Satan, the originator of sin. But Christ offers to place in us His own hatred for sin. This is what sets Christians apart from the world.

Unfortunately, little attention is paid to Satan among professed Christians today. On the one hand, Satan is an expert at perpetuating his lies about God and blaming all the troubles of life on Him. On the other hand, Satan works to make Christians feel comfortable with worldly pleasures. He is constantly trying to break down the barriers that separate God's people from the world.

Paul urges us to keep in mind that we are wrestling against the spiritual powers of unseen wickedness—the sinful influences of this world and wicked spirits that rule the unseen realm (see Ephesians 6:12). Peter warns us that Satan goes around like a roaring lion, seeking whom he may devour (see 1 Peter 5:8).

Key Thought: "The more nearly the Christian imitates the divine Pattern, the more surely will he make himself a mark for the attacks of Satan. . . .

"Satan assailed Christ with his fiercest and most subtle temptations, but he was repulsed in every conflict. Those battles were fought in our behalf; those victories make it possible for us to conquer. Christ will give strength to all who seek it. No man without his own consent can be overcome by Satan. The tempter has no power to control the will or to force the soul to sin. He may distress, but he cannot contaminate. He can cause agony, but not defilement. The fact that Christ has conquered should inspire His followers with courage to fight manfully the battle against sin and Satan" (*The Great Controversy,* p. 510).

Today's Lesson: God has promised that the Holy Spirit can make a way of escape for us from every temptation that comes to us. We do not have to be overcome by Satan.

DECEMBER 20

Agency of Evil Spirits

The Great Controversy, Chapter 31.

"Be sober, be vigilant; because your adversary the devil walks about like a roaring lion, seeking whom he may devour" (1 Peter 5:8, NKJV).

The connection of the visible with the invisible world, the ministry of God's angels, and the agency of Satan's evil spirits are plainly revealed in the Scriptures and inseparably interwoven with human history. There is a growing tendency today to disbelieve that evil spirits even exist. Others regard them as spirits of the dead. But the Scriptures not only affirm that angels exist—both good and evil—but that they are not the disembodied spirits of the dead.

Every follower of Christ has a guardian angel to shield him or her from the power of the wicked one. Evil angels were created sinless, equal in nature, power, and glory to the holy angels.

The New Testament clearly teaches that men and women can be possessed with demons. The persons thus afflicted were not merely suffering from a disease with natural causes. Jesus knew that He was dealing with the direct presence of Satan's evil angels.

Satan fears nothing so much as men and women becoming acquainted with his devices. He doesn't mind if he is ridiculed. He is well pleased to be painted as ludicrous or loathsome—a misshapen, half-animal, half-human object. This is all part of his clever mask.

Key Thought: "None are in greater danger from the influence of evil spirits than those who, notwithstanding the direct and ample testimony of the Scriptures, deny the existence and agency of the devil and his angels. So long as we are ignorant of their wiles, they have almost inconceivable advantage; many give heed to their suggestions while they suppose themselves to be following the dictates of their own wisdom. This is why, as we approach the close of time, when Satan is to work with greatest power to deceive and destroy, he spreads everywhere the belief that he does not exist. It is his policy to conceal himself and his manner of working" (*The Great Controversy*, p. 516).

Today's Lesson: We need to remind ourselves that in spite of Satan's power in our world today, we have a personal guardian angel who will keep us in his care.

Snares of Satan

The Great Controversy, Chapter 32.

"The coming of the lawless one is according to the working of Satan, with all power, signs, and lying wonders, and with all unrighteous deception among those who perish, because they did not receive the love of the truth, that they might be saved . . . that they all may be condemned who did not believe the truth but had pleasure in unrighteousness" (2 Thessalonians 2:9–12, NKJV).

As the end of time approaches, Satan redoubles his efforts to hold men and women in darkness and impenitence until probation closes. He watches as the pastor is preparing his sermon and then tries to control circumstances so the persons needing that particular message are prevented from hearing those words. In the worship service, he tempts men and women to think about their wishes or some business venture, all of which numbs their sensibilities to listen carefully to God's message.

Another snare is to convince men and women that feeling good about their religion is more important than sound doctrine. Or to keep minds constantly searching and conjecturing in regard to things God has not made clear—rather than accepting the truths the Bible does make plain.

Among Satan's most successful deceptions are the delusive teachings of spiritualism, the idea that Jesus is not eternal, that Satan himself is not a personal being, that prayer is not essential to the Christian life, that doubts are a sign of maturity, and that people go either to heaven or to an eternally burning hell when they die.

Distrust of God is a natural outgrowth of the unrenewed heart. But the Holy Spirit inspires faith. Faith will flourish if we cherish it. No one can become strong in faith without a determined effort. Leaning on God's promises builds more faith.

Key Thought: "Satan can present a counterfeit so closely resembling the truth that it deceives those who are willing to be deceived, who desire to shun the self-denial and sacrifice demanded by the truth; but it is impossible for him to hold under his power one soul who honestly desires, at whatever cost, to know the truth" (*The Great Controversy*, p. 528).

Today's Lesson: Resisting the devil requires a clear mind and a strong confidence in God's enabling power.

The First Great Deception

The Great Controversy, Chapter 33.

"You will not surely die" (Genesis 3:4, NKJV).

The big lie originated in Eden with the universe's greatest liar. Adam and Eve had been perfectly happy in obedience to God's law. They were a constant witness against Satan's claim that God's law is oppressive and contrary to the well-being of His creatures. Furthermore, Satan was envious as he looked upon the beautiful home prepared for the sinless pair. He determined to cause their downfall—to gain possession of the earth and establish his kingdom here in opposition to God.

Capturing Eve's curiosity, Satan engaged her in artful conversation, holding before her the chance to think like God Himself. Drifting farther into his trap, Eve forgot that trusting God was her greatest hedge against evil. Immortality, promised to the first couple on condition of obedience, was forfeited by distrust.

But Satan was not through. After the fall of Adam and Eve, Satan instructed his angels to make a special effort to foster the belief that humans are naturally immortal. At the same time, he taught that sinners would live in eternal misery. The chief result of these lies was a picture of God as a vengeful tyrant who enjoys the prospect of sinners writhing forever in unutterable anguish.

It is beyond the power of the human mind to estimate the evil that has been done by the idea of an eternal hell. The religion of the Bible, full of love and goodness, is darkened by superstition and clothed with terror. When we consider in what false colors Satan has painted the character of God, can we wonder that our merciful Creator is feared, dreaded, and even hated? The appalling views of God that have thus spread over the world have made thousands, yes, millions, of skeptics and infidels.

Key Thought: "The theory of the immortality of the soul was one of those false doctrines that Rome, borrowing from paganism, incorporated into the religion of Christendom. Martin Luther classed it with the 'monstrous fables that form part of the Roman dunghill of decretals' " (*The Great Controversy,* p. 549).

Today's Lesson: The better we know the truth about death, the more prepared we will be when faced with undeniable impersonations of dead loved ones.

Can Our Dead Speak to Us?

The Great Controversy, Chapter 34.

"He performs great signs, so that he even makes fire come down from heaven on the earth in the sight of men. And he deceives those who dwell on the earth by those signs which he was granted to do in the sight of the beast" (Revelation 13:13, 14, NKJV).

The doctrine of natural immortality, first borrowed from pagan philosophy and incorporated into the Christian faith during the darkness of the great apostasy, has replaced the plain scriptural truth that the dead know nothing. This great triumph of Satan's deceptive skills has prepared the way for modern spiritualism and the almost overwhelming delusions of the last days.

Satan has the power to bring before us the appearance of our dead friends and loved ones. His counterfeit is perfect—the familiar look, the words, the tone are all reproduced with marvelous authenticity. Many accept the manifestation as genuine and are comforted with the assurance that their loved ones are enjoying the bliss of heaven. Without any suspicion of danger, they listen to the lies of seducing spirits and the doctrines of devils.

These pretended visitors from the spirit world sometimes utter cautions and warnings that prove to be correct. Then, as they gain their victim's confidence, they present doctrines that directly undermine faith in the Scriptures.

Many try to account for these spirit manifestations as fraud or sleight of hand. But although trickery has sometimes been palmed off as a genuine spirit manifestation, many of these incidents are exhibitions of real supernatural power—the work of Satan's evil angels.

Key Thought: "Satan has long been preparing for his final effort to deceive the world. . . . Little by little he has prepared the way for his masterpiece of deception in the development of spiritualism . . . .

"Except those who are kept by the power of God, through faith in His word, the whole world will be swept into the ranks of this delusion. The people are fast being lulled to a fatal security, to be awakened only by the outpouring of the wrath of God" (*The Great Controversy*, pp. 561, 562).

Today's Lesson: It requires a deep confidence in the truths of the Bible not to be overwhelmed by Satan's deceptions.

DECEMBER 24

Liberty of Conscience Threatened

The Great Controversy, Chapter 35.

**"I saw one of his heads as if it had been mortally
wounded, and his deadly wound was healed. And all the
world marveled and followed the beast"
(Revelation 13:3, NKJV).**

L et the restraints now imposed by secular governments be removed
and Rome be reinstated to her former power, and there would
quickly be a revival of her tyranny and persecution. Of course, there
are sincere, genuine Christians in the Roman Catholic communion,
living up to the best light they have—just as there are good Christians
in every church.

But as a religious system, Roman Catholicism is no more in harmony
with the gospel of Christ now than it has been at any earlier period
in its history. The Protestant churches are in great darkness or they
would discern the solid growth of Catholicism throughout the world.
Protestants have made compromises and concessions which Catholics
themselves are surprised to see and fail to understand.

The Roman Catholic Church today presents a fair front to the
world, covering her record of cruelties with apologies. The papacy can
be winsome in its appeal, embracing two types of people—those who
want to be saved by their own merits and those who want to be saved
without giving up sin. This is a secret of Rome's power.

God has given us warnings in His Word of the dangers posed to
religious liberty in the last days. As freedoms are removed, those who
believe God and obey Him will suffer persecution.

Key Thought: "Protestants little know what they are doing when
they propose to accept the aid of Rome in the work of Sunday exaltation.
While they are bent upon the accomplishment of their purpose, Rome
is aiming to re-establish her power, to recover her lost supremacy. Let
the principle once be established in the United States that the church
may employ or control the power of the state; that religious observances
may be enforced by secular laws; in short, that the authority of church
and state is to dominate the conscience, and the triumph of Rome in
this country is assured" (*The Great Controversy*, p. 581).

Today's Lesson: Movements are taking place today that will
result in all the world looking to the papacy for spiritual guidance and
direction.

The Impending Conflict

The Great Controversy, Chapter 36.

"The dragon was enraged with the woman, and he went to make war with the rest of her offspring, who keep the commandments of God and have the testimony of Jesus Christ" (Revelation 12:17, NKJV).

From the very beginning of the great controversy in heaven Satan has tried to overthrow God's law. The last great conflict between truth and error will be only the last engagement in the long-standing war between Christ and Satan concerning the validity of God's commandments. The world is now entering upon this battle—the struggle between the religion of the Bible and the religion of tradition and fable.

No error accepted by the Christian world strikes more boldly against the authority of Heaven, none is more pernicious in its results than the idea so prevalent in today's world that God's law is no longer binding on men and women—that disobedience to God is unimportant.

Through the two great errors of the immortality of the soul and Sunday sacredness, Satan will attempt to bring the people under his deceptions. The first lays the foundation for spiritualism, and the latter creates a bond of sympathy with Rome. Protestants in the United States will be foremost in stretching their hands across the gulf to grasp the hand of spiritualism; they will reach over the abyss to clasp hands with the Roman power; and under the influence of this threefold union, this country will follow in the steps of Rome in trampling on the rights of conscience.

Key Thought: "Those who honor the Bible Sabbath will be denounced as enemies of law and order, as breaking down the moral restraints of society, causing anarchy and corruption, and calling down the judgments of God upon the earth. Their conscientious scruples will be pronounced obstinacy, stubbornness, and contempt of authority. They will be accused of disaffection toward the government. . . . In legislative halls and courts of justice, commandment keepers will be misrepresented and condemned. A false coloring will be given to their words; the worst construction will be put upon their motives" (*The Great Controversy,* p. 592).

Today's Lesson: We need to be preparing our minds and hearts now for the intense spiritual struggles that will take place just before Jesus comes.

DECEMBER 26

The Scriptures a Safeguard

The Great Controversy, Chapter 37.

"To the law and to the testimony! If they do not speak according to this word, it is because there is no light in them" (Isaiah 8:20, NKJV).

Every revival of spiritual godliness arouses Satan to more intense activity. He is putting forth his utmost efforts now for the final struggle against Christ and His followers. The last great delusion is soon to open before the world. Antichrist will perform his marvelous works for all to see. Satan's counterfeits will so closely resemble God's truth that we will be able to distinguish them only by comparing them to the truths of God's Word.

The biblical prophecies open the future before us plainly, just as Jesus' words opened the future to His disciples. The Bible clearly presents the events connected with the close of probation and the work of preparation for the time of trouble. But many people have no more understanding of these important truths than if they had never been revealed. When God sends warnings so important that they are represented as being proclaimed by holy angels flying in the midst of heaven, He requires every person on earth to pay attention to the message.

It is the first and highest duty of every rational being to learn from the Bible what is truth and then to walk in its light and encourage others to follow his example. We need to store Christ's teachings and promises in our minds, so the Holy Spirit will be able to bring them to our remembrance when we need them.

Key Thought: "Many are deceived as to their true condition before God. They congratulate themselves upon the wrong acts which they do not commit, and forget to enumerate the good and noble deeds which God requires of them, but which they have neglected to perform. It is not enough that they are trees in the garden of God. They are to answer His expectation by bearing fruit. He holds them accountable for their failure to accomplish all the good which they could have done, through His grace strengthening them" (*The Great Controversy*, p. 601.

Today's Lesson: God has given us in His Word everything we need to live for Him and to grow spiritually.

The Final Warning

The Great Controversy, Chapter 38.

"After these things I saw another angel coming down from heaven, having great authority, and the earth was illuminated with his glory" (Revelation 18:1, NKJV).

God still has people in Babylon, and before His judgments are visited upon the earth, these faithful ones must be gathered into His fold. He doesn't want the plagues of Babylon to fall on them. His call to His people to come out of Babylon—along with the third angel's message—is the final warning that will be given to the people living on the earth.

When the issues are clear and everyone has an opportunity to understand them, then whoever still chooses to disregard God and receive the mark of the beast will voluntarily accept the sign of allegiance to that power. God warns, "If any man worship the beast and his image, and receive his mark in his forehead, or in his hand, the same shall drink of the wine of the wrath of God" (Revelation 14:9, 10). But no one will suffer God's wrath until He knowingly rejects the truth and decides to disobey God's specific command.

God has His agents among the influential leaders of the world. In the last days, a few men will hold in check a powerful current of evil. When God's final warning is given, it will arrest the attention of these leading men, through whom the Lord is now working, and some of them will accept it and stand with God's people through the time of trouble.

Key Thought: "The message will be carried not so much by argument as by the deep conviction of the Spirit of God. The arguments have been presented. The seed has been sown, and now it will spring up and bear fruit. . . . Now the rays of light penetrate everywhere, the truth is seen in its clearness, and the honest children of God sever the bands which have held them. . . . Notwithstanding the agencies combined against the truth, a large number take their stand upon the Lord's side" (*The Great Controversy,* p. 612).

Today's Lesson: The preparations we are making today will enable us to stand for God and give His message in the difficult days at the time of the end.

DECEMBER 28

The Time of Trouble

The Great Controversy, Chapter 39.

"At that time Michael shall stand up, the great prince who stands watch over the sons of your people; and there shall be a time of trouble, such as never was since there was a nation, even to that time. And at that time your people shall be delivered, every one who is found written in the book" (Daniel 12:1, NKJV).

When Jesus leaves the Most Holy Place in the heavenly sanctuary, the wicked will have passed the boundary of their probation and removed themselves from His protecting care. They have persistently resisted God's Spirit, and now He has withdrawn Himself from them. Satan will then be able to plunge the people of earth into one great, final trouble. As the angels of God no longer hold in check the fierce winds of human passion, all the elements of strife will be let loose upon the earth. The whole world will be involved in ruin more terrible than the destruction that came upon Jerusalem.

Even in the absence of the Holy Spirit, the people will continue their religious forms. The satanic zeal with which they carry out the malignant designs of the evil one will in some respects resemble zeal for God. The Sabbath will become the special point of controversy; religious and secular authorities will combine to demand Sunday observance and enforce obedience to their requirements in this regard. Those who refuse to do so will become objects of universal hatred. It will be urged that they should not be tolerated, that it would be better for them to die than for the whole nation to suffer God's anger and be destroyed.

Key Thought: "The people of God will not be free from suffering; but while persecuted and distressed, while they endure privation and suffer for want of food they will not be left to perish. . . . While the wicked are dying from hunger and pestilence, angels will shield the righteous and supply their wants. To him that 'walketh righteously' is the promise: 'Bread shall be given him; his waters shall be sure.'. . . Isaiah 33:15, 16" (*The Great Controversy*, p. 629).

Today's Lesson: God will not abandon His people in their hour of greatest need. His angels will surround them with their protecting power.

God's People Delivered

The Great Controversy, Chapter 40.

"Then the seventh angel poured out his bowl into the air, and a loud voice came out of the temple of heaven, from the throne, saying, 'It is done' " (Revelation 16:17, NKJV).

When the protection of human laws shall be withdrawn from those who honor the law of God, there will be a simultaneous movement all over the world for their destruction. As the time specified in the decree for the death penalty to take effect draws near, the godless will conspire to root out these hated dissidents. They will determine to strike a decisive blow in a single night that will utterly silence the hated voice of these people.

As the angry multitudes are about to carry out the death decree against God's people, a rainbow, shining with glory from the throne of God, seems to encircle each praying company. The murderous mobs gaze fearfully upon this symbol of God's covenant and long to be hidden from its brightness.

The people of God hear a voice, clear and melodious, saying, "Look up." Looking up, they, too, see the rainbow. The black clouds that covered the sky are parted, and like Stephen, they can see into heaven itself and witness the glory of God and Jesus. From the lips of Jesus Himself they hear the request He makes to the Father in the presence of the holy angels, "I will that they also, whom thou hast given me, be with me where I am" (John 17:24).

Key Thought: "Graves are opened, and 'many of them that sleep in the dust of the earth . . . awake, some to everlasting life, and some to shame and everlasting contempt.' Daniel 12:2. All who have died in the faith of the third angel's message come forth from the tomb glorified, to hear God's covenant of peace with those who have kept His law. 'They also which pierced Him' (Revelation 1:7), those that mocked and derided Christ's dying agonies, and the most violent opposers of His truth and His people, are raised to behold Him in His glory and to see the honor placed upon the loyal and obedient" (*The Great Controversy*, p. 637).

Today's Lesson: Our highest desire should be to be among God's faithful people when Jesus returns.

Desolation of the Earth

The Great Controversy, Chapter 41.

"Behold, the Lord comes out of His place to punish the inhabitants of the earth for their iniquity; the earth will also disclose her blood, and will no more cover her slain" (Isaiah 26:21, NKJV).

The judgments that Babylon has called down upon herself will be horrible. In his fury, Satan has demonstrated the lengths to which evil will go when God no longer restrains.

The wicked are filled with regret, not because of their sinful neglect of God and their hatred of their fellow men, but because God has conquered. They lament the result, but they do not repent of their wickedness. They would still try to conquer if they could. The wicked see the very people whom they have mocked and derided and desired to exterminate, as they pass unharmed through pestilence, tempest, and earthquake.

Pastors and church members see that they have not had a right relationship with God. They have rejected truth and chosen to cherish error. No language can express the longing the disobedient and disloyal feel for that which they have lost forever—eternal life. Men whom the world has worshiped for their talents and eloquence now see these things in their true light.

The people see that they have been deluded. They accuse one another of having led them to destruction, but all unite in heaping their bitterest condemnation upon their pastors and religious leaders. Now, in despair, these teachers confess before the world their work of deception. The weapons that were intended to kill God's people are now employed to destroy their enemies. Everywhere, there is strife and bloodshed.

Key Thought: "Here is to be the home of Satan with his evil angels for a thousand years. Limited to the earth, he will not have access to other worlds to tempt and annoy those who have never fallen. It is in this sense that he is bound: there are none remaining, upon whom he can exercise his power. He is wholly cut off from the work of deception and ruin which for so many centuries has been his sole delight" (*The Great Controversy*, p. 659).

Today's Lesson: The wages of sin is death, and those who choose to identify themselves with sin will be destroyed with it.

The Controversy Ended

The Great Controversy, Chapter 42.

"Great and marvelous are Your works, Lord God Almighty! Just and true are Your ways, O King of the saints!" (Revelation 15:3, NKJV).

When Jesus returns at the end of the thousand years, the New Jerusalem settles on the earth, and Satan prepares for a last, mighty struggle for the supremacy. He sees the vast multitude of His followers after the wicked dead are raised to life, and he determines not to yield the great controversy. The wicked have no second chance at salvation, no second probation. They would still choose to follow self rather than God, given the opportunity to choose.

Satan inspires the vast throng with his own spirit and energy. He tells them that he has raised them to life by his power and assures them they are well able to overcome the city. As the wicked advance against the city, fire comes down from heaven and destroys them.

The fire that destroys sin and sinners purifies the earth. John says, "I saw a new heaven and a new earth: for the first heaven and the first earth were passed away" (Revelation 21:1). Paul says that human thought is unable to imagine the things that God has prepared for His people. A sinless universe stretches before them. An endless vista of new experiences awaits. And greatest of all—unbroken communion with their Savior who has made this all possible.

Key Thought: "The years of eternity, as they roll, will bring richer and still more glorious revelations of God and of Christ. As knowledge is progressive, so will love, reverence, and happiness increase. The more men learn of God, the greater will be their admiration of His character. . . .

"The great controversy is ended. Sin and sinners are no more. The entire universe is clean. One pulse of harmony and gladness beats throughout the vast creation. From Him who created all, flow life and light and gladness, throughout the realms of illimitable space. From the minutest atom to the greatest world, all things, animate and inanimate, in their unshadowed beauty and perfect joy, declare that God is love" (*The Great Controversy,* p. 678).

Today's Lesson: Am I looking forward to spending eternity with Jesus—to growing spiritually, mentally, and in every joy and happiness? Am I preparing today to live in heaven? All this is yours if you have accepted Jesus as your Lord and Savior.

Scripture Index

GENESIS
3:4 372
3:15.............11, 369
4:4 13
4:26 14
5:22, 24 14
6:5 15
8:13.....................16
11:5 18
12:1 19
12:2.....................19
13:2.................... 20
22:8.................... 21
22:18 115
24:67 23
27:3, 4 24
28:15..................25
32:26..................26
35:2 27
35:4 27
39:9....................28
45:4, 5 29

EXODUS
4:22, 23 32
7:1 31
14:31...................33
16:28 187
19:5, 6................41
19:6....................35
19:3-6.................35
23:14.................. 61
25:2 38
25:8 38
32:1....................36

LEVITICUS
27:30 59

NUMBERS
7:9 80
14:2.....................43
16:1-3.................44

DEUTERONOMY
1:15 42
1:45.....................43
3:2......................48
3:25, 26 51
11:19..................55
15:1 60
17:17 86
26:19................ 159
32:15..................46
33:25 157
34:5, 6 52

JOSHUA
1:5......................53
9:15, 16 56
10:40, 42 57
23:3 58
24:31..................58

JUDGES
1:28.....................62
14:3.....................63
16:30 63

1 SAMUEL
1:17 64
2:1-10 64
2:17.....................65
2:22, 34 65
2:26.....................64
2:30 123
3:1.......................66
7:12 .... 66, 157
8:7 68
8:19, 20 68
12:13 71
13:14 71
14:6.....................69
15:22, 23............ 71
16:1.....................72
16:7.....................72
16:18 73
22:2 74
24:6 75
28:5 76
28:12 76

2 SAMUEL
1:11, 12 78
1:19-27...............78
5:10.....................79
12:7, 9 82
12:14 81
24:14..................83

1 KINGS
3:9 84
4:32 84
11:31...................89
12:13, 14 89
13:5.....................90
15:11...................98
17:9.....................93
18:17 93
18:21...................94
18:39..................94
19:7.....................95
19:12...................96
19:18..................96

2 KINGS
2:8 100
2:19................... 101
2:21, 22............. 101
4:40....................103
6:16, 17 105
15:34, 35...........109
19:6.....................114
19:35..................114
21:16...................116
23:3 117

1 CHRONICLES
10:13, 14 77
19:13 80
21:11, 12 83
21:17 83

2 CHRONICLES
6 85
6:1, 2..................85
7:1.......................85
7:13, 14 92
9:5, 6, 8 87
14:5.................... 91
14:11.................. 91
18:5.....................98
20:20..................98
23:21...................99
30:26..................112
31:20, 21............112
32:8 114
32:7, 8 114
32:26..................113
33:9 116

EZRA
4:1, 2..................130
7:27....................134
9:6......................135
10:1....................135

NEHEMIAH
2:2 136
2:10 136
4:6......................137
5:6......................138
5:12....................138
6:8 139
8:12....................140
9:19-21...............45
13:8, 9................141

ESTHER
4:14...................133

PSALMS
40:8.................. 175

51........................81
61:2.....................46
62:7 46
78:15, 16 34
91:9..................... 16
119:11 167
119:46................350
119:105 280
119:130 349
119:172...............247
139:23, 24 147
144:12.................85
145:17 9

PROVERBS
3:5-8 157
7:26.....................50
9:10 67
14:12 81
14:34..................124
16:12 124
19:5....................104
20:28..................124
28:13..................148

ECCLESIASTES
2:10, 11 88
10:16................... 111

ISAIAH
1:18 10
5:20 39
6:3 109
8:10, 13, 14 111
8:20 376
13:12 241
24:1, 5............... 144
25:4 144
25:8 144
26:3 331
26:21 380
27:6 143
33:15, 16 378
38:10-20............113
43:2 125
44:28 129
45:1-3, 13...........129
48:9, 11 110
49:6 209
50:4 263
51:7.....................37
53:4 46
55:1 150
55:6, 7................ 110
56:7 281
61:1, 2 182

JEREMIAH
2:13.................366
6:16.................. 118
9:23, 24 84
20:9.................119
23:11.................120
25:12................. 129
29:11................. 129
29:13.................149
30:7.................26
30:11.................122
32:17-27 122
32:37-44........... 122
32:27................. 122
37:17.................121
44:28.................121

EZEKIEL
21:27.................120
28:15................. 368
33:11................. 90
36:26................150

DANIEL
2:21.................124
2:47 124
4:37 126
5:1.................127
5:17.................127
6:16.................128
6:28 128
7.................367
8:14 ....357, 362
9:24, 25 181
9:27 181
12:1.................378
12:2.................379

HOSEA
4:6 108
8:4 107

JOEL
2:28-32........... 284

AMOS
3:3 23
5:10, 12 107
7:17 107

JONAH
3:10 106

MICAH
5:2 142
7:2 111
7:18, 19 145

NAHUM
1:9.................368

HAGGAI
1:4, 5.................130
2:7 132
2:9 132

ZECHARIAH
3:3 131
3:4 131
3:4, 7, 8 131

MALACHI
3:1.................363
3:11 59

MATTHEW
1:23.................158
2:2 163
3:2 213
3:15.................169
4:1.................170
4:10 171
4:19.................183
5:1, 2.................247
5:13 101
5:17................. 248
6:1.................249
7:1 251
7:2 270
7:12.................229
7:21.............27, 273
7:24, 25 189
8:2, 3 185
8:8.................190
8:13.................190
8:26.................193
9:9 186
9:21.................194
9:22 194
10:6 195
10:16................. 195
10:32, 33 347
11:9.................180
11:28.................192
12:12 187
12:41.................106
12:50 191
13:23.................252
13:27, 28...........254
13:31, 32 255
13:44.................259
13:45, 46........... 260
13:47-50 261
13:52.................262
14:27.................198
15:19, 20 200
15:28.................201
16:12 202
16:13, 16 203
16:24................. 203
17:3 204
17:9.................205
17:20................. 132

18:4 206
18:21.................270
18:33 270
19:14 214
19:16................. 215
19:21.................279
19:22................. 215
20:14, 15...........279
20:26................. 218
21:11................. 221
21:19.................222
21:33.................274
22:8 275
23:3 225
23:38.................225
24:4 228
24:13................. 228
24:38, 39 15
25:6 361
25:10 280
25:15.................276
25:40.................229
26:13................. 220
26:29 231
26:63.................234
26:67 234
27:4 ....147, 235
27:17, 18 236
27:42 237
27:65, 66 239
28:6 240
28:18-20...........245

MARK
1:2, 3.................168
1:15 181
3:13.................188
4:26-29.............253
4:38, 39 193
5:31.................194
6:31.................196
6:43, 44 197
8:36 277
9:23, 24 205
9:35 206
11:17.................223
11:24.................263
14:34.................233

LUKE
1:6.................168
1:15.................168
2:10 161
2:29, 30 162
2:35 162
2:40 165
2:49 166
4:22 182
4:32 184
5:20 185
5:22, 23 185
6:5 187

7:9 190
7:13.................190
9:56 211
9:57 188
10:25, 29 278
10:36 212
10:36, 37..........278
11:1.................250
12:1 257
12:20, 21........... 271
13:6 268
13:20, 21...........257
14:23.................269
15:1, 2 266
15:20 267
16:8 277
16:13 277
16:26.................272
17:20, 21 213
18:7, 8.................265
18:9 264
19:9, 10.............219
19:41-44 340
20:25.................224
20:39, 40..........224
21:28 356
22:42 233
23:34 237
24:17.................242
24:25, 26 242
24:27.................358
24:36, 37 243
24:38.................243

JOHN
1:4, 9.................353
1:9.................115
1:11.................159
1:12 145
1:16 334
1:29.................169
1:36 172
1:50 172
2:4 173
2:16................. 174
3:3 ....156, 174
3:17.................268
3:19.................354
3:20 365
3:29, 30 176
4:13, 14 177
4:15.................207
4:48 178
5:8 179
5:14 179
5:19-47 179
5:30 179
6:26, 27 199
6:35, 48, 51.......199
6:37 47
7:16 352
7:17 208

383

7:19................ 208
7:37............46, 207
8:12.......... 209, 356
8:32................ 209
8:51, 52.......... 240
10:14................210
11:4.................. 216
11:12, 14............ 216
11:57................ 217
12:20, 21..........227
13:7................ 230
14:1, 3.............232
14:6...................146
14:12................ 282
14:16-18...........285
14:21................ 288
15:5..................152
16:33............... 288
17:3.................. 154
17:17-19 366
17:24.................379
18:38 236
19:22.................237
19:30.................238
20:15, 16...........241
21:1..................244
21:15................244
21:20 334

ACTS
1:8....................283
1:11...................246
2:1.................... 284
3:6 286
4:32 287
4:32, 34 218
5:5 287
5:29 288
5:34 288
5:41................. 288
6:3 289
6:7 289
6:8 290
7:25 30
7:58 290
8:5 291
8:6 291
9:6 292
9:22 293
10:1, 2..............294
11:21, 22 296
12:1, 2 295
13:45, 46..........297
14:2.................. 298
14:11................. 298
15:10.................299
15:14 255
16:1, 2 300
16:9...................301
16:30 119
17:4................. 302
17:11, 12 303

18:4 304
18:24, 25 306
18:26 306
18:28 306
19:1 307
19:21................308
19:28 308
19:40 – 20:1.... 308
20:10 317
20:30................ 317
20:33-35...........313
21:12 317
21:39, 40 318
24:26, 27 319
25:12 321
26:27-29..........322
27:31.................323
28:15.................324
28:30, 31 325

ROMANS
1:17 346
1:20 17
4:3 20
8:3 170
8:7 146
8:22 61
10:1 315
11:26 315
13:10 247

1 CORINTHIANS
1:1 293
1:10 309
1:23.................. 304
1:26, 27............255
1:27...................351
2:2 304
3:9 256
3:10-12 85
7:24 153
9:11-14 312
9:24, 25 310
10:4 46
10:11 97
14:33.................289
15:51, 52 100

2 CORINTHIANS
4:17...................336
4:17, 18 314
5:17.............151, 311
6:2 147
8:5 312
11:7-10 313
13:8...................345

GALATIANS
1:6, 7.................316
4:4, 5 160
5:6 248

EPHESIANS
1:4-10 281
2:14.................. 282
4:24...................326
5:11 307
5:14...................190
6:12...................369

PHILIPPIANS
1:13 325
2 326
3:7, 8 260
4:6 155
4:22 325

COLOSSIANS
1:13 190
2:6 152
2:9 132
3:1-3 326
3:4 240

1 THESSALONIANS
1:5-7..................305
3:1 303
4:3 336
4:13-18 305

2 THESSALONIANS
2:3, 4, 7 342
2:9-12 371
3:8, 9 313

1 TIMOTHY
1:2.................... 300
3:16...................132
4:1......................184
6:9 22

2 TIMOTHY
1:12 331
1:16-18.............328
2:3 348
3:12.................. 341
4:6-8.........330, 331
4:11...................328
4:16, 17 327

HEBREWS
3:7, 8 147
9 362
10:23 329
10:35, 36 361
11:7 15
11:30.................54
12:21..................35

JAMES
1:17 146
5:17 154

1 PETER
1:3, 4................332
2:1-3 152
5:8 ....369, 370

2 PETER
1:5-11 333
2:15, 16 49
3:11, 12...............333
3:12..........228, 253
3:15, 16 156

1 JOHN
1:1-4..................335
1:2.....................334
1:9.....................264
3:2, 3 334
3:11 218
3:13.....................62
4:16....................247

JUDE
24 247

REVELATION
1:7.............246, 379
1:9.....................337
2:10 341
2:25 343
2:26 344
7:9, 10...............339
11 354
11:8....................354
11:19......... 362, 364
12:4...................145
12:10.................265
12:17 375
13:3....................374
13:8..................... 12
13:11..................355
13:13, 14............373
14.......................363
14:4, 5...............338
14:6....................359
14:6, 7 360
14:6, 7, 12 108
14:6-14.............255
14:9, 10.............377
14:12 364
14:20 364
15:3...................381
16:17 379
18:1.......... 255, 377
18:4 360
19:8 275
20:12 367
21:1 381
22:12.................275